The Biblical Saga of King David

The Biblical Saga of
King David

John Van Seters

Winona Lake, Indiana
EISENBRAUNS
2009

www.eisenbrauns.com

Library of Congress Cataloging-in-Publication Data

Van Seters, John.
   The biblical saga of King David / John Van Seters.
      p.   cm.
   Includes bibliographical references and indexes.
   ISBN 978-1-57506-170-2 (hardback : alk. paper)
   1. David, King of Israel.   2. Bible. O.T. Samuel, 1st, XVI–
Kings, 1st, II–Criticism, interpretation, etc.   I. Title.
   BS580.D3V36   2009
   222′.4092–dc22

                                                    2009014642

Contents

Abbreviations

General

AN	Ark Narrative
D	Deuteronomy
DHG	*Davidshausgeschichte* ("The Story of David's House")
Dtr	Deuteronomistic (Historian)
DtrH	Deuteronomistic History (German: DtrG)
DtrN	Nomistic Dtr stratum or redactor
DtrP	Prophetic Dtr stratum or redactor
HDR	History of David's Rise
CH	Court History
J	Yahwist
LXX	Septuagint
LXX^B	Codex Vaticanus of the Septuagint
MT	Masoretic Text
OG	Old Greek
P	Priestly Writer
PH	Prophetic History
PR	Prophetic Record
REB	Revised English Bible
RSV	Revised Standard Version
SN	Succession Narrative

Reference Works

AB	Anchor Bible
ADAJ	*Annual of the Department of Antiquities of Jordan*
ATD	Das Alte Testament Deutsch
BAR	*Biblical Archaeology Review*
BASOR	*Bulletin of the American Schools of Oriental Research*
BN	*Biblische Notizen*
BWANT	Beiträge zur Wissenschaft vom Alten und Neuen Testament
BZAW	Beihefte zur Zeitschrift für die alttestamentliche Wissenschaft
CANE	*Civilizations of the Ancient Near East.* Edited by J. Sasson. 4 vols. New York: Scribners, 1995
ConBOT	Coniectanea biblica: Old Testament Series
CBQ	*Catholic Biblical Quarterly*
CBQMS	Catholic Biblical Quarterly Monograph Series
ICC	International Critical Commentary
IEJ	*Israel Exploration Journal*

Int	*Interpretation*
JAOS	*Journal of the American Oriental Society*
JBL	*Journal of Biblical Literature*
JHS	*Journal of Hebrew Scriptures*
JNSL	*Journal of Northwest Semitic Languages*
JSOT	*Journal for the Study of the Old Testament*
JSOTSup	Journal for the Study of the Old Testament Supplement Series
KAT	Kommentar zum Alten Testament
NCB	New Century Bible
NEA	*Near Eastern Archaeology*
OBO	Orbis biblicus et orientalis
OTL	Old Testament Library
PEQ	*Palestine Exploration Quarterly*
RB	*Revue biblique*
RGG	*Religion in Geschichte und Gegenwart.* Edited by H. Gunkel. 5 vols. Tübingen: Mohr, 1909–13
RGG[2]	*Religion in Geschichte und Gegenwart.* Edited by H. Gunkel and L. Zseharnack. 5 vols. 2nd ed. Tübingen: Mohr, 1927–32
SBLDS	Society of Biblical Literature Dissertation Series
SBT	Studies in Biblical Theology
SJOT	*Scandinavian Journal of the Old Testament*
SR	*Studies in Religion*
TA	Tel Aviv
TDOT	*Theological Dictionary of the Old Testament.* Edited by G. J. Bottenweck and H. Ringgren. Translated by J. T. Willis, G. W. Bromley, and D. E. Green. 8 vols. Grand Rapids: Eerdmans, 1974–2006
TLOT	*Theological Lexicon of the Old Testament.* Edited by E. Jenni, with assistance from C. Westermann. Translated by M. E. Biddle. 3 vols. Peabody, MA: Hendrickson, 1997
UF	*Ugarit-Forschungen*
VT	*Vetus Testamentum*
VTSup	Supplements to Vetus Testamentum
WBC	Word Biblical Commentary
WMANT	Wissenschaftliche Monographien zum Alten und Neuen Testament
WO	*Die Welt des Orients*
WZK-MUL	*Wissenschaftliche Zeitschrift der Karl-Marx Universität Leipzig*
ZAW	*Zeitschrift für die alttestamentliche Wissenschaft*
ZDPV	*Zeitschrift des deutschen Palästina-Vereins*

Preface

This book has been many years in the making. I first became fascinated with the David story and what scholars called the Succession Narrative when, as a student, I heard Gerhard von Rad lecture on it at Princeton Theological Seminary, where he was a visiting professor in 1961. His remarks on the Succession Narrative were part of a larger discussion of the rise of historiography in ancient Israel,[1] and it gave me a lasting interest in this subject. It was a number of years later, in 1974, when John Wevers of the University of Toronto organized a faculty seminar on ancient historiography, consisting of members from both the Department of Near Eastern Studies (A. Kirk Grayson, Donald Redford, and me) and the Department of Classics (Peter Derow and Timothy Barnes), with a guest scholar from the University of Chicago (Harry Hoffner). The intention was to publish the papers together in book form, but this did not work out. Three of the papers, by Grayson, Hoffner, and me, were subsequently published under the title "Histories and Historians of the Ancient Near East," in *Orientalia* 49-50. The rest appeared in various forms in other works.

My own study in this series, "The Israelites," along with valuable stimulation from Grayson in Assyriology, Redford in Egyptology, and Hoffner in Hittite studies, became the basis of my later work, *In Search of History* (1983). At the same time in the 70s, David Gunn and I were engaged in a lively exchange of views about the literary nature of the David story, and this resulted in a number of articles by both of us and in his provocative book, *The Story of King David* (1978). This discussion is also reflected in my treatment of the David story in *In Search of History*. Though my primary research in the 80s and 90s focused on the historiography of the Pentateuch, as reflected in my studies on the Yahwist, I did return from time to time to questions relating to the Deuteronomistic History and to the story of David in particular. In a symposium held in Berne in February, 1997, I was asked to offer my views on the Succession Narrative (or Court History) in dialogue with Otto Kaiser and others, and this debate was published in

---

1. This later appeared in English as G. von Rad, "The Beginnings of Historical Writing in Ancient Israel," in *The Problem of the Hexateuch and Other Essays* (Edinburgh: Oliver & Boyd, 1966), 166-204.

Die sogenannte Thronfolgegeschichte Davids (A. de Pury and T. Römer, eds.; 2000). My own contribution, "The Court History and DtrH," centered on the debate concerning the relationship of the Court History to DtrH, and I argued, as in *In Search of History* but in greater detail, that the Court History was a later addition to DtrH. This issue has been taken up again in a greatly expanded form in this study and extended to include the account of David's rise to power as well.

Consequently, I can safely assert that over the last three decades I have consistently maintained the view, against the consensus reflected in the works of L. Rost, G. von Rad, M. Noth, and many who have followed them, that a large part of the David story, including the Succession Narrative, is a late addition to DtrH and not a source and that it was produced during the Persian period. I have also attempted to follow the archaeological discussion as it has to do with appraising and reconstructing the period of David's reign and the development of the Judean state and as both of these relate to the sociohistorical context of the David story. What I could not have known in the 70s and early 80s, when I first began to develop this thesis, was that the archaeological evidence would so overwhelmingly confirm my position about the development of the David story. We now know with a high degree of confidence that the sociohistorical context reflected in the Court History of David simply cannot be supported by the archaeological evidence for the 10th century and must belong to a much later age. What Rost, von Rad, and Noth could not have known, namely, the great advances in archaeological evidence, this we can now use to understand and interpret the David narrative that has come down to us.

Once one has accepted the notion that the story of David was not inspired by or produced during a period contemporary with a ruler of Jerusalem in the 10th century but instead is the work of one or more authors of times far removed from that period, then the form of the story and its interpretation must be radically different from those proposed by earlier scholars. The accounts of David's rise to power in place of Saul and Solomon's eventual succession to the throne, usually construed as two documents, were understood as apologies written by members of the court in defense of the Davidic dynasty. This sort of understanding of the David story's genre and interpretation is no longer tenable. Already at the beginning of my study of the David story in the mid-70s, I raised questions about this mode of interpretation. But it still persists against all evidence to the contrary, so I lay out at some length in this work why it must be set aside and a different approach taken to understanding this literary masterpiece.

One other approach that has arisen, as a kind of steady piecemeal re-treat from the older position, is to relegate everything that might be con-strued as later in time than the original documents to the work of a series of "redactors." As a consequence, not only was Noth's Deuteronomistic Historian, who was thought by Noth to have used these earlier "sources" for his history, now construed as one of these "editors," but the whole of what was thought by earlier scholars as the finest example of classical He-brew prose is now fragmented into a myriad of small pieces and under-stood as endless additions to the original. And this literary process is stretched over a very long period of time. This makes it all too easy for some to despair of the historical-critical effort altogether and to opt for a holistic or final-form approach to the David story, and I sympathize with their frustration with critical scholarship. Nevertheless, I remain commit-ted to the historical-critical method of literary analysis on the one hand and, on the other hand, to an appreciation of the literary quality of a large part of the David story, as recognized by Rost, von Rad, and others. This work is an attempt to present a balance between these two goals.

Acknowledgments

I have benefited greatly from the discussion and dialogue of many schol-ars over the years, and I hope their contributions to the study of the David story are adequately reflected in this book. Without this scholarly dis-course forcing me to address important issues on this subject, I could not have produced this book and whatever merits it may be deemed to have. In particular, I want to thank those who have seen and commented on various parts of this book in the process of its writing. The assistance given me by Nadav Na'aman and Israel Finkelstein and their comments on historical and archaeological matters have been invaluable. They are, of course, not responsible for my views or any mistakes that may remain in the text. Oth-ers, such as Niels-Peter Lemche, Steven McKenzie, David Gunn, Kenton Sparks, Brian Schmidt, Paul Dion, Michele Daviau, and Peter Erb, have had to endure my most recent obsession with the biblical David and have been most generous with their comments and encouragement. They cannot be held responsible, however, for any errors or the views expressed in this book. In addition to these, there are two other scholars who have done much work on the David story and are worthy of special mention here: Walter Dietrich and the late Timo Veijola. Both have shown me much kind-ness and generosity in the past and have shared their publications with me.

In the course of doing research on this book, I presented a paper entitled "David: Messianic King or Mercenary Ruler?" at the Canadian Society of Biblical Studies in Saskatoon, Canada, in May, 2007, and another paper entitled "David the Mercenary" at the European Biblical Society in Vienna in August, 2007.[2] The content of these papers has been used in a modified form in the present book. I wish to thank my colleagues in both societies for granting me the opportunity to air my views on the dating and interpretation of the David Saga. Their discussion and criticisms were most helpful.

As in the past, Jim Eisenbraun has been most helpful in all aspects of the production of this book. In addition, the meticulous editorial work of Amy Becker at Eisenbrauns has rescued me from many errors and rendered the text more readable at many points, and for this she has my sincere thanks. Any errors that remain are entirely my own.

This book is dedicated to my European colleagues who have been so supportive of my work and have shown me so much friendship and hospitality over a period of many years. In particular, I single out Hans Heinrich Schmid, Niels-Peter Lemche, Otto Kaiser, and Thomas Römer, but there are many others who come to mind as well. Finally, as with so many other authors, it is my family who must put up with my obsession with a project such as this one, and my wife, Elizabeth, has been most patient and understanding during the writing of this book.

---

2. These papers are being published in collections of these conference papers, the first in *Community Identity in Judean Historiography: Biblical and Comparative Perspectives* (ed. G. Knoppers and K. Ristau; Winona Lake, IN: Eisenbrauns, 2009), 27–39; the second in *Israel in Transition: From Late Bronze II to Iron IIA (c. 1250–850 BCE)*, vol. 2: *The Texts* (ed. L. L. Grabbe; European Seminar in Historiography 8; London: T. & T. Clark, forthcoming).

Chapter 1

Introduction

The Scope of the Study

This study of the biblical story of David is limited in scope to the literary aspects of the biblical account contained within 1 Sam 16–1 Kgs 2 but excluding 2 Sam 21–24. The reason for the exclusion is that these chapters have long been regarded as a kind of appendix that is quite different from the narrative material that both precedes and follows and breaks the obvious continuity in the literary work between 2 Sam 20 and 1 Kgs 1. Furthermore, there is nothing in the rest of the story of David that depends on or even assumes knowledge of the material contained within this appendix. And the chapters of the appendix all have their own sets of literary-critical problems and peculiarities that would detract from the focus of this study. Consequently, what I hope to demonstrate in this study is that within this corpus from 1 Sam 16 to 1 Kgs 2, with the exception of the appendix of 2 Sam 21–24, are two extensive and competing presentations of David that extend from the beginning of David's career under Saul to the succession to David's throne by Solomon. These two narratives are obviously contradictory in the sense that the one idealizes David as the model king for all future monarchs, as embodied in the ideology of the messiah, Yahweh's anointed and chosen king, and the other regards both David's rise to the throne and the manner of his reign as typical of oriental despots and hardly a fitting model for a just society. I believe that it is possible to lay out the literary parameters of these two narratives and to demonstrate their relationship to each other. Once the limits of the works are made clear, then it will not be difficult to see that the narrator who is favorable to David is in continuity with the larger Deuteronomistic History (DtrH) where this idealization of David as the model king works as a theme throughout his treatment of the monarchy.

The relationship of the other corpus that presents David in a negative light is more difficult to delineate and to establish in relationship with the former Deuteronomistic (Dtr) narrative. The reason for this is that its vivid and highly realistic prose style has, since the 19th century, earned it the praise of a polished piece of early historiography that must have arisen close to the events that it records. Its interpretation, therefore, and its relationship to the other "Deuteronomistic" source is bound up with an extensive discussion of its particular social and historical context. This entails a preliminary investigation of historical questions about the early monarchy and the comparative social context and possible literary genre that support claims such as these to a primitive historiography in the 10th century B.C.E. These claims will have to be balanced against alternatives that suggest a quite different and quite late social context for the narrative in the late Persian period. Such a late dating for the narrative would require that it be viewed as a supplement to and revision of the earlier Dtr version of the David story.

In addition to the delineation of the two main narrative threads, there has also been much discussion about the "historical" or legendary sources used by these narrators. Though questions of this sort are primarily the concern of historians attempting to reconstruct the history of the early monarchy, they cannot be easily separated from the literary questions, and vice versa. Here charges of "minimalism" and "maximalism" in the matter of historical reconstruction have clouded the attempt at clarity on the level of literary analysis. Too often a social and historical context is put forward, and then the narrative sources are made to fit this context, and finally the fit is used to confirm the reality of the historical context—a complete circularity of argument. Any search for a controlling context for narrative sources or background must establish a sufficient level of confidence outside this hermeneutical circle to be effective. Consequently, I shall review and test the issue of primitive sources within the narratives concerning the degree to which they reflect archaic features or late anachronisms.

One particularly controversial source is that of the story of David and Goliath and how it relates to the larger narrative context. The attitudes about this unit vary greatly, from regarding it as quite primitive to its being a late addition to the narrative. The matter is also complicated by the fact that the MT and LXX texts of both this story in 1 Sam 17 and its sequel in chap. 18 contain significant differences, and this is also used to support different theories of compositional development. These issues have become so complex that the story of David and Goliath will be discussed in a separate chapter.

The beginning of the story of David, likewise, raises a number of historical and literary problems. On the literary side, it is clear that the introduction of David is closely tied to the prior story of Saul, specifically to the theme of Yahweh's rejection of Saul in favor of David. In addition, the early narratives about David all have to do with his service to Saul and his subsequent flight from Saul. Thus, a very large portion of the David story is told within the broader context of the story of Saul. Furthermore, this is complicated by the fact that there are three different introductions of David and two different versions of how David enters the service of Saul. Consequently, some attention must be given to the interrelation of the David story with the story of Saul. Regarding historical problems with the beginning of the David story, there have been serious questions raised in recent years concerning the common origin of Israel and Judah as a "United Monarchy." It now seems increasingly likely that the origins of the two states had little to do with each other, which means that the accounts of David succeeding to the throne of Saul, or indeed any connection between the two, is not historical and does not reflect a primitive tradition. If this is the case, it will have an important bearing not only on the various versions of David's beginnings under Saul but on the whole story of David. At what stage in the history of Israel and Judah did the traditions of the two states merge into a combined history of the Israelite people?

The History of Scholarship on David

It would be useful to review the recent history of scholarship on the David narratives in order to place the current study within the context of a variety of studies and approaches. There is no need to outline an extensive survey because these have been done before, but we only must highlight a selection that reflects the various methods and presuppositions that have dominated the field of study. These encompass the literary-critical approach, with special concern for the history of the traditions behind the text, its form or genre, and the history of its composition or "redaction." In contrast to these methods is the study of the literary qualities of the David narrative in its "final form," which has little concern for its diachronic development. Alongside the literary analysis is the historical approach to the text, with primary concern for the social and historical setting of the David story. It is, of course, the case that the concerns of many scholars overlap these areas of literary and historical concern or at least make assumptions about the results of work in one area while focusing on that of another. Nevertheless, it is important to understand how the investigation in each of these areas has had an impact on the study of the David story as a whole and to locate my own study within this matrix. Furthermore, the constant interplay among all of these methods of analysis, literary and historical, makes it difficult to treat them in isolation from one another. Consequently, in the introduction we will look first at the broad history of the literary approaches to the David story, and only in two subsequent chapters will we survey the various issues related to the social and historical contexts of the David story, which have had quite an impact on its interpretation.

The Literary-Critical Analysis:
Julius Wellhausen

It is quite remarkable how Julius Wellhausen set out in a few pages in the *Prolegomena* the main features for the critical study of the David narratives that were to become the basis for the development of future research by generations of scholars down to recent times.[1] Wellhausen identifies two complementary narratives: the first, contained in 1 Sam 16–2 Sam 8, is the story of how David rose to the throne and his principle achievements as king; the second is contained in 2 Sam 9–20 and 1 Kgs 1–2, and although it has a somewhat mutilated beginning, it is otherwise remarkably intact. The latter deals with the later years of the king's reign and tells of the struggle for the succession, ending in Solomon's successful palace coup to gain the throne of David. This work Wellhausen regards as a historical work reflecting events and circumstances with remarkable realism. The earlier narrative dealing with David's rise is no less a valuable source of historical events, but it is a more obviously biased account. It is also full of legendary modifications and tendentious insertions and revisions, many of these being reflected in doublets. Thus, he finds the whole of 1 Sam 15:1–16:13, which includes an introduction of David, to be parallel to the older introduction of David in 16:14–23, which has its original connection with 14:52. The primary introduction has its sequel in 18:6ff so that the story of David's encounter with Goliath in 17:1–18:5 is also a legendary accretion. In a similar fashion, Wellhausen attempts to evaluate a number of other doublets to determine which of them are primary and which are secondary.

Wellhausen uses a number of different criteria in making his decisions. Sometimes it is a matter of identifying what seems to be intrusive within the general narrative continuity of a literary unit. At other times, the differ-

---

1. J. Wellhausen, *Prolegomena to the History of Ancient Israel* (Gloucester, MA: Peter Smith, 1973), 262–69. See also idem, *Die Composition des Hexateuch und der Historischen Bücher des Alten Testaments* (4th ed.; Berlin: de Gruyter, 1963), 247–60.

ences between the MT text and the LXX, particularly in 1 Sam 17–18, suggest a preference of one version over the other. There are some cases in which Wellhausen used a history-of-religions approach to establish what is more primitive and what is later in terms of religious development. Often, he resorts to a kind of historical logic in terms of what one might expect David to have done in certain circumstances. In some instances, Wellhausen identifies scenes and episodes that have been created as imitations of those in the Saul narratives. These he finds to be particularly the case where Samuel comes into the story of David, as in 1 Sam 19:18–24, which presupposes the anointing of David by Samuel in 16:1–13, and both of these have parallels in the Saul story.

In this first part of the story of David, Wellhausen engages in a fairly typical form of 19th-century history-of-traditions analysis, trying to discern various levels in the history of the text. Yet, the analysis does not result in a final basic narrative but yields only a collection of stories loosely fitted together with a varied history of development. Only in 2 Sam 2–5 and 8 does Wellhausen sense an extensive literary continuity, apart from a few minor additions in chaps. 2–5 and the intrusion of chaps. 6–7. It was therefore left to later scholars to sort out his many suggestions in a more systematic way. One tendency among later scholars that was not reflected in Wellhausen's own work but grew out of the source analysis of the Documentary Hypothesis was the attempt to extend the same type of source analysis as that used in pentateuchal studies, identifying the same or similar parallel sources in the books of Samuel.[2]

Form Criticism:
Gunkel and Gressmann
Herrmann Gunkel built on the work of Wellhausen, accepting the basic analysis of the two narrative sources and their historical and literary qualities, but he applied to it the new method of form criticism with respect to their form or genre and their social setting.[3] For him, the rise of history

---

2. See the survey of these views in O. Eissfeldt, *The Old Testament: An Introduction* (New York: Harper & Row, 1965), 241–48, 268–81. Eissfeldt continued to hold a modified version of this view long after it was abandoned by most scholars. See also R. H. Pfeiffer, *Introduction to the Old Testament* (New York: Harper & Row, 1941), 338–73.

3. H. Gunkel, "Geschichtsschreibung im A.T.," *RGG* 2:1348–54; idem, *RGG*[2] 2:1112–15; idem, "Die isrealitische Literatur," in *Die orientalischen Literaturen* (ed.

writing in Israel was the result of a long evolutionary process, from early
legends about the ancestors of the people and heroic tales about shadowy
figures of the distant past, such as one finds in the book of Judges, to more
recent historical figures within living memory, such as Saul and David.
True historiography, however, is only achieved within the context of a literate society and a kingdom, such as that reflected in the time of David and
Solomon. Thus, the superb literary work that Wellhausen identified in the
story of David's reign, especially the account of the Absalom rebellion, is
for Gunkel the height of Israelite historiography. Its Sitz im Leben is the
court of Solomon, and it was probably written by a former member of David's court.

The views of Gunkel were taken over and expanded by Hugo Gressmann.[4] Thus, the early stories of Saul and David, though often arising out
of actual events of the recent past, take on the form of heroic tales.[5] In the
time of David's reign, however, something new happens, with a transformation of the literary form: "The literary narrative is given added depth
along the lines of the novella. The inner life of the heroes is presented in
the action more strongly than was previously the case, even if it is not explicitly described at great length. . . . This is the birth of heightened history
writing on the lines of the novella." Gressmann then explains why this particular form of literature should arise in this social setting. He states:

> It is no accident that this occurred in David's time. For it was natural that
> a sense for political events should awaken with the establishment of any
> empire, although the converse is certainly right also: when eyes were
> opened to political necessities, the monarchy was set up and people sub-
> jected themselves to the constraints of the state. In the time of David, in-
> dividual narratives began to be preserved in writing from their inception,
> and it was certainly not long before existing historical narratives of the
> present and the recent past were collected and written down.[6]

P. Hinneberg; 2nd ed.; Berlin: Teubner, 1925), 53–112. For a more extensive discussion of Gunkel's treatment of Israelite historiography, see my *In Search of History: Historiography in the Ancient World and the Origins of Ancient History* (New Haven, CT:
Yale University Press, 1983; repr. Winona Lake, IN: Eisenbrauns, 1997), 209–13.

4. See H. Gressmann, "The Oldest History Writing in Israel," in *Narrative and
Novella in Samuel: Studies by Hugo Gressmann and Other Scholars 1906–1923* (ed.
David M. Gunn; JSOTSup 116; Sheffield: Almond, 1991), 9–58.

5. Ibid., 17–18.

6. Ibid., 16.

Gressmann is primarily concerned with a literary appreciation of the form and character of the individual story units, not with continuous sources or collections, but with the evolution of the smaller story units into more sophisticated forms, including the development of history writing and the appropriate setting that would give rise to literary types of this sort.[7] Gressmann paid particular attention to a detailed analysis of the literary character of the various novellas within the Court History in 2 Sam 9-20 and 1 Kgs 1-2, and, while he acknowledged the historical character of much of the narrative, he also was concerned to bring out its novella-like qualities in his analysis of the individual units of the composition. Using this form-critical method, Gressmann resisted the older method of source division and instead emphasized the genres of individual stories and episodes within the Court History as a collection of novellas. For him, this form and style of writing was the hallmark of the Davidic-Solomonic period in particular.[8]

The Thematic Analysis of Leonhard Rost:
The Succession Narrative

Leonhard Rost's work on the David story in *Die Überlieferung von der Thronnachfolge Davids* (1926)[9] gives special attention to the work that scholars up to this point had characterized as the Court History of David in 2 Sam 9-20 and 1 Kgs 1-2. In this, he follows Wellhausen, except that he does not pay much attention to what Wellhausen describes as the story of David's rise to power in 1 Sam 16-2 Sam 5 and 8. Perhaps this is because he is not sympathetic toward the older source criticism, which split up the books of Samuel into parallel sources, a method that seemed to have some justification within the History of David's Rise (HDR) but was unsuitable for the Court History (CH). Rost followed the form-critical approach

---

7. In much of his discussion of the novella and its use as a form of historiography, he was anticipated by W. Caspari, "The Literary Type and Historical Value of 2 Samuel 15-20," in *Narrative and Novella in Samuel: Studies by Hugo Gressmann and Other Scholars 1906-1923* (ed. David M. Gunn; JSOTSup 116; Sheffield: Almond, 1991), 59-88.

8. For my earlier critique on Gunkel and Gressmann, see my *In Search of History*, 209-13.

9. Translated by M. D. Rutter and D. M. Gunn as *The Succession to the Throne of David* (Historic Texts and Interpreters in Biblical Scholarship 1; Sheffield: Almond, 1982). References to Rost and quotations will be taken from this translation.

of Gressmann and Caspari with their emphasis on the literary form of novella as it applied to the CH but, instead of viewing it as a collection of individual novellas, he argued for the thesis that all of 2 Sam 9–20 and 1 Kgs
1–2, with the exception of a few short additions, was a single composition.
In addition to this composition by a single author, he saw connections
made in 2 Sam 6:16, 20–23 to an earlier work, the story of the Ark in 1 Sam
4:1b–7:2 and 2 Sam 6, together with an original version of the Nathan oracle in 2 Sam 7:1–7, 11b, 16, 18–21, 25, 27–29 and the incorporation of an
old account of the Ammonite war in 2 Sam 10:1–11:1 and 12:26–31.[10]

The major contribution that Rost makes to the discussion of the CH is
his attempt to demonstrate the unity of the work against both form criticism and source analysis, which would divide it into pieces. This he does
by examining the style, structure, and interdependence of the various parts
as reflective of the genius and distinctive characteristics of a single author;
but, above all, he argues for the *thematic unity* of the composition. This
theme he finds most clearly expressed in the final section of the work, in
1 Kgs 1:20, 27: "Who will sit on the throne of my lord the king after him?"
All of the individual units are examined to see how they are related in one
way or the other to this particular theme. For this reason, Rost prefers to refer to this whole corpus as the Succession Narrative (SN), and many have
followed him in this designation. Now there can be no doubt that the issue
of David's successor and the fate of three successive crown princes, Amnon, Absalom, and Adonijah are closely interrelated, but it is not clear that
the particular question of which son of David will succeed him is the primary issue from the beginning. One would expect the theme to be clearly
expressed at the outset and not discovered at the end in retrospect as the
clue to a bewildering set of events. Moreover, there are a number of units
that do not fit this theme very well. After the Nathan prophecy in 2 Sam
7:11b, 16, there can be no reason to think that Mephibosheth, in 2 Sam 9,
has any serious hope of gaining the throne. The Ammonite war in 2 Sam 10
does not deal with this theme, so Rost makes it an older source, but reasons will be given to leave this judgment in doubt. Likewise, the revolt of
Sheba in 2 Sam 20 does not fit this theme either.

The point is that one must first try to establish the limits of the literary
work before one attempts to articulate the theme. More recently, scholars
have suggested that 2 Sam 2:8–4:12 also belongs to the CH and this would

---

10. These three earlier sources are dealt with in the first three chapters of Rost,
The Succession to the Throne of David, 6–64.

further limit the usefulness of the succession theme for determining the limits and unity of the composition. Furthermore, Rost does not address the relationship of SN to the account of David's rise to power (HDR). If the author of SN made use of the Ark Narrative (AN) as a prologue to his own work, why did he not use the story of David's rise, which Rost also believes existed before SN and was known to him? Rost's reply, "Why should he repeat things which every child knew?" is rather weak.

After Rost has established the limits of SN on the basis of the work's theme, he then supports this view by means of the other criteria, most notably the author's distinctive style. In comparison with other narrative sources, Rost states, "we are struck all the more by the individuality of our source. The sentences are longer, expression is fuller, the description is richer, the language is more sonorous and richer in imagery. The rapid flow of the narrative is restrained. Each individual scene is neatly detached from those adjoining."[11] Rost then gives a number of examples to demonstrate the richness of graphic detail, including the use of striking images, which he regards as particularly distinctive of this author. Another feature of style he regards as distinctive consists of the speeches that employ many different forms and the structuring of the speech for dramatic effect. Rost pays particular attention to the use of the messenger reports as they appear in SN, as compared with AN, especially the way in which SN develops these reports into dialogue, which is important for the whole development of the action. The speeches have a "scene-building capacity," which Rost illustrates with a number of examples.[12]

This discussion of style leads into the work's structure and the various means by which the work is tied together and connected by both subtle anticipation and references to past actions and events. Much of this is connected to the development of both major and minor characters, whose multiple appearances knit the whole work together in a remarkable way. As Rost states,

> The artistic skill in structure is especially shown in the manner by which people are introduced, keep intervening in the plot, and finally leave the stage. Of the main characters only David lacks proper introduction ... without family name or genealogy. Even the secondary characters are for the most part introduced fully. . . . All the main characters and most of

---

11. Ibid., 90.
12. Ibid., 96–97.

the minor characters also make a corresponding exit. Usually their fortunes are recounted until their death, as with David, Amnon, Absalom, Adonijah, Joab, Shimei, Amasa and Ahitophel, or until they leave the scene, as with Abiathar, or until they reach their zenith, as with Solomon. Especially in 1 Kgs 1 the characters crowd together to form a brilliant final tableau, which is extended and balanced somewhat by chapter 2.[13]

At this point in our review of Rost, we need to pause and consider the virtues and weaknesses of Rost's stylistic approach. There is no doubt in my mind that Rost's stylistic, structural, and artistic analysis of SN strongly supports the case for the unity of the work and for the literary skill of its author. Nor can there be any doubt that we are dealing with an author and not merely an editor of disparate sources or a collection of novellas. Even though Rost's understanding of the qualities of authorship may be influenced by the romantic understanding of individuality and creativity, the literary elements that he investigates are still useful in identifying the nature of this composition. If there is one weakness in Rost's stylistic approach, it is the fact that he limits his comparison with other texts primarily to the AN, which he considers a source, and does not address the more important issue of whether or not the same features could be found in some parts of HDR. Indeed, even when he finds cross references from SN to HDR, as in the case of David's recollection of Joab's murders of Abner and Amasa side by side (1 Kgs 2:5), he rejects the significance of the reference to Abner and consequently the inclusion of the whole block of texts in 2 Sam 2:8–4:12 because it would not fit the predetermined limits of SN based on the work's theme. Furthermore, close examination of a number of the stylistic features outlined by Rost can be made to fit remarkably well with at least some parts of HDR, although not so well with others. If Rost had begun with a stylistic analysis of the whole of the David story first and used it to establish the limits of the literary work in question before fixing the limits based on its theme, the results could well have been somewhat different.

Rost concludes his stylistic discussion of SN by stating, "The whole succession story reveals itself to be a lively extract from an eventful period. With the greatest skill and conscious planning, the characters are balanced against each other, their appearances determined, their actions linked one with another and connected with the major theme, the succession of David."[14] This leads into a discussion of the relationship of this artistry to the

---

13. Ibid., 102.
14. Ibid., 103.

historical reality, as he sees it, behind the events. Rost has already inherited from earlier scholarship, as far back as Wellhausen, the view that SN reflects an eyewitness report of actual historical events, but this must be modified by the artistic nature of the literary work. He states:

> On the one hand, it must be granted that everything gives an impression of probability and realism, so much so that one would most like to maintain that long stretches of the narrative come from immediate eye-witnesses. On the other hand, the possibility cannot altogether be rejected that a writer of particular sensitivity created this work with no too great consideration for the actual events. This latter possibility is supported by the fact that the whole dramatic structure is based on dialogue, by the artistic arrangement of the individual scenes, and by the internal consistency and the fine rounding-off of the whole complex.[15]

The arguments for its historical character are rather slim. In addition to the verisimilitude of the account, they consist of the close connection to the Ammonite war report in 2 Sam 10, which is taken as historical fact,[16] and the tale about David's adultery with Bathsheba, about which he says, "It can hardy be assumed that somebody would later have dared to expose David in this way without sound evidence." Yet, as we will see below, the Ammonite campaign is of doubtful historicity and does contain more "artistic construction" than Rost allows, and his argument about David's adultery only carries weight if the text belongs to the time of David or shortly thereafter. Apart from this affirmation on the basic historical facts, albeit "in a strongly stylized dress," Rost can point to no concrete evidence to confirm these "facts." He is merely content to assert that "fact and fiction join hands in this succession narrative as in every work of an artistically sensitive historiographer."[17] The author selects the events relevant to his story and groups them around a single theme, that is, the succession to the throne.

Rost places the author within the early years of Solomon's reign, and in his view it was written "to the greater glory of Solomon."[18] This opinion on the purpose of the narrative is given without any argument or justification in spite of much in 1 Kgs 2 that would lead to a quite-different conclusion. It is apparent that the dating of the work to the early Solomonic

---

15. Ibid., 104.

16. This view he takes over from Gressmann, "The Oldest History Writing," 23–25.

17. Rost, *The Succession to the Throne of David,* 104. His models seem to be those of Herodotus and Thucydides.

18. Ibid., 105.

period dictates its possible purpose and not anything decisive in the content. Rost spends more time on the possible identity of the author, as did others before him, as though a great literary work were in need of a name to make it great. Nevertheless, he concludes, "In the end it is simply an argument about names which cannot change the fact that the author is one of the best narrators in the Hebrew Language."[19]

Rost gives much attention to the theology of SN as a contrast to other parts of Samuel and Kings, with its infrequent reference to divine intervention and complete absence of the miraculous. He compares the portrayal of divine activity in history to "the Enlightenment's belief in providence,"[20] and this suggestion is picked up by other scholars as a reflection of the Solomonic age. In contrast to the few direct references to divine activity is the frequent mention of the deity on the lips of so many of the characters within the story. Here, there is a much greater similarity with remarks made by similar or the same persons in the parts of Samuel that Rost does not include within his work, but he does not deal with any comparison of this sort. This applies to important notions such as regarding the king as Yahweh's anointed, but it also has to do with the references to the king as the "angel of Yahweh," which seems rather distinctive within SN.[21] Yet Rost overlooks the fact that David is also compared to "an angel of God" in 1 Sam 29:9 by Achish, but in this case we know that the description is false. This raises the question of whether any of these characterizations are meant to be taken seriously and how we are to understand the religion of the story's characters as compared with that of the author himself.

Regarding the narrator's depiction of divine intervention, he states that Yahweh "works only in and through secondary causes."[22] Of course, he must allow for the obvious exception of Yahweh's sending the prophet Nathan to chastise David and predict the death of the child in 2 Sam 12. Nevertheless, he continues: "Nowhere does he intervene with a miracle, nor influence human events with miracles and prophecies. It is the secondary causes which Yahweh uses to give effect to his thoughts and to bring his plans into being. . . . Yahweh reveals himself in the course of events. His intervention is indirect."[23] Rost, however, does not explain why this narrator

---

19. Ibid., 106.
20. Ibid.
21. Ibid., 107.
22. Ibid., 108.
23. Ibid.

felt compelled to include within his work the Nathan oracle with its promise of a dynasty (2 Sam 7), even if this is taken from an older source, and
why so many references are made to it in 1 Kgs 1-2 in order to suggest that
Solomon's succession was the fulfillment of this prophecy. This looks very
much like the Dtr pattern of prophecy fulfillment, with the same prophecy
being fulfilled in the building of the temple (1 Kgs 8). However, this is not
the place to treat Rost's discussion of 2 Sam 7 in detail; we will leave this to
a later consideration below.

I have looked at Rost's treatment of SN in some detail because it has so
often become a generally accepted thesis or a point of departure for subsequent discussion of the David story, with numerous modifications suggested by later scholars. His forceful demonstration of the unity and literary
quality of SN won widespread approval, even though differences remained
about its exact limits. Thus, for instance, Martin Noth, in his *Überlieferungsgeschichtliche Studien* (1943),[24] accepts both HDR (1 Sam 16-2 Sam 5) and
SN (2 Sam 6-7*, 9-20; 1 Kgs 1-2; as defined by Rost) as older sources for
his DtrH, without further discussion. In his *Geschichte Israels*,[25] Noth treats
SN, as delineated by Rost, as a completely reliable historical source and
uses it as the basis for his characterization of the reign of David.

The David Story as the Beginning of History Writing:
Von Rad

Gerhard von Rad, in his essay "The Beginnings of Historical Writing in
Ancient Israel" (1944), adopts the form-critical position of Gunkel and
Gressmann on the evolution of historical thought and writing, from primitive etiological *Sagen*, through the stage of heroic tales of the Judges, to
the development of true historiography under the United Monarchy of David and Solomon.[26] Into this general scheme of Gunkel and Gressmann,
von Rad introduced at least two important qualifications. The first is the
distinctive character of Israel's historical way of thinking that arose out of

---

24. M. Noth, *The Deuteronomistic History* (JSOTSup 15; Sheffield: JSOT Press,
1981), 54.

25. Idem, *The History of Israel* (2nd ed.; New York: Harper & Row, 1960), 199–
204. (More on this below.)

26. G. von Rad, "The Beginnings of Historical Writing in Ancient Israel," in *The
Problem of the Hexateuch and Other Essays* (Edinburgh: Oliver & Boyd, 1966), 166–
204. For a more detailed discussion of von Rad's views, see my *In Search of History*,
213-17.

the nature of its faith. He states, "*The Israelites came to a historical way of thinking, and then to historical writing, by way of their belief in the sovereignty of God in history.*"[27] The second modification by von Rad was to accept Rost's analysis of SN in preference over Gressmann's analysis and to build on Rost's treatment his own literary and theological understanding of the narrative. Von Rad subscribes to Rost's broader limits of SN, including the episode of David and Michal in 2 Sam 6:16, 20–23, and therefore the connection of SN with the older AN, as well as the incorporation of the shorter version of the Nathan Prophecy in 2 Sam 7. He is persuaded by Rost's arguments from style for the unity of the work and the basic theme of the succession to the throne of David as the thread that ties the entire work together. Yet, like Rost, he skips rather lightly over some of the obvious interconnections between SN and HDR, and he has no place in his historiographic discussion for HDR.[28]

However, following Gressmann and especially Albrecht Alt,[29] von Rad placed a much stronger emphasis than Rost on the historiographic character of SN and the way in which the work reflects the new historical and political realities of the monarchy under David and Solomon. Von Rad adopts Rost's notion of a Solomonic "enlightenment"[30] and sees it as a time when older sacred orders were transformed by a new internationalism and a new way of thinking about religion. It is not surprising, therefore, that von Rad places great importance on what he sees as the theme of divine providence (as is illustrated in the emphatic quotation above), treated in a highly subtle and sophisticated way. Von Rad tries to make a distinction between this Israelite historiography and that of the Greeks. He admits that both the Greek historians and SN share in the notion of retribution, but on the matter of direct divine intervention and providence he cites Thucydides' "icy skepticism." Nevertheless, there is considerable evidence that divine providence

---

27. Von Rad, "Beginnings," 170. Emphasis is in the original text.

28. Later, in von Rad's *Old Testament Theology* (2 vols.; New York: Harper & Row, 1962), 1:49, he recognizes HDR (1 Sam 16:14–2 Sam 5:12) as the earliest of three histories of the Davidic-Solomonic period. This, of course, makes the question of the relationship of SN to HDR all the more important.

29. In particular, von Rad cites A. Alt's "Die Staatenbildung der Israeliten in Palästine" (1930), translated as "The Formation of the Israelite State in Palestine," *Essays on Old Testament History and Religion* (trans. R. A. Wilson; Oxford: Blackwell, 1966), 171–237. Alt's work will be taken up again below.

30. "Beginnings," 203.

did play a role in the work of some Greek historians, such as Herodotus and Polybius.[31] Furthermore, von Rad's early dating of this Israelite achievement in historiography predated the achievement of the Greeks by several centuries, and this fact very much colored the way in which SN was to be understood.

Consequently, the author of SN gave a theological, one could even say a confessional, interpretation of historical events in the time of the historian. Von Rad states, "A completely simple profession of faith underlies this work, and for this reason it must in every sense be reckoned a theological history, however worldly the colours in which it is painted."[32] This is based on the three texts in which the author, and not the characters within the story, expresses the theme of divine intervention (2 Sam 11:27, 12:24, 17:14), and he deals with these texts in considerable detail. As we shall see in a later part of this study, each of these texts has parallels in DtrH that are not merely verbal in character but are part of very similar stories. With such an early date for SN, von Rad could perhaps dismiss the need to consider these other texts, except to acknowledge that Dtr may be mimicking SN. But if SN is later than DtrH, as I shall argue below, then a comparison such as this cannot be avoided, and this may lead to a quite-different interpretation of the particular texts and the work as a whole.

The Succession Narrative and Wisdom:
Whybray

Following very much in the tradition of Rost and von Rad is R. N. Whybray's study of SN, in its seeing SN both as a literary masterpiece and as a work produced within the context of a Solomonic "enlightenment" by a member of the court.[33] Unlike von Rad, however, Whybray sees it not as a piece of historiography but instead as a carefully constructed political novel. Support for this he finds in Rost's treatment of the unity of theme, structure, use of dialogue, portrayal of character, and style. In addition, Whybray points to the strong emphasis throughout the work on wisdom themes, the value of good counsel, and a correspondence with other biblical didactic literature. He further adopts the view of those who see evidence

---

31. J. Van Seters, "Is There Any Historiography in the Hebrew Bible? A Hebrew-Greek Comparison," *JNSL* 28/2 (2002), 1–25, esp. pp. 9–17.

32. Von Rad, "Beginnings," 201–2.

33. R. N. Whybray, *The Succession Narrative: A Study of II Sam. 9–20 and I Kings 1 and 2* (SBT 2nd series 9; London: SCM, 1968).

of a strong Egyptian influence within the Solomonic court, especially in the development of a scribal class, and he looks for evidence of Egyptian literary genres that correspond to the kind of novelistic and sapiential literature that he finds in SN. From his comparisons with works such as the *Instruction of Amenemhet* and the *Story of Sinuhe*, he concludes that

> such models there must have been; and in view of the fact that the author was himself a scribe at the court of Solomon, at a time when foreign, and especially Egyptian, cultural and literary influence was strong, it is impossible to regard as irrelevant the fact that Egypt had produced, at a very similar time in its own history, a sudden burst of literary activity which bears marked resemblances to that of Israel's "enlightenment."[34]

This thesis ultimately rests on whether or not the arguments for this historical and social context can be maintained; and we shall see that other quite-different comparative models have been proposed.[35]

The History of David's Rise

The other legacy of Wellhausen cited above (p. 4), which has been rather neglected, is the History of David's Rise. The form-critics tended to view the stories in 1 Samuel and the early parts of 2 Samuel as a collection of *Sagen*, mostly *Heldensagen*, "heroic tales."[36] And as we saw above, the older style of literary criticism continued to divide up the text of Samuel into parallel sources, based on the many occurrences of parallel episodes in the text. Rost, in his study of SN, makes scant reference to HDR,[37] and

---

34. Ibid., 115.

35. Similar to the position of Whybray is that of E. Blum, "Das Ende der Thronfolgegeschichte," in *Die sogenannte Thronfolgegeschichte Davids* (ed. A. de Pury and T. Römer; OBO 176; Freiburg: Universitätsverlag, 2000), 4–37. Blum takes issue with the characterization of SN as historiography and regards it as much closer to the literary wisdom tradition. He sees it as quite distinct from the other material in the Pentateuch and Former Prophets, which he characterizes as "*Sagenschreibung*," a rather curious description, harking back to Gunkel's romantic notions about *Sagen* and oral tradition. Yet he regards the story of David's rise as a later attachment to the preexisting SN, with 2 Sam 2–4 being constructed as a bridge between the two. He too regards the David story as largely historical and contemporary but still characterizes it as "traditional narrative" (p. 37)! In my view, he has created many new problems and added little to their solution.

36. Gressmann, "Oldest History Writing," 17–18.

37. Rost, *Succession*, 105, 109.

von Rad does not make any references to HDR in his historiographic study of 1944. Later, in von Rad's *Theologie des Alten Testaments* (1958),[38] however, he recognizes HDR (1 Sam 16:14–2 Sam 5:12) as the earliest of three histories of the Davidic-Solomonic period. Noth acknowledged the existence of HDR (1 Sam 16:14–2 Sam 5:25, with many later additions) as an early source for DtrH, but he never gave any detailed analysis.[39] Noth also acknowledged the account of David's rise to power as "a connected narrative which deals with precisely this historical theme and traces David's progress from his beginnings up to the establishment of the Judean-Israelite state with obvious expert knowledge and a sure grasp of the underlying circumstances."[40] One can therefore say that by the late 1950s HDR had again come into focus alongside SN, encouraged by the views of the two most prominent German scholars of the day.

Consequently, it is from this time onward that a series of literary studies on HDR began to appear.[41] There is no need to consider these works in detail here but only to note some prevailing trends, as well as unresolved problems and issues.[42] A major problem has to do with the limits of the work, where exactly it begins and ends. Wellhausen had proposed 1 Sam 16:14 as the beginning of the story, regarding the whole of 1 Sam 15:1–16:13 as a later addition, and both Noth and von Rad, among others, followed him in this. A. Weiser, however, argued for 1 Sam 16:1–13 as integral to the larger story, but because it is difficult to separate chap. 15 from

---

38. Von Rad, *Old Testament Theology*, 1:49.

39. Noth, *The Deuteronomistic History*, 54.

40. Noth, *The History of Israel*, 179. Again, Noth acknowledged that, in spite of "some secondary additions . . . it was possible to reconstruct its original form with fair certainty" (ibid., n. 1). Both von Rad and Noth were influenced by the historical studies of Alt. See Alt, "The Formation of the Israelite State," 187.

41. H.-U. Nubel, *Davids Aufstieg in der frühe israelitischer Geschichtsschreibung* (Ph.D. diss., Rheinische Friedrich-Wilhelms-Universität, 1959); F. Mildenberger, *Die vordeuteronomistische Saul-Davidüberlieferung* (Ph.D. diss., Universität Tübingen, 1962); A. Weiser, "Die Legitimation des Königs David: Zur Eigenart und Entstehung der sogen. Geschichte von Davids Aufstieg," *VT* 16 (1966): 325–54; J. H. Grønbaek, *Die Geschichte vom Aufstieg Davids (1 Sam. 15–2 Sam. 5): Tradition und Komposition* (AtDan 10; Copenhagen: Munksgaard, 1971); T. N. D. Mettinger, *King and Messiah: The Civil and Sacred Legitimation of the Israelite King* (CBOTS 8; Lund: Gleerup, 1976), 33–47.

42. See my earlier survey, *In Search of History*, 264–71; also W. Dietrich and T. Naumann, *Die Samuelbücher* (Erträge der Forschung 281; Darmstadt: Wissenschaftliche Buchgesellschaft, 1995), 47–86.

what follows in 16:1-13, Grønbaek argued for its inclusion as well.[43]
F. Mildenberger, in his Tübingen dissertation, had earlier argued that in
fact the story of Saul could not be separated from the David story. The
problem of how the Saul and David stories are to be related to each other,
both on the level of their tradition history and as part of one or more literary works, becomes a constant issue in subsequent discussions. At the
other end of HDR, there is the question of exactly where it ends. Most
scholars believe that it ends somewhere in 2 Sam 5, but opinions differ as
to where this is. Some want to include 2 Sam 8 with chap. 5 as its original
continuation, while some want to include 2 Sam 7, which has important
lines of continuity with the earlier HDR and forms its climax.

The problem of the ending of HDR likewise raises the question of the relationship of HDR to SN. This becomes apparent whether one follows Rost
and sees 2 Sam 7 as a vital part of SN or follows Weiser and Nubel and sees
it as a part of HDR.[44] Mettinger wants to have it both ways, with the Nathan
Prophecy in both SN and HDR.[45] The matter was further complicated when
H. J. Stoebe proposed that SN included 2 Sam 2-4, so that HDR ended with
2 Sam 1, and in this he was followed by David Gunn and me.[46] This would
significantly change the character of both SN and HDR. Indeed, for Gunn,
it meant the inclusion of HDR into the story of Saul, and the whole of it he
called "The Fate of King Saul,"[47] with Saul being the primary focus of the
story and David's rise to the throne in 2 Sam 2 being merely part of the epilogue. This leaves out of consideration 2 Sam 5-8, which belongs to neither of the two literary works and is left in limbo.[48] Nevertheless, Gunn
does make a strong case for the inclusion of 2 Sam 2:8-4:12 within SN by

---

43. Weiser, "Legitimation," 325-29; Grønbaek, *Die Geschichte vom Aufstieg Davids,*
25-29. Mettinger follows Grønbaek here.

44. Weiser, "Legitimation," 342ff.; Nubel, *Davids Aufstieg,* 81-82.

45. Mettinger, *King and Messiah,* 32, 41-47.

46. H. J. Stoebe, *Das erste Buch Samuelis* (KAT 8/1; Gütersloh: Gütersloher Verlagshaus, 1973), 296ff.; D. M. Gunn, *The Story of King David* (JSOTSup 6; Sheffield:
JSOT Press, 1978), 66-68; Van Seters, *In Search of History,* 282-85. Gunn and I suggest that SN begins at 2 Sam 2:8 (or 2:12).

47. D. M. Gunn, *The Fate of King Saul* (JSOTSup 14; Sheffield: JSOT Press, 1980).

48. Gunn partly solves this problem by assigning at least 2 Sam 5:1-3* to SN
(*King David,* 70-76), along with 2 Sam 2:8-4:12, as an appropriate introduction to
2 Sam 9. Because Gunn omits 2 Sam 5:6-9 from SN, which seems necessary to account for the move from Hebron to Jerusalem, he must imagine an omission from
SN that included some remark about the move (ibid., 69). This does seem to be a
little special pleading.

using the same kind of stylistic arguments that Rost used for the unity of
SN, finding those same features in 2 Sam 2:8–4:12.[49] With these new limits
Gunn raises the problem of the *theme*, because the one proposed by Rost,
succession to the throne, would no longer be totally appropriate, and he argues that it does not entirely fit the other parts of the story as well.[50] His
own interpretation of the David story will be taken up below, pp. 39–42.

Nevertheless, one of the criticisms that Gunn makes against Rost, namely,
that he uses the predetermined theme of the work to determine its limits,
may also be raised against his work. Thus, he begins with the assumption
that it is an independent literary work that tells a story about David,

> how David gained the throne (it was given to him), how it was taken
> away from him but restored, though somewhat uneasily, and how finally
> he himself gave it away, or alternately, as we are invited to see it, how it
> is again, but now successfully taken from him. But it is not only the story
> of the kingdom and David the king. It is the story of David the man.[51]

While Gunn's interpretation of the subject or theme of the work attempts to
fit the contents and the limits of the work that he proposes, in two respects
it is still problematic. First, the beginning and the ending do not seem to be
entirely appropriate. Whether it begins in 2 Sam 2:8 or 2:12, this beginning
already assumes the account of how David gained the throne of Judah and
then focuses on a surviving son of Saul, and it is some time before David
even comes on the scene. This struggle between the two houses assumes far
too much to be a beginning. And why should we have so much said about
Solomon in 1 Kgs 2? From 1 Kgs 1:49 onward, Solomon, who has been a
minor character up to this point, now completely upstages David. Even the
remark about David's death in 1 Kgs 2:10–12 is problematic because it is
contained in a transition formula that belongs to Dtr. Second, the question
of the relationship of this story to what has gone before and what follows
must be addressed much more fully, because if it is in fact dependent on a
larger literary context, then this fact bears heavily on its theme and interpretation. Nevertheless, Gunn makes a significant contribution in opening
up new ways of understanding this work.[52]

---

49. Ibid., 76–81.

50. Ibid., 81–84.

51. Ibid., 110.

52. Gunn's treatment of the Saul story (*King Saul*, 11–19) takes a much different
tact and treats the story in its "final form." I will take up this issue below.

The New Redaction-Critical Approach:
Veijola

In contrast to the method of Rost and Gunn, in which the primary concern is to delimit clearly the story as a whole and to interpret its theme, Timo Veijola restricts his investigation to the Dtr editing and its interpretation of the David tradition.[53] Veijola accepts the view of Noth that Dtr has taken over the various earlier narrative units as outlined in Rost, but he feels that Dtr has been much more active in his intervention within the text, and in this way Dtr has sought to impose his own theme on the text, a theme that is articulated in 2 Sam 7 and numerous related texts, namely, the divine promise of the eternal dynasty to David. Following R. Smend and W. Dietrich, he also believes that one can distinguish within DtrH at least three levels: DtrG, DtrP, and DtrN, and he finds evidence of this distinction within the David story.[54] While most of the texts that he includes within the Dtr corpus belong to DtrG, part of Nathan's speech in 2 Sam 12 is attributed to DtrP, and this allows Veijola to explain away the apparent contradiction between the idealized David of DtrG and David the sinner in DtrP.

As in the case of Rost, Veijola starts with an analysis of the end of the story in 1 Kgs 1-2, but for quite-different reasons, because this is the part of the David story that has the most obvious indications of Dtr "additions." Not only is this true for 1 Kgs 2:1-4 and 10-12, but Veijola also recognizes as Dtr references back to the theme of the divine promise in 2 Sam 7, found in some of the speeches, in which the author uses key Dtr terminology (1 Kgs 1:30, 35-37, 46-48; 2:24, 31b-37b, 44-45). This leads to other earlier texts in the David story that also anticipate David's divine choice as king (1 Sam 25:23-34; 2 Sam 3:9-10, 17-19; 5:1-2; 6:21). This suggests to him the Dtr theme of the *eternal dynasty of David*, as articulated in 2 Sam 7. The problem with this method of analysis, however, is that it must first assume the priority of all of these stories of HDR and SN in order to regard all of these thematic texts as secondary. If, however, the story in 1 Sam 25

---

53. T. Veijola, *Die Ewige Dynastie: David und die Entstehung seiner Dynastie nach der deuteronomistichen Darstellung* (Suomalaisen Tiedeakatemian Toimituksia Annales Academiae Scientiarum Fennicae Series B 193; Helsinki: Suomalainen Tiedeakatemia, 1975).

54. For this purpose, Veijola also includes 2 Sam 21-24 within his study as having been edited by Dtr (see ibid., 94-126). For reasons that will be obvious in the latter part of this study, I cannot follow him in this, so I will not make reference to this part of his study.

and the CH, as Gunn and I have delimited, are later than DtrH, then use of this theme by a later writer is entirely possible. Furthermore, Veijola pays little attention to how the theme of the eternal dynasty is being used in the particular contexts. As we will see, there is much to suggest that the author parodies the theme and deliberately subverts it. The very narrative contexts make a complete mockery of it to the extent that Dtr could never have inserted it into the texts as they now stand.

The second major point that I want to stress regarding Veijola's method is that, once one begins to remove some of the texts of the story as Dtr revisions, then one also completely undermines the stylistic analysis that Rost used to argue for the unity of the work, and it breaks once again into fragments. For instance, Veijola regards 1 Kgs 2:5-9 as part of the Dtr addition to the text, and this leads him to identify other texts that are linked to this text as secondary. For Rost, on the other hand, it was very important to use these links in arguing for the way in which the author tied his work together. In addition, the deletion of supposed Dtr texts from speeches also destroys many of the examples that Rost gives to argue for the literary technique and artistry of the author of SN. What this kind of analysis in Veijola's work does is to shift the emphasis in some treatments of the David story away from the compositional critique in the style of Rost and Gunn to a redaction-critical analysis that completely dismembers what was once regarded as a literary masterpiece. However, many of the individual points raised by Veijola will be taken up again in the appropriate place in this scrutiny of the various parts of the story of David.

The Prophetic History of David

Kyle McCarter, in his very influential commentaries on 1 and 2 Samuel,[55] follows the lead of Rost in identifying the two major blocks of the David story as HDR, which he limits to 1 Sam 16:14-2 Sam 5, and SN, but he rejects the inclusion of 2 Sam 6 as part of the original AN and hence its place within SN. Following Noth and Veijola, he accepts that HDR and SN were included into DtrH and attributes to Dtr 2 Sam 7 as "the capstone of the history of David's rise to power,"[56] along with a few other Dtr texts in

---

55. P. K. McCarter, *I Samuel* (AB 8; Garden City, NY: Doubleday, 1980); idem, *II Samuel* (AB 9; Garden City, NY: Doubleday, 1984).

56. McCarter follows Cross in identifying a double redaction of DtrH, rather than the triple redaction of the Göttingen school of Veijola. But Dtr2 plays almost no role in the analysis of the David story. See idem, *I Samuel*, 17.

HDR, as a way of integrating these accounts into his larger history. However, McCarter follows the suggestion of Bruce Birth that prior to DtrH there was a Prophetic History (PH) whose author put together the major blocks of material in the books of Samuel.[57] These included the AN, the older story of Saul in 1 Sam 9-14, and the story of David's rise, "older sources systematically reworked to produce a continuous prophetic history of the origins of monarchy in Israel. . . . The prophetic writer who incorporated them into his history amplified them and reworked parts of them, sometimes with considerable license, to reflect his particular *Tendenz*."[58] This view is heavily dependent on the role of Samuel within 1 Sam 1-15, but it hardly works very well for the story of David. McCarter admits that the figure of Samuel in 1 Sam 19:18-24 is not pre-Dtr, but he ascribes the anointing of David in 1 Sam 16:1-13 to this source, as well as a reworking of the story of Samuel's ghost in 1 Sam 28:3-25.[59] Within 2 Samuel, McCarter attributes an early version of 2 Sam 7 to the PH, along with the story of David and Bathsheba in 2 Sam 11:2-12:24.[60] Because Veijola, following Dietrich, attributed these same texts to DtrP, it is not clear how one distinguishes between Dtr and PH, except as support for a literary theory.

Concerning HDR in 1 Sam 16:14-2 Sam 5:10, McCarter regards it as the oldest narrative source the purpose of which "was to show the legitimacy of David's succession to Saul as rightful king of all Israel, north as well as south."[61] McCarter formulates this theme, based on the assumption that the events portrayed are contemporary and historical, and then matches his interpretation to these events. He states, "HDR is a document from the time of David himself, written before the development of the theology of dynastic promise under Solomon and directed toward those conservative elements in the north, especially in Benjamin, who were suspicious of the new king."[62] For support of this view, McCarter appeals to an example of Hittite propagandist literature, the *Apology of Hattusilis*, which then leads him to interpret all the events in the story of David as containing a strong apologetic bias. Likewise, McCarter interprets SN as a similar royal apology in fa-

---

57. Ibid., 18-23. See B. Birch, *The Rise of the Israelite Monarchy: The Growth and Development of 1 Samuel 7-15* (SBLDS 27; Missoula, MT: Scholars Press, 1976).
58. Ibid., 18.
59. Ibid., 20-21.
60. *II Samuel*, 7-8.
61. *I Samuel*, 28.
62. Ibid., 29.

vor of Solomon's succession.[63] It is again assumed that all of the episodes mentioned correspond to actual historical events that were "publicly known and could not be baldly denied."[64] It is clear that McCarter's interpretation of the story of David rests very heavily on his assumption that the episodes, with few exceptions, are based on actual historical events, and the task of the exegete is to make sense of them within this particular context. This issue will be taken up below (pp. 54–60).

A champion of the pre-Dtr PH is Anthony Campbell, who identifies what he calls the Prophetic Record (PR) within 1 Samuel–2 Kgs 10.[65] To do this, he must carve out of the Dtr texts a pre-Dtr prophetic redaction, much of which is derived from Dietrich's DtrP. As with McCarter, Campbell includes HDR, and to do this he must identify 1 Sam 16:1–13 as PR's introduction to the David story, as well as 28:17–19a.[66] He ignores the fact that the whole of 28:3–25 does not fit well within its context. All that he can say about the rest of HDR is that "[a]s a paradigm of Yahweh's action in history, it could be pressed into the prophetic service."[67] This reconstruction has little to commend it. The major focus is on 2 Sam 7, most of the text of which, in agreement with McCarter, is attributed to PR. (This will be examined in detail below, pp. 241–256.) Regarding SN, he can find so little for its inclusion that he must construe most of it as a later addition.[68] There is, of course, an obvious problem with the notion of "prophetic editors" in the 9th century creating a lengthy literary history of the monarchy. The fact is that no collections of prophetic oracles were made before the mid-8th century, so it seems quite unlikely that "prophetic editors" would be writing a prophetic history a century earlier. It must remain a quite-speculative conjecture with little evidence to support it.

---

63. *II Samuel*, 9–16.

64. Ibid., 15. See also idem, "'Plots, True or False': The Succession Narrative as Court Apologetic," *Int* 35 (1981): 355–67. One could, of course, show from historical examples how crimes and assassinations by usurpers can be easily covered up and "baldly denied" by court historians. An argument such as this is very weak.

65. A. F. Campbell, *Of Prophets and Kings: A Late Ninth-Century Document (1 Samuel 1–2 Kings 10)* (CBQMS 17; Washington, DC: Catholic Biblical Association, 1986).

66. Ibid., 70–71.

67. Ibid., 71.

68. Ibid., 82–84. Note that I had earlier proposed that SN was a later addition to DtrH (*In Search of History*, 277–91).

The Literary/Final-Form Approach

One of the literary approaches to the narrative analysis of the David story is to set aside the diachronic investigation of literary strata and to focus on the "final form" of the text. One scholar of this sort who has given particular impetus to this method of analysis is David Gunn, in his work *The Fate of King Saul*.[69] In an earlier work, *The Story of King David*, he consciously confined his study to what he believed to be a self-contained literary work, corresponding largely to SN. In this later study, however, he departs from this approach "partly because I do not believe that anyone has succeeded in delineating the constituent sources of 1 Samuel and partly because I happen to be interested this time in the 'final form' of the text."[70] He seeks to justify this approach over against the study of the history of the text by stating that "when it comes, however, to reading the text in the form in which we have it now, seeking an integrated interpretation, it is not surprising to find such discussion to be often of relatively little assistance. Unless the compilation of the material has been made purely mechanically, or redactional material inserted that is totally out of sympathy with the "basic" material, then it is likely that there will be an overall flow and coherence in the final product—and this is what I have found in looking closely at the Saul story."[71] Gunn is quite aware of the fact that a claim of this sort is not without problems, but he suggests that his reading of the story of Saul, which for him extends from 1 Sam 8–2 Sam 2, has its own coherence, which, in spite of tensions, results in "a complex but artistically satisfying whole."[72] This approach makes a basic assumption about the compositional nature of the "final form," its being the responsibility of a particular author and this author's ability to fashion all of his disparate materials into a consistent thematic unity. But this is far from obvious and will need to be tested in particular cases in the study that follows.

Gunn likewise begs the question about what the relationship of this narrative unit is to the larger Deuteronomistic History, particularly the parts of it that are most closely related to DtrH in content and narrative continuity. Thus, scholars have long identified a major break between the story of Saul's career up to the end of 1 Samuel 14 and the rise of David to power in what follows in 1 Sam 16:14–2 Sam 5. What happens between these two

---

69. D. M. Gunn, *The Fate of King Saul*.
70. Ibid., 13.
71. Ibid.
72. Ibid., 14.

is a radical shift from the primary focus's being on Saul in the first unit to its being on David in the second, with the quite-secondary connection between the two being the double reference to Saul's rejection in favor of David in 1 Sam 13:8–15a and 1 Sam 15:1–16:13, which has its obvious fulfillment and completion in David's becoming King of all Israel in place of Saul in 2 Sam 5:1–3. How Gunn comes to terms with these texts that deal with the theme of Saul's rejection, which is central to the study as a whole, will be the primary test of his thesis and method.[73]

A work that follows very closely in the same mode as that of Gunn is Diana Edelman's *King Saul in the Historiography of Judah*.[74] In this study, Edelman also claims to be working with the "final form of the text," but in her case this "final form" happens to be part of a larger complex that is identical with the Deuteronomistic History, so that the genre of the text of the story of Saul is defined by this context. This means that Dtr is effectively "the last 'hand' that made adjustments to [the story]."[75] The limits that Edelman sets to the Saul story, 1 Sam 8–2 Sam 1, are virtually the same as those of Gunn, so that the same problem of how to account for the ending without dealing with David's enthronement and indeed the Dtr climax in 2 Sam 7 applies in this case also. From 1 Sam 16 onward, it is the story not of Saul but of David, and this makes a fundamental difference in how the story is to be understood. Edelman defends the limits she sets to the narrative boundaries by claiming that they were not determined beforehand but "resulted from my completion of the literary analysis."[76] Given the fact that by her own admission the study is part of a larger project on the historical evidence for the reign of King Saul, the limits seem to be much too convenient.

Edelman's method of literary analysis I also find rather curious. She states, "I will analyze the narrative sequentially, as if I were hearing or reading it for the first time. This means that I will not use later story developments, occurrences of idioms, *Leitwörter*, or literary techniques to influence my interpretation of preceding ones."[77] But how can she even know where to begin and end the story without establishing its limits by using all of

---

73. See below, pp. 126–130.
74. D. V. Edelman, *King Saul in the Historiography of Judah* (JSOTSup 121; Sheffield: Sheffield Academic Press, 1991).
75. Ibid., 13.
76. Ibid., 14.
77. Ibid.

these methods? The story itself not only makes reference to a greater past but often anticipates a certain future, for example, that David will become king in place of Saul, a future that she arbitrarily refuses to recognize. Once one acknowledges that the story of Saul and David is an integral part of the larger DtrH, then ending the story at Saul's death seems to be quite arbitrary. Furthermore, what must also be established is whether or not there is a substantial part of this story of David and Saul that is later than DtrH, and if this is the case then it would have a major bearing on how the present story, its "final form," is to be understood.[78]

Another example of a final-form approach to the story of David is represented by the work of Kurt Noll in his book *The Faces of David*.[79] Though the main body of the book deals with the parts of the David tradition that will not be treated in my own work, the first two chapters do lay out his methodological approach, which merits a few remarks here. The study as a whole is written from the viewpoint of a synchronic analysis, making use of recent literary theory and engaging in a critical appraisal of others who share the same "final-form" or "literary" approach to the text. The approach is offered as an alternative to the older historical-critical method of source analysis.

Noll first introduces his theory of biblical narrative that will govern his treatment, which is that the author sets forth his concerns by means of the narrator's writing within his own story-world, and whatever he says about the long past of this story-world must be understood from within his own place in this world. But there is evidence, so he asserts, that this narrator is not consistent or is contradictory in the presentation of his story, and this leads Noll to suggest the possibility that in addition to the narrator there is also the "implied author," who has deliberately introduced material into the narrative that complicates and even subverts the judgments and ideology of the narrator. Consequently, unlike many others, who operate with only the single level of narrator and reader/audience, Noll makes use of a second level, "implied author," who addresses an "implied reader," who is reflected in a "value system" different from that used by the narrator. It is

---

78. There are many other studies of various parts of the story of David in its "final form," but these are of no concern in this study, which is focused on the diachronic analysis of the text.

79. K. L. Noll, *The Faces of David* (JSOTSup 242; Sheffield: Sheffield Academic Press, 1997). See also idem, "Is There a Text in This Tradition? Readers' Response and the Taming of Samuel's God," *JSOT* 83 (1999): 31–51.

this scheme that allows Noll to overcome the problems in the text that older literary critics have used in the past to identify sources and literary strata in the history of the text's composition and transmission. This leads Noll to review the various literary theories and their relationships to his own method of approach, especially as it has to do with the story of David.

In order to illustrate the distinction between narrator and implied author, Noll points to the example of Mark Twain's *Adventures of Huckleberry Finn*, in which Twain uses the literary conceit of Huck as the narrator, who suggests that he is not in entire agreement with the author. However, when the narrator is a character within the story, he is a fiction created by the author for his own literary purposes, and no serious reader would confuse his limited perspective with that of the author. There is nothing comparable to that literary technique in the story of David. Is Noll suggesting that DtrH is a deliberate fiction created by the author and that any serious reader should be able to identify this *narrator* (Dtr) as a special literary construction employed by the "implied author" in order to offer his critique on Dtr morality and theology? I hardly think that this is likely. I would not deny that characters within the story of David can make speeches that may serve the purpose of parody on the religious themes of DtrH, but this is quite another matter.

Consequently, Noll's critique of scholarship, especially as it has to do with those who opt for a plurality of authors in the text, does not stand up. Here, his remarks are primarily addressed to Noth and his successors in the Cross school of Dtr editors, but they do not address the approach I took in my previous work or the one reflected in this book. What Noll identifies as the *narrator* and the *implied author* I would simply construe as two (or more) authors, the earliest being Dtr (regardless of what sources he may or may not have used for his account), and at least one major author who made an extensive addition to Dtr, much of it attempting to subvert the earlier work. These two authors cannot be said to share the same storyworld, nor do they reflect the same social context. Each must be understood in his own right and in juxtaposition to the other.

In keeping with Noll's notion of interplay between the good David of the narrator and the more human David of the implied author, he views the Former Prophets as just "strung together to function aesthetically."[80] This is similar to David Gunn's suggestion about "serious entertainment." As we

---

80. Noll, *The Faces of David*, 37.

shall see below in a discussion of genre (pp. 39–49) this suggestion of "serious entertainment" or "aesthetic presentation" of tradition has considerable merit. If one wanted to pursue this notion, one could compare the
various plays of the Greek dramatists dealing with the same theme, such as
the murder of Agamemnon. How different are the treatments of tradition
and the heroes by the three greats, Aeschylus, Sophocles, and Euripides.
They all live in a somewhat different story-world, and the youngest certainly
seems to subvert the perspective or theology of the oldest. The works of all
three were certainly meant for entertainment of a large audience and had a
significant impact, to the extent that all of them became "canonical," even if
the more iconoclastic Euripides became the most popular in a later period.
He spoke to the age. This strikes me as a better model than the one suggested by Noll, in which an older, more "traditional" author is satirized by
a younger one. Dtr represents the traditional view of David; the later author
is a highly iconoclastic revisionist.

Part of the problem with Noll's theory of an interplay between the narrator (Dtr) and the implied author (CH) is that it comes to a climax and end
in 1 Kgs 2. While scholars identify DtrH as continuing on throughout the
rest of Kings, there has never been an inclination to continue the work in
CH beyond that final scene. The rest of the story of Solomon is of an entirely different character. Nor is there anything that is the least bit comparable in the books of Chronicles, even when the Chronicler takes over the
older material from Samuel–Kings. He simply excises what does not fit his
ideology. Nevertheless, in spite of my rejection of Noll's literary theory, his
work has considerable merit in that it clearly recognizes that there are two
voices in the text of the David story, which are clearly at odds with each
other, and that it is the voice of the second author (his implied author) that
is making a parody of the traditionalist Dtr (his narrator). This has allowed
him to see these two quite-distinct perspectives and the primary role that is
played in the narrative by the satirical and realistic portrait of David. My
own literary theory attempts to account for this same observation of the
two conflicting voices in a different way.

Redaction-Critical Disintegration of the
Old Consensus: Dietrich

In contrast to the final-form approach is that of redaction criticism, in
which the literary unity of HDR and SN have been dissolved not only into
the pieces of individual stories of the older form criticism but also into various layers of literary expansion. This includes the methodological analysis

of Walter Dietrich, which builds on Veijola's treatment of extensive editing by multiple Dtr redactors.[81] This is not surprising, given the fact that both Veijola and Dietrich, along with Rudolf Smend, were the initial creators of the so-called Göttingen school of criticism of DtrH. Whereas Dietrich acknowledges, with Veijola, that the Deuteronomists were responsible for some of the linkage between the major blocks of the David story, the development of the story of David was much more complex. For him, this is evident in the numerous links between HDR and SN that cannot all be accounted for by Dtr redactors, as well as the internal complexity of HDR. For him, this means that we have to do with a literary development that stretches between a basic document, or documents, from Davidic times down to the post-exilic period. Furthermore, this was not merely the uniting of independent literary works, but much of it was a process of expansion and revision. Following a number of other scholars, Dietrich is willing to acknowledge that a large part of the interconnection between HDR and its larger context in both the Saul story, which precedes it, and SN, which follows, was the product of pre-Dtr redactions. This is primarily in response to the growing number of scholars, such as McCarter and Campbell, who championed a PH prior to DtrH.

Dietrich's diachronic analysis rests on the assumption that there was a basic document of the Davidic era, reflected within SN, along with some other materials in the rest of the David story, so that the whole story expanded in stages from this base. He also insists that the interconnections between HDR and SN must be taken seriously. He concludes:

> [T]he so-called Rise of David Narrative probably never existed as a single work on its own but was conceived as an additional layer to the Succession Narrative. Or, more carefully, it was conceived together with a secondary textual layer in 2 Samuel 10–20 + 1 Kings 1–2 not least in order to shed more favorable light on gloomy memories and messages that were detrimental to the dynasty of David.[82]

The attempts to sort out the pro- and anti-dynastic/Davidic/Solomonic layers in the text and to decide which belong to the original composition and

---

81. W. Dietrich, *Die frühe Königszeit in Israel: 10. Jahrhundert v. Chr.* (Biblisch Enzyklopädie 3; Stuttgart: Kohlhammer, 1997), 202–73; W. Dietrich and T. Naumann, "The David–Saul Narrative," in *Reconstructing Israel and Judah: Recent Studies on the Deuteronomistic History* (ed. G. N. Knoppers and J. G. McConville; Sources for Biblical and Theological Study 8; Winona Lake, IN: Eisenbrauns, 2000), 276–318.

82. Dietrich and Naumann, "The David–Saul Narrative," 313.

which are editorial has become a major fixation in the diachronic analysis of the David story.

In his latest analysis of SN, Dietrich moves more radically in the direction of redaction criticism and retreats from Rost's view of SN to the older view of individual pieces.[83] Thus, he concludes that the Bathsheba episode in 2 Sam 11–12 together with the account of the palace intrigue and crowning of Solomon in 1 Kgs 1–2, minus the numerous later revisions and additions, was an independent early story of Solomon written by a contemporary witness to the events. All of the texts that form interconnections with earlier events, and they are very many, are removed as secondary additions. By the same token, the rest of SN is split up into several pieces of ancient David stories, and all of their interconnections, both internally to the rest of SN and externally to HDR, are redactional. All of these, together with most of what Veijola was inclined to attribute to Dtr are now attributed to a Prophetic Historian. This even replaces Dietrich's own DtrP in the Bathsheba story, and the limits of this historian also embrace the material in HDR, as well as the earlier material in 1 Samuel and later material in Kings. This is much more ambitious than McCarter's modest proposal, and Dietrich dates this historian a century later to the late 8th century, after the fall of the Northern Kingdom. This is based on the assumption that after 722 B.C.E. there was a flood of refugees into the south, and the author is using his history of the "united kingdom" to appeal for the unity of these Israelites with Judah into a single entity.

Without going into detail on particular texts, let me make the following comments on these proposals. First, in the process of his analysis of redactional additions, Dietrich has, of course, quite done away with many of Rost's strongest arguments for the high literary qualities of SN, including the very complex pattern of interconnection, which now becomes merely evidence of redaction. What is quite remarkable is that this whole system of elaborate interconnection is never duplicated outside the David story either before HDR or after SN. Second, some scholars' attributing "redactional" additions to Dtr, others' to PH, and still others' to many different hands, whatever suits their particular literary theories with no apparent control, is quite intolerable. Third, the Prophetic History/Record was invented originally to account for Samuel's role in 1 Samuel, but under Camp-

---

83. W. Dietrich, "Das Ende der Thronfolgegeschichte," in *Die sogenannte Thronfolgegeschichte Davids* (ed. A. de Pury and T. Römer; OBO 176; Freiburg: Universitätsverlag, 2000), 38–69.

bell it grew into an extensive history down to the 9th century. Dietrich dates this PH a century later but restricts it to a history of the early monarchy, and within the David story Dietrich gives it an entirely different character from that suggested by McCarter and Campbell. Fourth, the reason for dating PH to the late 8th century rests on the notion of an invasion of refugees from the Northern Kingdom after the fall of Samaria, to whom the work is intended to appeal. Recently, however, Na'aman has seriously called into question any such migration from the north during the period of Assyrian domination as against state policy.[84] Fifth, by accepting the various archaic sources within the story of David as being from the 10th century, Dietrich must confront the growing scholarly opinion that there never was a "United Monarchy" and that a viewpoint such as this, which permeates the whole corpus, cannot possibly be removed as "redactional." Indeed, Dietrich and many other redaction critics are so caught up in their literary theories that they have not taken seriously the numerous anachronisms that permeate the whole of the David story, but especially SN.

One recent effort to understand the literary continuity between SN and HDR in a different way is a proposal put forward by Ina Willi-Plein, in which she advocates a literary stratum containing elements from both and which she calls "the Story of David's House" (*Davidshausgeschichte* = DHG).[85] The criteria for establishing the outlines of this source are rather vague, apart from the exclusion of Deuteronomistic additions, following the identification of texts such as these by Veijola. Her main criterion is the distinction between the roles of Jonathan and Michal in their relationship to David. Michal plays a very significant role within the DHG, whereas the Jonathan texts, in her view, all belong to a later and much shorter addition. Willi-Plein places a strong methodological emphasis on not adopting a literary theory or mode of analysis that leads to circular argument, but one has the sense that this has also happened in her case as well. There are some rather serious tensions, contradictions, and doublets within the corpus of texts devoted to the relationship between David and Jonathan that she does not

---

84. N. Na'aman, "When and How Did Jerusalem Become a Great City? The Rise of Jerusalem as Judah's Premier City in the Eighth–Seventh Centuries B.C.E.," *BASOR* 347 (2007): 21–56. (I will discuss more on this below, pp. 82–83).

85. I. Willi-Plein, "1 Sam 18-19 und die Davidshausgeschichte," in *David und Saul im Widerstreit: Diachronie und Synchronie im Wettstreit* (ed. W. Dietrich; OBO 206; Freiburg: Academic Press / Göttingen: Vandenhoeck & Ruprecht, 2004), 138–77; see also idem, "Michal und die Anfänge des Königtums in Israel, " in *Congress Volume, Cambridge 1995* (ed. J. A. Emerton; VTSup 66; Leiden: Brill, 1997), 401–19.

address. Even the texts that present Michal as David's wife, which are her primary concern, demonstrate very contradictory portraits of the relationship of David and Michal; those in the story of David in the court of Saul differing radically from those in the CH. These differences are, in my view, too easily glossed over.[86]

The consequences of the analytical method of redaction criticism, as reflected in Dietrich and others, can be seen in the recent work of Thilo Rudnig, in which, in my view, the number of editors and revisers has proliferated to the point of absurdity.[87] He first reduces SN to include only the Bathsheba affair (2 Sam 11-12), the revolt of Absalom (chaps. 15-19), and the succession of Solomon (1 Kgs 1-2). The basic text consists of very short fragments within these three divisions, which may go back to the Davidic-Solomonic period.[88] These have been subject to over a dozen identified redactions, as well as innumerable glosses and additions, some quite large, and this redactional process extends over a period from the first redactor in the 9th century to the latest addition in the 3rd century B.C.E. The result is that any possible literary coherence or artistry, which so impressed earlier scholars, has been completely demolished. The text is a product of mere chance with so many different parties and concerns, reflecting so many different social contexts, that the final product, viewed by many as the finest piece of biblical prose, can only be regarded as a miraculous coincidence.

This approach by Rudnig represents a return to the worst abuses of redaction criticism by German biblical and classical scholarship in the 19th century.[89] This goes directly against the literary analysis of Rost, who rejected attempts of some earlier scholars to divide SN into a number of independent sources. He states:

> Against this we should note that no peculiarities of language or style can
> be discerned and that in terms of content the threads are interwoven. So
> the most likely solution is that we should recognize just one *author*, in
> which case the somewhat unlikely possibility exists that we should attrib-

---

86. These issues will be taken up again in chap. 5, pp. 165-171.

87. T. A. Rudnig, *Davids Thron: Redaktionskritische Studien zur der Thronnachfolge Davids* (BZAW 358; Berlin: de Gruyter, 2006).

88. The basic source text for the conquest of Rabba in 2 Sam 11-12 is 11:1*; 12:29, 31b; for the Absalom revolt in 2 Sam 15-19 is 15:1*, 12b; 17:22a*; 18:1a, 6, 9b, 15*, 16a, 17a*; for the birth and succession of Solomon is 2 Sam 11:2, 4*, 5, 27a*; 12:24b*; 1 Kgs 1:5, 7, 8*, 38, 39*, 40*.

89. See my *Edited Bible: The Curious History of the "Editor" in Biblical Criticism* (Winona Lake, IN: Eisenbrauns, 2006).

ute the present form of the whole text to a final redaction by this same writer. . . . But just one look at the uniform style or the structure of the succession story proves that there is a unifying plan underlying the whole text which does not owe its origins to the industrious hands of some *editor.*[90]

The rest of his discussion is an attempt to demonstrate just this thesis, and it won the support of both Noth and von Rad, among many others.

Consequently, the redactor has been introduced into the literary analysis, not on the usual basis of source criticism, that is, differences of style, vocabulary, and content, but to address the problem of the relationship of SN to Dtr and the attempt to date all or part of SN as early. Nevertheless, apart from the very small source fragments that Rudnig identifies as base texts and a very minimal editing of these into a single composition, which was then taken up by Dtr into his work by the addition of 1 Kgs 2:10-12, the rest of the expansion of this small corpus belongs to the post-DtrH period.[91] According to Rudnig, the first major revision is a criticism of the Davidic dynasty. This would appear to be a concession to my own long-standing view that the CH, which takes a negative view of the Davidic monarchy, is a post-Dtr work. Yet there seems to be some strong desire to ground this postexilic work in events that took place many centuries earlier, as reflected in his source fragments, but without any way of controlling an earlier date such as this. This very restricted corpus of early texts seemingly eliminates most of the anachronisms in SN, but not all of them. In the final scene relating to Solomon's coronation, Rudnig is compelled to include in the original source a reference to Solomon's supporters in 1 Kgs 1:8 and 38, among whom are Benaiah, the son of Jehoiadah, and the Cherethites and Pelethites. However, as we shall see below,[92] this body of Greek mercenaries, which appears to serve here as the palace guard, cannot possibly be dated to the time of David and instead reflects the late Persian period. And this means that everything else in these two chapters belongs to the same era. Nor is it possible to solve the problem by eliminating this figure and his group as "redactional," because Benaiah is clearly necessary as a counterpart to Joab, the commander of the army in Adonijah's party. The

---

90. Rost, *The Succession,* 67 (my emphasis).

91. There is, of course, not much point in speaking of a redaction of SN after the David story has become part of Dtr's larger history. One would then need to speak of the "editing" of DtrH as a whole.

92. See chap. 3, pp. 99-118.

texts all belong to the same late level of composition, and the divisions made by Rundig are quite arbitrary.

As we have seen above, the present form of redaction criticism, as reflected by Dietrich and Rudnig, has led to a complete disintegration of the consensus position, developed by Rost and strengthened by von Rad, that within the David story, particularly in SN, we have evidence of remarkable artistic gifts, the work of a skilled author. The method of redaction criticism in biblical criticism generally is to replace all these skilled authors with editors and all signs of literary artistry with pedantic scribal techniques.[93] Dietrich's method is to accommodate every other possibility, except of course, the method that calls into question the whole notion of these editors and their techniques.[94] Willi-Plein attempts to solve the problem of this disintegration of documents by suggesting a new literary configuration in DHG that embraces parts of both HDR and SN as a base text, with subsequent layers of redaction. But this ultimately leads to the same kind of literary fragmentation of the former SN.

A Different Approach to the David Story:
Van Seters

At this point I will set forth my earlier treatment of the David story and some critical responses to it. In my discussion of the story of David's rise in *In Search of History*,[95] I considered it a work put together by the historian Dtr. It begins with 1 Sam 16:14, which was a continuation of 14:52, and therefore I regarded the whole of 15:1–16:13 a later addition to the Dtr account. Dtr's story of David extends to 2 Sam 2:7, 5:1–25. This is also in direct continuity with Dtr's account of the restoration of the ark in 2 Sam 6 and the Nathan Prophecy in chap. 7, the whole of which I attributed to Dtr.[96] The military campaigns in 2 Sam 8:1–14 and 10:15–19a also belong to Dtr. The only other piece to belong to Dtr's story of David is in 1 Kgs 2:1–4 and 10–12. All the rest is a later literary expansion. Consequently, I advocated the view that it was Dtr who first put together the story of David, and there was never an earlier HDR as a source for his work. This was a radical departure from the prevailing view of the David story and one that

---

93. See most recently K. van der Toorn, *Scribal Culture and the Making of the Hebrew Bible* (Cambridge, MA: Harvard University Press, 2007).

94. See my *Edited Bible.*

95. Idem, *In Search of History,* 264–71.

96. Ibid., 271–77.

was largely ignored in subsequent treatments. Furthermore, in this earlier study I did not regard the parallel episodes in HDR as pointing to parallel documents or "sagas" (*Sagen*), as Klaus Koch had argued[97] but attributed all of the episodes to the same source. However, my reevaluation of this problem of parallels has led me to quite-different conclusions in the present study, and these will be examined in detail below.[98]

With regard to SN, which in my earlier study I preferred to call the Court History (CH), I largely followed the treatment of Rost regarding the limits of the work and its general character, except with respect to its beginning. By including 2 Sam 2:8–4:12, which contains the war against Ish-bosheth, I considered Rost's proposal of the theme of the succession to David's throne no longer appropriate. Furthermore, the problematic account of Saul's death by the hand of the Amalekite in 2 Sam 1:5–10, 13–16 I also regarded as belonging to CH. However, if these texts are also part of CH, then it is clear that CH is later than Dtr and dependent on it, and much in the rest of CH points in this same direction. In particular, the transition from David's rule in Hebron to his kingship over all Israel in Jerusalem, which is recounted in Dtr, is presupposed by CH in 2 Sam 9–20. I also argued that Dtr's ending of David's reign and transition to Solomon in 1 Kgs 2:1–4, 10–12 likewise requires that CH is later than Dtr because it is presupposed in the rest of the narrative in 1 Kgs 2. This was a radical break with earlier scholars who viewed SN as a primitive document contemporary with the events portrayed. A post-Dtr dating of CH suggests, in fact, that all of the episodes presented in this document are fictional and not based on any historical record. Such a late dating of CH likewise indicates that it has nothing to do with the legitimization of David's and Solomon's reigns or succession. Its whole intent was in fact antimonarchic or even antimessianic.

My later study, "The Court History and DtrH," was written in response to a number of scholars who disputed my late dating of this corpus.[99] In

---

97. K. Koch, *The Growth of the Biblical Tradition:The Form-Critical Method* (trans. S. M. Cupitt; London: Black, 1969), 138–41.

98. I also note with some embarrassment that I often refer to Dtr as author/editor or author/redactor and his literary activity as redactional. Mea culpa! This language I now consider inappropriate. See my *Edited Bible*.

99. J. Van Seters, "The Court History and DtrH," in *Die sogenannte Thronfolgegeschichte Davids* (ed. A. de Pury and T. Römer; OBO 176; Freiburg: Universitätsverlag, 2000), 70–93.

this study on the relationship of CH to DtrH, I focused on three issues. The first was what I consider "the clearest and strongest argument against the priority of the Court History and its use as a source by DtrH. This is the fact that we have a basic contradiction between the behavior of David in the Court History and Dtr's Judgment of David that he was the epitome of the just and righteous king who was completely obedient to Yahweh and who was the model for all the subsequent kings to follow."[100] To illustrate this point, I drew a comparison between David's adultery with Bathsheba and the murder of Uriah in CH, and Dtr's treatment of Ahab's murder of Naboth in 1 Kgs 21 in order to show how utterly unlikely it is for Dtr to regard Ahab as the worst of all the kings of Israel and for his dynasty to be condemned as a result of this act and yet for Dtr to consider David the best of all the kings of Israel and Judah in spite of his crimes. Dtr could not plausibly have known of this episode and included it in his history because it would have made a mockery of all his positive statements about David. Later, I will take up a more detailed comparison between the Bathsheba episode in CH and a number of stories in Dtr that I believe the writer of CH imitates.

The second point that I discussed is the literary relationship between CH and Dtr as it has to do with the beginning and the ending of the account. Because the beginning of CH depends so clearly on Dtr's presentation of David's anointing as king over all Israel and his move from Hebron to Jerusalem in 2 Sam 5:1-12 and because the ending of CH (in 1 Kgs 2:5-9, 13-48) is incomprehensible without Dtr's transition of the monarchy from David to Solomon in 1 Kgs 2:1-4, 10-12, scholars have shown remarkable ingenuity in trying to overcome these difficulties. They have claimed that the beginning of SN was lost or replaced by Dtr and the transition in the ending formula was merely modified by Dtr. There are also explicit statements in CH, particularly in the succession account in 1 Kgs 1-2 that reflect the Dtr language of 2 Sam 7, but these have all been bracketed as Dtr glosses. In a similar fashion, there are allusions throughout CH to episodes in the larger Dtr history, a work that is clearly familiar to the author of CH. These must also be removed by invoking a Dtr redactor. Yet, I have tried to show that the dependence goes well beyond just these few details but reflects whole episodes that have been structured in imitation of similar episodes in Dtr.[101] These will be taken up in detail below.

---

100. Ibid., 71.
101. See also my "Creative Imitation in the Hebrew Bible," *SR* 29 (2000): 395–409.

The third issue that I addressed is the quite-different royal ideology that is reflected in DtrH and CH. Dtr is at great pains to lay out the basis on which Yahweh chose David, as the man after God's own heart, to succeed Saul, and because of David's exemplary rule Yahweh promised to establish his dynasty in perpetuity. The climax of this ideology, therefore, is reflected in 2 Samuel 7. The whole of CH seeks to undermine this ideology by demonstrating first that David himself was quite unworthy of the divine promise because of his adultery and murder early in his reign and that each successive crown prince was likewise tainted. The final succession by Solomon was the result of a palace intrigue followed by much bloodshed, all of which was intended to completely undermine this royal ideology. These presentations of kingship in DtrH and CH are so utterly incompatible that Dtr could not have included CH in his portrayal of David and his house. The Chronicler simply removed them from his record to maintain his idealization of David and Solomon, and there would have been nothing to compel Dtr to include them. Once CH is understood as a later addition to DtrH, then Dtr's history of David with 2 Sam 7 as its capstone and ending becomes clear and consistent within the larger work.

In an extended response to my position on the CH, Otto Kaiser takes up a number of issues about which I will make a few remarks here.[102] As is obvious from the title of his essay, Kaiser follows a number of scholars who recently dispute the existence of a Deuteronomistic History and merely treats the supposed Dtr elements within CH as a redactional layer or layers. Kaiser also accepts the view of Wellhausen that CH rests on eyewitness accounts, but these belong to a series of independent stories within the base narrative that experienced successive redactional additions. Kaiser is concerned to identify a particular pre-Dtr, prodynastic revision that attempts to modify the older accounts of the actual (?) events, which Kaiser dates, on the basis of the dating formula in 2 Sam 11:1, to the late 8th to 6th centuries B.C.E. This seems to be a modification of the older notion of the Prophetic History, but with quite a different character. Thus, in 1 Kgs 1 the texts that Veijola regarded as Dtr and Dietrich viewed as PH, Kaiser ascribes to his prodynastic revision.

---

102. O. Kaiser, "Das Verhältnis der Erzählung vom König David zum sogenannten deuteronomistischen Geschichtswerk: Am Beispiel von Kön 1–2 untersucht. Ein Gespräch mit John Van Seters," in *Die sogenannte Thronfolgegeschichte Davids* (ed. A. de Pury and T. Römer; OBO 176; Freiburg: Universitätsverlag, 2000), 94–122. The details of his analysis on 1 Kgs 1–2, as distinct from my own, will be taken up in a later chapter.

The whole scheme seems highly implausible. One would need to assume that the negative eyewitness accounts from the 10th century were faithfully retained and transmitted by royal scribes from one generation of kings to the next for no apparent reason, and only with the end of the monarchy did someone bother to bring all of the stories together into one composition and give them a positive spin. Furthermore, the earlier arguments used to interpret certain remarks within CH as pro-Davidic or pro-Solomonic depend entirely on identifying CH as a royal apology and dating the texts soon after the events portrayed. Once one removes the text to a time centuries later, the editorial addition of an apologetic element is pointless. One certainly cannot assume that the base texts were in the public domain in some form and were therefore well known. Furthermore, what seems equally incredible is how so many redactional layers in the text, added over an extended period of time, could produce a work of such great unity and uniformity of literary style that it is frequently considered the finest example of narrative literature in the Hebrew Bible.

Another response to my views within the same volume was put forward by Steven McKenzie, which was of quite a different kind.[103] McKenzie wants to salvage the older view that a large part of HDR and CH reflects early apologies of David that were used as base texts for Dtr. However, in answer to the objections I raised above to viewing CH as a source for Dtr, he admits that the story of Bathsheba in 2 Sam 11–12 is so completely at variance with Dtr's view of David that this must be a later post-Dtr addition to the David story. Consequently, in his view it was not originally part of CH that followed in 2 Sam 13–20. He also accepts my view that 1 Kgs 2:1–4, 10–12 reflects the Dtr transition formula, which is presupposed by the rest of the narrative in 1 Kgs 1–2; so he takes the whole of these chapters as the work of Dtr. Having met these two objections of mine, he then attempts to view the rest of the material as not incompatible to Dtr's view of David. In his view, it is Dtr who is responsible for putting together a number of sources in HDR as well as those in 2 Sam 9, 13–20, (21:1–14), which were pro-Davidic apologies that arose out of the particular historical events to which they refer. Just how many original apologies he has in mind, all apparently using the same technique in their defense of David, is not at all clear. Because there is nothing Deuteronomistic in any of this material in

---

103. S. L. McKenzie, "The So-Called Succession Narrative in the Deuteronomistic History," in *Die sogenannte Thronfolgegeschichte Davids* (ed. A. de Pury and T. Römer; OBO 176; Freiburg: Universitätsverlag, 2000), 123–35.

CH, it is difficult to see how he can attribute to Dtr the collection and editing of these "sources." Why would Dtr's treatment of the sources in CH be different from Dtr's presentation of David in 2 Sam 5–8? Furthermore, there remains, as with Kaiser, a very long gap between the creation of these sources and Dtr's discovery of them in some "archive" (?) or as the repository of literary texts within the courtly scribal tradition and then used by him as material for his history. In either case, the possibilities for filling the gap between 10th-century origins of apologetic texts and the combined document of the 6th century seem highly improbable. Finally, McKenzie passes rather lightly over my discussion of the somewhat sardonic references to divine election and the succession promise of 2 Sam 7 within 1 Kgs 1–2. These references completely subvert the basic theme of DtrH and can hardly belong to Dtr.

McKenzie's case rests entirely on the viability of the dating of the so-called apologies in HDR and CH to the time of David, and this matter will be taken up below (chap. 2, pp. 53–60). But in addition, McKenzie has completely ignored Rost's argument from style and the obvious unity throughout the CH. The style and mode of characterization is so similar between 2 Sam 11–12 and what follows in CH and also between CH and 1 Kgs 1–2, with the complex interconnections throughout all of these units, that they cannot be ignored. And it is inconceivable that Dtr could have written the treatment of Solomon in 1 Kgs 2, which McKenzie must admit is rather negative, and then presented a quite-different pious and humble Solomon in 1 Kgs 3. Nothing in what follows in 1 Kgs 3–11 resembles in the slightest way the style and character portrayal of 1 Kgs 1–2 or the CH in general. Gone is the court life so ubiquitous in CH; gone is Bathsheba and the royal family; gone are the generals; gone are Nathan the prophet and Zadok the priest, except in the lists. This also applies to 2 Sam 5–8, which has the same colorless style without any secondary figures that populate the whole of CH. Nathan appears in 2 Sam 7 merely as spokesman for the deity and nothing more. The one exception is the scene of David and Michal in 2 Sam 6:16, 20–23, precisely because this is an *addition* by CH, as Rost recognized.

The Genre Debate

When it comes to a discussion about what genre designation is most suitable as a characterization of the story of David, there have been a variety of suggestions, based either on the supposed dating of the work and

specific historical purpose or on certain literary characteristics and the perceived function or role of the story in its social setting. As we saw in the
above historical review, the earlier dating of the David story and the perception of it as a literary work of the court led scholars to characterize it as
historiography and to identify it with certain apologetic genres with the intent of legitimating David as successor to Saul and Solomon's succession of
David. Various Near Eastern parallels were invoked to support this general
approach, and this understanding of the David story's form still influences
many studies today. These treatments of genre rest heavily on questions of
social and historical context, which will be taken up in the next two chapters, and will not be anticipated here. It is enough at this point merely to
state that the social and historical context of the story of David as we have
it provides very little warrant for characterizing it as an apology by the
court, directed at a contemporary audience within the living memory of
David and Solomon. Furthermore, the specific characteristics of royal inscriptions, on which so much of the genre comparison is based, bear little
resemblance to all but a very small part of the story, such that these characteristics give us no help in understanding the matter of genre.

A quite-different approach was undertaken by David Gunn in his study
The Story of King David, in which he gave considerable attention to the
question of genre.[104] After reviewing various proposed genres (history writing, apology, wisdom literature, and didactic narrative or *Königsnovelle*),
Gunn finds none of these satisfactory, and proposes something in a quite-
different direction.[105] While he grants to Whybray that there is some merit
in the designation of the David story as a "novel," he prefers to use the
more general classification "a story, told in a traditional vein as a work of
art and entertainment."[106] He rejects the form-critical designation "saga" to
reflect this traditional character in order to avoid confusion with the older
debate about what is meant by this term in the general discussion of sagas
in the Pentateuch and historical books and settles on the classification "traditional story." The traditional character of the story is understood in two
senses. On the one hand, it may refer to the traditional content of details
within the story, which, through the medium of oral tradition, would give
it some continuity with an archaic past. On the other hand, it may refer to

---

104. D. M. Gunn, *Story of King David*, 19–62.
105. On these forms see the earlier study by R. N. Whybray, *The Succession Narrative*; Gunn, *Story of King David*, 37–62.
106. Ibid., 38.

elements of structure, plot, or shape, "rather in the manner of a motif," and it is "traditional motifs" of this sort that become his primary concern in the matter of genre.[107] Gunn, in his study, makes frequent reference to a vigorous discussion and debate that existed between him and me over the nature of these "traditional motifs." The debate need not be repeated here, except to say that I consider most of the stock scenes or traditional motifs not to reflect oral tradition but to be either the result of direct literary imitation of an earlier example or the invention and repetition of a particular motif by the same author. In other words, unless the identification of stock scenes can be used to mark the text as derived from oral tradition, I do not think that it assists us in the genre classification of the David story. This issue will, of course, need to be clarified further in the analysis of the David story that follows in the rest of this book.

Consequently, I cannot accept Gunn's conclusions, based on his discussion of the traditional motifs: "There is evidence in the story of King David that significant elements in it have been derived from an existing storytelling tradition. . . . Accordingly we may speak of the story as a traditional story. I have argued, furthermore, that this story probably stands not far from an oral stage of transmission, though its precise relation to oral storytelling is impossible to determine."[108] I do not deny that oral tradition makes use of traditional motifs as a story-telling technique, but literary works of great sophistication often imitate techniques of this sort and develop new motifs that become traditional in a particular genre. As a result, the mere repetition of the same motif in a story does not necessarily imply a direct dependence on an oral source.

Nevertheless, what Gunn has to say about the purpose of the story of David is, in my view, quite significant. This purpose he describes as "serious entertainment," and it is this character of the story that makes it a work of art. Whether or not this piece of entertainment is fiction or, as Gunn believes, a story that "is about a former king and a civil war, among other public events" and "the author [of which] believed himself to be recounting in essence what actually happened"[109] must await the following study.

---

107. Quotation: ibid. Gunn is working along the lines of R. C. Culley, *Studies in the Structure of Hebrew Narrative* (Philadelphia: Fortress / Missoula, MT: Scholars Press, 1976). Culley's study of "stock scenes," which are the equivalent of Gunn's "traditional motifs," is done within the context of his work on oral transmission of prose stories, and this is what Culley means by "traditional story."

108. Gunn, *Story of King David*, 61.

109. Ibid.

However, disagreement on this issue does not negate the fact that a large part of the David story is serious entertainment.

In order to illustrate what he means by serious entertainment, Gunn draws attention to the Icelandic "family sagas" and their combination of history and fiction. He states:

> With the Icelandic stories a similar problem arises: there is good reason to believe that the genre was treated by authors and audience as though it yielded what we might call "historical" truth, yet scholars are able to detect demonstrably fictitious or highly conventional elements in the stories. The solution is not to describe the sagas as either fictitious "novels" or historical records of the utmost reliability handed down verbatim over generations, but to understand that stories based on historical incidents can be subject to reshaping in tradition while yet retaining for teller and audience the character of "truth."[110]

My own reading of the Icelandic sagas and of studies about them would affirm this observation and the usefulness of the comparison between them and the David story. However, it becomes clear in this comparison, which Gunn does not chose to explore more deeply, precisely how the fictitious and conventional elements of the Icelandic sagas as works of literature relate to their traditional sources and written historical records and how they are then similar to the biblical story of David.

Rather than adopting the classification "traditional story" as both too vague and suggesting too close a connection with a body of oral tradition, I want to propose the term *saga* in the specific meaning of the Icelandic and Norse sagas as the most appropriate comparative literature for the David story. This takes up Gunn's suggestion of some similarity between the David story and the Icelandic "family sagas" as demonstrating the same kind of "serious entertainment" in the treatment of a period in the nation's past, as quoted above. It is this comparison between these two bodies of texts that I want to explore further as justification for using the term *saga* as a genre designation for the David story. I want to emphasize at this point that I am not using the term *saga* as the equivalent of the German term *Sage*, which is much too closely associated with oral tradition,[111] but I will use the designation *David Saga* as reflecting precisely the kind of written literature that one finds in the Icelandic sagas.

---

110. Ibid., 61–62.

111. See my *Abraham in History and Tradition* (New Haven, CT: Yale University Press, 1975), 136–37.

The first point of comparison that I wish to make is the fact that the Icelandic sagas are based on prior "historical" sources and a body of historiographic literature that developed in Iceland about a century or more before most of the sagas were written. One of these works was a concise history of Iceland by the historian Ari Thorgilsson, written shortly after the rise of literacy in Iceland and within a couple of generations of the Saga Age. The history covers the time from the settlement of Iceland (ca. 870 c.e.) down to his own time in the early 12th century. Robert Kellogg describes Ari as "very much an author in the modern sense. He cites in detail the oral sources of the information that he has written down, including such remarkable things as a list of names and periods of tenure of the Lawspeakers." He further points out: "As the founder of Icelandic historical writing Ari was cited as an authority by others,"[112] although often such citations were simply a rhetorical device to give authority and credence to a saga as the "truth." A second historical source was the *Book of Settlements*, "which describes the settlement of Iceland and the establishment of the original families, region by region around the country."[113] This work includes thousands of names, including many of the original settlers who figure as the main characters in so many of the sagas. Indeed, one of the prominent features of the sagas is their use of genealogies, either derived directly from this work or constructed in imitation of it, which are vital to understanding the role of the many different characters within the sagas. In addition, there were many other written sources dealing with the kings of Norway and other nations so that there was a significant body of written historiography at the disposal of the saga writers. Alongside the written sources there continued to be a strong oral story-telling tradition that was used by the saga writers.

In making a comparison with the *David Saga* it must, of course, be admitted that the biblical writer did not have such a sophisticated historiography at his disposal, but it will be argued in later chapters that he did make use of DtrH as his historical source. It is Dtr's historical framework that has been incorporated into the *David Saga* and used as the point of departure for the author's own work. Likewise, one finds within the David story lists of David's sons and wives, which are used in ways very similar

---

112. R. Kellogg, introduction to *The Sagas of Icelanders: A Selection* (London: Penguin, 2001), xxiii.

113. Ibid., xxiv.

to the Icelandic genealogies, that is, to understand how persons in the story are related to each other.

One of the distinctive features that the Icelandic sagas share with many biblical writers but that is quite different from much other medieval literature is the saga writers' anonymity. The question is what does this mean? What it does *not* mean is that they were merely editors and not authors. Nothing of the kind has been suggested in the literature on sagas that I have seen. They are uniformly regarded as authors in spite of this feature. Indeed, their anonymity is regarded as a quite-conscious element of their style. It is a deliberate literary device used by the narrator to exhibit his complete "fidelity to the events, or to others' accounts of them and their judgments on those who were involved."[114] This is the case even when it is clear that there is considerable fiction in their accounts. In further support of this view, is the use of a strict chronological style of presentation and the frequent use of placing poetic verses into the prose, a practice that "probably began as an authenticating device."[115] The author may have made use of some archaic pieces and composed others by imitation of style and language and then placed them in the mouths of prominent persons in the saga. What the sagas attempt to do by their deliberate use of anonymity, therefore, is to present a more "realistic" portrayal of the Saga Age and the principal figures in it than the mere reporting of events that are found in the history of the times.

I believe that much the same can be said for the anonymous style of the biblical writers, especially as it has to do with the presentation of "historical" events. The writers are at pains to convey the impression that they are giving a faithful presentation of the past, whatever their sources might have been and however creatively they tried to represent that time. What is most characteristic of the *David Saga* is its apparent "realistic" quality, which, as we have seen, led so many scholars to regard it as historiography. It is precisely this quality, however, that puts it in the same genre as the saga and accentuates its artistic literary qualities. It is the author as artist rather than historian that comes across in the work.

This brings us to Gunn's suggestion of the David story as "serious entertainment." The same assessment of the sagas is made by Magnus Magnusson: "From the thirteenth-century sources it is clear that sagas were re-

114. Ibid.
115. Ibid., xxvii.

garded at the time as what one might call 'serious entertainment,'"[116] and then he cites a number of these sources that recount the reading of a saga before an audience as a form of entertainment. He goes on to argue from this that a purpose of this sort is reflected in the saga's form:

> The emphasis on *reading* aloud is interesting, for it suggests that the sagas were specifically designed for public, rather than private, reading. It also suggests an explanation of the characteristics of oral style which some scholars have found in the sagas; what appears to be transcription of an existing oral tale is much more likely to have been a deliberate simulation of the earlier oral style. Formal story-telling had developed into formal saga-reading many years before *Njal's Saga* was written, and the saga bears constant marks of the concern the author showed for the listener as well as the reader.[117]

This point is important because there are a large number of literary conventions that are shared by the sagas, and they are comparable to what Culley calls "stock scenes" and what Gunn calls "traditional motifs" in the David story. Yet it is difficult to say in either case the extent to which they go back to earlier traditions of oral story-telling. There has been a long-standing debate within Icelandic studies as to the extent of their dependence on oral tradition and therefore their continuity with actual historical events, on the one hand, and the extent to which they are works of fiction with little historical basis, on the other. Most scholars seem to occupy a position between these two extremes, often depending on the particular saga and where it would be placed on the rather vague spectrum of early to late in the saga-writing age.[118] What is clear from the Icelandic sagas, however, is that the "traditional motifs" have become shared *literary* conventions, and the same is probably true of the David story. Literary conventions such as these cannot be used as evidence for the traditional *content* of the episodes in which they occur.

---

116. M. Magnusson and H. Palsson, *Njal's Saga* (Harmondsworth, UK: Penguin, 1960), 24

117. Ibid., 25–26.

118. The literature is very extensive, but see P. Hallberg, *The Icelandic Saga* (Lincoln: University of Nebraska Press, 1962), 49–69; T. M. Andersson, *The Problem of Icedandic Saga Origins: A Historical Survey* (New Haven, CT: Yale University Press, 1964); idem, *The Growth of the Medieval Icelandic Sagas (1180–1280)* (Ithaca, NY: Cornell University Press, 2006); L. Lönnroth, *Njáls Saga: A Critical Introduction* (Berkeley: University of California Press, 1976), 42–103.

Magnusson not only emphasizes the way in which the sagas are written and used as entertainment but why he characterizes the entertainment as "serious." It is for this reason that he is inclined to describe *Njals saga* as a "homily." He explains,

> Throughout the saga there is a bitter conflict between the forces of good and evil; physical violence is the symptom of this constant friction. In the saga, evil is consistently generated by self-aggrandisement, by the attempt to gain power or wealth. . . . In this homily, the only answer to the violence aroused by evil is active will towards good. Christianity comes to Iceland half-way through the action; and it is the Christian virtues of self-sacrifice and humility that eventually stem the tide of evil, not the pagan virtues of heroism and pride.[119]

What is significant in these remarks for the purposes of this study is that the saga offers a critique on nostalgia for the past and its values and an acceptance of a new reality under Christianity and foreign (i.e., Norwegian) political control. This is done without making this message explicit but entirely by means of the persuasive power of artistic presentation.

Recently, Andersson takes a somewhat different view of *Njals saga*, although he too is in agreement that it is a critique of the saga age. He reads *Njals saga* as a case of "demythologizing the tradition" and states his thesis as follows:

> By common agreement, *Njáls saga* occupies a transcendent place in the Icelandic tradition as the greatest, if not quite the latest, of the classical sagas. It represents such a pinnacle of style, range, and drama that it tends to overshadow the earlier sagas and relegate them to the status of preliminary attempts at a form that matures only in *Njáls saga*. My approach departs from this perspective. Rather than viewing *Njáls saga* as the crowning achievement, I suggest that it consciously subverts the narrative positions constructed in the earlier sagas. I consider the author less as the master architect perfecting inherited forms than as a satirist and caricaturist who holds these forms up to searching gaze, revealing what is doubtful and even fraudulent about the older conventions. This reversal is accomplished by isolating patterns in the inherited narratives and inverting them in such a way as to reveal quite different perspectives.[120]

Andersson supports his thesis by comparing a number of traditional motifs and conventions that are typical of the saga form and then shows how these

---

119. Magnusson and Palsson, *Njal's Saga*, 26–27.
120. Andersson, *Growth*, 183.

highly traditional elements have been quite deliberately subverted by the author of the *Njals Saga*. He concludes by saying: "The argument offered here is that *Njáls saga* persistently subverts a series of traditional narrative patterns and the authorial perspectives they imply."[121] This revisionist presentation involves the treatment of Iceland within its historical context and ultimately the kind of national identity that the earlier saga tradition created, the construction of heroic characters who are seriously compromised, the effectiveness of Icelandic institutions, and the theme of great foreign adventures, which in the *Njals saga* so often end in failure.

One can perhaps see this subversion most clearly in the convention of the feud, which occurs as a motif in all of the sagas and provides the principal motivation for the action. These feuds arise as a grievance between two leading families among the Icelanders, based on an act of violence, an injustice, or violation of honor, which calls for revenge. Rivalries of this sort spread through the families and close associates and lead to numerous episodes of bloodshed, which can go on for years and even generations. They run their course and are ultimately resolved and tranquility is restored, usually through the mediation of institutions and conventions of compensation payments. In *Njals saga*, however, the feuds are particularly frequent, violent, and ugly, and they are never resolved until the tragic end of the heroes, Gunnar and Njal. The institution in Iceland that was intended to mediate disputes such as these, the Althing or General Assembly, is shown to have been easily intimidated by the supporters of one or the other party in the dispute. Thus, *Njals saga* calls into question the whole heroic character of the founding age of the Icelandic sagas. Andersson sums up *Njals saga*'s treatment of the earlier saga tradition by stating that

> by the time the author of *Njáls saga* went to work, the Icelandic past had become seriously problematical. The glittering vision of the past was extinguished, and the great historical figures had become not only ironically but genuinely ambiguous. Tragedy had become more interesting than triumph. Marriage patterns, the feud system, and legal processes were open to question. Many of the sequences read like parodies of traditional narrative conventions. . . . The total effect of *Njáls saga* is to problematize the whole tradition of saga writing during the preceding century.[122]

In the study that follows, I shall try to demonstrate that in the story of David, and particularly within the *David Saga*, one will find this same quality

---

121. Ibid., 200.
122. Ibid., 208.

of serious entertainment and representation of the past glory of the days of David and Solomon. As I have argued in the past, there is a stratum within the story of David that reflects an attempt to "demythologize the tradition" that is similar to what is evident within *Njals saga*. This stratum, which is reflected in the so-called Court History, presents a complete subversion of the older idealized David in DtrH and a parody of many of its major themes, and it does so by means of the same artistic qualities of character portrayal and "realistic" recreation of the past that one finds in *Njals saga*. The same can be said about its presentation of older traditions and conventions, many of which are similar to those of the sagas. This is particularly the case with the feud, which in one form or another is the most basic structural device in the composition of the saga.

Within the *David Saga*, the case could also be made that feuds and rivalries permeate the whole work. There are the initial rivalry between the house of Saul and the house of David and the rivalries among the sons of David—the feud between Amnon and Absalom and the struggle for the throne between the parties of Adonijah and Solomon—leading to much bloodshed. There are the feuds and rivalries between the military commanders—Abner and Joab, Amasa and Joab, Benaiah and Joab—all of which end in murders. There are also a struggle between David and Joab for the control of the realm and the feud between David and Absalom leading to open war, as well as other minor rivalries. Indeed, it can also be said of the *David Saga* that these feuds and rivalries form the basic structure of the work and the motivation for the various episodes within it. Like the *Njals Saga*, the reconciliations are merely momentary and overcome by subsequent violence, and the final resolution is only reached when the last members of the feuds, Adonijah, Joab, Shimei, are all murdered off, and only Solomon and his supporters are left.[123]

In addition to feuding, the major characters in the sagas of Iceland are frequently engaged in carrying out Viking raids in their ships in Denmark, England, and Scotland or raiding expeditions over land on the Nordic mainland. Their object is to gain wealth from booty, and in their wake they leave a trail of death and destruction. They also hire themselves out as ruthless mercenaries to foreign kings. In similar fashion, we find within the *David Saga* references to David and his men carrying out raids for booty and

---

123. In the book of Genesis, there are stories of rivalries, such as Jacob and Esau's or Joseph and his brothers', but like the older sagas they are resolved by peaceful reconciliation. But this is not the case in the *David Saga*.

engaging in mercenary activity or the use of foreign mercenaries in military service under David and Solomon. In both cases, it adds to the general portrait of the founding period as a particularly violent and lawless age.

One could multiply the similarities of other minor motifs, and these will be noted in the analysis that follows. However, I think that what we have seen is sufficient to justify characterizing the David story as a saga. This is not to suggest that there are no important differences between the biblical story of David and the Icelandic sagas, but we may use the term *saga* to refer to a literary work that has the following features.

1. The story deals with the principal figures and families of the founding age of the nation and extends over more than a single generation of that period.
2. It is based on an older written historical record, but it supplies extensive fictional details to make the "historical" account more vivid and realistic.
3. The author is anonymous as a matter of style and convention and uses this style along with various other conventions, such as chronology, genealogy, place names, and memorial markers, to persuade his audience that he is giving a "true" portrayal of the past.
4. The work is intended as serious entertainment, to use the artistic presentation to make a judgment about the nation's past and its appropriate expectations for the future.
5. The work uses a number of literary conventions, above all, rivalry and feud, to integrate numerous episodes over an extended period of time and to motivate the action of the story.
6. While in most cases the saga tends to glorify a certain period of the past as a heroic age, it is also possible for a work of particular literary brilliance to parody and subvert that same literary tradition.[124]

Given all of these shared features, I think it is reasonable to adopt, as a working hypothesis, the view that the story of David from his first introduction into the service of Saul to the final transfer of power to Solomon (1 Sam 16–2 Sam 20, 1 Kgs 1–2) is a saga in form and intention. I will attempt to substantiate this view in the analysis that follows.

---

124. One is also reminded of the brilliant but often satirical works of Euripides in comparison with the earlier dramatists in their presentations of the heroic age of the Greeks. These were also works of "serious entertainment."

Summary

There is little point in adding further to this review the many additional studies on the David story. A number of them will surface in the course of addressing particular texts and issues. What is clear is the fact that running through so many of these studies is a limited number of issues that may be summarized in the following way.

1. Since Wellhausen, there has been a very strong tendency to identify a large portion of HDR and SN/CH as consisting of primitive historical documents from the 10th century. The judgment regarding their historicity was based primarily on the realistic quality of the literary presentation and their verisimilitude in the presentation of court life. This judgment was later supported by arguments from historical parallels that suggested a motive for these documents as apologetic, written to legitimate David's succession to Saul's throne and Solomon's succession in preference to his older brother.

2. Form-critical study raised the question of whether or not one should consider HDR and CH collections of smaller units of tradition, hero tales, and novellas instead of larger literary works, much as was also the case with the study of the Pentateuch. Against this trend in form criticism, Rost's very influential work attempted to recover, at least for CH, a unified and highly artistic literary masterpiece, SN, and similar efforts were made to recover a unified story of David's rise (HDR). Von Rad accepted Gunkel's form-critical understanding of the rise of historiography from smaller units of tradition to the apex of historiography in the account of David's court, and this approach he combined with Rost's literary analysis of SN. Von Rad associated this achievement of Israelite historiography with a Solomonic enlightenment.

3. The literary approach of Rost tended, in later studies, to be reflected increasingly in those treatments of the text that were concerned with the "final form" and the artistic qualities and thematic concerns of SN and, to a lesser degree, HDR. By contrast, the application of redaction criticism tended to revert to the earlier form-critical position of viewing the original sources as small units of tradition that were combined in stages to produce the final product. Some of the literary techniques that Rost had identified as artistic literary devices of the author were transformed into editorial strategies to create unity out of individual pieces.

4. Once Noth established the thesis of a Deuteronomistic History with both HDR and SN as sources used by the historian with little change, the

relationship of DtrH to HDR and SN became a matter of discussion. With the splitting of DtrH into two or three recensions and with the possibility of an earlier pre-Dtr historical work within Samuel–Kings being proposed, such as the Prophetic History/Record, the redaction history of HDR and SN became increasingly complex. There is even the recent tendency to do away with DtrH altogether and make Dtr little more that a redactional layer with a distinctive linguistic usage and theological bias.

My own approach to the story of David has been quite different from those reviewed above, and therefore it has been largely excluded from the scholarly discussion or at least marginalized as merely idiosyncratic. In my view, the reasons for dating HDR and CH/SN so early were always rather weak and this opinion is becoming even more apparent today than it was in Wellhausen's day. This early dating of HDR and CH unduly prejudices the whole literary analysis of the David story. I have accepted the basic validity of Noth's thesis of a DtrH, but the one perceived weakness in the proposal of a DtrH was the lack of any sign of it in so much of the books of Samuel, especially within the story of David. What constituted a major problem was the rather negative portrayal of David within CH that could hardly be viewed as a source of DtrH. I found strong reasons to regard CH as a later addition to DtrH, and its removal left a clearly defined Dtr corpus of texts (in 2 Sam 5–8; 1 Kgs 2:1–4, 10–12) dealing with David's reign. I also viewed the HDR as basically a work of Dtr, with some late additions to it, so that one can reconstruct a fairly clear continuity in DtrH between Saul, David, and Solomon, with a consistent theme and language.

I have a great deal of sympathy for the studies of Rost, von Rad, and Whybray, who take seriously the artistic qualities of the stories in SN, and studies such as Gunn's and Edelman's, which have extended this same literary sensitivity to HDR as well; they have added many important insights. Nevertheless, I am concerned that the emphasis on artistic and thematic aspects of the story of David has often been at the expense of important issues having to do with the diachronic development of the text. One simply cannot assume that the "final form" of the text is homogeneous or the reflection of a single mind. On the other hand, I have less sympathy for the redaction-critical approach to the story of David, which completely dismembers the text into many layers and fragments, using very weak criteria to distinguish between the layers, with little hope of agreement. Redaction criticism pays little attention to the artistic qualities of the text and quite ignores the fact that the story of David from his first appearance in 1 Sam 16 to his death and Solomon's succession represents a remarkable story with a sequence of interrelated events that scarcely has any precedent in the rest of the Hebrew Bible. The closest parallel, perhaps, is the work of the Yahwist in the Pentateuch, and von Rad argued strenuously against the form-critics that it could not have grown into a literary product of this sort by random chance, a criticism that applies equally to the redaction critics.

Finally, following the suggestion of Gunn, I have argued for the merits of considering the story of David in its entirety as sufficiently similar to the saga in form and intention, and I will use this hypothesis as a way of understanding the artistic qualities of the story. At the same time, I will give serious attention to the diachronic aspects of the story's development in the literary analysis that follows.

Chapter 2

The David Saga *within Its Social and Historical Setting, Part 1*

As we have seen in our survey of the past scholarship on the story of David, the predominant assumption since Wellhausen and the late 19th century has been to read the biblical stories against the historical background of the 10th-century B.C.E. reigns of David and Solomon, and this assumption has continued until the most recent publications on David.[1] However, they merely follow a long list of attempts to find evidence to be used in support of an early date for the narrative. These have generally adopted the view that the literary genres in which the story of David is written, whether as a form of historiography or as royal apology, reflect forms of narrative that would be contemporary with the events and offer important information on the reigns of David and Solomon. On the basis of the biblical story, it was assumed that the kingdoms of David and Solomon represented a period of political and imperial power during a time when Egypt, Assyria, and the Hittites all experienced an eclipse of power that allowed Israel to dominate the region of Syria-Palestine and establish all the trappings of a monarchy. Notions such as these about the reigns of David and Solomon were developed in the absence of archaeological evidence to the contrary, and when archaeological evidence gradually came to light it was then simply interpreted in agreement with the biblical record, creating a complete circularity of argument. Thus, the archaeological data of a particular stratum at Megiddo, Hazor, and Gezer were dated to the Solomonic age because it was understood as reflecting of the description of Solomon's achievements in 1 Kgs 9:15–19, which in turn was used to confirm the biblical picture of the United Monarchy. If, however, this archaeological evidence is proven to be problematic, then all of the arguments based on

---

1. See S. L. McKenzie, *King David: A Biography* (New York: Oxford University Press, 2000); B. Halpern, *David's Secret Demons: Messiah, Murderer, Traitor, King* (Grand Rapids: Eerdmans, 2001).

notions of great literature produced by a Solomonic enlightment, including historiography and the genre of royal apology, could lose their validity.

It was the archaeological exploration of Kathleen Kenyon in 1960s, followed by the work of Y. Shiloh (1978–84) and then numerous subsequent probes, that began to raise serious questions about a great kingdom in the 10th century. The region of the southeastern hill known as the Ophel, or City of David, showed very sparse remains and hardly what one would have expected of the capital of a great kingdom. Some scholars discounted this evidence on the grounds that too little of Jerusalem could be excavated and suggested that the 10th-century evidence of other sites should be given greater weight. Other scholars took a more "minimalist" view to suggest that the biblical tradition should be viewed more critically as the later glorification of a very modest beginning. Thus, since the early 1990s the battle lines have been drawn between two competing groups of scholars. At stake for the purposes of this present study is how to assess the evidence for the periods in which the various parts or versions of the story of David were written. To do this, we will need to look at both sides of the argument and the dates proposed for the narratives, regardless of the danger of getting bogged down in the great detail of studies that this involves. We will begin by looking at the older argument of the literary genre thought to be reflected in the story of David and then move to the archaeological debate and its consequences.

Historical Documents from the David-Solomon Era

The concern to understand the social and historical context for the story of David arises, first of all, out of the attempt to recover and evaluate possible contemporary sources from the time of David within the biblical narrative. The belief among critical scholars that a recovery of primitive sources such as this was possible was already present in the earliest days of historical criticism when Richard Simon proposed that the account of the monarchy in Samuel–Kings was dependent on the editing of archival accounts retrieved from the palaces and temples of the monarchies, including those of the time of David and Solomon.[2] The appeal to these supposed archival sources and scribal editors has remained a persistent notion in biblical scholarship ever since. Only recently, with the socioarchaeological evaluation of the nature of Jerusalem's polity in the 10th century B.C.E. and the

---

2. J. Van Seters, *The Edited Bible*, 185–86.

level of its literacy, has the notion of an assumed administrative and scribal culture such as this been seriously questioned, as we shall see below.

In the late 19th century, Wellhausen, among others, regarded parts of the David story, particularly the part that was later known as the SN, to be an eyewitness account of events of David's reign and therefore of high historical probability. The model for this was the view of classical Greek historians that the task of history writing was to deal with recent events and not with myths and legends of the distant past. This concern for a narrative reflecting an eyewitness account of events was a shift from speaking merely about archival sources to the evolution of the literary genre of historiography, and it was this form-critical question that was taken up by Gunkel and Gressmann, as we have seen above. They assumed the validity of the view of Wellhausen that the account of David's reign was contemporary and historical, written within the social context of an imperial court, and were primarily concerned to map out the social evolution of literary forms of this sort from the primitive premonarchical period to the great Solomonic age.[3] Von Rad, taking up Rost's literary analysis of the SN and combining it with the form-critical notions of Gunkel and Gressmann, formulated his grand essay on the rise of historiography in the Davidic-Solomonic age. As we have seen above, this laid the groundwork not only for the later literary analysis of the David story but also for the assumptions about its social context.[4]

As though to confirm a 10th-century social context, there was a concern to find a more appropriate Near Eastern genre than the Greek model of historiography, and one that would be much earlier, as a way of explaining the nature of the narrative in both HDR and SN. The genre that was seized on was the "royal apology." The use of the apology form as a way of explaining the nature and intention of a large part of the David story has become so pervasive in the critical discussion of the David narratives that it calls for some detailed discussion here.

Important as a genre model of the royal apology is the so-called *Apology of Hattušili III*, a Hittite king of the 13th century B.C.E.[5] The document is an autobiographical account by the king describing his early career and rise to a position of authority as governor of the northern regions of the Hittite realm under the rule of his brother and as a devotee of the goddess Ishtar.

---

3. Idem, *In Search of History*, 209–20.
4. See above, pp. 4–15.
5. Ibid., 118–19.

After the death of the ruler he helped the king's son succeed to the throne but subsequently became a rival to the new ruler and usurped the throne. In the light of this violation of the constitution, the *Edict of Telepinu*, which laid down the rules of succession, he justifies his actions in this testimonial. It is an apology only in the vague sense that it is a record of the events related to his usurpation of power, to set the record straight for the benefit of posterity as a just and pious king, made long after the events in question. It is autobiographical only in the sense that it uses first-person narration in the same way as do all other annals and royal inscriptions.

A number of scholars have suggested parallels between the *Apology of Hattušili III* and the David story, particularly citing HDR, and have even argued for a direct literary connection between Hittite historiography and the rise of early Israelite history writing.[6] We may quickly dismiss any direct dependence of the David story on Hittite texts as entirely unlikely, in spite of the reference to a "Hittite" in David's court. This sort of dependence must presume some transmission of Hittite cultural heritage between David's "empire" and the remnants of Hittite civilization in northern Syria, assumptions that are quite unwarranted. Some, like McCarter, merely use the comparison as evidence of a common Near Eastern genre to explain the nature of HDR. Thus, McCarter describes HDR as "a document from the time of David himself, . . . and directed toward those conservative elements in the north, especially Benjamin, who were suspicious of the new king. . . . Its purpose was to justify the succession as a reflection of Yahweh's will and offer rebuttal to charges made against David." In this way, McCarter can describe HDR as "a special category of ancient Near Eastern literature in which the accession of a ruler whose right to the throne is somehow suspect is shown to have been in accordance with the will of the gods and therefore lawful."[7] He then cites the *Apology of Hattušili* as the best example of this genre of literature, but he does not make use of such a genre comparison in the case of SN, although he does call SN an "apology."

---

6. H. Hoffner, "Propaganda and Political Justification in Hittite Historiography," in *Unity and Diversity: Essays in the History, Literature, and Religion of the Ancient Near East* (ed. H. Goedicke and J. J. M. Roberts; Baltimore: Johns Hopkins University Press, 1975), 49–50; idem, "Histories and Historians of the Ancient Near East: The Hittites," *Orientalia* 49 (1980), 315–16; H. M. Wolf, *The Apology of Hattušiliš Compared with Other Self-Justifications* (Ph.D. diss., Brandeis University, 1967); H. Cancik, *Grundzüge der hetittischen und alttestamentlichen Geschichtsschreibung* (Wiesbadden: Harrassowitz, 1976).

7. McCarter, *I Samuel*, 29.

Following a study by H. Tadmor, "Autobiographical Apology in the Royal Assyrian Literature,"[8] T. Ishida seeks to use a royal inscription of Esarhaddon containing an "apology" as a parallel to the Succession Narrative.[9] What is most remarkable about his comparison is that the apology of Esarhaddon makes it abundantly clear that this younger son of Sennacherib was clearly identified by divine oracle and by the recognition of his father as the legitimate heir, whereas the complete opposite is the case with SN. Nowhere does the deity identify Solomon as the rightful heir and nowhere does David establish Solomon as the crown prince until the moment of the final coup in 1 Kgs 1, which makes the whole event suspicious. The two examples could not be more different. In an earlier article, Ishida suggested quite a different comparison, one between SN and the inscription of Kilamuwa, king of Y'dy, who reigned in this north Syrian kingdom toward the end of the 9th century.[10] This too becomes an example of apologetic literature. The point of the comparison seems to be to demonstrate that "there were common features in the political development in the early–inexperienced–monarchies in the national kingdoms of Syro-Palestine at the beginning of the first millennium B.C."[11] The fact is that this inscription belongs to a group of royal inscriptions with common features that go by the name of "Memorial Inscriptions" because they generally sum up the king's career at a point late in his life or after his death, to ensure that future generations will regard him highly.[12] The much-better-known Mesha Stela, dated about the same time, also belongs to this group.[13] There is nothing actually "apologetic" about them, and the treatment by Ishida is quite misleading. For comparative purposes, they should be treated as a group, belonging primarily to the 9th and 8th centuries, not the 10th century B.C.E.

---

8. In *History, Historiography and Interpretation: Studies in Biblical and Cuneiform Literatures* (ed. H. Tadmor and M. Weinfeld; Jerusalem: Magnes, 1983), 36–57.

9. T. Ishida, "The Succession Narrative and Esarhaddon's Apology," *History and Historical Writing in Ancient Israel: Studies in Biblical Historiography* (Leiden: Brill, 1999), 175–85.

10. Idem, "Solomon's Succession in the Light of the Inscription of Kilamuwa, King of Y'dy-Śam'al," in *History and Historical Writing in Ancient Israel: Studies in Biblical Historiography* (Leiden: Brill, 1999), 167–74.

11. Ibid., 174.

12. Van Seters, *In Search of History*, 192–93; F. M. Fales, "Kilamuwa and the Foreign Kings," *WO* 10 (1979): 6–22.

13. J. M. Miller, "The Moabite Stone as a Memorial Stela," *PEQ* 104 (1974): 9–18.

More recently, an attempt has been made by Baruch Halpern to find a Near Eastern parallel to the David story.[14] His focus is primarily on the wars of David in 2 Samuel 8; he regards the treatment of these wars as based on a contemporary document, which he compares with the Assyrian royal inscriptions, particularly those of Tiglath-pileser I, a contemporary of David. Halpern sees in Tiglath-pileser's inscriptions a style of presentation of historical events characterized by exaggeration and self-promotion that he labels the "Tiglath-pileser principle" and attributes this same style to David's scribes. Thus, in the light of this scribal tendenz, one should read these texts "against the grain," and by doing so one can recover the historical kernel from these documents. Once Halpern establishes this scribal method and tendency on the basis of the military campaigns of 2 Samuel 8, he then moves on to applying this same principle to the quite-different narratives in the rest of the David story. They must be "deconstructed" by means of the "hermeneutic of suspicion" in order to uncover the real David.

Fortunately, we need not take long in dealing with this suggestion, because in a recent article Steven Holloway has written a rather devastating critique of Halpern's Tiglath-pileser principle by examining the full range of Assyrian royal inscriptions, and he finds no basis for Halpern's thesis.[15] Holloway sees Halpern's choice of Tiglath-pileser I's inscriptions for comparison with the biblical text as merely "chronological apologetics" in order to date the Samuel texts early and contemporary with David. Furthermore, Halpern explains that the biblical texts both in the David story and in the Assyrian inscriptions correspond to the type known as the "display" inscription, which is arranged topically rather than chronologically. This allows him to rearrange chronologically the items in 2 Samuel 8 and the other events in the David story to overcome apparent contradictions and to accommodate his imaginative reconstructions. The fact of the matter is, however, that the Tiglath-pileser text that he refers to so often is not a "display" inscription but the beginning of a new style of annals in which the events *were* arranged chronologically.[16] The entire comparison is without merit as anyone familiar with the Assyrian royal inscriptions would readily recognize.[17]

---

14. B. Halpern, *David's Secret Demons*, 107–226.

15. S. W. Hollaway, "Use of Assyriology in Chronological Apologetics in *David's Secret Demons*," *SJOT* 17 (2003): 245–67.

16. A. K. Grayson, *Assyrian Royal Inscriptions* (vol. 2; Wiesbaden: Harrassowitz, 1976), 1–3.

17. A much more cogent comparison can be made between David's wars and those of the Aramean kings of Damascus, as has been done by Nadav Na'aman, reaching very different conclusions, and this will be taken up below.

Furthermore, one can say of all these examples cited above that the scholars who use them seriously abuse the form-critical method. All of the Near Eastern parallels are royal inscriptions in the first-person style given as the direct words of the king, and the apologetic genre would need to undergo a rather radical transformation in order to produce the third-person style of historical narration that we find in the biblical text. This does not happen in either Hittite or Assyrian literature; it only comes into vogue in the chronicles of the Neo-Babylonian period contemporary with the time of the Dtr Historian, a fact that these scholars ignore or lightly dismiss. Furthermore, the third person chronicle style does not exhibit any of those "apologetic" or "propagandistic" features found in the Hittite and Assyrian royal inscriptions. In addition, the argument involves a serious circularity of reasoning, because the apology form only has relevance if one can be certain that the narrative is contemporary with the events described. If the dating of the David story is contested, then one cannot use the parallels to also date the story. If the stories of David and Solomon are significantly later than the 10th century, then they cannot be interpreted as apologies for the reigns of these two kings. This is simply another case of "parallelomania" so common in an earlier generation of biblical scholars of the "biblical archaeology" movement. If one wants to find comparable stories about life in the royal court of a great king, then one should look at the stories about the Persian kings in Herodotus's *Histories*.

As we have seen above in our review of scholarship on the David story, there is increasing skepticism that one can isolate extensive primitive documents, such as HDR and SN, which could have served as political apologies during the reigns of David and Solomon. At the most, it is suggested that we have to do only with some individual stories, which may have had apologetic tendencies, and that these were used by the later writers for their own purposes. Nevertheless, this still seems to allow McKenzie to assume a strong apologetic character to both HDR and SN, as he redefines them, and then to read these narratives "against the grain," following McCarter, in order to extract from them enough "history" to write a "biography" of David.[18] However, unless one can firmly establish the fact that the events mentioned in the story actually took place and are not fictitious, one cannot read a story such as this "against the grain" any more than one can read any work of fiction against the grain. Even the royal inscriptions of Assyria cannot be treated in this way, unless one has additional concrete

18. S. L. McKenzie, "The So-Called Succession Narrative in the Deuteronomistic History," 123–35; idem, *King David: A Biography*, 26–36.

evidence that is contrary to the claims contained in them, which in some cases one does have. But in the biblical story of David, we have no other evidence regarding the events described. Reading biblical narrative texts "against the grain" is an exercise in sheer fantasy, as some of the more re- markable examples found in Halpern's *David's Secret Demons* illustrates. Halpern, in his "deconstruction" of the text, using the "hermeneutic of sus- picion," is able to uncover the skillful work of the apologists in Solomon's court. Thus, he finds that all of the deaths of important figures from which the biblical story exonerates David, that is, Saul, Abner, Ishbosheth, Am- non, and Absalom, are nevertheless to be laid at David's door, while the one death for which David is held reponsible, namely, Uriah the Hittite, he did not cause! The supposed reason for this latter deception is that Solo- mon was not David's son, but actually the son of Uriah the Hittite, and the story of David's murder and adultery were invented by Solomon's court apologist 25 years after Solomon came to the throne, in order to prove that Solomon was David's son. This fiction is then used to explain the cause of the revolt of Absalom, rather belatedly it would appear. Halpern, however, fails to note that the same apologist would have been responsible for the curse that is uttered through Nathan, the prophet, on the entire dynasty of David: "the sword shall not depart from your house forever." The whole re- construction of the activity of these apologists becomes completely absurd, and one must give up the notion of treating the story of David as an apol- ogy for his reign or that of Solomon.

All of these proposals regarding the kinds of historical documents that lie behind the story of David have been based on the assumption, through- out most of the 20th century, that the archaeological evidence supported the kind of imperial monarchy that was reflected in the biblical record. Therefore they saw nothing that was inappropriate to a context of this sort in their proposals of royal apologies, inscriptions celebrating victorious armies, and the like. In the last two decades, however, this kind of confi- dence in these archaeological assumptions has come under attack and given rise to a quite-different approach to the biblical tradition. It is to this approach and the new archaeological perspective that we will now turn.

The David Tradition and the
Biblical Archaeology Debate

Regarding the matter of the social context for the David story, the view that dominated scholarship from the 1930s until the present was the one that argued for a great Davidic/Solomonic kingdom, which included "all Israel," from Dan to Beersheba, and which controlled the whole of Syria-Palestine. This was based on the correlation of remarks about Solomon's realm in the biblical text with certain impressive archaeological finds from excavations in Palestine. In particular, the statement that Solomon built the cities of Hazor, Megiddo, and Gezer as store-cities and cities for his chariots and cavalry (1 Kgs 9:15, 19) is thought to refer to Stratum VA–IVB at Megiddo, Stratum X at Hazor, and Stratum VIII at Gezer. These "Solomonic" cities are characterized by large buildings that made use of ashlar masonry, great four-entry (six-chambered) gates, and pillared buildings, which have been interpreted as stables. This remarkable correlation seemed to confirm the historicity of the particular details in Kings, supporting the idea of a Davidic-Solomonic empire and serving as the appropriate context for a narrative such as one finds in SN. This kind of interpretation of the archaeological evidence is reflected in many standard textbooks of the history of Israel and was widely accepted throughout the discipline of biblical studies in historical, archaeological, and literary studies of the Davidic-Solomonic period.[19]

This view of a powerful Davidic-Solomonic state that dominated the whole region of Syria-Palestine in the 10th century was a consensus view until about two decades ago. How did this consensus come about and why did it gradually come apart?[20] When Megiddo was being excavated by the University of Chicago in the 1920s and 30s, the excavators uncovered in Stratum IV a large solid city wall with a six-chambered gate, a "governor's residence," and a number of pillared buildings that were interpreted as "stables." All of this seemed to the director of the expedition, P. L. O. Guy, to correspond to the description of Solomon's building activity in 1 Kgs 9:15–19, so he dated the stratum to the Solomonic age. As a consequence, any stratum at another site that contained architectural features corresponding to those of Stratum IV was deemed to be "Solomonic." This was

---

19. K. Kenyon, *Royal Cities of the Old Testament* (New York: Schocken, 1971); A. Lemaire, "The United Monarchy: Saul, David and Solomon," in *Ancient Israel: A Short History from Abraham to the Roman Destruction of the Temple* (ed. H. Shanks; Washington, DC: Biblical Archaeology Society, 1988), 85–109; A. Mazar, *Archaeology of the Land of the Bible: 10,000–586 B.C.E.* (New York: Doubleday, 1990), 368–402.

20. See the convenient review of this development of the Solomonic dating of archaeological features in G. J. Wightman, "The Myth of Solomon," *BASOR* 277–78 (1990): 5–22.

a case of pure "biblical archaeology" in which the dating of archaeological remains was simply made to accommodate agreement with the biblical text. Thus, when Yigael Yadin excavated Stratum X at Hazor in the 1950s, he also found a six-chambered gate in connection with a casemate wall and a pillared building, which he likewise dated to the Solomonic period. The stratigraphy of both sites was entirely governed by the practice of matching architecture with the Bible. Furthermore, as Wightman points out,

> the biblical passage 1 Kgs 9:15 was subtly reinterpreted: Solomon did not build a wall only around Jerusalem; he also built walls around Hazor, Megiddo, and Gezer. This biblical passage was now held to refer specifically to fortifications. Yet 1 Kgs 9:15 gives no indications of the nature of Solomon's building at Hazor, Megiddo, or Gezer: *hormat* refers only to Jerusalem; the other cities are direct objects to the verb *libnôt*.

Thus, the biblical texts were made to say much more than was actually stated. Nevertheless, this same error of interpretation, which renders 1 Kgs 9:15 as a reference to the fortifications of Hazor, Megiddo, and Gezer, continues to be made by later defenders of the Solomonic date of these structures.[21]

Once Yadin had identified the six-chambered gate as a distinctive Solomonic feature, he found one at Gezer in the older site reports of Macalister's earlier dig there, which had previously been undetected. This completed and confirmed for many the link to these three sites, Megiddo, Hazor, and Gezer, mentioned in 1 Kgs 9:15. However, to make the symmetry complete, Yadin returned to Megiddo to look explicitly for a "Solomonic" casemate wall that he could associate with the six-chambered gate, because the casemate wall was deemed earlier than the solid wall. What he found was a casemate wall under the so-called "stables" belonging to a new intermediary stratum, now numbered VA–IVB, but this wall was connected with a quite-different gate; and it was no longer associated with the pillared buildings of Stratum IVA. Furthermore, at Samaria casemate walls were associated with a massive construction work carried out by the Omrides; and in subsequent excavations at Lachish, Ashdod, Tell Balash, and Tel 'Ira, the

---

21. See W. G. Dever, *What Did the Biblical Writers Know and When Did They Know It?* (Grand Rapids: Eerdmans, 2001), 131. Cf. the criticism of Dever by I. Finkelstein and N. A. Silberman, "The Bible Unearthed: A Rejoinder," *BASOR* 327 (2002), 67–68.

six-chambered (four-entry) gates continue to be built in levels later than the 10th century.[22]

Notwithstanding these growing questions about "Solomonic" architecture, in the 1960s and 70s a series of excavations was begun under G. Ernest Wright and carried on by William Dever at Gezer specifically to investigate Yadin's proposed "Solomonic" six-chambered gate. The full plan of this gate was uncovered with meticulous stratigraphy by John S. Holladay, detailing the ceramic dating of the gate's foundation and usage.[23] Nevertheless, because of the earlier excavation by Macalister, no firm connection was made between this gate and any casemate wall. Furthermore, while the relative ceramic chronology was now clear, its absolute dating was still in dispute. After all of his ceramic analysis, Holladay attempts to address the problem of the absolute dating for the various strata of Gezer. He states, "The key stratum seems to be Gezer Field III Phase UG3A [the six-chambered gate], which is both very short and historically exceptionally well positioned. It comes after the Solomonic building period, richly documented by biblical and historical data and secured by comparative regional archaeological and architectural criteria." With respect to his ceramic chronology, he states that "new stratigraphic data make it possible to pinpoint the introduction of early Iron Age burnishing on red slips to a date early in the period between the Solomonic foundation at Gezer and the subsequent Palestinian campaign of Sheshonq in 926 B.C.—in round terms, about 950 B.C."[24] This manner of dating Gezer VIII is a case of completely circular reasoning because the biblical text is being used to date the stratum at Gezer and other related sites, which are then cited as confirming the historicity of the biblical text. The Solomonic stratum is viewed by Holladay and Dever as sandwiched between two violent destructions caused by Egyptian invasions: the one by a pharaoh who was the father-in-law of Solomon and who, after destroying the city and its inhabitants, gave it to his daughter as a dowry (1 Kgs 9:16); the other by Sheshonq as stated above. There is no

---

22. D. Ussishkin, "Notes on Megiddo, Gezer, Ashdod, and Tel Batash in the Tenth and Ninth Centuries B.C.," BASOR 277-78 (1990): 71-91. See also the six-chambered gate with casemate wall attached at Khirbat al- Mudayna in Jordan: R. Chadwick, P. M. M. Daviau, and M. Steiner, "Four Seasons of Excavations at Khirbat al-Mudayna on Wadi ath-Thamad, 1996-1999," ADAJ 44 (2000): 257-70. This gate is clearly dated by pottery, artifacts, and C14 to Iron II (810-760), p. 267.

23. J. S. Holladay, "Red Slip, Burnish, and the Solomonic Gateway at Gezer," *BASOR* 277-78 (1990): 23-70.

24. Ibid., 63.

information from Egyptian sources as to who the first of these pharaohs might have been, and there is much reason to suspect that the remark is a very late fiction.

The site of Gezer calls for some additional comment, because William Dever, the excavator of this site, has made it something of a test case in his defense of the "age of Solomon." In an extended critique of the Gezer excavation, I. Finkelstein criticizes Dever for the same kind of circular reasoning in the dating of the "Solomonic" gate that Holladay used in the quoted text above.[25] Quoting from two recent publications by Dever,[26] Finkelstein states:

> Describing his reconstruction of the archaeology of the United Monarchy, [Dever] says: "The careful reader will observe that in the case I have tried to make here for a 10th century 'Israelite state', including, of course, the institution of kingship, I have made no reference to the biblical texts as evidence. . . . My evidence throughout has been archaeological." In another place he argues: "The pottery from this destruction layer included distinctive forms of red-slipped and slipped and hand burnished (polished) pottery, which have always been dated to the 10th century. . . . Thus, on commonly accepted *ceramic* grounds—not on naïve acceptance of the Bible's stories . . .—we dated the Gezer Field III city walls and gates to the mid-late 10th century." The "careful reader" will certainly recognize that the opposite is true! Dever's entire reconstruction rests on biblical testimony. If not for his adherence to 1 Kings 9:15, how could he date the six-chambered gates to the days of Solomon? How could he collect the evidence for his 10th-century strata if not for the specific type of pottery, which he dated to that period because it was found in relation to the "Solomonic" gate?[27]

As Finkelstein points out, Dever is guilty of the same naïve and uncritical acceptance of biblical statements which he accused early "biblical archaeologists" of using in their treatment of earlier periods of biblical history. Archaeology is simply made to fit the biblical text of the age of Solomon (and David); it is not used to offer a critical evaluation of the biblical portrayal of the "united kingdom."

---

25. I. Finkelstein, "Gezer Revisited and Revised," *TA* 29 (2002), 262-96.

26. Quoted from W. G. Dever, "Archaeology and the "Age of Solomon: A Case Study in Archaeology and Historiography," in *The Age of Solomon: Scholarship at the Turn of the Millennium* (ed. L. K. Handy; Leiden: Brill, 1997), 251; and then idem, *What Did the Biblical Writers Know and When Did They Know It?* 132.

27. Finkelstein, "Gezer Revisited," 272-73.

The Socioarchaeological Approach and Its Advocates

Nevertheless, some discordant voices were raised against a too-easy connection between the archaeological data and the biblical accounts of this period and in support of a much more sophisticated use of archaeological method in the evaluation of the biblical stories. In many ways, the turning point in the discussion came about with the dissertation of David Jamieson-Drake, *Scribes and Schools in Monarchic Judah* (1988),[28] in which he used a socioarchaeological approach to investigate the rise of a state in Judah that could support a scribal class and a bureaucracy necessary to administer a political structure of this sort. Contrary to the many earlier studies about the rise of the state in 10th-century Judah, he came to quite-different conclusions. After a meticulous examination of the material evidence available, he concluded:

> There is little evidence that Judah began to function as a state at all prior to the tremendous increases in population, building, production, centralization and specialization which began to appear in the 8th century. The limited quantity of data could only account for this finding if a reason could be found for differential recovery of 10th- and 8th-century materials. Lacking such an explanation, the disparity in rates of recovery of 10th- and 8th-century materials is best explained as reflecting the rates of deposition of those materials. A comparison of the listings of societal traits expected to be found in stratified societies . . . with our data will show that these traits are almost completely absent from our region in the 10th century. Even in the 8th and 7th centuries, the periods of greatest development seen through the lens of our data, evidence for some traits, namely professional, skilled artisanship, inter-regional trade, and population of the scale expected to characterize a state . . . must be characterized as weak. . . . The primary problem is one of scale: the levels of the production and population were just too small in 10th-century Judah to suggest the presence of the full-scale state; they seem more appropriate to a chiefdom.[29]

Jamieson-Drake made a critical evaluation of a number of earlier studies on the rise of the "state" in the Davidic-Solomonic period, including that of

---

28. D. W. Jamieson-Drake, *Scribes and Schools in Monarchic Judah: A Socio-Archeological Approach* (JSOTSup 109; Sheffield: Almond, 1991). Coming to quite-similar conclusions was the work of H. M. Niemann, *Hershaft, Königtum und Staat: Skizzen zur soziokulturellen Entwicklung im monarchischen Israel* (Tübingen: Mohr, 1993).
29. Ibid., 138–39.

T. N. D. Mettinger,[30] whose work will be taken up below. However, he did not make a detailed analysis of the biblical material itself.

Thomas Thompson, in his methodological study on the correlation of archaeological evidence and written sources of the early Israelites,[31] made use of Jamieson-Drake's study to affirm this thesis: "It was not until the last quarter of the eighth century and especially in the second half of the seventh, that Jerusalem began to take on some of the trappings of a dominant regional state power."[32] Niels-Peter Lemche also came to the support of Jamieson-Drakes's conclusion that there was no state in Judah until the late 8th century, which he found quite compatible with his own sociological magnum opus.[33] Lemche acknowledged the criticism of Jamieson-Drake's work, namely, that it relied too heavily on the archaeological data in older reports that were not sufficiently controlled or up-to-date, but he went on to point out that more recent work by Israel Finkelstein and others tended to confirm and support the thesis rather than undermining it. In particular, as we shall see below, it is the regional archaeological surveys of the Palestinian highlands that have been most important in resolving the discussion of the nature of the polity in Judah in the 10th century B.C.E.

In a short period of time, a number of scholars joined the great debate about the nature of the "state" under David and Solomon, with the discussion often degenerating to a very vitriolic level. It is not my intention to chronicle this exchange. What is important is the fact that the focus shifted to a new appreciation of the archaeological material remains as they relate to the nature of the Judean state from the 10th to the 6th centuries B.C.E. The problem that the archaeological evidence posed was this: on the one hand, the archaeological material recovered from Jerusalem from the 10th century showed a very small town that could hardly serve as a state capital; on the other hand, as we have seen above, the northern cities of Megiddo, Hazor, and Gezer, said by the Bible to be under Solomon's control, were thought to give confirming evidence in certain strata, which were dated to

---

30. T. N. D. Mettinger, *Solomonic State Officials* (Lund: Gleerup, 1971).

31. T. L. Thompson, *Early History of the Israelite People: From the Written and Archaeological Sources* (Leiden: Brill, 1992).

32. Ibid., 333.

33. *Early Israel: Anthropological and Historical Studies on the Israelite Society Before the Monarchy* (Leiden: Brill, 1985). See idem, "From Patronage Society to Patronage Society," in *The Origins of the Israelite States* (ed. V. Fritz and P. R. Davies; JSOTSup 228; Sheffield: Sheffield Academic Press, 1996), 106–20; idem, *The Israelites in History and Tradition* (Louisville: Westminster John Knox, 1998), 65–86.

the same period, of being large and important administrative centers, worthy of a powerful state.

Stepping into the middle of this debate with an attempt to offer a viable archaeological solution to this contradiction were Israel Finkelstein, David Ussishkin, and Nadav Na'aman of the "Tel Aviv School."[34] The dating of archaeological strata to corresponding social and historical chronology is faced with a number of controversial issues, which this group of scholars attempt to address. The first of these is the correlation of the ceramic sequence in Iron I with the end of the Egyptian hegemony in Palestine (late 12th century) and the settlement of the Philistines in the southern coastal

---

34. I. Finkelstein and N. A. Silberman, *David and Solomon: In Search of the Bible's Sacred Kings and the Roots of the Western Tradition* (New York: Free Press, 2006); eidem, *The Bible Unearthed* (New York: Simon & Schuster, 2001); eidem, "Temple and Dynasty: Hezekiah, the Remaking of Judah and the Rise of the Pan-Israelite Ideology," *JSOT* 30 (2006): 259-85; I. Finkelstein, "The Archaeology of the United Monarchy: An Alternative View," *Levant* 28 (1996): 177-87; idem, Bible Archaeology or Archaeology of Palestine in the Iron Age? A Rejoinder," *Levant* 30 (1998): 167-74; idem, "State Formation in Israel and Judah: A Contrast in Context, a Contrast in Trajectory," *NEA* 62 (1999): 35-52; idem, "Omride Architecture," *ZDPV* 116 (2000): 114-38; idem, "The Rise of Jerusalem and Judah: The Missing Link," *Levant* 33 (2001): 105-15. David Ussishkin, "The Credibility of the Tel Jezreel Excavations: A Rejoinder to Amnon Ben Tor," *TA* 27 (2000): 248-56; idem, "Solomon's Jerusalem: The Text and the Facts on the Ground," in *Jerusalem in the Bible and Archaeology: The First Temple Period* (ed. A. G. Vaughn and A. E. Killebrew; SBLSymS 18; Leiden: Brill, 2003), 103-15; idem, "Excavations at Tel Lachish 1973-77: Preliminary Report," *TA* 5 (1978): 1-97; idem, "Excavations at Tel Lachish 1978-1983: Second Preliminary Report," *TA* 10 (1983): 171-73. Nadav Na'aman, "Historical and Literary Notes on the Excavations of Tel Jezreel," *TA* 24 (1997): 122-28; idem, "The Contribution of the Amarna Letters to the Debate on Jerusalem's Political Position in the Tenth Century B.C.E." *BASOR* 304 (1996): 17-27.

I use the term *Tel Aviv School* to encompass a group of like-minded scholars in archaeological and historical studies at the University of Tel Aviv whose work is relevant to the discussion of the David story. This is not to suggest that there are no differences of opinion among them, but what they have in common is quite different from the approach of the earlier group that we have considered. Their method is not to presuppose that the biblical stories of David and Solomon are contemporary accounts of historical events and then fit the evidence to suit this view but rather to understand first the nature of the state in Jerusalem and the surrounding region of Judah in comparison with that of Israel to the north and with the later periods of Judean history, using both the archaeological evidence and the relevant historical texts that relate directly to the region. Only then is an attempt made to fit elements of the David tradition into this picture.

plain. Finkelstein argues that the monochrome pottery that marks the
beginning of the Philistine development is subsequent to the demise of
the Egyptian rule of Palestine and that this was followed by a period of
bichrome ware, which lasted until the early 10th century, and a post-
Philistine or "Canaanite" ware that characterized the basic assemblage of
the 10th century, based on the best ceramic sequence for the period at Megiddo. It is the cultural continuity from the Late Bronze age down through
Stratum VIA (10th century) that is the reason for characterizing this phase
as "Canaanite." This covers Iron I, and then there is a decisive break, followed by a new ceramic sequence of Iron IIA. In the Megiddo sequence
after a poor Stratum VB, we have the famous Stratum VA–IVB with its monumental "Solomonic" architecture, which, according to Finkelstein, must
now be dated to the early 9th century. Because Finkelstein begins with the
generally held chronological assumption that the reigns of David and Solomon are from the 10th-century B.C.E., Megiddo Stratum VA–IVB can no
longer be Solomonic. This would make Sheshonq/Shishak the one responsible for the destruction of Megiddo VIA, followed by the meager remains
VB, and Omri would be the builder of VA–IVB.[35]

Once it is understood that Megiddo VA–IVB, Hazor X, and Gezer VIII all
belong to the 9th century and are the work of Omri and not Solomon, then
one is immediately drawn to comparisons with the close parallels in the architecture of Samaria and Jezreel, two sites that were first built by the Omride dynasty and not before. The founding of Samaria by Omri and the role
of both Samaria and Jezreel as royal cities by the Omrides is attested in the
Bible. Furthermore, unlike the case of David and Solomon, the greatness of
Omri and Ahab is independently confirmed by external sources, such as
the Assyrian inscriptions of Shalmaneser III and the Mesha stela. The correlation of Megiddo, Gezer, and Hazor with the single-period site of the
Jezreel compound is particularly important because it seems quite certain
that this site must be dated to the middle portion of the 9th century.[36] Not

---

35. In a private communication, Finkelstein informs me that "recent ^{14}C results
seem to indicate that the end of the late Iron I in the valleys was a gradual process
and therefore not the result of a single military campaign, e.g. Sheshonq I."

36. In addition to the publications in n. 34, see also H. G. M. Williamson, "Jezreel in the Biblical Texts," *TA* 18 (1991): 72–92; N. Na'aman, "Historical and Literary Notes on the Excavations of Tel Jezreel," *TA* 24 (1997): 122–28; I. Finkelstein,
"Addendum: Ben-Tor's Dating of Hazor X–VII," *TA* 27 (2000): 240–44; D. Ussishkin, "The Credibility of the Tel Jezreel Excavations: A Rejoinder to Amnon Ben Tor,"
TA 27 (2000): 248–56.

only is there a direct correspondence in architecture but the ceramic evidence is also in close agreement. This would make it most unlikely that the strata of Megiddo VA–IVB, Hazor X, and Gezer VIII could be dated to the time of Solomon, about a century earlier. This "low chronology" proposed by Finkelstein is further confirmed by new advanced use of ^{14}C dating that confirms the later dating of the Iron IIA samples.[37]

When it comes to considering the archaeological evidence from Judah and Jerusalem, the result is a strong confirmation of the position presented by Jamieson-Drake, which we noted above. After all of the excavations by K. Kenyon, Yigal Shiloh, and others, the result, as Ussishkin has pointed out,[38] is that all signs of a large and prosperous capital of the Davidic-Solomonic era are completely missing. There are no remnants of monumental architecture and few pottery sherds of the period. All indications are that it was a rather small town of not more than a thousand inhabitants. As Finkelstein states, "The most optimistic assessment of the negative evidence is that tenth century Jerusalem was rather limited in extent, perhaps not more than a typical hill country village."[39] Margreet Steiner, who worked on the publication of the Kenyon excavations, has a slightly more favorable view of size and significance of Jerusalem in this period.[40] She associates part of the stepped store structure to this period as the foundation for a fortification and perhaps some administrative structures and therefore something beyond the "villages" of the rest of Judah, with a population of as much as 2000 inhabitants. However, she does not consider a United Monarchy to be likely. In addition, she dates this phase of the city's architecture,

37. Finkelstein and Silberman, *The Bible Unearthed*, 141; also I. Finkelstein and E. Piasetzky, "Recent Radiocarbon Results and King Solomon," *Antiquity* 77 (2003): 771–79; I. Sharon et al., "Report on the First Stage of the Iron Age Dating Project in Israel: Supporting a Low Chronology," *Radiocarbon* 49 (2007): 1–46. Halpern's special pleading on Jezreel (*David's Secret Demons*, 452–53) to get around this ^{14}C dating by stretching out the ceramic data over 75 years to cover both Solomon and the Omrides does not solve the problem. Furthermore, Jezreel is not one of the cities listed by Sheshonq among the other sites of the region in his campaign for the obvious reason that it did not yet exist as a significant city.

38. D. Ussishkin, "Solomon's Jerusalem: The Text and the Facts on the Ground," in *Jerusalem in the Bible and Archaeology: The First Temple Period* (ed. A. G. Vaughn and A. E. Killebrew; SBLSymS 18; Leiden: Brill, 2003), 103–15.

39. Finkelstein and Silberman, *The Bible Unearthed*, 133.

40. M. L. Steiner, *Excavations by Kathleen M. Kenyon in Jerusalem 1961-1967: The Settlement in the Bronze and Iron Ages* (Copenhagen International Series 9; London: Sheffield Academic Press, 2001), 42–53, 113–15.

based on the ceramic pottery, to the rather vague 10th to 9th centuries, which is intended to cover both the high and low dating, and if one opts for the lower chronology of the 9th century for these wares, then it still lies outside the Davidic-Solomonic range. In any event, the city of Iron IIA was still only about one-fifth of the size of the 7th-century city.

Furthermore, the most important city of Judah during the monarchy, in addition to Jerusalem, was Lachish, situated on the edge of the Shephelah, and it was not inhabited between the end of the Late Bronze Age and the end of the 10th or early the 9th century (Lachish V). When it was finally re-built in Stratum IV as a fortified city, it imitated some of the architectural features of the northern site, with a six-chambered gate, solid walls and an elaborate palace, but it did not make use of ashlar masonry. This city preceded the major city of the region in Stratum III (late 8th century)—the one destroyed by Sennacherib in 701 b.c.e.[41]

More recently, Eilat Mazar, the current excavator in Jerusalem's "City of David" has made another attempt to identify certain architectural features found in the excavations with David's palace.[42] After finding certain fragments of massive walls in the reports from previous excavations combined with additional wall fragments in her own excavation adjacent to these, she reconstructs a "Large Stone Structure" from a single building that she identifies as David's palace. This archaeological reconstruction, however, has been challenged by L. Singer-Avitz, Z. Herzog, Finkelstein and Ussishkin.[43] They argue that (1) the walls unearthed by Mazar do not belong to a single building, (2) the more impressive wall fragments belong with those uncovered by Macalister and Duncan in the 1920s, to be dated to the Hellenistic period, and (3) the massive "stepped stone structure," understood as the foundation built to support the palace, belongs instead to at least two phases of construction, the lower part of which may be Iron IIA (9th century by late chronology) and the upper part belonging to the Hellenistic period. As a consequence, all of the pieces do not fit together to produce a palace of the 10th century. The scholars conclude by showing how all the references to Jerusalem in the Bible from Genesis on down to the time of

---

41. D. Ussishkin, "Excavations at Tel Lachish 1973-1977: Preliminary Report," *TA* 5 (1978): 1-97; ibid., "Excavations at Tel Lachish 1978-1983: Second Preliminary Report," *TA* 10 (1983): 171-73; Finkelstein, "Rise of Jerusalem," 109.

42. E. Mazar, "Did I Find King David's Palace," *BAR* 32/1 (2006): 16-27, 70.

43. I. Finkelstein, L. Singer-Avitz, Z. Herzog, David Ussishkin, "Has David's Palace in Jerusalem Been Found," *TA* 34 (2007): 142-64.

David are made by Mazar to fit the archaeology, in the tradition of the old "biblical archaeology" movement. In a summary they state:

> The biblical text dominates this field operation, not archaeology. Had it not been for Mazar's literal reading of the biblical text, she never would have dated the remains to the 10th century B.C.E. with such confidence. This is an excellent example of the weakness of the traditional, highly literal, biblical archaeology—a discipline that dominated research until the 1960s, that was weakened and almost disappeared from the scene in the later years of the 20th century, and that reemerged with all its attributes in the City of David in 2005.[44]

In addition to this negative evidence from the excavations at Jerusalem and Lachish are the extensive *surveys of settlement patterns* in the region of Judah in the 10th century.[45] These yield the same result of a very limited population for the whole region of the Judah highlands. As Finkelstein states, the sparse remains from Jerusalem "meshes well with the rather meager settlement pattern of the rest of Judah in the same period, which was composed of only about twenty small villages and a few thousand inhabitants, many of them wandering pastoralists."[46] By comparison, the settlement of the northern highlands of Israel for the 10th century presents a quite-different picture, reflecting a different historical development. As Finkelstein states, "Out of a total of approximately forty-five thousand people living in the hill country, a full 90 percent would have inhabited the villages of the north. That would have left about five thousand people scattered among Jerusalem, Hebron, and about twenty small villages in Judah, with additional groups probably continuing as pastoralists."[47] In the northern highlands, with its much greater population base and much richer resources, the region developed much more rapidly toward statehood, so that a quite-strong kingdom arose in the 9th century under the Omrides. This happened at the same time in various regions in the rest of Syria and Transjordan during the 9th century with very similar features, far in advance of more remote places such as Judah and Edom, which lagged a century or more behind.[48]

---

44. Ibid., 162.
45. Finkelstein, "State Formation," 42.
46. Finkelstein and Silberman, *The Bible Unearthed*, 133-34.
47. Ibid., 143.
48. Another recent attempt at articulating an explanation of the rise of the Israelite state is made by A. Faust, "Abandonment, Urbanization, Resettlement and the Formation of the Israelite State," *NEA* 66 (2003), 147-61. In this article, Faust attempts

What the archaeological record and the demographic surveys of settlement patterns reveal, as Finkelstein and Silberman state, is that "the evolution of the highlands of Canaan into two distinct polities was a natural development. There is no archaeological evidence whatsoever that this situation of north and south grew out of an earlier political unity—particularly one centered in the south."[49] Judah's small monarchy developed slowly in the shadow of the north and very much under its control. This is a very important point when it comes to critically evaluating not only the early history of Judah, including the reigns of David and Solomon, but also the literary history of the stories about these two kings. In particular, it raises the difficult question of how we are to understand the relationship of the Judean king David to the Benjaminite king Saul, and the tradition about David's succession to the throne of Saul and his rule of all Israel, to say nothing about his far-flung conquests of kingdoms that as yet did not exist in the 10th century.

Another kind of correlation between archaeological finds and their social contexts must be briefly mentioned here, and this has to do with epigraphic materials and their relationship to a scribal class and its role within the state or society in which it is located. In a recent study, Ryan Byrne has attempted to make this kind of correlation of epigraphic evidence both with respect to the Late Bronze Age, the time of the Egyptian Empire, and the subsequent Iron I period, corresponding to the period of David's rule.[50] Regarding the former period, he notes that it was cuneiform that formed the scribal language in a standardized western form, serving the empire both for political and commercial purposes. Once the empire came to an end, so did this scribal practice, which left scarcely a trace in the subsequent period. This was also the case for the more local state-supported alphabetic cuneiform of Ugarit. The parallel development of the Canaanite alphabetic script, as a kind of rival to cuneiform, was very slow in developing and, even with the disappearance of the empire, did not evolve into a standardized epigraphic form until the rise of the Palestinian states in the

---

to use archaeology in support of the biblical presentation of the United Monarchy. The article is severely criticized by I. Finkelstein ("[De]formation of the Israelite State: A Rejoinder on Methodology," *NEA* 68 [2005]: 202–8) as a typical case of biblical archaeology, making the material evidence fit the presentation of Israelite history in the biblical text.

49. Ibid., 158. See also Finkelstein, "State Formation."

50. R. Byrne, "The Refuge of Scribalism in Iron I Palestine," *BASOR* 345 (2007): 1–31.

Iron II period. Thus, even though examples of early alphabetic script have been found belonging to the 10th century, their lack of any standard epigraphy argues strongly against any state-supported scribal institutions. This would seem to agree with the Jamieson-Drake hypothesis of state development, as well as the other "minimalist" archaeological evidence, namely, that there was no Judean state in the 10th century.

Comparison between the Amarna Age and David's Reign: La longue durée

This argument from the epigraphic evidence has considerable relevance for Nadav Na'aman's critical response to Jamieson-Drake and the "minimalists" (by which he means Thompson and Lemche, but we must also include Finkelstein) and their characterization of Davidides' rule in Jerusalem as a simple illiterate chiefdom until the 8th century.[51] Na'aman appeals to Albrecht Alt's method of using *la longue durée*, also used by Finkelstein, which sees a strong similarity between Jerusalem of the 14th and the 10th centuries, and specifically with the rule of ʿAbdi-Heba of Jerusalem and the time of David and Solomon. Na'aman rejects the negative appraisal of the archaeological evidence, against the evaluation of his colleagues Finkelstein and Ussishkin, because the archaeological picture for Judah and Jerusalem in the Late Bronze Age is no more impressive than and quite comparable to that of Iron I. Yet the epigraphic evidence reveals a more sophisticated state for LB II than what the archaeological evidence would suggest, and for Na'aman this means that 10th–9th century Jerusalem could also have been more sophisticated than what has been suggested by Jamieson-Drake.

Before proceeding with Na'aman's specific arguments, some comments on the use of *la longue durée* are necessary. The problem with its use is that it can give one some useful information about repetitive social trends, but if the nature of other factors from the two periods is different or unequal, then it can be misleading. Thus, in a comparison between LB II and Iron I, it can be asserted that the southern and northern highlands are not a single homogeneous region but regularly divide into two separate entities, the northern being the stronger, more densely populated, and more prosperous of the two. Politically, it is the northern region that would tend to dominate the southern. As Finkelstein has shown, this basic understanding of

---

51. N. Na'aman, "The Contribution of the Amarna Letters to the Debate on Jerusalem's Political Position in the Tenth Century B.C.E.," *BASOR* 304 (1996): 17–27.

the development of the two regions holds not only for the first millennium but also for the second and third millennia as well.[52] However, the one important element that is present in LB II, which is missing in the 10th century, is the Egyptian Empire with its complete political control of the region. This foreign entity dictated the political configurations of each small unit and its boundaries; it imposed its bureaucracies and lines of communication; it provided military garrisons and policing of the region; it appointed the rulers who served at the pharaoh's pleasure.[53] All of these things were missing in 10th-century Palestine. Furthermore, the archaeological and epigraphic evidence does suggest a long cultural continuity of city-states preceding LB II and the Amarna age, whereas there is a radical disjunction between LB II and Iron I, corresponding to the loss of Egyptian control of the region, so that one cannot assume a social continuity, at least not at the elite level represented by the Egyptian presence in the region.

Let us consider for a moment the place of Jerusalem in the Amarna age. As Redford points out,

> In the fourteenth century during the Amarna period, Egypt conceived of these highlands [of Palestine] as encompassing two spheres of responsibility, the *mâtat Urusalim*, "the lands of Jerusalem," centered upon Jerusalem and synonymous with the Judean highlands; and the northern hill country controlled from Shechem. Since these thinly settled uplands constituted ideal staging areas and terrain for settlement of renegades, *some* kind of imperial presence was necessary to save the valleys and coastlands from marauders. Both areas, however, the Egyptians were content, if not obliged, to leave in the hands of local dynasties.[54]

Redford goes on to describe the appointment of ʿAbdi-Heba in Jerusalem, the younger son of the previous ruler, who had been sent to Egypt for his education and military training and who considered himself a "soldier," able to command the pharaoh's troops in the region under his authority. His correspondence to Pharaoh constantly appeals for receiving additional troops so he can do his job of protecting the lands against hostile elements, primarily marauding bands, for the benefit of Egypt.[55]

---

52. I. Finkelstein, "The Emergence of Israel: A Phase in the Cyclic History of Canaan in the Third and Second Millennia BCE," in *From Nomadism to Monarchy* (ed. I. Finkelstein and N. Naʾaman; Jerusalem: Israel Exploration Society, 1994), 150–78.

53. One can also point to the comparable impact on Israel and Judah with the rise of Assyrian control of Syria-Palestine in the late 8th and 7th centuries.

54. D. B. Redford, *Egypt, Canaan, and Israel in Ancient Times* (Princeton: Princeton University Press, 1992), 269.

55. Ibid., 270.

What becomes abundantly clear is that in the highlands, north and south, this Egyptian cultural veneer was quite antithetical to the culture of the general population and constantly under threat from the local population of predominantly Shasu and ʿApiru, and once Egyptian power in the region faltered, it was easily annihilated. The archaeological picture for the transition between LB II and Iron I is far from clear in Jerusalem, but at Lachish there is a significant gap between the end of LB II and the renewed occupation in the 9th century.[56] In the southern coastal plain, it is the Philistines and other "Sea Peoples" who fill the void in Iron I, a population significantly different from those living in the highlands region. The picture at Shechem is not entirely clear for this transition period, due to the character of early excavations at the site.[57] Nevertheless, there does seem to be a significant break in occupational continuity, with a destruction of Stratum XIII (late 13th century), then some revival of the Late Bronze Age in Stratum XII and gradual transition to Iron I in XI (late 10th century). After a short occupation gap, Stratum X reflects Iron IIA in the early 9th century.[58] All of this suggests that one must exercise considerable caution in the way one makes use of the Amarna-period textual evidence four centuries before the 10th-century "monarchies" of these two regions.

Let us now return to Naʾaman's argument based on a comparison between the Amarna age and the 10th century. His description of ʿAbdi-Heba's rule in the Amarna age is as follows:

> According to the Amarna tablets, Jerusalem was the seat of a king nominated by the Pharaoh. . . . He lived in a palace (*bitu*) . . . , and an Egyptian garrison of about 50 soldiers was temporarily stationed in the place. Egyptian messengers came quite often to the court of Jerusalem . . . , and the king sent rich caravans with tribute and gifts to the Pharaoh. . . . Jerusalem's territory extended from south of Bethel in the north to Hebron in the south, and from the Jordan in the east to the Shephelah hills in the west. . . . The place of Jerusalem in the Egyptian province of Canaan was similar to that of other lowland Canaanite city-states, although its society,

---

56. See D. Ussishkin, "Excavations at Tel Lachish 1973–1977," 91–93; idem, "Excavations at Tel Lachish 1978–1983," 168–70.

57. R. G. Boling and E. F. Campbell, "Jeroboam and Rehoboam at Shechem," in *Archaeology and Biblical Interpretation* (ed. L. G. Perdue et al.; Atlanta: John Knox, 1987), 264–72.

58. For an extensive review of the published archaeological data, see I. Finkelstein, "Shechem in the Late Bronze and the Iron I," in *Timelines: Studies in Honour of Manfred Bietak* (ed. E. Czerney et al.; OLA 149; Leuven: Peeters, 2006), 349–56.

economy, and internal organization must have been quite different from those of its western neighbors.[59]

What this description *seems* to suggest is that there is some cultural continuity, as well as similarity in the material development, between the two periods. This impression is strengthened by an argument used by Na'aman to support his view that there was continuity in scribal traditions between the end of the Egyptian empire in Asia and the 10th century. He states that "hieratic numerals and signs appear in epigraphic documents of the kingdoms of both Israel and Judah in the eighth-seventh centuries B.C.E. but do not appear in documents of Israel's neighbors. Goldwasser . . . has shown that they must have entered the Hebrew script before the division of the monarchy, namely, in the tenth century B.C.E."[60] However, what Goldwasser's study makes clear is that this use of hieratic numerals came into Israel and Judah by way of the southern lowlands of Philistia, which may have inherited it along with the Canaanite script from the former population of the region. Exactly when it found its way into Israel and Judah is a matter of debate, because it does not show up in that region until the 8th and 7th centuries. It is more likely that this came about in the 9th or 8th century than the 10th. At any rate, what Goldwasser and Na'aman do not assert is any scribal continuity in Jerusalem itself, and this is confirmed by Byrne's study, as noted above. Whereas in LB II there was a strong and uniform scribal tradition in cuneiform throughout the whole of the Levant imposed by the Egyptian Empire, there is a complete lack of any epigraphic standardization of this sort in Iron I, suggesting the complete lack of the corresponding state institutions to support it.

Consequently, lest there be any misunderstanding that the views of Na'aman support the widespread idea that there was, in fact, a cultural continuity in Jerusalem that went back to the Amarna age, Na'aman has assured me in a recent private communication that this was not his intention. He states (e-mail, 18 July 2008): "In light of the enormous demographic and cultural difference between the Amarna and Iron Age I period, no sensible scholar would suggest similarity between the kingdom and court of ʿAbdi-Heba and that of David. The similarity between the 14th and 10th century is only in the overall structure, not in regime, society, administration or culture." He merely wanted to raise the *possibility* that there was a

59. Na'aman, "The Contribution of the Amarna Letters," 20.
60. Ibid., 22. He sites O. Goldwasser, "An Egyptian Scribe from Lachish and the Hieratic Tradition of the Hebrew Kingdoms," *TA* 18 (1991): 248–53.

monarchy with a court in the 10th century, in spite of the lack of material remains, just as there is a similar lack of material evidence for the court of ʿAbdi Heba.

Naʾaman offers two additional arguments in support of a court in Jerusalem such as this during the reigns of David and Solomon. First, he places a lot of weight on the reference to Shishak's campaign against Jerusalem in Rehoboam's fifth year and the transfer of Solomon's golden shields to Shishak and their replacement with copper shields (1 Kgs 14:25–28). He takes this as evidence of a written text from that period, but it is difficult to understand what the point of a contemporary text such as this would be; it seems to me to be a fiction of Dtr.[61] The major problem with this scheme is that Shishak never mentions Jerusalem or the Kingdom of Judah in his victory inscription. Second, Naʾaman cites the lists of officers of the court of David and Solomon, which include references to scribes (2 Sam 8:17, 20:25; 1 Kgs 4:3), as evidence of written sources from that period. However, there is good reason to regard these lists as suspect, and they will receive more detailed treatment below.

In Naʾaman's characterization of the Davidic "state," he assumes the view that this included a "united kingdom" of both the southern and northern highlands, as well as the highlands of Transjordan in the time of Iron IIA (the high chronology).[62] This increases the size of the kingdom many times and even makes an "empire" possible. It allows him to make the further claim that "the scope of settlement in the highland areas is also relevant for the discussion of the so-called 'Davidic empire.' According to the biblical account, David conquered Philistia, Aram, Ammon, Moab, and Edom and brought all these kingdoms under his yoke. But the great kingdom was short-lived and fell apart immediately after David's death."[63] Naʾaman chides the "revisionist" scholars who have questioned an "empire" such as this, and he refers to

---

61. See also Finkelstein and Silberman, *David and Solomon*, 71–81. More on this below.

62. Ibid., 23–24. Naʾaman wants to use Isa 7:17a as an 8th-century witness to this former united kingdom, but it is not at all clear how to understand what is meant by "the day that Ephraim departed from Judah," and it is circular reasoning to interpret it as a reference to the split of the kingdom in the time of Rehoboam. What is awkward about an interpretation such as this is that it turns the good news of v. 16 into a threat. It could just as easily refer to a time in the more recent past when the domination of the Omrides over Judah came to an end and Judah was permitted to prosper on its own. See also his general summary, p. 25, point d.

63. Ibid., 23.

the activity of Lab'ayu, king of Shechem, whose kingdom was much smaller and yet could extend his influence far beyond his own realm. As we shall see in the next chapter, however, Na'aman rather drastically qualified this position by suggesting in his later work that most of this military activity was the creative invention of the historian who imitated the conquests of Israelite and Aramean kings of a later time.[64]

Two remarks are in order here. The first is that, though Na'aman criticizes Thompson for not using the principle of the *longue durée*, he himself has only used it selectively. As Finkelstein has so strongly emphasized, the *longue durée* has made it clear that the north and south highland regions should be understood as separate regions, with the north being the dominant one in all periods. It would be a complete anomaly for a ruler of the southern region with a tenth of the population and so much less in resources to be able to dominate the northern highlands and those of Transjordan too. The example of Lab'ayu proves, if anything, the opposite of Na'aman's position, because 'Abdi-Heba of Jerusalem was certainly no match for Lab'ayu. Second, as we have seen above, Finkelstein's low chronology for Iron IIA to the time of the Omrides makes this period fit the *longue durée* very well. He argues for the domination of the northern highland kingdom over the whole Palestinian highland region, with the small kingdom of Judah as subordinate. Just like Lab'ayu, but to a far greater extent, the Omrides extended their control into Transjordan as far as Moab, over the Jezreel Valley and Megiddo, north to Dan, and over the Shephelah to Gezer. In this respect, Finkelstein's position seems to confirm the views of the "revisionists" and furnish strong archaeological support for it.

More recently, Finkelstein and Na'aman have together written a piece comparing Shechem of the Amarna period with Samaria of the Omri-Ahab age of the Kingdom of Israel, which expresses their agreement in the application of the *longue durée* principle to the northern state of Israel.[65] However, the article is completely silent about how the *longue durée* principle applies to the Southern Kingdom of Judah, and to David in particular. Only in the introduction do they both affirm that "it has become clear in recent years that the biblical description of a great tenth-century United Monarchy is an ideological construct of the time of the authors, who lived centuries after the 'events' they described. . . . This means that the first fully-

---

64. See below, pp. 97–99.

65. I. Finkelstein and N. Na'aman, "Shechem of the Amarna Period and the Rise of the Northern Kingdom of Israel," *IEJ* 55 (2005): 172–93.

developed territorial state of ancient Israel was the Northern Kingdom of the time of the Omrides in the first half of the ninth century B.C.E."[66] In other words, over the last decade, Naʾaman has modified his position in response to the constant accumulation of new evidence, much of it based on his own research, to the point that his views are not so different from those of the "minimalists" whom he earlier criticized.

Finkelstein and Silberman have their own way of using the Amarna age and the *longue durée* as a way of understanding the David story. They first attempt to use the knowledge of ancient settlement patterns from archaeological surveys in order to find the one that is most appropriate as a historical background for the David story or parts of it. They accept the critical position that the story of David in its literary form was the product of a later day, based on oral tradition of the earlier period. They state:

> Since evidence of extensive literacy is lacking in Judah before the end of the eighth century B.C.E., "The History of David's Rise" is unlikely to have been put into writing less than two hundred years after David's time. Is it possible that the narrative was composed at that time and that the general settlement patterns and population distribution described in the story of David's rise reflect the situation at *the time of writing*—and have no real connection to the situation in the tenth century B.C.E.?[67]

They answer this question by suggesting that the story of David's rise and flight from Saul reflects a time when Judah was rather sparsely populated and it makes no mention of such sites as Beer-sheba, Arad, Lachish, and Beth-shemesh, which became important to Judah in the 9th century.[68] In their view, "the description of a 'wild south'—of lawlessness and banditry in the fringe areas of Judah, so central to the David story—does not fit the situation in the earliest possible period when 'The History of David's Rise' was put into writing."[69] They also point to the prominence of the city of Gath in the David story and the fact that this city was an important regional power in the 10th and 9th centuries but lost this position in the late 9th century. Consequently, in their view, the HDR reflects oral traditions that stem from the 10th century that were only put into written form two centuries later.

Finkelstein and Silberman likewise invoke the parallel of the Amarna age and the reign of ʿAbdi-Heba of Jerusalem. The reason for doing so is

---

66. Ibid., 172.
67. Finkelstein and Silberman, *David and Solomon*, 37.
68. Finkelstein, "The Rise of Jerusalem," *Levant* 33: 105–15.
69. Finkelstein and Silberman, *David and Solomon*, 38.

that both the 14th and 10th centuries have the same basic settlement pattern of "'dimorphic' chiefdoms, denoting a single community stretching over a significant territory, in which two forms of subsistence, farming and herding, existed side by side."[70] At this point, however, the comparison becomes somewhat confused. On the one hand, they compare the nature of ʿAbdi Heba's chiefdom with that of David; on the other hand, they are more concerned to compare David and his men with a particularly troublesome group of the Amarna age, that of the ʿApiru. They describe this group in the following way: "The Apiru were uprooted peasants and herders who sometimes turned bandits, sometimes sold themselves as mercenaries to the highest bidder, and were in both cases a disruptive element in any attempt by either local rulers or the Egyptian administration to maintain the stability of their rule."[71] This group was particularly troublesome for ʿAbdi-Heba, a loyal representative of the Egyptian administration. Finkelstein and Silberman acknowledge that the ʿApiru were particularly hostile toward Egyptian authority, which may have been largely responsible for the conditions that led to the formation of bandit gangs of mercenaries such as these. It is just this kind of band that they wish to compare with David and his men, and they cite various passages in the David story that they see as fitting this description.

Once again, there are some problems with this use of the *longue durée*. As we have seen above, what is missing from the 10th century that was true in the Amarna period is the Egyptian Empire and the great social impact that it had on the region. There is no reason to believe that in the 10th century the same conditions prevailed that gave rise to the phenomenon of the ʿApiru in the 14th century. The term ʿApiru does not persist into later times. Furthermore, it is a fact that conditions similar to those of the 14th century arose in later periods under the Assyrian and Babylonian domination, which did give rise to mercenary bands of this sort and could just as easily have served as a model for David and his men. Naʾaman has made a strong case for the depiction of these bands of mercenaries in the David story and elsewhere as reflecting the conditions in the time of the Assyrian Empire, which were familiar to the later writers of these stories, and specifically to Dtr.[72] In applying the use of the *longue durée*, one could say that the more

---

70. Ibid., 41.
71. Ibid., 44–45.
72. N. Naʾaman, "Ḫabiru-like Bands in the Assyrian Empire and Bands in Biblical Historiography," *JAOS* 120 (2000): 621–24. More on mercenaries below.

accurate parallel with the period of the Egyptian Empire in Asia is the Assyrian Empire in Syria-Palestine and its impact on the region. Once one admits that there are details in the story of David that could reflect a time of composition much later that the 8th century proposed by Finkelstein and Silberman, then the conditions of Judah reflected in the story may relate to the Exile and Postexilic Period, when the population of the region was again very sparse for an extended period of time.

Finkelstein also attempts to make another comparison between the stories in Samuel and the Amarna age by comparing Lab'ayu, a ruler of Shechem in the 14th century, with Saul, "the last Labayu," in the 10th century.[73] Finkelstein views the stories about Saul and David as a mixture of traditions from the north (positive toward Saul) and south (negative toward Saul in favor of David), which were first brought together in written form in the late 8th century. Because the stories of Saul center so directly on Benjamin and not on the more northern region of Shechem and Samaria, Finkelstein argues that they must come from the period before the rise of Samaria. Furthermore, he regards the rises of the two states, Judah and Israel, as quite separate from each other, so that the myth of a "united kingdom" was only created by this 8th-century combination of the northern and southern traditions after the fall of Samaria when refugees from the Benjaminite region came into Judah. This led to viewing David as the successor of Saul and hence to David's rule over all Israel as well as Judah. This also means that the chronology of Saul's reign cannot be controlled by that of David and Solomon, and Saul's reign can only be viewed as occurring sometime in the 10th century.

Finkelstein's thesis of Saul as the "last Labayu" is that, like Lab'ayu, Saul's chiefdom in Benjamin extended far beyond this region to include Jabesh-Gilead and the Jabbok valley in Transjordan and the Jezreel valley in the north. This was perceived as a threat by the Egyptians under Shishak (Sheshonq), who had aspirations of regaining their lost control of Canaan-Palestine. He even thinks that there may have been a coalition between the Philistines and the Egyptians that is no longer remembered in the biblical

---

73. I. Finkelstein, "The Last Labayu: King Saul and the Expansion of the First North Israelite Territorial Entity," in *Essays on Ancient Israel in Its Near Eastern Context: A Tribute to Nadav Na'aman* (ed. Y. Amit et al.; Winona Lake, IN: Eisenbrauns, 2006), 171–87; also Finkelstein and Silberman, *David and Solomon,* 61–89. In Finkelstein and Na'aman, "Shechem and the Amarna Period," 181–87, Lab'ayu is compared more appropriately with the Omrides.

tradition. Consequently, in Saul's fateful battle in the Jezreel valley near the city of Beth-shean (an Egyptian administrative center in the time of the empire), it was the Egyptians and not the Philistines who defeated Saul there. This reconstruction of events links certain areas of conquest in the Sheshonq victory stela, namely, the Benjamin plateau, the Jabbok valley, and the Jezreel valley, with the domain of Saul.

There are, however, some serious problems with the territorial dimensions of Saul's rule on which the whole thesis depends. The basic Saul tradition lies within 1 Sam 9–14, and this clearly restricts his rule and activity to the Benjaminite region with his main objective to win freedom from the Philistines. There is no justification in viewing the Philistine garrisons of this region as Egyptian because the Egyptian presence in Canaan had long ended. The account of Saul's rescue of Jabesh-Gilead never suggests that he became ruler of this region, and in any event, there was likely no kingdom of Ammon at this time against which to fight. The story more likely reflects a 9th-century reality when Jabesh-Gilead was closely associated with the Omrides. The use of the territorial markers in 2 Sam 2:9 belongs to CH and is a postexilic fiction full of anachronisms.[74] The final battle at Jezreel is part of the David-Saul story, and, as Finkelstein admits, against the Philistines it makes no sense, so he makes Sheshonq responsible for Saul's death. But if Sheshonq attacked Saul's homeland of Benjamin as well, why was Saul not defending that region instead of the one so much further north? In fact, as we shall see, the model that the author (Dtr) used for this conflict was the Omrides against Hazael in this same region. Furthermore, by selecting proof-texts somewhat arbitrarily and uncritically to construct the dimensions of Saul's realm, Finkelstein risks engaging in "biblical archaeology," which he so strongly criticizes in others.

Even if one grants that the Saul and David traditions were once separate from each other and that Saul could have been a chieftain of Benjamin anytime in the 10th century, it is still not so clear when these traditions came together. This needs much more critical literary analysis than Finkelstein has given it. There are certainly other possibilities than the late 8th century. The principal reason for the choice of the late 8th century for the ideological construction of a United Monarchy is the belief that there was a substantial influx of refugees from the north after the destruction of the Kingdom

---

74. The reference to Jezreel is a case in point. It was built as a royal city by the Omrides. The Assurites probably refer to Assyrian transplants in various regions after the fall of Samaria. On the dating of this text, see below, pp. 271–272.

of Israel. This view, however, is strongly disputed by Naʾaman, who argues that a movement of population such as this would have been strongly resisted by the Assyrian authorities.[75] Instead, he accounts for the temporary influx of population into Jerusalem at the end of the 8th century as the result of the Sennacherib invasion and destruction of so many cities, creating homeless Judean refugees who flooded into Jerusalem. If this is correct, it would suggest that the amalgamation of northern and southern traditions did not come about until some time later. Furthermore, once one limits the territory of Saul's rule to the Benjamin region, then there is no need to make Saul another Labʾayu and the reason for Sheshonq's invasion of Palestine. Whatever this pharaoh's intention was, the whole scheme of his campaign was very short lived. It cannot help us much with the David story.

A quite-different perspective on *la longue durée* has been suggested by the work of Keith Whitelam in *The Invention of Ancient Israel*.[76] Whitelam's primary concern is that the whole discussion of the archaeological approach to the history of the Palestinian region is that it has been dominated by the quest for the origins of Israel, and though Finkelstein and Silberman reject the rather crass use of the Bible in "biblical archaeology," they still fall prey to the same error of circularity in their use of Israel as a starting point. The whole point of using *la longue durée* was precisely to find the real Israel by means of this process. By contrast Whitelam proposes an alternative. He states:

> The pursuit of Palestinian history is dependent upon freeing it from the temporal constraints imposed upon it by the discourse of biblical studies. Braudel's concept of *la longue durée* offers a perspective which overcomes the neat periodization of biblical histories. It is a temporal perspective which helps to illustrate that Israel is but an entity in the sweep of Palestinian time. Concentration on the short term, the Iron Age to Roman period or the present, obscures the fact that Israel is but one thread in the rich tapestry of Palestinian history. It is the perspective of *la longue durée* which allows the historian to decide whether the settlement patterns of, say, the Early Iron Age in Palestine are unique or conform to similar patterns at other times. Only then is it possible to ask if there might be similar factors at work affecting the shift in settlement or

---

75. N. Naʾaman, "When and How Did Jerusalem Become a Great City? The Rise of Jerusalem as Judah's Premier City in the Eighth-Seventh Centuries B.C.E.," *BASOR* 347 (2007): 21–56, esp. pp. 35–38.

76. K. W. Whitelam, *The Invention of Ancient Israel: The Silencing of Palestinian History* (London: Routledge, 1996).

whether it has to be explained in terms completely different from any other period in the history of ancient Palestine. From this perspective, Palestinian history becomes the pursuit of the whole gamut of social, economic, political, and religious developments within Palestine, rather than a preliminary or exclusive concern with how such developments relate to and explain the emergence and evolution of Israel.[77]

In the same way, Whitelam argues that it is the ideological identification of the whole of Palestine as the equivalent of the biblical Davidic kingdom "from Dan to Beersheba" that has resulted in the interpretation of so much of what lies within this region and its archaeology as "Israelite" from the Iron Age onward.[78]

Following this perspective, if the concern is with a comparison between the whole region of Palestine (what the Egyptians called Canaan and the Bible calls the land of Canaan) in the Amarna age, and the same region in the later Iron I–IIA period, then the focus should not be exclusively on Jerusalem and its ruler in the south or Shechem and the central highlands in the north. There were a lot of little states in the region more important that ʿAbdi-Heba of Jerusalem. Any history that focuses exclusively on ʿAbdi-Heba to the exclusion of the rest in order to explain the rise of David is in danger of falsifying the larger picture. To take the larger picture seriously, one might rather suggest that David was also merely one of a number Palestinian chieftains or petty rulers of the region, and certainly not the most significant. Nor is there any clear evidence that ʿAbdi-Heba was the ruler of a territorial state, as Naʾaman suggests, and there is no evidence apart from the anachronistic biblical accounts that David was also a territorial ruler. We simply have no contemporary evidence to indicate the extent of any ruler who may have ruled from Jerusalem in the 10th century B.C.E.

Furthermore, there is nothing in the archaeological record that would allow us to identify the ethnicity or self-identification of the inhabitants of the southern highlands region. All the indications of cultural continuity between the Late Bronze Age and Iron I, as well as with groups outside of the highland region, do not permit us to draw any conclusions about the inhabitants as "Israelites" or "Judeans" distinct from the "Canaanites." If there is a disruptive element within the region of Palestine at the end of the Late Bronze Age, it is the well-documented arrival of the Sea Peoples in general and the Philistines in particular, accompanied by the decline of the

77. Ibid., 66–67.
78. Ibid., 39–58.

Egyptian Empire and the withdrawal of the Egyptian presence in Palestine. In the highland region of Palestine, the hinterland of the new Philistine presence, one could expect to find continuity with the older Palestinian population of the Late Bronze Age, and that is what appears to be the case, in spite of the biblical tradition to the contrary.

In addition, Na'aman and Finkelstein acknowledge that the "united kingdom" of Israel and Judah is a late ideological construct, which means that David was never the king of a population known as "Israelites." He may have been a leader of the tribe of Judah who managed to take control of Jerusalem, but this should not be construed as part of the history of Israel. The rise of Israel to the status of a state must be restricted to the northern highlands region. All of this is implicit in the archaeological and historical research of the Tel Aviv School, even though they still use the language of biblical archaeology in speaking of David as an Israelite king. Consequently, the quest for the origins of Israel in the time of David is a hopeless endeavor. It is the identification of Israel in the biblical tradition with archaeological remains in Iron I in Palestine that permits Finkelstein and Silberman to make that connection.

Having established a radically different archaeological basis for their treatment of the social context of the David story from those studies that we reviewed in the first part of this chapter, Finkelstein and Silberman attempt to explain the stories of David and Solomon as a multilayered tradition, reflecting different historical and social contexts. [79] These can be distinguished by comparison with what is now known of Judah's and Israel's social development from the 10th to the 4th centuries B.C.E. [80] In contrast to the earlier studies, this one is based first and foremost on a critique of the archaeological data used to support the "Solomonic" remains at sites such as Megiddo, Hazor, and Gezer.[81] As we have seen above, the supposed Solomonic features are redated to a period about a century later, which radically changes the whole understanding of political development in Syria-Palestine during the 10th century B.C.E., to which David and Solomon are dated. In addition, Finkelstein and Silberman critically evaluate the archaeological evidence available from Jerusalem itself, dealing with its

---

79. I. Finkelstein and N. A. Silberman, *David and Solomon: In Search of the Bible's Sacred Kings and the Roots of the Western Tradition* (New York: Free Press, 2006).

80. We will not be concerned here with David tradition in Judaism and Christianity as treated by Finkelstein and Silberman in part 3 of their book.

81. Ibid., 275–81.

development from the 10th to the 6th century, independent of the biblical
tradition about David and Solomon, to reconstruct a social context against
which the multiple layers of the David tradition may be compared and understood. Thus, in contrast to the "biblical archaeologists," the archaeological and other historical data are used as a control to interpret the Davidic
tradition and not vice versa.

The strength of this approach to the David story, therefore, is the degree
to which they allow the use of archaeological and historical evidence to understand the social and historical development of ancient Palestine independent of the biblical tradition. Just how that biblical tradition of David
relates to our increased knowledge of the social history of the highland regions of Palestine, which they identify as Israel,[82] then becomes the main
focus of discussion. The great achievement of the work of Finkelstein and
his colleagues is their significant contribution to the social history of this
region through their archaeological work. Yet when it comes to relating the
various strata of the David tradition to this social history, Finkelstein and
Silberman revert to the same basic categories (HDR, SN, PH, DtrH) that we
saw previously in the work of Kyle McCarter but now place them in the various social strata of Jerusalem's history, which they have uncovered. Thus,
HDR in oral form is placed in the 10th century; SN, also in oral form, in the
9th century; the first literary combination of these traditions as an early history in the late 8th century (= PH); and an edited version by Dtr in the late
7th century, and an exilic Dtr redaction in the 6th century. Slight modifications in these four categories are made in order to fit their social history
scheme. While they respect the science of historical criticism, unlike many
"biblical archaeologists" who deal with the Solomonic age, Finkelstein and
Silberman borrow the four basic literary strata from others and do not engage with it critically.[83] The problem, of course, is that much of this literary
stratification is based on prior historical assumptions that they do not accept. Furthermore, apart from some scattered examples of items in the tra-

---

82. See the remark regarding the population components of the Iron I period
(ibid., 21): "And in the highlands long remembered as the birthplace of Israel and
the home of its royal traditions, a dense network of rustic hilltop farming villages in
formerly sparsely inhabited regions marked the emergence of a culture and a society whose members would later identify themselves as "Israelites." The evidence for
that "memory" is entirely biblical and, in the case of the southern region of the highlands, very late and an ideological invention. The identity is completely anachronistic for the Davidic period. This is still a case of biblical archaeology.

83. They do, however, modify the 10th-century date of SN to the 9th century.

dition that may be assigned to particular levels, no detailed analysis of the stratification of the tradition is attempted. Consequently, one does not know in the case of any particular text that is not specifically mentioned just where they would fit a particular item or episode.

Nevertheless, it should be clear, from the above, that the two approaches to locating the David story within its sociohistorical context, namely, those based on comparison with "historical documents" and those based on a critically reconstructed socioarchaeological context, are not compatible. Not only is there a fundamental disagreement about the nature of the social context in which the story was first produced in David or Solomon's court, but there is a radically different evaluation of the literary character of the David tradition. The one view holds that HDR and SN are contemporary literary works of the most sophisticated narrative kind by accomplished scribes living in the time of David and Solomon; the other view regards HDR and SN as a collection of oral legends and ballads, handed down for centuries before they were committed to their written form. However, we have already suggested in the introduction that the literary stratification being used by both groups of scholars is problematic. What is needed, therefore, is a new literary-critical evaluation that is also compatible with the recent critical reconstruction of the social history of Judah, and this is the task that I will undertake in the present study.

Summary

Let me summarize the results of this archaeological survey thus far. Until the late 1980s, the old "biblical archaeology" method was used to support the biblical view of the great united kingdom of David and Solomon, particularly by using architectural finds at Megiddo, Hazor, and Gezer, which were correlated with the building activities of Solomon as recorded in 1 Kgs 9:15. Even those who criticized the practice of "biblical archaeology" for earlier periods of biblical history, such as Dever, still made use of it in this instance. This application of biblical archaeology, however, was challenged by a new "socio-archaeological analysis" of the material finds at Jerusalem itself, in the study of Jamieson-Drake, which cast serious doubt on whether the very small settlement at Jerusalem in the 10th century B.C.E. could sustain the kind of state necessary to administer the biblical empire of David and Solomon. The study concluded that it was not until the late 8th century B.C.E. that Judah actually became a state that could sustain a cultural and literate elite and an administration of government and military officials.

This made all literary portrayals of such a state in the earlier periods historically suspect, especially the Solomonic Age presented in 1 Kings. A number of scholars, including Thompson and Lemche, immediately offered support for the Jamieson-Drake position, namely, that David's rule was little more than a very limited chiefdom, and these scholars were soon labeled as "minimalists" by the former "biblical archaeologists."

Into the middle of this controversy stepped the Tel Aviv School, supported by their prodigious and highly respected archaeological activity. They reevaluated the ceramic chronology of the controversial sites of Megiddo, Hazor, and Gezer by means of comparative data from Samaria and Jezreel to prove that the former 10th-century B.C.E. pottery should be dated to the 9th century, contemporary with the time of the Omrides. This gave a quite-different historical horizon to the finds at all of these sites. It was also clear from Ussishkin's excavations at Lachish, coordinated with the results from Jerusalem, that Judah did not begin to develop as a state until the late 9th and early 8th centuries B.C.E. and only came into its own in the late 8th century as Jamieson-Drake had suggested. In addition, the ceramic surface surveys of archaeological sites to estimate the demographic distribution throughout the northern and southern highland regions of Palestine likewise confirmed the conclusions from excavation regarding the late flowering of the state in Judah.

Nevertheless, Na'aman raised some reservations against the views of Jamieson-Drake and the "minimalists," which he viewed as based too narrowly on the sparse archaeological record of Jerusalem and the demographic surveys. If the same arguments were used in the case of the sparse archaeological remains of the LB II period and the low demographics for Judah in this period, then there should not have been a kingdom in Jerusalem in the 14th century B.C.E. Yet, as Na'aman points out, there was a regional kingdom with a small administrative structure and the use of a scribe for royal correspondence. Na'aman's view was that the same *possibility* of a monarchy in Jerusalem exists for the 10th century as well. While he regards a "United Monarchy" as possible in his 1996 article, he considers this only a late ideological construct in his 2005 article. However, what must be emphasized, in my view, is the asymmetry between the two periods, namely, the presence of the Egyptian Empire in Palestine-Canaan, which largely dictated the nature and extent of the various polities throughout the region. Egypt's loss of their Egyptian Empire, followed by the significant influx of Philistines and other Sea Peoples, led to a major disruption in the material culture of most of the region, including the highlands. Though Na'aman acknowledges the complete cultural dissimilarity between the two periods, in his use of the *longue durée* he did not adequately take these factors into account.[84]

Finkelstein's use of the *longue durée* and his comparison with the Amarna age argues against any United Monarchy in David's time. Based on the obvious superiority of the Northern Kingdom of Lab'ayu of Shechem over that of 'Abdi-Heba of Jerusalem, he regards it as highly unlikely that the polity of Jerusalem and Judah could have dominated the much richer and more populous northern highlands, to say nothing of the Jezreel Valley and Transjordan. The Omride period clearly demonstrates the opposite with their control of these regions from Samaria and their domination of the southern highlands. For Finkelstein, the *longue durée* is decisive as evidence against any "united kingdom" under David and Solomon and for a quite-modest chiefdom in 10th-century Jerusalem. Nevertheless, Finkelstein also attempts to use the rule of Lab'ayu of Shechem during the Egyptian Empire as a model for the reign of Saul, which he dates to the time of Sheshonq I. He sees Saul as ruling over a region comparable to that of Lab'ayu and likewise viewed as a threat to Egyptian control of the region, making it the reason for Sheshonq's invasion of Palestine. In this case, however, the two periods are not in any way comparable. The literary evidence for Saul's control of territory beyond Benjamin is very weak; nor is their any evidence of Sheshonq's control of Palestine beyond his one campaign. This sort of reconstruction of the Saul and David traditions is, in my view, quite untenable. This, however, does not negate Finkelstein's broader use of the *longue durée* to establish the relative strengths of the two highland regions and the separate development of Israel and Judah into states in the 9th and 8th centuries, respectively.

Furthermore, while members of the "Tel Aviv School" are sensitive to the need for the use of historical criticism when they attempt to relate the biblical text to archaeological data, they may, as in the case of Finkelstein and Silberman, make use of a literary stratification that is based on assumptions about the sociohistorical context, which they do not accept. What is needed is to construct a literary analysis that will more clearly reflect this new understanding of Judah's social history.

---

84. In fact, there would appear to be very little difference between his view and that of the "minimalists" at the present time.

Chapter 3

The David Saga within Its Social and Historical Setting, Part 2

The Search for Historical Sources within the David Story

In the previous chapter, we reviewed the various forms of *external* evidence that have been used in the past to help date the composition of the David story or various layers of tradition within it. This consisted of either comparative literary genres or the archaeological contexts that are appropriate for the various strata of the David tradition. In this chapter, I wish to address the debate about *internal* evidence that may be used to date the narrative in which it is found. These consist of two kinds: one kind is possible historical documents that were used by the writer for his history of the period; the other is the occurrence of anachronisms, which give the most precise clue to the time of literary composition.

The Lists of David's Officials, His Sons, and His Military Officers

In the past, the primary focus on internal evidence as a way of controlling the historical context of the story of David has been the effort to find remnants of historical sources embedded within the narrative that relate to the time of David and Solomon. In a recent study of the sources for the history of David, Nadav Na'aman argues for the possibility of written records, however rudimentary, in this period.[1] For David's reign, he cites the following:

1. Lists of officials (2 Sam 8:16–18, 20:23–26)
2. Lists of wives and sons (2 Sam 3:2–5, 5:13–16)
3. A list of military officers and heroes (2 Sam 23:8–39)

---

1. N. Na'aman, "Sources and Composition in the History of David," in *The Origins of the Ancient Israelite States* (ed. V. Fritz and P. R. Davies; JSOTSup 228; Sheffield: Sheffield Academic Press, 1996), 170–86.

These lists, however, do not inspire much confidence as official records. The general assumption has been that the lists reflect written archival sources contemporary with the kings in question, and therefore all the discussion about them has to do with understanding them in terms of the social context of the early monarchy.[2] Some allowance is made for their "editing" to make them fit the appropriate literary unit to which they are attached, usually at a fairly early stage in the development of the stories of David, so that few other possibilities are considered beyond these parameters. Nevertheless, many questions and problems exist within the lists that call for further investigation. Let us look at these lists in turn.

Regarding the lists of David's officials in 2 Sam 8:16–18, 20:23–26, there are both inconsistencies and overlap between the two, so that there is some literary connection, but they are hardly just variants of the same list in two different sources. There is also internal inconsistency in form and content within the lists themselves so that it is hard to see how either list could have served a particular bureaucratic function. Nevertheless, the lists are still used to support the notion of a bureaucracy in the time of David, whose officials were responsible for the production of historical documents and their preservation in royal archives. Perhaps the most detailed treatment of these lists is that of T. N. D. Mettinger, whose work is frequently cited in support of the historical authenticity of the lists for the Davidic period.[3] Thus, a few general remarks about this study are in order. Mettinger begins with this assumption: "There is no reason to doubt that these lists originate in the royal chancellery in Jerusalem and that they are most important historical sources."[4] This means that all of his comparative analysis attempting to identify the significance of the titles of the officials is governed by this dating of the lists, and parallels that may be made with Assyrian royal officials of a later period are dismissed as not relevant.

---

2. More recently, Naʾaman has acknowledged the difficulty of assuming the existence and use of archival sources for historiography in the ancient period. See N. Naʾaman, "The Sources Available for the Authors of the Book of Kings," in *Recenti tendenze nella ricostruzione della storia antica d'Israele: Convego internazionale, Roma, 6–7 marzo 2003* (ed. M. Liverani; Rome: Accademia nazionale dei Lincei, 2005), 106; see also my *In Search of History*, 4, 40–51, 195–99; R. Thomas, *Oral Tradition and Written Record in Classical Athens* (Cambridge: Cambridge University Press, 1989), 60–94; ibid., *Literacy and Orality in Ancient Greece* (Cambridge: Cambridge University Press, 1992), 132–44.

3. T. N. D. Mettinger, *Solomonic State Officials* (CBOT 5; Lund: Gleerup, 1971).

4. Ibid., 7. Here he makes reference to and builds on the view of M. Noth.

Nevertheless, there are many reasons for disputing this assumption and the whole edifice of discussion built on it.

1. There is no analogue for such lists of court administrators in Near Eastern and Egyptian sources, and it is difficult to see what the point of a list such as this would be. The lists are so short with no hint of ranking and no idea of how it would be used or why a "memo" such as this would be preserved. The notion that it is an official list of the king's "cabinet" is a ludicrous anachronism.

2. The bureaucracy envisaged by Mettinger in Jerusalem during the time of David and Solomon is an imperial state with a high level of literacy, but as we have seen above there is increasing archaeological evidence to suggest that a state of this sort was not possible in Judah before the mid-8th century. Mettinger himself makes use of evidence drawn from the end of the monarchy and simply assumes continuity back to the beginning of the monarchy, but bureaucratic institutions of the late monarchy are anachronistic for the time of David and Solomon.

3. Mettinger follows A. Cody and others[5] in placing great weight on presumed Egyptian parallels for the various royal officials. This is especially the case for the various forms of the name of David's scribe. One form of the name in 2 Sam 8:17 is שריה, which is a fairly common Hebrew name in late texts, although Mettinger insists on trying to find some Egyptian origin for it. The other form occurs in a number of variants, but Mettinger argues for שישא (1 Kgs 4:3) as the original form and identifies it with the Egyptian term for "scribe" (sšš⁽.t), and he suggests that the title was later construed as a proper name.[6] This, however, does not really tell us how we could arrive at the present texts if they all go back to originals in the time of David and Solomon. In a similar fashion, Mettinger attempts to see the term מזכיר "recorder" (2 Sam 8:16) as reflecting the Egyptian term whm.w.[7] D. B. Redford, however, strongly disputes this claim and regards both proposed correspondences between the Hebrew titles and their Egyptian counterparts as quite misleading and unlikely.[8]

---

5. A. Cody, "Le titre égyptien et le nom propre du scribe de David," *RB* 72 (1965): 381–93; R. de Vaux, "Titres et fonctionaires égyptiens à la cour de David et de Salomon, " *RB* 48 (1939): 394–405.

6. Mettinger, *Solomonic State Officials*, 25–30, 45–51.

7. Ibid., 58–62.

8. D. B. Redford, *Egypt, Canaan, and Israel in Ancient Times* (Princeton: Princeton University Press, 1992), 369–74. R. Byrne (in "The Refuge of Scribalism in Iron I

4. In addition, Mettinger points to a supposed close relationship between the Davidic-Solomonic monarchy and Egypt in the 21st Dynasty as the means by which this cultural transfer was made. There is, however, nothing in the story of David that suggests any such connection. Everything depends on the references to Solomon's marriage to an Egyptian princess who is presumed to be the daughter of a pharaoh of the 21st Dynasty. But all the references to the Egyptian princess are late secondary additions to the DtrH and are historically quite worthless. Shishak of the 22nd Dynasty is portrayed as quite hostile. By contrast, it is the period at the end of the monarchy that shows close connections with both Assyria and Egypt, so that if there was any foreign influence on Judah's bureaucracy it was in this period and not sooner.

From these observations one must conclude that a good case has not been made for understanding these lists as official documents reflecting the period of David and Solomon. What is necessary is to reconsider the literary character of these lists within the contexts of the story of David.

The two lists in 2 Sam 8:16–18 and 20:23–26 are often characterized as comprising David's cabinet or inner circle of officials, but none of the stories or episodes present them in this way. For the later kings, no such lists of officials are given. Instead, we learn of the existence of various officials only through their roles in the narratives, and from these we can hardly reconstruct their place in the larger bureaucracy. In no case do they function as a "cabinet" or inner circle of advisors. It is much more likely, it seems to me, that the lists were created by drawing on figures from the larger story context and by imitation of officials found in the historical narrative of later kings. Regarding the first list in 2 Sam 8:16–18, the remark about the priests in v. 17 is curious because Zadok is given a patronymic, Ahitub, which appears with his name nowhere else in Samuel–Kings, but Ahitub belongs to the lineage of Abiathar, and Abiathar's genealogy is inverted.

Palestine," *BASOR* 345 [2007]: 1–31) comments on the references to scribes in the lists of David's officials. He states: "Some have taken this to represent a larger bureaucracy (or worse still, an Egyptian derivative), but the text makes more sense at face value. David retains a scribe when scribes are curiosities. . . . These scribes were less administrators than hagiographers" (p. 23). Byrne accepts without argument that these lists are historical records from the time of David, and he implies that their only function was to write the kind of accounts about David that we have in the books of Samuel. Neither of these assumptions is acceptable, and no evidence on scribal activity in Iron I Palestine that he presents would support them.

Thus, scholars usually reconstruct his name as Abiathar the son of Ahi-
melek the son of Ahitub (see 1 Sam 22:6–23, 23:6, 30:7).[9] Zadok, as one of
David's priests, does not appear on the scene until the Court History, so
that the addition of his name in the list alongside Abiathar may account for
the confused genealogy by scribal copyists. The remark about Benaiah
along with the Cherethites and the Pelethites in v. 18 are also anachronistic. Benaiah is characterized in the list of David's heroes (2 Sam 23:20–23)
as being in charge of David's "bodyguard," which is just another way of referring to him as commander of the foreign mercenaries. This also points
to some connection with CH.[10] Finkelstein has recently argued that the
Cherethites and the Pelethites are to be identified as Greek mercenaries,
and Greek mercenaries were known to have been used by the Egyptians in
the late 7th century B.C.E.[11] However, as we shall see below, these particular groups of Greek mercenaries were only used in Asia from the 4th century onward. Thus, the references to these groups as mercenaries and a
royal bodyguard are anachronistic before the late Persian period. The remark in v. 18b that "David's sons were priests" is also quite enigmatic. It is
of a quite-different form from the rest of the list; no names are given and
the verb היה is used only in this instance. It also contradicts the earlier
statement naming Zadok and Abiathar as priests, unless one is to understand that the royal sons were only of a lesser rank, in which case there is
little reason for their being in the list at all. No other king of Judah seems
to follow this practice of appointing sons as priests. The remark can only
be viewed as highly suspect.

The list is introduced in 2 Sam 8:15 by the statement "And David
reigned over all Israel and David maintained the law and acted justly towards all his people." This statement is clearly intended to sum up David's
career, so that it likely comes toward the end of the story of his life. What
one expects to follow is the account of his final words to Solomon in 1 Kgs
2:1–4 and his death in 2:10–12. Instead, what follows 2 Sam 8:15–18 is

---

9. According to the literary analysis presented below, all these texts in which
Abithar appears belong to the *David Saga*, a post-Dtr addition to the David story.

10. The form of the entry ובניה בן־יהוידע והכרתי והפלתי corresponds exactly to the
references to Benaiah in 1 Kgs 1:38, 44.

11. I. Finkelstein, "The Philistines in the Bible: A Late-Monarchic Perspective,"
JSOT 27 (2002): 148–50. Finkelstein understands all of the references in the David
story as Dtr and 7th century in date. I consider them all post-DtrH and of Persian
date. See below, pp. 105–109, 115–118.

the CH account of David's reign in 2 Sam 9-20, which completely contradicts this general assessment in 8:15 at so many points, and this in turn is ended by a repetition of the list of David's officials in 2 Sam 20:23-26, just before the final scene of David's life in 1 Kgs 1. Thus, what we have in the second list is a case of *Wiederaufnahme*,[12] which suggests that the whole of the CH in 2 Sam 9-20 and 1 Kgs 1-2 (minus 2:1-4, 10-12) is a later addition to the earlier Dtr account of David's life. The second list is therefore an imitation and modification of the first list, both of them by the author of the CH.

The second list begins in 2 Sam 20:23 with the two rival commanders, Joab and Benaiah, who have a prominent role in what follows in 1 Kgs 1-2, with Benaiah murdering Joab at the instigation of Solomon and ultimately replacing Joab as the head of the army (1 Kgs 4:4). In 1 Kgs 1:38 and 44, Benaiah is linked with the mercenaries, the Cherethites and the Pelethites, as he is in this list. In v. 25b, Zadok and Abiathar are mentioned without patronymics and they also play a role in the rivalry for the throne in 1 Kgs 1-2. The *mazkîr* and the scribe are taken over from the earlier list, with a variation in the name of the scribe, but a new figure is introduced in v. 24a, Adoram, the one in charge of the forced labor. This notorious person is familiar from the revolt of the northern tribes against Rehoboam (1 Kgs 12:18) and implies that the practice of forced labor dates back to the time of David. Finally, a "foreigner" is introduced in v. 26, Ira the Jairite (or Jethrite; see 2 Sam 23:38), who is named as David's priest. The point of introducing such a person is not clear. This entry, beginning with וגם, "and in addition," and using the verb היה, does not conform to the style of the list. This suggests that it has a similar function to that of the last entry in the previous list in 2 Sam 8:18, namely, to call into question David's religious practices.

The two lists of the sons of David (2 Sam 3:2-5, 5:13-16) are often regarded as late interpolations within their present narrative contexts, but many still believe them to have been drawn from early archival sources. The first list (2 Sam 3:2-5) includes the names of the sons born in Hebron, given in the precise chronological order of birth, along with the names of the mother of each son, and the list is directly related to the larger narrative. It is a highly artificial construction, very likely composed by the author of

---

12. See H. J. Stoebe, *Das zweite Buch Samuelis* (KAT 8/2; Gütersloh: Gütersloher Verlagshaus, 1994), 448. Stoebe recognizes this important literary structure but then fails to understand the implications of it for the analysis of the lists.

CH.[13] The first two wives, Ahinoam of Jezreel and Abigail of Carmel, are likewise closely linked in the earlier narrative (1 Sam 25:39-43, 27:3, 30:5; 2 Sam 2:2), and the list makes a direct reference back to the episode in 1 Sam 25.[14] Quite remarkable is the fact that David's third wife and the mother of Absalom is the daughter of a king of Geshur. This anticipates later events in CH in which Absalom flees to Talmai, his father-in-law, the king of Geshur. The fourth son is Adonijah, the son of Haggith, who, after Absalom's death, is the next presumed heir to the throne, 1 Kgs 1:5-8, until he is displaced by Solomon in a palace coup. The list is simply too convenient to the plot of CH to be anything but a creation of the author of that work.[15]

By contrast, the second list (2 Sam 5:13-16) ignores any mention of the mothers of David's sons born in Jerusalem and seems to lump together the offspring of both wives and concubines in no particular order. This also applies to Solomon. It is not even clear that the list includes only sons and not daughters as well. The two lists could hardly belong to the same "archival" source; and it is also hard to imagine any useful bureaucratic function for such lists. Yet the second list does seem to refer back to the earlier list, and therefore it was likely an addition made by the same author. It seems to suggest that none of these sons (and daughters) had any claim to the throne.[16] The lists are no older than CH and therefore postexilic in date.

The list of David's heroes (2 Sam 23:8-39) also seems like a very artificial literary construction from various sources with some anecdotes similar to those collected in 2 Sam 21:15-22. The anecdotes deal entirely with the period of conflict with the Philistines and particularly with Gath and are not easy to reconcile with the other narratives about David. They glorify the themes of single combat as in 1 Sam 17 and feats of military prowess as in the Samson stories; they are quite different from the wars against the Philistines in 2 Sam 5:17-25. The lists of 2 Sam 23:8-39 contain a number of problems and hardly constitute an official record.[17] The list of the "thirty"

---

13. Ibid., 119-22. Stoebe, however, interprets CH as a historical document.

14. The connection of these narratives with SN/CH will be dealt with below.

15. W. Dietrich (in *Die frühe Königszeit in Israel,* 212) argues that both lists of David's sons belong to SN. However, he dates SN (= CH) to the 10th century, so that the lists were official documents used by the author of CH at that time.

16. However, Stoebe suggests (in *Das zweite Buch Samuelis.,* 175) that the name of Solomon's mother may have been originally present, based on 1 Chr 3:5, but this seems altogether unlikely. 1 Chronicles 3:9 also adds the name of the one daughter known from CH.

17. Why is there no separate entry for Joab? Abishai gets two entries and Asahel, as brother of Joab, gets one, and even the armor bearer of Joab gets an entry, but not

is not so easy to reconstruct and clearly has some additions at the end, consisting mostly of foreigners. Judging from the place names from which those belonging to the thirty originate, the list assumes David's control of a rather large territory.

David's Wars

The major problem with the historical sources of the Davidic period, however, lies not with these lists but with the larger narrative units. Those often viewed as of primary importance are the accounts of military activity in 2 Sam 5:17-25 and 8:1 against the Philistines, which were primarily defensive, and the campaigns of conquest against the neighboring countries in 2 Sam 8:2-14. Na'aman has examined the campaigns against the Arameans, the Moabites, and the Edomites rather carefully and observes that the details resemble closely corresponding military activity by Arameans and Israelites of the Northern Kingdom in the 9th and early 8th centuries. From this, he concludes that this is a case of "borrowing military outlines of an actual event to depict an episode of the early history of Israel."[18] (These will be considered in greater detail below.)

Concerning the Philistine wars, Na'aman is more confident that these reflect historical reminiscences from the time of David. The primary argument for this is the prominence of Gath in the David stories as the leading Philistine city, which, as Na'aman argues, had lost its military power and political status by the late 9th century.[19] Thus, according to Na'aman, the most that we can say is that the stories of struggles against Gath were put together by the late 9th century when the memory of its prominence was still strong. There is, however, some reason for caution on this point. First, there are lots of examples in which the names of places that were once prominent in the past retain some memory of this fact long after their importance has diminished. Thus, one cannot, for example, date the poems of Homer based on their geography.[20] Second, once a name is associated with a particular tradition, such as David's struggles against the Philistines of Gath, then this

---

Joab himself. Some entries seem dependent on the larger narratives; others contradict them. In fiction, anything is possible. Cf. ibid., 461-68, 495-512.

18. Na'aman, "Sources and Composition," 179; see also idem, "In Search of Reality behind the Account of David's Wars with Israel's Neighbours," *IEJ* 52 (2002): 200-24.

19. Ibid., 210.

20. M. I. Finley, *The World of Odysseus* (New York: New York Review of Books, 2002), 39-41.

name could be picked up and used by any later author as well, and some references, as we shall see, are very late. Third, the name of Gath's ruler, King Achish, seems to reflect the name of the ruler of Ekron in the 7th century.[21] Consequently, references to Achish of Gath in the so-called HDR could not belong to an early collection on David, and Gath is not mentioned in the wars of 2 Sam 5.[22]

These accounts of military activity in 2 Sam 5 and 8 Naʾaman attributes to a "chronicle of early Israelite kings," the author of which lived in the 8th century, and this document was later used by the Dtr historian.[23] The idea of a "chronicle of early Israelite kings" is an interesting one because it invites comparison with a similar group of Babylonian chronicles that also deal with the distant past history of Mesopotamia down to the 8th century. One of these is the "Chronicle of the Early Kings," which covered a millennium of time from Sargon the Great to Agum III, ca. 1450 B.C.E.; a second is the so-called Chronicle P, which takes up where the previous chronicle left off and covers the Kassite period; a third, the so-called Eclectic Chronicle, continues this history from where Chronicle P leaves off down to the rise of the Neo-Babylonian dynasty in the 8th century, at which point the Babylonian Chronicles series takes over.[24] I argued some years ago that these three "early" chronicles were actually part of the same literary composition that was put together in the Neo-Babylonian period in order to fill the gap between the earliest period of Mesopotamian history and the rise of the Neo-Babylonian dynasty.[25] The sources of these chronicles of early

---

21. See I. Finkelstein, "The Philistines in the Bible," 133–36.

22. The possible exception is 2 Sam 8:1.

23. This "chronicle" is not to be confused with the so-called PH as a precursor to DtrH, to which Naʾaman does not subscribe.

24. A. K. Grayson, *Assyrian and Babylonian Chronicles* (Locust Valley, NY: Augustin, 1975; repr. Winona Lake, IN: Eisenbrauns, 2000), 45–49, 56–59, 63–65 (= Chronicles 20, 22, 24). There is a fourth text, numbered Chronicle 25, published by C. B. F. Walker, "Babylonian Chronicle 25: A Chronicle of the Kassite and Isin II Dynasties," in *Zikin Šumim: Assyriological Studies Presented to F. R. Kraus on the Occasion of His Seventieth Birthday* (ed. G. van Driel et al.; Leiden: Brill, 1982), 397–417. This text seems to belong to the same set of chronicles dealing with early times and fills a gap between Chronicle P and the Eclectic Chronicle.

25. *In Search of History*, 84–88. One may note the obsession of the Neo-Babylonian period, especially Nabonidus, with historical connections between early Mesopotamian history and the Neo-Babylonian period. See P.-A. Beaulieu, *The Reign of Nabonidus King of Babylon 556–539 B.C.* (New Haven, CT: Yale University Press, 1989), 138–43.

times consisted primarily of standard literary works of the library collections, such as omen texts, historiographic works, epic texts, and other comparable sources. When one compares these sources, one finds that the historian(s) of the chronicles had no qualms about making changes to suit his Babylonian bias. This was not a case of "archival research" as we would understand it but a matter of "plagiarizing" earlier works in the scribal library for the greater glory of Babylon.

If we now apply this analogy to the "early chronicles of Israelite kings" as suggested by Na'aman, then we should think in terms not of archival sources or contemporary annals but rather of collections of legends about David's Philistine wars along with some written copies of 9th–8th-century memorial-style inscriptions from the Northern Kingdom of Israel that served as scribal models,[26] all of which were used by the later historian for his literary composition. As Na'aman suggests, some parts look like almost verbatim quotations, whereas others were extensively modified. This was clearly the case with the Babylonian "Chronicles of Early Kings" and was likely the case here as well. However, I remain rather skeptical of an 8th-century date for an "early chronicles of Israelite kings," with all of these components included, as Na'aman suggests.

David the Mercenary and the Use of Mercenaries in Greece and the Near East

When we come to consider *internal* evidence concerning social institutions that may be dated in a fairly clear and unequivocal way, we will find it in the practices of the military and, in particular, in the use of mercenaries. Throughout the story of David there are abundant references to mercenaries. This applies to the role of David as the leader of a mercenary band, as well as to David's use of foreign mercenaries as regular part of his military force after he became king. In addition, there are references to other nations using mercenaries against David in his wars with foreign enemies. All of this is quite significant because, as we shall see in the discussion that follows, it is extremely unlikely that there was any widespread use of mercenaries in the early first millennium B.C.E. There are very few references to mercenaries in the later monarchy, and there is no clear evidence that any other kings of Judah and Israel made use of them. The few references to

---

26. On memorial style inscriptions, see my *In Search of History,* 191–95.

mercenaries that one does find in the rest of Kings are quite suspect as anachronisms. It appears to be the case, therefore, that references to mercenaries within the story of David reflect the time of the author of these narrative accounts and not some ancient tradition. Thus, if we can gain some clear idea about the rise of the phenomenon of mercenary use in the Near East in the first millennium,[27] then we may be able to use this understanding of the role of mercenaries to date the narratives in question and to perhaps distinguish the parts that refer to mercenaries from those that do not. What I hope to show is that the abundant references made to mercenaries give us one of the best controls over the date and extent of the source in which they are found.

The Assyrian Period

There is an extensive body of literature on the military use of mercenaries from antiquity to modern times with a fairly clear picture of when and how this phenomenon arose, the social conditions that produce mercenary soldiers without a state, and the need for states to employ professional soldiers of this sort within their military institutions.[28] The conditions that resulted in a widespread use of mercenaries in the Near East in the first millennium may be said to have arisen with the Neo-Assyrian Empire. Some scholars do begin with the time of David, but that is because they accept the texts of 1 and 2 Samuel as historical and contemporary with David.[29] This is problematic for the many reasons presented in this study. So we will begin with the Assyrians.

---

27. I am not concerned about the use of mercenaries in the second millennium because there is no evidence of a continuity of their use in Syria-Palestine from the second to the first millennium. Thus, the Ḫabiru bands of the second-millennium Levant are no longer mentioned in first-millennium sources.

28. No exhaustive bibliography will be attempted here, but the following major studies will be cited: H. W. Parke, *Greek Mercenary Soldiers: From the Earliest Times to the Battle of Ipsus* (Oxford: Clarendon, 1933). G. T. Griffith, *The Mercenaries of the Hellenistic World* (Cambridge: Cambridge University Press, 1935); F. E. Adcock, *The Greek and Macedonian Art of War* (Berkeley: University of California Press, 1957), 19–25; Yvon Garlan, *War in the Ancient World: A Social History* (New York: Norton, 1975), 93–103; Serge Yalichev, *Mercenaries of the Ancient World* (London: Constable, 1997); R. Waterfield, *Xenophon's Retreat: Greece, Persia and the End of the Golden Age* (Cambridge: Harvard University Press, 2006). In the early modern period, one finds extensive use of mercenaries during the Thirty Years War; see C. V. Wedgewood, *The Thirty Years War* (New York: New York Review of Books, 2005).

29. Yalichev, *Mercenaries*, 62–69.

Prior to the time of Tiglath-pileser III, the Assyrian army was made up of militias of part-time soldiers recruited from the local population of the various provinces and regions.[30] With Tiglath-pileser, this changed into the professionalization of the army with a large, central, highly trained force as the backbone of the military. This permanent army was committed in absolute loyalty to the king and greatly increased his control of the realm. Plunder from military activity was the primary means of maintaining this system, which encouraged the continuous growth of the empire. The need for increasing manpower to sustain this force was met by the deportation of large elements of the population, among whom were trained soldiers who could then be used in other parts of the empire for military and garrison use. These foreign forces were not mercenaries in the usual sense of employment of bands of military adventurers under contract with their own leaders but prisoners of war who were coerced into service to the victorious regime. Thus, the Assyrians could add to their own citizen army the best of the troops that they conquered, such as in the cavalry corps, the members of which became mercenaries not by choice so much as by necessity.[31] Only in special circumstances did the Assyrians hire foreign troops as auxiliaries, such as the Sythians, known as expert horsemen. In order to pay for the large professional army of native soldiers and foreign mercenaries, the Assyrians began the habit of campaigning on an annual basis. Toward the end of the Assyrian Empire, the economic chaos that resulted from the constant invasion of armies created increasing numbers of desperate bands of men who were willing to submit to Assyria as mercenaries in return for a regular meal or who engaged in marauding and brigandage.

The Saite Period

The decline of the Assyrian Empire in the mid-7th century permitted the recovery of Egyptian autonomy and the rise of the 26th Dynasty of Saite rulers, beginning with Psammetichus I (664–610 B.C.E.), who was able to unite much of Egypt once again under his control. He then entered into an alliance with Gyges of Lydia (655 B.C.E.), who sent him mercenaries from Ionia and Caria that were under his control, and thus, the Greek mercenary first arose not as an aspect of warfare in Greece itself, but in foreign

---

30. Ibid., 70–79.

31. See S. Dalley, "Foreign Chariotry and Cavalry in the Armies of Tiglath-Pileser III and Sargon II," *Iraq* 47 (1985): 31–48. Foreign troops of this sort included Israelites from Samaria.

service.[32] It was acknowledged that the Greek infantry was superior both in terms of its use of heavy armor and its deployment of these troops in battle, so that Egypt under the Saites was among the first to employ these hoplite soldiers from Ionia and Caria as mercenaries.[33] These Greek mercenaries were stationed in fortifications in the eastern Delta, most notably at Daphnae on the Pelusiac branch of the Nile, and later Greek settlers and traders established a permanent colony at Naukratis in the Delta. Herodotus (book 2, chap. 163) claims that Apries had 30,000 Ionians and Carians under his employ. They also served as the Pharaoh's personal bodyguard in the Saite period. The Greek mercenaries played a major role in the final struggle of Egypt against Cambyses and the Persians, but with the Persian victory the employment of Greek mercenaries in Egypt came to an end (ca. 525). It was only much later, after the Greek-Persian War, that Greek mercenaries began to be used by Persian satraps and rulers.

The unity of Egypt under a single administrative control and the encouragement of foreign trade with Greek states and the Phoenician coast brought great prosperity to the Saite rulers, who were then able to hire mercenaries from many different regions, not only from Ionia and Caria but also from the Levant and Syria. In addition to the military camps of Greek mercenaries in the eastern Delta, Greek and other foreign garrisons were also set up on the Egyptian frontier.[34] The Saite rulers likewise attempted to extend their rule over the Levant as far as Phoenicia and establish a provincial control of the region using garrisons, with the local rulers as vassals. Military control of this region was largely in the hands of mercenaries. As Redford explains,

> In the event Saite Egypt became a highly desirable employer for Asiatics as well as Greeks. Syrians came to Egypt and are found in communities at Migdol, Athribis, Memphis, Thebes, and Aswan, and at special encampments in the Delta. . . . It is clear, then, that the prime function of all these enclaves was paramilitary, although nothing prevented any of them from engaging in commerce. They were organized into 'garrisons' and paid salaries from the royal treasury.[35]

---

32. See Redford, *Egypt, Canaan, and Israel*, 433, 441.
33. Parke, *Greek Mercenary Soldiers*, 4–6.
34. Note the presence of the Jewish mercenary colony of Elephantine.
35. Redford, *Egypt, Canaan, and Israel*, 443.

Redford further argues for the extension of this same military policy into Asia. He states:

> In the context of Psammetichos's reassertion of control over the Levantine coast, the mercenary troops he had acquired were also used to garrison the strongpoints. One such post has come to light through excavation at Mesad Hashavyahu on the coast not far from Ashdod. Here Greek pottery of the period 625–600 B.C. attests the presence of Hellenic occupants. . . . Southeast, similar pottery has come to light at Tel Melah in the Negeb.[36]

Redford also interprets a reference to *Kittiyim* ("Greeks") in the texts from Arad belonging to this same period as Greek garrison troops from Egypt, rather than Greek mercenaries employed directly from their Aegean source by the Judean king. With the rise of Babylon the control of the Levant was contested between Egypt and Babylon, a dispute in the middle of which Judah was caught, to its great detriment. Babylon was not able to conquer Egypt or to entirely subdue the Phoenician cities of the coast. The mercenaries, as the backbone of the Saite military strength, allowed these kings to survive until the conquest of Egypt by Cambyses in 525. However, it must be emphasized that acquisition of a mercenary force and their retention of a standing army in the 7th and 6th centuries, as reflected in Assyria and Egypt, is a very expensive proposition. It is highly unlikely that the kings of Israel and Judah made any extensive use of mercenaries throughout the period of their monarchies. This assertion may appear to be contradicted by the mention of Carians as part of the palace guard in 2 Kgs 11:4, 19.[37] The reference, however, is clearly anachronistic for the 9th century and must represent the invention of this episode in the 6th century, when Carian mercenaries were being used as part of the bodyguard of the Saite pharaohs. This biblical episode cannot be used to prove that the Judean kings actually did make use of Greek mercenaries; it only demonstrates that this practice was known at the time of writing.

The Rise of Mercenaries in the Greek World

The mercenary has been characterized by Garlan in the following way: "The mercenary is a professional soldier whose behaviour is determined

---

36. Ibid., 444.
37. See Finkelstein, "The Philistines in the Bible," *JSOT* 27 (2002): 149.

not by his membership in a political community but by the lure of profit. The combination of three characteristics—being a specialist, an expatriate and a wage earner—was peculiar to this type of man in the ancient world as in the modern."[38] There were always professional soldiers with specialties requiring training, drawn from certain areas, such as archers from Crete. In the archaic period before the wars with Persia, the number of mercenaries in Greece was quite small, serving primarily as personal bodyguards for tyrants. It was only in the rather special circumstances of the Saite deployment of Ionian mercenaries that significant numbers of Greek mercenaries were used in the Mediterranean region. The development of a reliance on Greek mercenaries, especially the Greek hoplites with heavy armament (as portrayed in Goliath's weapons), was particularly important in the evolution of warfare in the Mediterranean region. The diffusion of mercenaries and Greek colonization in the eastern Mediterranean went hand in hand during this period until ca. 525, when there was a hiatus in Greek mercenary activity in Asia for about a century.

As Garlan points out, a major factor in the use of mercenaries by any city or larger political entity is the ability to pay the wages of the soldiers.[39] In the older period of Greek history, wars between city states were basically conducted by citizen armies, and states, such as Sparta, whose whole way of life depended on the development of its citizens in the art of warfare, obviously had an upper hand. Sparta continued to be famous for its excellence in warfare. In the great wars against Persia, it was primarily a coalition of citizen armies of individual states against a superior power. These were primarily wars of defense in which service was limited to the length of the campaign and the citizens themselves bore much of the expense of equipment and supplies. It was only certain rich states, such as Egypt under the Saites, who could hire Greek armies with special expertise in battle tactics and superior military equipment, and in these cases mercenaries became a major factor in the conduct of war.

Payment for service was a constant source of difficulty between mercenary and employer, whether king or tyrant, and delays in payment could lead to revolt with serious consequences for the state involved. The need for guarantees of remuneration led to the practice of formal contractual agreements similar to treaties between foreign powers. Thus, the arrangements of remuneration for service were laid out and guaranteed by a sol-

---

38. Garlan, *War in the Ancient World*, 93.
39. Ibid., 95-98.

emn oath sworn by both parties.[40] Another way of trying to ensure loyalty
was by means of land grants. This kind of military colonization is already
known to have existed in the Saite period of Egypt and continued into later
periods as well. It could have involved the founding of new settlements and
the integration of these foreigners into the realm. It gave these landless adventurers property and a stake in the realm, which they did not have when
they took up their military careers in the first place. Of course, the mercenaries also shared in the booty that resulted from specific military campaigns, as well as direct payment for service that was stipulated in the
agreement.

The social causes of the mercenary system resulted from the impoverish-
ment of many small landowners who sought relief through colonization
and military adventure. The rise of the rule of tyrants also created a need
for private bodyguards, loyal only to the tyrant, who could assist the tyrant
in the control of the populous that he ruled. These conditions were particularly in evidence in both the archaic period and from the late 5th century
onward. It was, however, not only or primarily the demand of tyrants and
foreign rulers but the supply of many who had experienced war and who,
when the war came to an end, had no other means of livelihood. Citizen
armies, consisting of farmers, land owners, and artisans, could not tolerate
long campaigns without suffering financial ruin. Prolonged warfare thus
created a great flood of mercenaries from various parts of the Greek world,
especially after the 30-year-long Peloponnesian War (431–404). This conflict created the long "habit and discipline of war"[41] as well as the need for
a continuous supply of soldiers. And the more the war was prolonged, the
more the land was impoverished, which left little else but to earn a livelihood as a soldier in further conflict. This in turn gave rise to a heavy dependence on mercenaries in the conduct of war from the late 5th century
onward, both in Greece itself and also in the use of Greeks and non-Greeks
in Asia.

The Persian Period

After the Peace of Callias (449 B.C.E.), which ended the hostilities between
the Persians and Greeks, and following the Peloponnesian War, Greek mercenaries again became employed in great numbers in Asia. The most notable example, among many, of the employment of Greek soldiers in foreign

---

40. See ibid., 96–98, for examples.
41. Griffith, *The Mercenaries of the Hellenistic World*, 4.

service is the more than 10,000 Greek mercenaries that were used by Cyrus the Younger (401–400) in his failed attempt to gain the throne of Persia, as well as the Greek forces that were also employed by the Persian king, as recorded in great detail in Xenophon's *Anabasis*. The later Persian kings as well as the satraps of the western satrapies made abundant use of Greek mercenaries down to the time of Alexander. Alexander the Great made extensive use of mercenaries, not only in his war against the Persians but also in the establishment of military colonies through the Asian lands that he conquered, and this practice was continued by the Ptolemies and Seleucids. The distinction between these two periods, the first in the 7th and 6th centuries and the second from the late 5th century onward, is important and can be seen most clearly in the increasing specialization in military personnel between the heavily armed hoplites, who formed the main body of the assault troops, and the light-armed auxiliaries, the archers, slingers and spear-throwers. In addition to these foot-soldiers was the cavalry. Among the light-armed troops, most effective in skirmishes and swift attacks, were the Cretan archers and the *peltastai* of Thrace, known by their use of the small shield (πελτη).[42] As Griffith points out, the end of the 5th century gave rise to a different kind of warfare, that of prolonged skirmishes in a warfare of attrition, for which the light infantry of the mercenaries were best suited, rather than the citizen hoplites used in a single decisive battle. Thus, it was precisely the light-armed peltast who most represented this form of mercenary and who played an increasingly important role in the 4th century. So ubiquitous is the mention of the peltasts in the references to mercenaries in the second period and so completely lacking is it in the accounts of the earlier period that it becomes an easy marker of texts that use this reference to Greek mercenaries.

Regarding the peltasts, Adcock notes that these rather barbarian Thracians were especially known for their skill at spear throwing and their brutality and he refers to Thucydides, who gives a vivid picture of the raiding and massacre of small communities by bands of mercenaries such as these (book 7, chap. 29): "The Thracians burst into Mycalessus, sacked the houses and temples, and butchered the inhabitants, sparing neither the young nor the old, but methodically killing everyone they met, women and children alike, and even the farm animals and every living thing they saw."[43] These

---

42. See Finkelstein, "The Philistines in the Bible," 148–50.
43. Thucydides, *The Peloponnesian War* (trans. R. Warner; Harmondsworth: Penguin, 1972), 495. See Adcock, *The Greek and Macedonian Art of War*, 21.

groups tended to fight in small battle formations under their own professional leaders.

Furthermore, Adcock makes the point that mercenary light-armed troops could be used more easily than regulars in a variety of terrain and conditions, and they could also garrison strongholds and fortified positions away from the city centers, which were the homes of the citizen armies, because they were basically homeless. Citizen troops fought during a particular campaign season and then returned to their homes and regular occupations. Mercenaries had no local patriotism and therefore no political attachments; thus, they were most useful in the service of tyrants and foreign kings. Their loyalty was entirely to those who paid them. It is also the case that the generals of mercenary forces, with their widespread foreign experience in many different situations and their continuous engagement in military activity, became superior to the traditional generals of national armies and their conservative tactics of warfare. This even happened in actions against the vaunted Spartan hoplites.[44]

In his book *Xenophon's Retreat*, Robin Waterfield gives us a vivid and detailed view of the role of Greek mercenaries with the Persian armies at the end of the 5th century B.C.E. Regarding the insurrection by Cyrus the Younger, he states:

> In all, Cyrus hired some 10,600 Greek hoplites, and about 2,300 peltasts. They came in several units, depending on their ethnic loyalties and on their recruiting officers, and each soldier's first allegiance was to the fellow members of his own unit and to his commander, who secured his men's fickle loyalty by being the channel through which pay from Cyrus would reach them. Until they were forced by the defeat at Cunaxa to unite against a common enemy, relations with other Greek units tended to be tense and divisive (and the Greeks as a whole also kept themselves aloof from the Persians and other non-Greek troops—but then, members of elite regiments have always acted with haughty disdain towards other units).[45]

Included among the peltasts was a small contingent of 200 Cretan archers. The latter became increasingly important as mercenaries in the Near East, so that by the Hellenistic period, as Griffith states, "By far the most prominent Greek soldiers throughout the Hellenistic period were the Cretans."[46]

---

44. Ibid., 22–25.
45. Waterfield, *Xenophon's Retreat: Greece, Persia, and the End of the Golden Age* (Cambridge: Harvard University Press, 2006), 79.
46. Griffith, *The Mercenaries of the Hellenistic World*, 245.

As Waterfield indicates, both the Greek officers and their rank and file were "an unsavoury bunch," "hardened fighters" who were looking for a big payday from Cyrus, if they won, and the chance of "marauding their way back again afterwards." The reason why the Persian leaders employed these "thugs" is that they were simply the best warriors and in great demand as such. Even after Cyrus was defeated, the battle "advertised to the Persians the value of Greek mercenaries, and both satraps and kings used them in increasing numbers in the fourth century." And conditions in the Greek homeland were such that the supply from all the different regions of the country was equal to the demand, both in hoplites and in the light-armed peltasts. One of the dangerous social side-effects of this form of employment was that when they returned home to Greece they would either continue their pillaging there or create military tyrannies and provoke unwanted wars for further employment.[47] Waterfield refers to Isocrates' description of mercenaries as "vagabonds, deserters and criminals, given to praying on others. Unattached mercenaries, exiles from their native cities, formed bands, lived in caves in the mountains of Greece or Asia Minor, and survived by scavenging and brigandage."[48]

Waterfield goes on to point out that "since mercenaries worked for pay, it was a common belief, with a solid factual foundation, that they would desert for better pay, or if they calculated that the odds against them were too great."[49] They lacked the sense of loyalty of the citizen soldiers who had a stake in defending their own community and property. However, increasingly these landowning citizens were inclined to hire mercenaries and "fight by proxy." Thus, the older traditional system of states relying on alliances and allies to supplement their own resources gave way to hiring mercenaries instead. "The fourth century saw amateur soldiering give way almost entirely to the professionalism of mercenaries, whenever there was an important battle or war to be fought."[50] From this extended discussion of the mercenary soldier and his role in the Persian period, a clear picture emerges on the rise of this phenomenon in the Near East and the degree to which it reaches a peak in the Persian period, and this allows us to set the frequent references to mercenaries in the David story against this social background.

47. Waterfield, *Xenophon's Retreat*, 79–81.
48. Ibid., 81.
49. Ibid.
50. Ibid. It is quite remarkable how similar this situation is to the character and behavior of the mercenaries and their use by European states in the Thirty Years War. See Wedgewood, *The Thirty Years War*.

There is one more feature that is characteristic of ancient warfare in general and mercenaries in particular, the phenomenon of the baggage train that accompanied an army on campaign. Waterfield gives a vivid picture of the baggage train that followed Cyrus's army from Asia Minor to the battlefield of Cunaxa in the region of modern Baghdad.[51] He estimates that there were about as many noncombatants as there were soldiers, as well as a large number of animals, both for food and for transport of supplies, in addition to the cavalry horses and the fodder to maintain them. Provisions, equipment, weapons, and booty were carried on carts and by slaves; and the amount of goods and personnel that accompanied an army on the move was immense. The farther the expedition and the more prolonged the campaign, the greater the entourage. There were a large number and variety of artisans for cooking food and making and repairing equipment, clothing, and weapons; there were personal slaves for officers, wives and concubines for personal sexual needs and women for shared sexual use. During the campaign there was also the accumulation of booty and prisoners, the latter to be sold as slaves. A moving city such as this also attracted merchants to sell food and other commodities and to purchase prisoners of war for the slave trade.

What makes this understanding of the baggage train particularly relevant for the discussion of mercenaries is that there is an obvious difference between a short war entailing a single battle by citizen soldiers within a small region and in defense of a city, on the one hand, and the prolonged adventurous campaigning by mercenaries with no fixed abode, on the other. In the former case, the baggage train was of much more limited scope and duration, whereas with mercenaries, the military entourage was a way of life. Even in the case of large professional armies, such as the Assyrians and the Persians, there was a tendency to ensure the success of campaigns with provincial and outlying supply centers along the main military roads. But mercenary armies fighting in hostile terrain were much more dependent on the baggage train and on local marauding for all their needs.

Mercenaries in the Story of David

David and His Band of Mercenaries

There are many direct references to mercenaries and the activities in which these persons engage in the story of David and, once this fact be-

---

51. Waterfield, *Xenophon's Retreat*, 103-9.

comes clear then many additional details in the story become explicable as part of this phenomenon in the light of this social context. These references, with one exception, all belong to the same late source, and this will be our primary concern. First, however, we will deal with a reference in the earlier source in 1 Sam 22:2, which gives us a description of David forming a band of men over whom he becomes leader.[52] It states, "Everyone who was in difficult circumstances, everyone who was in debt, and every malcontent, gathered to [David]; and he became their commander. About four hundred men followed him." This describes very well the social situation that arose in the late monarchy from Sargon and Sennacherib down to the time of Nebuchadnezer, as we have seen above; thus, the description of David's group reflects a common social feature of this period. These persons live in caves and other wild regions of the country, living a very hand-to-mouth existence and often preying on small communities. David and his men, however, are presented in a positive light as saviors of the small town of Keilah, which was under attach by marauding Philistines (1 Sam 23:1–5). Thus, the author suggests that during this period when David is in hiding in Judah from Saul, he is engaged in just this kind of activity, that he and his men are not actually employed as mercenaries but live on booty taken from the Philistines, acting on behalf of the people of Judah. After David becomes king and engages in military activity against the Philistines, the Moabites, the Arameans, and the Edomites (2 Sam 5:17–25, 8:1–14, 10:15–19), there is no further suggestion of mercenaries used either by David or by his opponents. All the armies involved are national armies of citizen soldiers, and when some of these states find it necessary, they enter into political alliances with other kings or use troops from vassal states, as in 2 Sam 10:15–19. These accounts all belong to a time when the use of mercenaries was not yet a pervasive military fact of life.

References to mercenaries in the later version of the David and Saul story are quite numerous, so we will begin with the most obvious, David's employment in the service of Achish, king of Gath, as a leader of 600 mercenary soldiers (2 Sam 27:1–28:2, 29:1–30:31). David arrives in Gath with all of his men and their entire entourage, because as mercenaries they are stateless (27:2–3), and he reaches an understanding with Achish that, in exchange for his service, he will accept the border town of Ziklag in which to settle his company of soldiers and camp followers, in order not to be a burden on the capital city. Ziklag will thus become his personal domain. In this

---

52. In chap. 6 below I will attribute this text to Dtr.

capacity, he serves as Achish's "servant" or vassal. From this base of Ziklag, David carries out raids against the local inhabitants of the region, in a fashion all too typical of mercenaries as we have seen above, in which he engages in totally ruthless massacres of the communities he attacks in order that none can report to his employer exactly what he has done (27:8-12). All of the livestock and goods of the destroyed communities become the booty of the mercenaries and thus their wages. When David returns to Achish to report on his activity, he pretends that he has been engaged in military activity against the Judeans of the region, the enemy and rivals of the Philistines and the purpose for which he is hired, thus completely deceiving his employer, who commends him for his efforts against Judah. And who is to report otherwise, for those attacked are all dead? Achish does not question David's reports, because mercenaries are notorious for caring little about loyalties toward their own people. Greek mercenaries killed other Greeks just as easily as they killed foreigners.

Many commentators on this text find ways to commend David for his activity because he fought against Israel's traditional enemies, the aboriginal peoples of the region, and then deceived the Philistines, all of whom were fair game.[53] This suggests that our narrator had much less human sensitivity than Thucydides (quoted above, pp. 106) to the atrocities regularly committed by mercenary bands, which did them purely out of greed and concern for booty. I think this is not the case. The author repeats the remark about the wanton massacres and says that it was David's custom for the whole period that he was under the Philistines (27:11). The deceit about David's attacking the southern regions of Judah conceals his future ambition to become king of Judah and leads Achish to trust him and believe that he would always be his mercenary vassal. Given the widespread contempt for the brutality and complete unreliability of mercenaries and their leaders in antiquity, there can be little doubt that the narrator presents David in this same negative light. Furthermore, when Achish invites David to participate in the Philistine war against Israel, David immediately agrees, and this leads Achish to promise that such participation will be rewarded by elevating David to the status of the king's personal bodyguard (28:1-2). Mercenaries were often used by kings and tyrants as the palace guard (similar to the Swiss-guard in modern times) and personal bodyguard. Achish reasons that if David is already alienated from Judah and be-

---

53. See McCarter, *I Samuel*, 416. His remarks are typical. See also D. V. Edelman, *King Saul in the Historiography of Judah*, 232-37.

comes further alienated from Israel in the forthcoming battle against Saul, David will have little choice but to serve under his employ.

When Achish brings David and his mercenaries to the joint Philistine muster (29:1–11), matters are quite different. The various commanders of the other contingents are suspicious of the mercenary leader and his group of Hebrews, and rightly so, as the narrator has made clear. The commanders of citizen soldiers are always suspicious of mercenary leaders, and quarrels were common in joint campaigns of this sort, as is vividly described in Waterfield's treatment of the expedition of Cyrus.[54] The other commanders are fearful of the possibility that David, with his mercenary band, might desert to his former employer in the heat of battle, a possibility that is all too common with mercenaries who have no loyalties to the state for which they are fighting. The "tyrants" of the Philistines have their way, and Achish must report the bad news to David that he is not to fight in this battle but must return to his post in Ziklag. The whole discussion between Achish and David is full of irony. Thus, David protests his innocence, although the reader knows just how guilty and unfaithful he is—an all-too-typical mercenary who is only out for himself. Achish even begins his remarks to David by reciting an oath in the name of Yahweh, which seems to reflect a similar oath of his loyalty made by David to Achish. Why else would Achish invoke the name of David's god? Oaths of personal loyalty, sworn by mercenaries, were very important in lieu of any other guarantee.[55]

It must also be understood that David and his men are recognized throughout this episode as highly skilled professionals with a lot of battle experience, having been engaged in fighting constantly for a year and four months. They are not just a rag tag group of malcontents. Achish considers them a great asset, while the other leaders regard them as very dangerous. The usual practice is that they not be used in combination with the other soldiers but fight as an independent group, under David's sole command. In circumstances of this sort, there should not be any doubts about their commitment to the Philistine cause, and the other leaders were not willing to take that risk.

David returns to Ziklag only to discover that a disaster has taken place in his absence. The Amalekites, who have suffered frequent massacres at

---

54. See Waterfield, *Xenophon's Retreat*, 91–102.

55. For examples of oaths of this sort between rulers and mercenaries, see Garlan, *War in the Ancient World*, 96–98. The oaths by both parties invoke the same gods.

the hands of David's men, now retaliate with a raid of their own on Ziklag while David and his men are far to the north in Aphek, having left the home base unguarded, a very grave mistake (30:1–6). Yet what is quite remarkable is that the raiders, who completely sacked the city, took the entire population captive, but "they killed no one" (v. 2). This is stated in such explicit and marked contrast to David's own behavior, that for the narrator it must be significant. It simply points up the bloodthirsty character of David and his men toward these same Amalekites. The blame for the grievous oversight in not protecting those left in Ziklag is placed on David to the point of mutiny (v. 6), which is only averted by David's appeal to an oracle that calls for immediate action and full pursuit (vv. 7–10). Without corpses in the ruins of Ziklag, it was apparent that the wives and children had been taken captive, no doubt to be sold as slaves, which was a common result of raids such as this. The oracle merely stated the obvious and took David "off the hook."

A number of details in this episode are noteworthy. First, there is the remark about how 200 of the 600 soldiers were too exhausted to continue the pursuit (vv. 9–10) and stayed behind at the Besor River, while the rest continued the pursuit. Yet, on David's return from the raid this group is somehow converted into a guard for the baggage-train, which as we know from the earlier discussion is a regular feature of campaigns of this sort (vv. 21–25). It was, of course, a military necessity to always supply a guard for the baggage and all the more necessary for mercenary armies that traveled as vagabonds most of the time (see also 25:13). The division of the spoil with those who guard the baggage made sense. The saying attributed to David and thus recognized as a statute "to this day" is a quite-fictional etiology that simply recognizes a universal practice for this kind of warfare.

In pursuit of the Amalekites, David and his men come across an Egyptian who was a personal slave to one of the leaders of the Amalekite raiding party and was abandoned when he became ill, a not-unusual practice of an army on the march. Sick slaves and animals that could not carry their load were expendable. But a person such as this was invaluable to David in terms of providing intelligence about the activities and whereabouts of the raiding party. One place that is mentioned as having been raided by Amalekites is a community of Cherethites in the Negev (v. 14). This use of Cherethites (Cretans) is often compared with the references to Cherethites in Ezek 25:16 and Zeph 2:5. In these prophetic texts, *Cherethites* is used as a synonym for *Philistines*, perhaps in a derogatory sense, reflecting an older tradition about Philistine origins in Crete (Amos 9:7). However, this does not seem to be the case in 2 Sam 30:14. These are not Philistines but Cretans who elsewhere in this source are Greek mercenaries. The remark, therefore, may have in mind colonies or outposts of Greeks that had been set up by the Saite rulers to control the coastal region between Palestine and Egypt. However, there is no indication that the Saites ever used Cretans for this purpose, so that a Cretan colony in the region is probably a fiction of the narrator.

With the information given by the slave, David is able to find the raiding party and make a surprise attack, which results in a complete recovery of all the persons and goods and much additional booty (30:11–20). As with his former practice, he executed all the enemy combatants except those who escaped on camels. This great booty is then brought back to Ziklag, and much of it is distributed as gifts to the friends and elders of Judah in the cities of the region for obvious political purposes. It is usual in the case of booty acquired by military means, even by mercenaries on raids, to dedicate a tenth of it to the deity in recognition of divine assistance. Although David also recognizes divine assistance and describes the booty as "that which Yahweh has given us" (30:23) and "the spoil of the enemies of Yahweh" (30:26), no dedication of a portion of the booty to Yahweh is mentioned. It is clear that, throughout chaps. 27, 29–30, David is being portrayed as a typical but also very astute mercenary leader. As such, he is ruthless and deceptive, seeking his own interests and those of his men. He displays no concern for a higher cause or principle and uses religious legitimization for his actions only when it suits his purpose.

The narrator of David's employment by Achish in 2 Sam 27, 29–30 has not introduced this band of mercenaries de novo for these episodes alone but has already anticipated their existence in the previous episodes that he narrates. David's 400 men in the early version have become 600 men of a well-organized and well-equipped fighting force (23:13, 25:13) within the later narrative. The episode in 2 Sam 25 is very revealing. David and his men demand from one of the rich landowners of the region in southern Judah "protection pay" for not raiding his flocks. Nabal dismisses David as someone of no consequence and his motley freebooters as runaway slaves. David's response is to have his men prepare for a massacre. It is of interest to see that David's forces are divided into two groups, 400 who will engage in the actual raid and 200 who will guard the baggage train (v. 13). This is exactly the same arrangement that we saw above with respect to David's raid on the Amalekites and suggests that David is already the leader of a well-organized and experienced band of mercenaries. There is basically no difference in David's behavior before and after he becomes employed by Achish.

The disaster is averted by a young servant's recognition of the great danger and his warning to Abigail, Nabal's wife, who immediately intervenes with a lavish present of food to buy David off. She seduces David with a lot of pious words that appeal to David's ambition as a future king of the region, in which he will have cause to regret such bloodshed within Judah. Her remarks about preventing David from "shedding innocent blood" (v. 31) and of "fighting the battles of Yahweh" (v. 28) are surely ironic when it comes to his subsequent career under Achish. David and his men are mercenaries, and, as such, it is their nature to pillage and to shed the blood of their innocent victims. Furthermore, when David acquires Abigail as his wife he does not settle down on a large estate, because, as Abigail has suggested in her speech, she is aware that he has much greater ambitions and so must remain a mercenary until the opportune time.

In David's second encounter with Saul (2 Sam 26), also belonging to the late version, in which he spares Saul's life, David's band of warriors and Saul's elite corps of 3,000 fighting men are a case of two professional armies confronting each other. The mercenary band, although outnumbered five to one, has a tactical advantage in fighting on its own turf. What is also of interest is that among David's mercenaries are foreigners, such as Ahimelech the Syrian (Hittite[56]), who seems to rank at the same level as Abishai. This is the same ethnic mixture in the army that one will find in CH and is entirely typical of West Asian monarchies and satrapies in the Persian period. Furthermore, David's protest about being driven out of the "heritage of Yahweh" to "serve other gods" is rather empty in that as a mercenary he willingly goes to Achish when he is no longer pursued, and it is clear from Achish's invocation of Yahweh in 2 Sam 29:6 that David need not serve any other gods but his own. There is no indication that mercenaries ever needed to swear allegiance to any other country or their gods, as did vassal states. The arrangement between mercenary and overlord was entirely monetary.

The Use of Mercenaries in King David's Army
After David receives word that Saul and his sons have been killed by the Philistines, David moves to Hebron, and according to the late narrator he

---

56. The term *Hittite* is used in late texts as a reference to a non-Israelite aboriginal member of the population of Syria-Palestine. See my "Terms 'Amorite' and 'Hittite' in the Old Testament," *VT* 22 (1972): 64–81.

brings up with him the same body of men as his personal army, along with the entire entourage that he had as a mercenary leader, and settles them in the region of Hebron (2 Sam 2:1–3). According to the late source, David is made king of Judah at that time (v. 4), but he continues to be at war with the house of Saul, and his forces are under the same leadership, the sons of Zeruiah who were with David prior to his coronation (2:12–32). The forces of Saul under Abner are regularly characterized as the "men of Israel" or "Benjamin," while the forces under Joab are consistently designated as the "servants of David," that is, his personal professional army. Furthermore, on the occasion when Abner conspires to transfer the allegiance of all Israel and Benjamin to David in a private agreement, 2 Sam 3:12–25, the narrator states that Joab and the servants of David, that is, his mercenaries, had just arrived back at court "from a raid, bringing with them an abundance of booty." According to the narrator, it would appear that they still continued their old habits of marauding and slaughter. Joab, who already had a grudge against Abner for the death of his brother in combat, now was in danger of being overshadowed by Abner, who commanded the whole of the forces of Israel and Benjamin, while Joab was only the commander of the army of mercenaries, so Joab murdered him. This would not be the last time that Joab did such a thing. The point that I wish to make from all of this is that this sort of behavior reflects the same social milieu that was characteristic of military life in the Persian period. The narrative is all of a single piece reflecting the same social conditions.

After David becomes king of all Israel, he continues to use his professional army to do his fighting for him in CH, in contrast to the earlier source, DtrH, which always has David leading his forces in battle. However, in addition to his regular professionals, CH also has David employing foreign mercenaries. In both lists of David's officials there occurs the figure of "Benaiah the son of Jehoiada [who] was over the Cherethites and the Pelethites" (2 Sam 8:18, 20:23), and this was in addition to Joab as commander of the regular army. There can be no doubt that the Cherethites and Pelethites are none other than Greek mercenaries, the Cherethites being Cretan archers and the Pelethites being the famous peltasts, light armed spearmen, so common in the 4th century. So important does the narrator consider these mercenaries that Benaiah, their commander, is a serious rival to Joab in the story of Solomon's succession and the one who, as a supporter of Solomon, eventually murders Joab and replaces him as general of the army (1 Kgs 1–2; cf. 4:4). In another tradition (2 Sam 23:23), this mercenary force is also identified as the palace guard, which is most appropriate for the role that he plays in the Solomonic coup of 1 Kgs 1. These same Greek mercenaries also played a role in the Absalom revolt as part of David's loyal forces (2 Sam15:18) and in the revolt of Sheba (2 Sam 20:7).

In addition to the Greek mercenaries are a band of 600 Philistine mercenaries from Gath under their own commander, Ittai (2 Sam 15:18-22).[57] The scene, set at the beginning of David's flight from Absalom, is most instructive on the role of mercenaries in David's army. David acknowledges that Ittai has only recently arrived from Gath as a foreigner and an exile, and he suggests that perhaps he should return to Jerusalem and serve Absalom (vv. 19-20). The comparison with David's own former service as a mercenary in Gath is obvious, but Ittai makes a solemn oath of loyalty in the name of Yahweh that he will serve David to the death and he becomes part of David's entourage (vv. 21-22). Note that as a mercenary band all of the dependents must accompany the soldiers. This is also the case for David himself and his men. Furthermore, it is noteworthy that in the arrangements for the final battle, one third of the command is placed under Ittai the Gittite, the core of which was undoubtedly his own men (18:1-2). One must also reckon that the Cherethites and the Pelethites were thought of as being under the command of Abishai (cf. 20:7). Throughout the whole account of the war between David and Absalom, the narrator leaves the reader with the clear impression that David's army consists of a core of professionals augmented by a large body of foreign mercenaries. Absalom's army, by contrast, is constantly referred to as the "men of Israel," so that one is left with the impression that it consists entirely of citizen soldiers. They vastly outnumber David's army, but the latter are battle-hardened professionals, so that the Israelite conscripts are no match for them. The casualty figure of 20,000 is, of course, totally unrealistic and is derived by imitating the figure that Dtr gives for the dead in the Aramean and Edomite wars (20,000, 22,000, and 18,000 in 2 Sam 8:4-5, 13).

At the end of the revolt of Absalom, when David attempts to reclaim the throne and be reconciled with the elders of Judah and Israel, David seeks once again to replace Joab, this time with Amasa, the general of the joint forces of Judah and Israel under Absalom (2 Sam 17:25, 19:9-14). However, a dispute breaks out between the citizen forces of Judah and the citizen forces of Israel over royal prerogatives (19:40-43), and this results in

---

57. Cf. N. Na'aman, "Ittai the Gittite," *BN* 94 (1998): 22-25. Na'aman offers a quite-different understanding of this episode, one that is much more sympathetic to David than the one offered here.

a breakaway group of Israelites under Sheba who lead a second revolt. Amasa, the newly appointed general of the army, is delayed in his efforts to call up the recruits from Judah on short notice, so that David is forced to rely on his professionals and Greek mercenaries to deal with the situation (20:1-7). When Amasa does show up, he is murdered by Joab, and there is little that David can do about it. According to the narrator of this source, the monarchy has become completely dominated by the commanders of the professional army and the mercenaries with the king as a mere figurehead. In his final speech to Solomon, David advises his son to get rid of the ruthless Joab (1 Kgs 2:5-6), and Solomon does so (vv. 28-35), but this only leaves Benaiah, the commander of the mercenaries and murderer of Joab, in his place.

This totally fictional account of David's monarchy presents a vivid picture of the militaristic regimes of the Persian period, with an elite professional core and heavy dependence on mercenary armies, with specialized tactical skills such as those of the Cretans and the peltasts, under the control of their own leaders. The old citizen armies were no longer any match for these professional killing machines. These wealthy regimes, such as Persia, could invest fortunes in buying protection. The Davidic monarchy is viewed as a state with these resources, and the author sets out to recreate what life would be like in a state of this sort. His knowledge and understanding of the life of a mercenary and regimes that make use of them is quite remarkable and realistic when judged against the background of the social milieu of the 4th century B.C.E. There is no other period that provides such an appropriate context for this portrayal of a Near Eastern monarchy than this particular period.[58]

Conclusion

The institution that most clearly defines the sociohistorical context in which a large portion of the story of David is set is the military, both its nature as a professional and mercenary army and its role within the Davidic monarchy. Not only does this militaristic portrait of David's power base permeate the whole of what I have previously called the Court History, but

---

58. The attempt by Finkelstein and Silberman to fit CH into the social context of the 9th century (*David and Solomon*, 91-117) ignores too many of these anachronisms, which are inappropriate for their own reconstruction of the rather limited polity of Jerusalem in this period.

it also encompasses a large part of HDR in the form of David's role as a mercenary leader prior to his becoming king of Israel. This means that a very large portion of the David story must be viewed as a literary composition of the late Persian period, some time in the 4th century B.C.E. Once this setting is understood, there are many other anachronistic story details that become clear within this social setting. The fact that the story makes such explicit reference to certain Greek mercenaries whose social context within the Near East can be so precisely dated by a large body of literature from the Greek world makes the dating of this corpus a near certainty.

In contrast to this body of closely controlled data, we have reviewed all the various alternative types of evidence that have been used to identify the social context in which the stories of David in Samuel–Kings took shape. In particular, we have seen that the evidence for the composition of contemporary documents is flawed because the arguments based on parallels to royal apologies or memorial inscriptions or other works of court propaganda are unconvincing for the 10th century. Even the existence of brief archival sources or building inscriptions is unlikely, because there is strong reason to doubt the existence of any supporting state bureaucracy in this period. One cannot use the *longue durée* argument from the Amarna age, as comparable to the time of David's reign, because the small bureaucracies in little cities such as Jerusalem in the earlier period were totally dependent upon the presence in the region of the Egyptian Empire and its larger administrative structure. With the demise of the Egyptian Empire in Asia, the region reverted to illiteracy. None of the *external* comparative evidence or *internal* written "documents" can help us date the social context of the David story.

The archaeological evidence from Jerusalem and Judah, on the other hand, does furnish us with valuable negative evidence in that it strongly confirms that there was no royal monarchy or court, such as the David story suggests, and it is equally unlikely that there was any "united kingdom" of all Israel, let alone an empire. The origins of the two states of Israel and Judah were quite independent, with the Israelite state of the 9th century eventually dominating the region of Judah. Not until the late 8th century was Judah sufficiently advanced as a state that it could produce any written records, and not until the end of the monarchy did it make any attempt, in the form of the DtrH, to construct a "history" of its past, including an account of the reigns of David and Solomon. Even so, the initial story of David by Dtr was likely quite brief, because the evidence that a large portion of the David story was composed in the late Persian period is so clearly confirmed by the portrayal of mercenaries, both in David's rise to power and in his Court History.

All of this discussion about the social and historical background to the David story, therefore, calls into question most of the earlier critical analyses of the relevant texts in Samuel–Kings and their interpretations of the David story. These are based heavily on assumptions about a base text or texts that were thought to reflect (or distort) actual historical events to which they refer, and these assumptions, as I have tried to show, are quite unjustified. What is required, therefore, is a new literary analysis that takes into account the historical and archaeological conclusions outlined above, in order to produce a quite-different understanding of the David story in the biblical text and the evolution of the David tradition.

Chapter 4

David and Saul:
The Problem of Multiple Accounts

The Beginning of the Story of David

The beginning of the story of David has long been recognized as problematic by virtue of the fact that there appear to be three introductory episodes: the secret anointing of David by Samuel in 1 Sam 16:1-13; the initiation of David as a warrior into the forces of Saul in 1 Sam 16:14-23; and the story of David and Goliath. The last of these three will involve a rather extended discussion that will be taken up separately. I will begin, therefore, by examining the first two and their relationship both to each other and to the larger narrative context in which they are set. In the case of both introductory episodes in 1 Sam 16, there is the inevitable problem of their relationship to the "story of Saul," however this entity is to be understood. While the analysis of the Saul story in 1 Sam 9-15 lies outside the scope of the present study, some discussion of its relationship to the David story and to the episodes in 1 Sam 16 is unavoidable, because it bears directly on our understanding of the David story, and especially on the theme of David as a divine replacement for the rejected Saul. It also bears on the question of whether or not we can speak of an independent story of David's rise to power (HDR).

We begin with 1 Sam 16:14-23. It would seem to be the case, on the one hand, that the context for this episode is the protracted conflict between Saul's forces and the Philistines and hence Saul's need to develop an elite corps of warriors for this purpose, as reflected in 1 Sam 14:52. The immediate sequel to David's appointment by Saul, on the other hand, is to be found in 1 Sam 18. Consequently, two large blocks of narrative (1 Sam 15:1-16:13 and 17:1-18:4) have been inserted into the older narrative, both of which contain parallel introductions to David. In addition, there is in 16:14-23 the theme of the spirit of Yahweh abandoning Saul and being replaced by an evil spirit that troubles him, which requires someone who is able to play a lyre that can sooth Saul's spirit; David is the one who fills this need. This theme looks backward to the previous story of Saul in 1 Sam 9–14 and forward to the period of David's service under Saul in 1 Sam 18–19. The departure of the spirit of Yahweh is linked to the account of Saul's divine election in 1 Sam 9:1–10:16, in which the anointing (10:1) is directly related to the gift of the spirit (10:6–7, 9–10). However, it is also qualified by a command in 10:8, disobedience to which leads to Saul's rejection in 13:8–15a, and the subsequent departure of the spirit of Yahweh in 16:14. Along with Saul's rejection is the revelation in 13:14 that Yahweh had already chosen another to succeed him and the identity of this person becomes clear by the introduction of David in 16:18–23. Within this particular network of texts, however, it is not revealed to anyone in the story just who this successor will be, although the larger context of the history never makes this fact a matter of doubt. The theme of Saul's warfare against the Philistines and of David's place in his service is also taken up in 1 Sam 18–19, so that 1 Sam 16:14–23 is firmly situated within this sequence of texts. This is clear both in David's role as Saul's musician, who plays for him to overcome the effects of the evil spirit (18:10–11, 19:9–10) and in the frequent references to David's military exploits (18:5, 13–15, 30; 19:8).[1] As I have previously argued in *In Search of History*, these texts belong to the basic account of the story of Saul and David in DtrH.[2] We shall test this assumption in the analysis that follows.

A few further observations on 1 Sam 16:14–23 are in order. As we have seen, the departure of the spirit of Yahweh is related to the theme of Saul's rejection, of which we have two accounts, the immediately preceding one in 1 Sam 15:1–16:13 and the one in 1 Sam 13:8–15a, but these doublets cannot belong to the same source. It would be easy to read 1 Sam 16:14 as a continuation of v. 13 concerning the spirit of Yahweh descending on David when it departs from Saul, but arguing against continuation by the same writer is the obvious fact that 1 Sam 16:1–13 is a doublet to what follows in 16:14–23. Furthermore, 16:1–13 clearly represents a continuation of the account of Saul's rejection in 15:1–35, so that 16:14–23 must be linked instead to the unit in 13:8–15a. Another link is the fact that possession by the spirit is often manifested similarly to ecstatic prophecy (1 Sam 10:6, 10–12), and the evil spirit could have a similar, though quite negative, effect (18:10–11).

---

1. The particular analysis of 1 Sam 18–19 and its relationship to 1 Sam 17 is complex and will be dealt with in a later unit of this chapter.

2. Van Seters, *In Search of History*, 264–70.

In this basic account of David's introduction (1 Sam 16:14-23), it should be noted that David is the only son of Jesse who is mentioned, and all his qualities both as a skilful musician and as a warrior are enumerated, while his occupation as a shepherd is mentioned only rather incidentally (v. 19) as something known to Saul in his request to Jesse. The fact that a skilful warrior should also have another occupation, such as a shepherd, should not be regarded as exceptional because armies were regularly drawn from artisans and farmers, and it was only the most skilful of these that would be selected as part of an elite corps, useful especially in the event of a long-standing conflict, as reflected in 1 Sam 14:52. In this account of David's introduction, Jesse sends a present of food directly to Saul along with David; he enters Saul's service and is given the status of permanent enlistment as armor-bearer and court musician in the closest possible association with the king (16:20-23). As we shall see, this brief introduction will conflict in the most basic way with the story of David and Goliath. But before we can turn to this episode, we will need to look at the other introduction to David in 1 Sam 16:1-13.

David's first appearance in 1 Sam 16:1-13 is part of a much larger unit in 15:1-16:13 dealing with the rejection of Saul and must be considered within this context. This pericope is a later addition to the base text, interrupting the original continuity between 14:52 and 16:14. The fact that in 16:13, following David's anointing, we have the statement that "the spirit of Yahweh came mightily upon David from that day onwards," indicates that the writer has dovetailed his account into the earlier one to make it appear that the anointing of David and the gift of the spirit coincided with the departure of the spirit from Saul. So it is clear that 16:1-13 was not an independent tradition about David's election, and we must therefore look at its relationship to the earlier base text.[3]

The episode begins, quite out of the blue, with Samuel's issuing a divine command to Saul to eradicate the Amalekites (15:1-3). Even though this does not immediately follow from the remarks about warfare with the Philistines in 14:52 and ignores all of the events in chaps 13-14, it nevertheless makes a direct allusion back to Samuel's earlier anointing of Saul in 10:1 (cf. 13:16) for the purpose of defeating Israel's enemies, particularly the Philistines. Here, however, the enemy to be avenged is the Amalekites.

---

3. See my earlier discussion in ibid., 258-64. It is likely that the author of 16:14 regarded the departure of the spirit of Yahweh from Saul as taking place at the time of his rejection by Yahweh in 13:13-14.

Samuel recalls the episode of the Amalekites' harassment of the Israelites during the wilderness journey (Exod 17:8–16, Deut 25:18), so that the present command is viewed as the fulfillment of an ancient obligation. The details of the command (15:3) correspond to the law of *ḥerem* in Deut 20:16–18, although it is not clear that the Amalekites fall into the category of peoples to be exterminated. The model for the *ḥerem* is obviously Joshua's conquest of Jericho (Josh 6:21, 24) although it fits this exemplar very poorly. Furthermore, 14:48 suggests that Saul had already taken care of the Amalekite threat. One should also note that the prophetic command does not correspond to a salvation oracle issued before a battle to encourage the king to victory but has to do with a specific obligation derived from divine law. Samuel's prophetic role is to oversee obedience to the Torah as reflected in Deuteronomy.

Saul responds to this command by mustering a huge force of two hundred thousand infantry (from Israel?), with ten thousand from Judah (15:4). The numbers, of course, are grossly exaggerated, but they seem to correspond in size to those of Saul's war against Ammon in 11:8, where we read of 300,000 men of Israel and 30,000 men of Judah. The later episode, therefore, may be a deliberate imitation of the earlier one. This great force of citizen conscripts advances on the "city of Amelek." It is curious that this action is viewed as taken against a particular city, which is presumably ruled by the king who is later taken captive. The Amalekites are generally viewed as a nomadic people that inhabited a large arid region in northern Sinai and not in Judah proper. Merely to capture one settlement would hardly deal with the threat of these marauders. The whole scenario, therefore, is quite artificial, perhaps to make it correspond more closely to deuteronomic law. Living among the Amalekites are said to be another group, the Kenites, who belong to the Negev region. They are advised to withdraw from the region during the conflict so not to be caught up in the massacre. The reason they are spared in contrast to the Amalekites is that they "acted kindly to all the people of Israel when they came up out of Egypt" (v. 6). This must be an allusion to the visit of Moses' father-in-law in Exod 18:1–27 and Num 10:29–32 (cf. Judg 1:16),[4] in direct contrast to the Amalekites in Exod 17. Saul is then presented as carrying out a thorough ethnic extermination of the Amalekites over the extended region of northern Sinai

---

4. What seems quite remarkable is the fact that the author also seems to be aware of the very late identification of Moses' father-in-law with the Kenites and their settlement in the Negev in Judg 1:16.

from the Saudi Peninsula to the border of Egypt. However, they spared the
king as a trophy of war and some of the choicest of the animals (v. 9), and
this was viewed by the deity as a serous violation of the divine commandments and the basis for Saul's rejection as king.

This leads us to make a comparison with the earlier scene in 13:8–15a,
in which Saul is also rejected by God through the prophet Samuel. As I indicated in my earlier discussion,

> the following features are common to both stories. Saul's rejection arises
> out of a command by Samuel to Saul that is not *totally* obeyed. The scene
> of rejection in both cases is set in Gilgal, and includes the offering of sac-
> rifices, of which Saul's are rejected. When Samuel arrives on the scene,
> Saul greets him (*brk*) as if nothing is wrong. Samuel rebukes Saul with an
> accusing question and Saul immediately makes an excuse expressing
> fear or weakness. Samuel then tells Saul that he has disobeyed the divine
> command and as a consequence has been rejected by God in favor of an-
> other, bringing his own kingdom to an end. The two men part company
> and go their separate ways. While the divine command and the subse-
> quent offense by Saul are somewhat different in the two versions, the
> theme that "obedience is better than sacrifice" is still implicit in the first
> story and explicit in the second.[5]

The degree of similarity on so many essential points in both stories means
that the similarity cannot be fortuitous. Yet I think it is safe to say that the
two stories were not by the same author, because there is no credible reason
that an author would recount two different occasions of the deity's rejection
of Saul's kingship. Nor can it be a case of two independent accounts of the
same story or event, because the occasions that give rise to the rejection are
so entirely different. Yet they are treated in remarkably similar fashion. This
leaves only one plausible solution, that the one is a deliberate imitation of
the other. Furthermore, there can be little doubt about the direction of the
dependence of the later account (1 Sam 15:1–35) on the earlier (13:8–15a),
because the story of Saul's war against Amalek also makes use of so many
other literary works, both in DtrH and in the Pentateuch, in the elaboration
of his narrative; therefore it must be the later version.

If this is a case in which an author created a new scene to present God's
rejection of Saul, then we must ask why he wished to do so and how it is
related to his creation of a new introduction to the story of David in 16:1–
13, which is so closely attached to it. The reasons for the double parallel

---

5. *In Search of History,* 260–61.

must be closely related. Indeed, they both have to do with the theme of Yahweh's anointed; the one recounts the rejection of Saul as Yahweh's anointed, while the other tells of the selection and anointing of Saul's future replacement, David. However, once this obvious fact is acknowledged, there remains a number of subthemes that seem to reflect a set of theological problems and contradictions that make it difficult to come to terms with what the author of this unit is trying to say. Let us look at some of these. The first has to do with an apparent transformation in the nature of prophecy. The form of the prophetic address by Samuel in his opening speech to Saul (1 Sam 15:1–3) is an anomaly. The usual form is that a king planning a campaign or under threat from a foreign power consults a prophet for guidance or encouragement. This is clearly the situation in the earlier account in 1 Sam 13, in which Saul is already at war with the Philistines and Samuel's role is to give support to Saul. Saul's only mistake is that he did not wait long enough to receive that support and guidance. Here in 1 Sam 15, it is the prophet who commands the king to undertake a quite-different campaign, and he gives Saul very precise directions to carry it out. As indicated above, the divine command has to do with the implementation of a deuteronomic law, which involves the redefinition of the prophetic role as the guardian of deuteronomic law (Deut 18:15–19), and the fulfillment of an "ancient" obligation. Samuel plays the role of an ayatollah, whose word is sacred law above that of the king. He is a terrifying figure who chops down the Amalekite king with his own hands. Saul is left a broken man, begging for his support, at least to save face before the people. This view of the prophet has nothing in common with the older tradition of prophecy and is a completely artificial construction. There is no precedent for this kind of prophecy elsewhere in DtrH or the prophetic literature. It seems to me to parody the conception of prophecy that is put forward in Deut 18:15–22.

The second problem is to try to understand what great sin Saul has committed that he deserves to lose the kingship.[6] Saul is commanded by Samuel to attack and wipe out the Amalekites as an act of revenge, because of what their ancestors did centuries earlier, but also as part of the holy war against the aboriginal population of the region. This is reflected in the repeated use of the verb *ḥrm*. Not only all the humans but even the animals

---

6. See D. Gunn, *The Fate of King Saul*, 33–56. His discussion of "Saul's failure" in 1 Sam 13 and 15 becomes for him the key to understanding the whole story of Saul.

are involved in the sacred ban. Saul indeed conducts a massive campaign against them, in which he is careful not to involve the Kenites. He and his forces massacre the entire population, with the exception of the king and some of the best of the animals. Now it is these exceptions that get Saul into trouble. The command that Samuel gives does not strictly correspond to the deuteronomic law that deals with ḥrm (Deut 20:16-18), which is rather vague about what should be included within the phrase "nothing that breathes" as those who should be killed. In only one instance in Joshua, the city of Jericho, does this include all of the animals, but in all of the other cases the animals could be taken as booty (Josh 6:17; cf. Deut 13:15-17). Furthermore, in the case of Ai (Josh 8:29) and in the campaign against the cities of Judah (Josh 10:16-19, 22-27), the kings were spared until after the battle was over and then they were slain and hanged. The king of the Amalekites also experiences a similar fate. Thus, it is hard to see that Saul has done anything that is so different from the holy war tradition.

Likewise, the animals that were spared were said to be reserved for the specific purpose of offering them as a sacrifice of devoted animals (1 Sam 15:9, 21). Consequently, if they are sacrificed in this way, then they still fulfill the requirement of the law, even in its strictest sense. The violation of the command seems to rest on the very fine theological quibble of the distinction between what is devoted to Yahweh and what is sacrificed. Now it is precisely this notion that the animals that were taken are to be used for sacrifice that provokes the oracular response by Samuel (v. 22):

> Does Yahweh delight in burnt offerings and sacrifices, as he does in obedience to Yahweh? To obey is better than sacrifice and to listen to him than the fat of rams.

This resembles the reuse of a common theme of the 8th-century prophets and their critique of sacrifice, except that here it seems quite inappropriate. The command of Yahweh, after all, had to do with a massive slaughter of both humans and animals that were dedicated to the ban as a kind of sacrifice; thus, the charge against Saul is that the sacrifice was not done properly or was not complete. It therefore becomes absurd to say that the deity is not concerned about the sacrifice of the animals as much as the obedience to his commandments when the command is that the animals be slaughtered in the *ḥerem* in the appropriate way as a ritual slaughter. Does the narrator wish us to construe the whole event as a parody on deuteronomic law and on this traditional way of understanding the deity? Furthermore, as we shall see below, in the case of David's frequent raids on the Amalekites and other aboriginal peoples, he and his men also engage in massacres, but not for any religious motive, and David always keeps the booty of animals and other goods for his own purposes. Saul, in fact, looks like a religious zealot by comparison. He is hardly rebellious and stubborn, as Samuel charges (v. 23). It is as if, for all his religious zeal, Saul is not quite good enough in his obedience to the law.

The complete triviality of Samuel's charge against Saul is similar to his charge in 1 Sam 13:8-14, with the same consequence. There too, the original command, like in 10:8, was that Saul go to Gilgal and wait there for Samuel seven days until Samuel came to offer burnt offerings and wellness offerings. The command is ambiguous because it can be interpreted that Saul is to wait until Samuel comes, even if it takes seven days, or that Saul is only to wait seven days, and then do whatever he needs to do. Because Saul is under considerable pressure in the circumstances to act decisively or have his men desert him, he chooses the second option and is condemned for it. In both cases, as Gunn points out, the judgment on Saul's actions seems to be an excuse for the deity to reject him from being king.[7]

There are, however, some important differences between the two accounts, apart from the brevity of the first and the greatly expanded and detailed treatment of the second, and it is these differences that are important to our understanding of the account in 1 Sam 15:1-16:13. First, the warfare against the Philistines as presented in 1 Sam 13-14, both in its execution and in its ultimate success, has nothing to do with the episode in 13:8-15a, which merely uses the war as a convenient occasion for the rejection scene. By contrast, the execution of the war against the Amalekites in 1 Sam 15 is integral to the theme of Saul's rejection and the continuation in 16:1-13. Second, after Samuel accuses him of wrongdoing, in the first account, and declares to Saul that Yahweh has rejected him from being king over Israel (13:13-14), Saul says nothing. He does not admit his mistake, nor does he ask for forgiveness. In contrast to this, in the second account, we have Saul acknowledging his mistake and pleading for forgiveness, but he is bluntly refused any possibility of pardon (15:24-31). This refusal is directly related to the statement that the deity does not change his mind, even though it is previously stated that in rejecting Saul from being king Yahweh has in fact changed his mind (15:10-11). These

---

7. Ibid., 33-40.

differences are quite significant because it means that the authors have very different concerns.

The author of the first account, Dtr, has inherited traditions about Saul, the first king of Israel and David, the founder of the Davidic dynasty of Judah, and he has integrated these into a history of a "United Monarchy" of the mythical twelve tribes. This means that Saul is understood as chosen by Yahweh to be the first king and he serves the people well; his career is summarized in 14:47–48. Only at the end of his career is he rejected because of a mistake, a misunderstanding of a command given many years earlier, so that his dynasty can give way to David, the new founder of the united kingdom. Since David's dynasty lasts until the end of the Judean monarchy, it is a perpetual dynasty. Nevertheless, Solomon, in spite of his being the temple builder, violates Yahweh's commandments, and so his successors are rejected from ruling over Israel. The Kingdom of Israel is torn from him and given to Jeroboam (1 Kgs 11:9–13, 26–40); only Judah remains under the house of David, according to the special covenant with David. This pattern is repeated for the Northern Kingdom, in which Jeroboam is chosen by Yahweh and promised a secure house as was David, if he keeps his commandments, but Jeroboam also fails. It is clear, therefore, that what governs the theme of rejection for disobedience in 1 Sam 13:8–15a is not the fate or destiny of Saul, as Gunn argues, but the pattern of the larger history that is imposed on the independent northern Saul tradition in order to integrate it into the larger whole. There never was an "original" connection between Saul and David. This was the design of the Dtr Historian.

With the account of Yahweh's rejection of Saul in 1 Sam 15, the matter is altogether different, and here Gunn is on safer grounds.[8] In this account, we are told that Yahweh has had a change of heart about Saul, because he has not kept his commandments, although Saul claims that he has done exactly what was asked of him. Then, when Samuel has rebuked Saul and Saul has confessed to his errors and pleads for forgiveness, Samuel explains that Yahweh's rejection is irrevocable, because, unlike a human being, the deity cannot change his mind. There have been a variety of attempts to overcome this blatant contradiction, as Gunn has pointed out,[9] and there is no need to review them all here. Instead, we will look at this notion of the deity regretting past action, or relenting on an announcement of judgment, or changing his mind about someone. All these are expressed by the verb *rḥm*

---

8. Ibid., 41–56.
9. Ibid.

in the Niphal.[10] Within the Pentateuch, there are two primary examples of this theme. The first is in the Yahwist's flood story, in which Yahweh regrets (*rḥm*) having made mankind because of their wickedness and plans a judgment by flood to destroy every living thing (Gen 6:5–6), but then he makes an exception in the case of Noah and his family with a selection of the animals. And he further changes his mind about the very idea of a complete destruction (Gen 8:21), although in this case the verb *rḥm* is not specifically used. The second case is the story of the golden calf, in which Yahweh threatens to destroy the entire nation (Moses excluded) because of their idolatry, but in response to Moses' intercession, God "repents of the evil" (*rḥm* Niphal + ʿ*l hrʿh*) (Exod 32:12, 14). Consequently, it is possible that the intercession of a prophet can change the deity's mind with respect to a sentence of judgment or at least mitigate the sentence. See also Num 14:20–25.

This notion of Yahweh as a God of mercy who "repents of the evil" is reflected in prophetic literature in which the prophet acts as intercessor (Amos 7:3, 6; cf. Jer 15:1). More often, it is the situation in which Yahweh responds to the people's confession of sin and relents on his sentence of judgment (Jer 18:8, 10; 26:3, 13, 19; Jonah 3:10; 4:2). In Joel 2:12–14, the prophet pleads with the people to confess their sins and show remorse so that the deity will respond and avert the coming judgment. He characterizes Yahweh as a god who is "gracious and merciful, slow to anger, and abounding in steadfast love, and repents of evil" (cf. Exod 34:6–7, Ps 103:8–14). It is this theological dilemma between the justice of God and his mercy that is taken up in 1 Sam 15, but the whole motif is turned upside down. Now it is a case of the deity turning from favor toward Saul to disfavor and judgment, in which the confession of sin and plea for forgiveness by Saul does *not* cause God to "repent of the evil" that he plans against Saul, and no show of grief (intercession?) on Samuel's part can avail (cf. 1 Sam 12:19–25, Jer 15:1). Samuel uses as justification for Yahweh's lack of mercy the statement "the everlasting one of Israel does not deceive or change his mind; for he is not a human that he should change his mind" (1 Sam 15:29). This is a virtual quotation from the Balaam oracle: "God is not a man that he should deceive, or a human, that he should change his mind" (Num 23:19). The situation in the Balaam story, however, is the reverse of

---

10. See H. Simean-Yofre, "רחם *rḥm*," in *TDOT* 9:340–55 for a survey of all examples and usage. The discussion is influenced by an early date for the Pentateuch examples and the text in 1 Sam 15. See also H. J. Stoebe, "רחם *rḥm* pi. to comfort," in *TLOT* 2:734–39.

that in Samuel in that the prophet declares that once God has determined to bless Israel he cannot be persuaded by any means to curse his people.

What becomes clear from this comparison is that the whole presentation of this theme of God changing his mind in both the Pentateuch and the prophetic literature is that God can be persuaded by the intercession of prophets, especially Moses and Samuel (Jer 15:1), and by the confession of sin to change his mind and show mercy. However, in this unit the reverse is claimed, that is, once Yahweh has entered a sentence of judgment, nothing can change that. Yahweh is not merciful and compassionate toward sinners as humans may be. Samuel, for his part, while at first refusing to accompany Saul, does change his mind and go with Saul to worship the deity and even to grieve at length over Saul's rejection. Indeed, there is a deliberate contrast between the deity, who is angry with Saul and then changes his mind to reject him, and Samuel, who is angry and passes judgment on Saul but then changes his mind and grieves over Saul's fate because Yahweh had changed his mind and rejected Saul. This seems to me to make a parody of the theme of divine mercy and forgiveness and the role of the prophet as the one who can mediate divine commands and sentences of judgment but who declares himself impotent to intercede for the penitent. Under these conditions, Saul does not have a chance and he is to be pitied. It is this complete reversal in the theme of God's not being able to reverse a sentence of judgment that dooms Saul, no matter what he does. This is Saul's fate.

There is a sequel to this encounter between Saul and Samuel, which is hinted at in the very ambiguous statement that "Samuel did not see Saul again until the day of his death," which is linked to the story of the witch of Endor in 1 Sam 28:3–25. This episode begins with a reference to Samuel's death and burial and then a reference to preparations for the final battle between the forces of Saul and the Philistines.[11] The mustering of all the Philistine forces in preparation for attack leads Saul to seek divine guidance, but Saul can get no response from the deity by all the usual means of dreams, Urim, or prophets. This is the case in spite of the fact that he has carried through a religious reform, as did Josiah (2 Kgs 23:24), by ridding the land of all the mediums who consulted spirits of the dead in accor-

---

11. We will argue below that this episode in 28:3–25 has been displaced from its original location in 25:1 in order to accommodate the addition of the material in 25:1b–28:2. The confrontation between Samuel and Saul in 1 Sam 19:18–24 is also part of a later addition.

dance with deuteronomic law. Ironically, in desperation it is to one such medium that he now turns for help, and unlike the legitimate means of consultation, she does not fail him. The ghost of Samuel appears before Saul, and Saul bows before him and pours out his desperate plight, that he can receive no answer or help from the deity. To this, Samuel replies that since Yahweh has rejected Saul and become his enemy because he disobeyed the commandment concerning the Amalekites, his fate is sealed. Yahweh has given his kingdom to David, who is now specifically identified as his successor. He and his army will be defeated by the Philistines and he and his sons will die. Of course, what Samuel does not reveal to Saul is the fact that it was he who anointed David before David even entered Saul's service to begin his career as a military leader.

The final scene shows Saul utterly despondent at this revelation of his fate, lying prostrate on the ground, and it is only with great effort that the woman, in the role of a caring person, along with Saul's servants, are able to revive him and get him to eat. The woman goes to great lengths to prepare a meal that is fit for a king. The fact that the author spends so much time on this demonstration of compassion toward Saul is significant. Humans may be compassionate, but the deity is not. The whole episode is completely ironic. Saul, who is a devout follower of Yahweh and a strict reformer of religious practice according to deuteronomic law to the very end of his life, must still suffer his cruel fate for his one mistake. It is only when he resorts to an illegitimate method of inquiry concerning the will of the deity and future events that he receives a message from the dead Samuel. So the illegitimate means is effective, whereas the legitimate ones are not. The medium assists Saul at the risk of her life and then comforts and feeds him before he goes to his death. She is not an evil person any more than is Saul. Once Yahweh has become the enemy of Saul, he is doomed and nothing can change that. In stark contrast to the woman, Yahweh is presented in both episodes as completely without compassion, one whose fierce anger required the total and immediate annihilation of all the Amalekites and their animals. Almost out of spite for Saul's one mistake,[12] Yahweh will not support his people in their holy war against the Philistines.[13] The ironies and contradictions of the two additions in 1 Sam 15:1-35 and 28:2-25

---

12. It is clear that this source knows nothing of the massacre at Nob in 1 Sam 22:11-19. More on this below.

13. The Philistine wars are regarded elsewhere as wars of Yahweh. See 1 Sam 7, 9:16, 10:1.

raise the serious possibility that they are intended as a parody on DtrH and its construction of Israelite history.

If this reading of the account of Saul's rejection in 1 Sam 15 is correct, then it raises a serious question as to whether we are to understand the anointing of David as Saul's replacement in 16:1–13 in the same way, because it follows directly from the former episode as part of the same unit. Samuel is commanded to stop his crying over the fate of Saul and to go to Bethlehem in order to anoint Saul's successor from among the sons of Jesse. To do so is, of course, an act of treason against the reigning king and therefore Samuel fears for his life. So Yahweh provides Samuel with a plan of deception, which includes the pretence of presenting a sacrifice to Yahweh, which, of course, makes this ritual act of sacrifice for political purposes completely disingenuous. The fearsome prophet of Yahweh, who accused Saul of deception in his use of sacrifice, now becomes fearful and deceptive in a most serious matter of state, using a similar means of sacrifice to disguise his intentions. Those invited to the sacrifice, such as the city elders and Jesse's family, are completely unaware that they are being duped as part of this treasonous act. They could be placed in grave jeopardy.[14]

Jesse's sons are asked to appear before Samuel, and he reviews them individually. Samuel is immediately impressed with the eldest, Eliab, and considers him the anointed one because of his stunning appearance. However, Yahweh replies that he does not look on a person's outward appearance or his stature, but sees into the heart. This is directed at the remark that Saul, the one chosen by lot, is especially noted for his great stature (1 Sam 10:23–24), and when Saul was anointed it was Yahweh who gave Saul another heart (10:9). After Samuel is made to review and reject all seven of Jesse's sons who are present, Jesse is forced to admit that there is one additional son, not present, who is tending the sheep, and David is summoned.[15] In spite of the earlier remark about appearances, David is described as very handsome (16:12; cf. v. 18). Once David receives divine approval, he is anointed by Samuel and receives the spirit of Yahweh as a permanent endowment. The whole process of David's election and anointing is made to contrast with that of Saul. Unlike Samuel's explicit statement to Saul about being anointed as leader (*nāgîd*) of his people (10:1), David and his family are not actually told exactly what the anointing signifies, although the con-

---

14. Cf. the similarities in the case of the revolt of Absalom in 2 Sam 15:9–12.

15. This detail about David, his being the one among the brothers who takes care of the sheep, will appear again in the David and Goliath story. More of this below.

text suggests that he is anointed as king (*melek*). In Saul's case, there was no prior king, and the act was carried out by Samuel who was at the same time the judge and ruler of the people. With David, Saul is already king and remains king for some time. Two anointed ones at the same time over the same people is anomalous. Furthermore, Saul is anointed in complete privacy with even his servant excluded, but here David's anointing is witnessed by his family. And were the elders who attended the sacrifice also present for this event and therefore party to what it implied? Does this action cast all of David's subsequent activity as the servant of Saul into a different light and compromise his supposed loyalty? If the outward appearance of the events, a sacrificial feast made on the occasion of a visiting religious dignitary (cf. 9:11–14, 22–24), looks innocent enough, what is hidden from view is much more sinister. It rather makes a mockery of the maxim: "man looks on the outward appearance, but Yahweh looks on the heart." The one chosen by Yahweh as "the man after Yahweh's own heart," according to Dtr, is merely characterized in 15:28 as someone "who is better than you [Saul]," not necessarily more upright, but one who will fulfill the divine purpose.

The ceremony of anointing is likewise rather odd because Samuel does not make any declaration as to its significance, that is, that Yahweh has anointed David as king over Israel. Consequently, do those who witness the anointing recognize David as the future king and successor to Saul? In the case of Saul's anointing (10:1), Samuel makes clear the divine appointment as *nāgîd* and the one chosen by God to save the people from their enemies, and the next two episodes in the story are intended in this context to confirm Saul's appointment as king.[16] In 1 Sam 15:1–3, Samuel makes a connection between his prior anointing of Saul and the divine mission he has been given. In Second Isaiah, Cyrus as the anointed one of Yahweh has the mission of liberating Yahweh's people from the Babylonian power (Isa 45:1–3). The figure in Isa 61:1–4 is anointed and endowed with the spirit of Yahweh to carry out another mission of liberation. However, in David's case, nothing is said of any mission. Furthermore, if David was anointed by Samuel to be king, then why must he be anointed again? He is anointed as king of Judah (2 Sam 2:4) and of all Israel (5:2–3).[17] Saul was not anointed again publicly after the secret anointing by Samuel. There is likewise an-

16. See also 1 Kgs 1:32–40.
17. The anointing of David in 2 Sam 5:2–3 is Dtr's version and seems to closely associate David's mission with the prior task of Saul in 1 Sam 10:1 and a continuation of what he had begun under Saul.

other instance of a secret anointing by a prophet, that of Jehu in 2 Kgs 9. When the prophet arrives at the camp of the Israelites in Ramoth-gilead and asks for Jehu, they retreat to private quarters and he is anointed with oil as king over Israel and is given his marching orders, which are to wipe out the house of Ahab and to secure the throne. This is an act of high treason. Jehu is a usurper, whether anointed or not. The comparison with the anointing of David by Samuel leads to the inescapable conclusion that Samuel, the house of Jesse, and David are all conspirators and part to a coup d'état. It casts a shadow over all that David says and does. What is obviously lacking is the declaration of kingship and the instigation of a mission, that is, the actions and procedures by which David becomes king in actuality.

All of these features tend to confirm the view of Gunn that the author of 1 Sam 15:1–16:13 and 28:3–25 regards the recipient of the office of king and the dynastic succession as a matter of *fate* or *fortune* that has little to do with the inherent goodness or fine qualities of the recipient.[18] It is the inscrutable will of the deity that cannot be changed by deeds or persuasion. There is a certain degree of cynicism toward the events described and an extensive parody of Deuteronomy, DtrH, and the Pentateuch in its reference to laws and historical events and in its treatment of prophecy. The number of instances of blatant contradiction or reversal of what could traditionally be expected makes this conclusion inescapable. However, even though this author may intend to impose this understanding of events on the story of Saul that he has inherited, namely, DtrH, one must be cautious about reading this perspective back into Dtr's own view of the matter, which is quite different. And as we shall see, this reviser of Dtr does not have the last word. There is yet a later revisionist account of the stories of David and Saul that presents quite a different view of the whole matter of kingship, and it is misleading to interpret his additions from the perspective of this account of Saul's rejection.

The Story of David and Goliath

Before engaging in a detailed literary analysis, a few short remarks should be made about a problem related to the history of the tradition about David's killing Goliath. This has to do with the reference in 2 Sam

---

18. Gunn, *The Fate of King Saul*, 115–31. For Gunn, this interpretation applies to the whole of the story of David and Saul in 1 Sam 16–31, whereas I believe that is was the interpretation imposed by a later writer on the earlier Dtr narrative.

21:19 to one of David's heroes, Elhanah of Bethlehem, having been the one who killed the giant Goliath of Gath. Commentators have debated the relationship between this account and that of the David and Goliath story, and most conclude, correctly in my view, that the tradition in 2 Sam 21:19 is the older one and the David and Goliath story is derivative.[19] The reasons would appear to be obvious: first, it seems unlikely that the lesser-known figure, Elhanan, would borrow his feat from the more famous David; second, Elhanah's feat is merely one of a series of encounters with the giants of Gath and not the decisive victory that it becomes in the David story; third, the distinctive feature of Goliath in 2 Sam 21:19 is his spear "like a weaver's beam," and this object is borrowed and integrated into the description of Goliath's hoplite armor in 1 Sam 17:7. As I shall argue below, because the story is a very late literary composition, there is nothing that speaks against a direct literary borrowing of this story from the earlier collection and applying it to David. Our primary concern in this study, however, is the literary character of the David and Goliath story and its relationship to the larger whole. To this we will now turn.

The story of David and Goliath is by far the most difficult problem that scholars face within the narratives that make up the larger story of David and Saul, for a number of reasons. First, there are rather remarkable textual differences between the MT and the Old Greek of the LXX in the story of David and Goliath and its sequel in 1 Sam 18, about which textual critics have strong differences of opinion. Second, the story of David and Goliath seems to contradict completely 1 Sam 16:14–23 as to the circumstances under which David entered the court of Saul and joined his service. Third, the whole story of David and Saul that follows the Goliath episode seems to have almost nothing in common with that story and makes only a few passing references to it. David's military career is presented as if it had never happened. The way in which scholars address these problems, or completely ignore them, usually has much to do with how they view the compositional history of the story of David and Saul. It seems best, therefore, to address these issues head on at the outset of this study before undertaking a literary analysis of the rest.

---

19. McCarter, *I Samuel*, 291; R. W. Klein, *1 Samuel* (WBC 10; Waco, TX: Word, 1983), 173; cf. H. W. Hertzberg, *I & II Samuel: A Commentary* (OTL; Philadelphia: Westminster, 1964), 146.

The Problem of the Textual Differences in
Hebrew and Old Greek

The story of David and Goliath in 1 Sam 17 and its immediate sequel in chap. 18 is unique in the books of Samuel in the fact that there is such a large portion of the Hebrew text that has no equivalence in the Old Greek of the LXX as reflected in LXX[B]. This has led to a great deal of speculation among scholars as to why this should be the case, with rather strong differences of opinion. On the one side are those who view the differences between the MT and LXX as reflecting two different versions in the Hebrew, a shorter text, used as the *Vorlage* of LXX, that was the original version of the story, and a longer text, as the archetype of the MT, that reflects an expansion of the original, either as an editorial conflation of two parallel versions of the same story or as a literary amplification and embellishment of the earlier story. On the other side are those who regard the longer story as the original one and the shorter story as an abridgement either by the Greek translator or by a Hebrew copyist prior to its use in the Greek translation. This yields at least four distinctive positions, with the result that arguments used by one side may not address all of the options presented by the other side and vice versa.

The four basic positions may be outlined as follows. First, there is the position articulated by McCarter in his 1 Samuel commentary:

> The material collected here [1 Sam 17:12-31, 41, 48b, 50, 55-58; 18:1-5, 10-11, 17-19, 29b-30], though it appears in the received Hebrew text (MT) . . . , is missing entirely from the Codex Vaticanus (LXX[B]), the most direct witness to the Old Greek in 1 Samuel. It seems clear, then, that it was not in the Old Greek. It is easiest to conclude, moreover, that it was also absent from the Hebrew tradition behind LXX and indeed from the primitive text of Samuel itself, having been introduced into the tradition behind MT at some point after its divergence from the ancestral tradition of LXX in the fourth century B.C.[20]

McCarter disputes the claim of those, such as Wellhausen, who argue that the Greek text reflects an attempt at harmonization by means of the elimination of contradictory statements. He argues that "there is no thematic unity in the received text of 17:1-18:30 . . . , and a number of duplications exist especially in the two accounts of David's introduction to Saul in

---

20. McCarter, *I Samuel*, 306.

16:14-23 . . . and 17:57ff."[21] In his view, the effort at harmonization is far from complete or adequate. Furthermore, he states,

> Most damaging to the 'shortening' hypothesis, however, is the fact that the materials missing from LXX[B], when collected by themselves as they are here [in his commentary], can be seen to form a more or less complete narrative of their own. This strongly suggests that they represent the bulk of a full account of David's arrival and early days at court that was interpolated *in toto* into the primary narrative at some time subsequent to the divergence of the ancestral textual traditions that lie behind MT and LXX.[22]

As we shall see below, those scholars who maintain the theory of harmonization in LXX or its *Vorlage* are willing to defend this view with examples that McCarter claims do not exist, and they also argue for a thematic unity to the version in MT that McCarter denies. However, the argument that he considers the strongest, namely, that the pluses in the MT, when taken by themselves, result in a complete and independent narrative, may be seriously contested. While there is a rather long and repetitious introduction of David and how it came about that he arrived at the camp of Saul and took up the challenge of Goliath (1 Sam 17:12-31), nothing is said about how David actually becomes the one to accept the challenge, such as we have in vv. 32-40. Indeed, McCarter must invoke the notion of "harmonization" by a later editor for the remark in v. 31 that "when David's remarks were overheard, they were reported to Saul and he sent for him," which makes a smooth transition between the two scenes. The actual scene of the combat is so brief (vv. 41, 48b + 50) that it tells us nothing about what happened. The summary statement merely says that "David prevailed over the Philistine with sling and stone; there was no sword in David's hand." Yet in v. 57, ascribed to this same source, David appears before Saul "with the Philistine's head still in his hand." This seems to contradict the explicit statement in v. 50 and refer back directly to the description in v. 51 of Goliath's decapitation in the other source!

---

21. Ibid., 307. Wellhausen's position, however, seems to be much more ambivalent than McCarter suggests. See J. Lust, "The Story of David and Goliath in Hebrew and Greek," in *The Story of David and Goliath: Textual and Literary Criticism* (by D. Barthélemy et al.; OBO 73; Göttingen: Vandenhoeck & Ruprecht / Freiburg: Éditions Universitaires, 1986), 5-6.
22. Ibid.

Emanuel Tov

Emanuel Tov, in his study of the composition of 1 Sam 16-18,[23] undertakes a meticulous comparison between the MT and the LXX[B] or Old Greek, in which he pays attention, not only to the large pluses of the MT, but also to the smaller variant readings and a number of pluses in LXX, "ranging from single words to complete sentences."[24] Tov's primary purpose is to refute the view that the Greek text reflects a harmonizing abridgement of an earlier Hebrew text, and in particular, one that was the work of the Greek translator, although he concedes that some exponents of the abridgement theory "stressed that the translator was not likely to omit such large sections and that he therefore probably found a short Hebrew text in front of him."[25] Tov undertakes to examine the "translation technique" of the Greek translator in order to determine whether he used a "free approach" to the text and therefore would be more inclined to harmonistic revision or whether his translation is "literal" and thus less inclined to change the text or introduce into it his own exegetical interpretations of the Hebrew. Tov examines five aspects of the Greek translator's technique: "(1) linguistic versus exegetical renderings of individual elements in the text; (2) adherence to the word order of the Hebrew text; (3) qualitative representation; (4) consistency in translation equivalents; and (5) Hebraisms in the translation."[26] Based on an examination of these criteria, he concludes that "the analysis shows that the translator of 1 Samuel 16-18 remained relatively faithful to the Hebrew text, and it is therefore unlikely that he would have omitted 44 percent of the text. In other words, the Greek translation was based on a short Hebrew text containing only that part of the story presently found in the LXX . . . ; the remaining material, now found *only* in the Masoretic Text, had not been added to that short text."[27]

---

23. E. Tov, "The Composition of 1 Samuel 16-18 in the Light of the Septuagint Version," in *Empirical Models for Biblical Criticism* (ed. J. H. Tigay; Philadelphia: University of Pennsylvania Press, 1985), 97-130. See also an earlier version, although published later, idem, "The Nature of the Differences between MT and the LXX," in *The Story of David and Goliath: Textual and Literary Criticism* (by D. Barthélemy et al.; OBO 73; Göttingen: Vandenhoeck & Ruprecht / Freiburg: Éditions Universitaires, 1986), 19-46.

24. Tov, "Composition," 99.

25. Ibid., 100.

26. Ibid., 106.

27. Ibid.

These arguments are quite persuasive and seem to clearly rule out the possibility that the Greek translator was responsible for any abridgement of the Hebrew text that he had before him. However, it does not rule out all the possibilities that the LXX reflects a shortened text, such as the view of exponents of the abridgement theory who see the shortening and harmonization as the work of a Hebrew scribe, resulting in an abridged Hebrew text that was then used by the Greek translator. Tov does acknowledge that there is some parallel between the Qumran text of 1 Sam 11 in 4QSam[a] and MT (as well as LXX) in which the Qumran text has five additional lines in 1 Sam 11:1. What he does not say is that in this case there are strong arguments for the long text being the more original, in spite of all the other textual witnesses to the shorter text. This matter will need to be taken up below. The only argument that Tov offers against the theory that the abridgement took place on the level of the Hebrew text is that the motive of harmonization explains not all of the minuses in the LXX but only a few of them, and it does not account for the fact that so many other doublets and contradictions were allowed to remain in the shorter text.[28] This is certainly a valid argument that will need to be addressed.

In addition, Tov's view does not even rule out the possibility that a Greek translator originally translated faithfully a long text as reflected in the MT but subsequently an editor tried to correct the text by eliminating what was regarded as unnecessary duplication. This is the critique of Tov's view suggested by D. W. Gooding, and he points to the scholarship of the Alexandrians in their treatment of Homer.[29] It is not certain, however, whether these scholars of Homer are a suitable parallel. It is true that they marked many passages in Homer with critical signs as un-Homeric, but they did not actually remove them or produce a new standard text on that basis.[30] And the reasons for all of their decisions are not entirely clear. A development such as this could hardly have taken place before the mid-2nd century B.C.E., and the theory would further suggest that biblical scribes and scholars emulated Homeric scholarship in their treatment of the Greek Bible. If the eminent scholars of Alexandria could not create a shortened text of Homer as the standard text, then it is unlikely that this

---

28. Ibid., 117–18.
29. "Response by D. W. Gooding," in *The Story of David and Goliath: Textual and Literary Criticism* (by D. Barthélemy et al.; OBO 73; Göttingen: Vandenhoeck & Ruprecht / Freiburg: Éditions Universitaires, 1986), 99.
30. See my *Edited Bible*, 35–46

could have happened in this way with the LXX. Therefore, if the LXX represents an abridgment, then it probably occurred in the Hebrew *Vorlage*.

Like McCarter, Tov opts for the view that the differences between the pluses of the MT and the LXX stories represent two different, self-contained versions, without actually addressing any of the problems noted above. This means that he must employ the services of a redactor as the one who conflated the two versions. The shorter text of the LXX was his basic text into which he fitted details from the second text, even though they were contradictory to the first. Tov cannot explain why he added this second source, apart from the vague notion of preserving "certain traditions and details that were not in version 1."[31] The redactor must be held responsible for creating the problem of contradictions by this editorial activity but also for alleviating some of them by means of a few additions of his own. He also suggests that the editor added some of his own ideas, such as 17:50, but in that case there is nothing at all in the second version that tells how David killed Goliath. There is therefore no firm evidence to suggest that the second version was a self-contained story.

An alternative would be to suggest that all of the pluses in MT were the work of an author who deliberately expanded the older account represented by the text of the Old Greek. No redactor is necessary to account for the additions. These additions would need to be viewed as occurring very late in the transmission process and would not represent any "old traditions." The reasons for the additions would need to be sought within the content of the additions themselves.

Johan Lust

Another advocate of the view that the LXX represents the original text is J. Lust.[32] However, Lust wishes to modify our understanding of the extent of the LXX text by appealing to another witness to the Old Greek, that found in the *Sermo Hippolyti*, which has a reference to Jonathan's love for David (18:1b, [3], 4), when he "sees David carrying the head of Goliath in his hand."[33] This leads Lust to suggest that 18:1b, (3), 4 was part of OG but was lost through *parablepsis*, so that it followed on directly from 17:54 and

---

31. Tov, "Composition," 122.

32. See J. Lust, "The Story of David and Goliath in Hebrew and Greek," in *The Story of David and Goliath: Textual and Literary Criticism* (by D. Barthélemy et al.; OBO 73; Göttingen: Vandenhoeck & Ruprecht / Freiburg: Éditions Universitaires, 1986), 5–18.

33. Ibid., 7.

hence was part of the original version of the story. The importance for including 18:1b, (3), 4 into the original short version for Lust is that it now
accounts for how Jonathan in 20:8 can make a reference back to the covenant in 18:3. Because 20:8 is present in OG, the inclusion of 18:3 in OG as
well would solve a serious problem for advocates of the shorter original
text. This conclusion, however, is not quite so clear. First, the reference to
Jonathan's seeing David carrying the head of Goliath "in his hand" looks
like a more direct reference to 17:57b, and because the sermon is not a direct quotation at this point, it would rather argue that Hippolytus was familiar with the whole unit in 17:55–18:4. In addition, Barthélemy points
out in his response to Lust that there is strong evidence that Hippolytus
made use of other forms of the biblical text in addition to the OG, as did
Josephus.[34] Consequently, the problem of the reference to the prior covenant in 20:8 still remains.

Lust admits that McCarter's argument that the pluses in the MT can be
read as an independent story is weak, and he states, "Not all the arguments
against the shortening hypothesis are equally valid. Nevertheless, the basic
ones remain sufficiently strong. Intentional shortening is unlikely."[35] Lust
also admits, following Wellhausen, that 1 Sam 17, even in the short version, does not easily follow 16:14–23 and therefore must be a later insertion into the story. Lust further proposes that the MT may represent an
expanded, long text, of the type that one finds at Qumran among pentateuchal texts, and that both text types existed side by side, the shorter
text type leading to the LXX and the longer one to the MT. Without evidence that long and short texts of 1 Samuel did exist at Qumran, this becomes quite hypothetical.

On the level of literary analysis, Lust attempts a number of schemes in
which he sees a kind of concentric structure, with 17:1–11 balancing vv.
32–40, leaving the "addition," vv. 12–31, in the middle, which he views as
interrupting the sequence. However, one could argue that precisely because
of its central position and its theme of introducing the hero who changes
the whole momentum of the events, the block of text is vital to the whole.
Lust also treats the literary art reflected in the combat scene in vv. 42–54, to
which the epilogue in vv. 55–58 does not belong, but vv. 42–54 has a differ-

34. "Response de D. Barthélemy," in *The Story of David and Goliath: Textual and
Literary Criticism* (by D. Barthélemy et al.; OBO 73; Göttingen: Vandenhoeck & Ruprecht / Freiburg: Éditions Universitaires, 1986), 97.
35. Ibid, 11.

ent structure from the rest of the short text. And Lust must also strain to make 18:1, 3–4 belong to the literary structure of the short text as well.

Regarding the plus vv. 12–31 in the MT, Lust makes much of the comparison with 1 Sam 9:1–10:16, in order to understand the literary genre of the story. He is primarily concerned with the older level of this Saul story and not its later development by Dtr, and sees it as a kind of "fairy tale" or "romantic epic." This comparison will be greatly developed by Auld and Ho, discussed below, so I will not comment on this comparison here. However, in a response to Gooding, Lust does make some observations about how the original story in 17:12–31 was made to fit the larger literary context, especially with respect to the similarities between 17:12–16 and the parallel in 16:1–13.[36] He is able to show that the older introduction of David in the Goliath story has been subtly changed to make it conform to the episode in 16:1–13. This observation would, of course, apply whether one preferred the hypothesis of the short text or the long text as original. To my mind, Lust's literary observations are his most important contribution to the literary discussion, and I will give more attention to it below.

Ralph Klein

A position similar to that of Lust in support of the view that LXX[B] represents the oldest version of the story is reflected in the approach of Ralph Klein.[37] The primary difference that Klein has with McCarter is that he does not see the pluses of the MT as reflecting a separate, independent account.[38] He therefore also rejects the view that 17:14b–16, 23b, and 31 (as well as 18:10–11, 17b, 29b) are redactional harmonizations. Klein further argues that 17:41 and 49b are lacking in the LXX because of *parablepsis*, which would make McCarter's case even weaker. Klein states his solution to the textual problem: "the Hebrew text has been expanded in 17:12–31, 50, 55–58 and 18:1–5 by a series of excerpts from one or more alternate accounts."[39] This would also hold true for the pluses in 18:6a, 10–11, 17–19, and 29b–30, as well as some shorter glosses within 18:8, 12, 21, 26–28.[40] Klein continues: "Since these additions are not internally consistent nor do we know their extent or their non-canonical function, it is futile to interpret

---

36. Ibid., 90–91.
37. Klein, *1 Samuel*, 168–83. Klein's view is quite independent from Lust's treatment.
38. Ibid., 173–74.
39. Ibid., 174.
40. Ibid., 187.

them separately from their present context."[41] While this clearly rejects Mc-Carter's approach to print and interpret the pluses in the MT as a separate story, it is used by Klein to treat the "recension" in the MT as a final canonical form. Klein accepts the fact that the additions are no earlier than the 4th century B.C.E., but he wants to allow for the possibility that their composition may be much older than their addition to the Hebrew. An early dating for these additions is strongly disputed, as we will see below. It also assumes that the additions were drawn from a corpus of earlier texts and not composed at the time when the additions were actually made.

Graeme Auld and C. Y. S. Ho

A. G. Auld and C. Y. S. Ho begin their study of the David and Goliath story with a review of Barthélemy, Gooding, Lust, and Tov to clarify the current positions on the composition of this story.[42] They side with Lust and Tov on the text-critical evidence that the shorter version is the more original but not on the view that they reflect two separate stories. Auld and Ho do not believe, against Tov, that the LXX proves that a truncated version could not have taken place prior to the Greek translation, and they complain that no reason is given for the fact that the "editor" wanted to "create an amalgam out of the two stories."[43] Concerning Barthélemy and Gooding, who opt for the longer version, Auld and Ho point out that, whereas Barthélemy allows for this version to be the result of several sources, Gooding emphasizes there is less discrepancy within the story and its context than is emphasized by scholars and a much greater unity to the whole. However, this position of the literary unity of a longer text Auld and Ho reject.

The way in which Auld and Ho address the argument for the unity of the text is to suggest the possibility "that the pluses may be expansions by a skilful editor."[44] This creates a kind of self-confirming argument. When there are contradictions and tensions in the text, it is evidence of an unskillful editor conflating different stories, but when the story shows a clear unity, in spite of the text-critical evidence, then it is evidence of a "skilful" editor. "Artistic qualities and internal consistency can be explained in terms of either original unity or good editing."[45] In place of a parallel ver-

---

41. Ibid., 174.
42. A. G. Auld and C. Y. S. Ho, "The Making of David and Goliath," *JSOT* 56 (1992): 19–39.
43. Ibid., 20.
44. Ibid., 21.
45. Ibid., 21–22.

sion of the David and Goliath story, Auld and Ho suggest another possibility: "What about literary creation by a redactor out of existing material in 1 Samuel?"[46] That seems to me a case of special pleading and rules out any kind of evidence that would argue decisively for the role of an author.[47]

Following the earlier suggestion by Lust, noted above, Auld and Ho proceed to demonstrate a number of similarities and interconnection between the pluses in the MT and other texts in 1 Samuel, particularly those in the accounts of Saul's anointing in 1 Sam 9:1–10:16. The supposed parallel between David and Saul is particularly important to Auld and Ho for their understanding of the redactor's intention in modifying the earlier short version of the story. The basic list of similarities that are proposed and based on which Auld and Ho elaborate their discussion is the following:

a. A man has a son (9.1 // 17.12).
b. He sets a minor task to his son (9.3 // 17.17–18).
c. The hero meets the leader of his country (9.17ff. // 17.55–58).
d. 'On that day' is used in 9.24 and 18.2.
e. The hero succeeds the leader.[48]

One is rather struck by the complete triviality of this list. There are many references to men having sons and in 1 Sam 16 it is already mentioned in two different literary units that David was the son of Jesse. The parallel with 16:1–13 is particularly close and requires special attention, which is largely ignored by Auld and Ho. The tasks set for the two sons are also altogether different. The search for the lost donkeys in the Saul story is not trivial but basic to the whole story. It is the primary motivation for the action throughout the story, including the encounter with Samuel, and although it ultimately becomes subordinated in the present form of the story, it still remains a feature in the story until the end in 10:14–16. Nor is there any suggestion in the story that Saul's mission was a failure. Indeed, the asses were found and that is what was important. In the case of David's task, it is merely an excuse used by the narrator to get David from tending the sheep to the battle line, 17:17–22; it has nothing to do with the rest of the action and is not the reason for David's encounter with Saul. In fact, because David

---

46. Ibid., 24.

47. But this is just the long-standing abuse of the notion of editor. There is, in fact, no need for any editor, whether skilful or unskillful. The roles attributed to editors in the whole discussion are totally inappropriate. See my *Edited Bible*.

48. Auld and Ho, "The Making of David and Goliath," 24.

merely deposits the items with the "keeper of the baggage," he does not himself actually distribute the items as he was told, and he certainly does not return a report to his father concerning his brothers' welfare. So David can hardly be commended for fulfilling his errand as Auld and Ho suggest.

A much closer parallel to David's errand is found in the Joseph story, in which Joseph, the second youngest, is sent by his father to find his older brothers who are rather hostile to him and to report to their father on their welfare. It is also the case that this errand, from which he does not return, changes his whole destiny. There is no need to think that there is any direct connection between the Saul story and the Joseph story, and therefore the same applies to the Saul and David stories, as I have suggested above (p. 129). Even the similarity between the Joseph and David stories may simply be the use of a common folktale motif and nothing more.

Regarding item c above, the Saul story in 1 Sam 9:1–10:17 does not actually present Samuel as the leader of the country but portrays him only as a local seer. It is the larger context in 1 Sam 7–8 supplied by Dtr that gives to Samuel this role as well as the task of king-maker. Samuel is actually the rejected leader in 1 Sam 8. Samuel's role in his encounter with Saul is entirely different from David's role in his encounter with Saul in 1 Sam 17:55–58. In fact, the meeting between David and Saul has its obvious parallel in 1 Sam 16:14–23, with its repeated emphasis on David as "the son of Jesse." To this parallel we will return below. We may also quickly dismiss, in item d above, the fact that the phrase "on that day," ביום ההוא, occurs in both stories. The phrase is so common in Samuel that its presence in the two texts cannot be viewed as significant. This also applies to the occurrence of questions in the stories. Finally, concerning item e above, the hero's succession as leader occurs so much later outside the narrative in both cases that it can hardly be used for comparison between the two units themselves.

There are, in fact, quite a number of parallels in 1 Samuel, most of them within the David and Saul story, and many of them have nothing to do with long and short texts. While there are a number of them within 1 Sam 17:55–18:30, there is only one significant one in 1 Sam 17:1–54, and that is within the unit 17:12–15, the introduction of Jesse and his sons, which is parallel to the introduction of Jesse and his family in 1 Sam 16:1–13. Furthermore, the dependence of 17:12–15 on 16:1–13 is fairly obvious. The fact that Jesse has eight sons is important in the development of the narrative in 16:6–13, but the reference in 17:12 is incidental and leaves one to wonder why one of the sons who was not preoccupied with the sheep could not carry out the errand. In 16:6-9, the three oldest sons are named and the rest of the sons are left anonymous, and it is just these three sons, the author having given both their names and their order of birth, who are in the army under Saul in chap. 17. This can hardly be a coincidence. However, there is no reason in the second story for us to know their order of birth as there is in the first. Thus, it is clear that the story in 17:1-54 is entirely aware of the anointing of David in 16:1-13. But this episode, which is part of the much larger story in 15:1-16:13, is a later addition to the earlier introduction of David and his incorporation into Saul's army in 16:14-23.[49] So if 17:15 was intended to somehow take into account this earlier introduction, then it was part of the introduction of 17:12-15 as a whole and not just a later "redactional" addition of this verse alone.

The question that remains to be decided is whether the pluses in 17:1-54 belong to a "redactional" addition or the unit as a whole is the work of a single author. Once this issue is decided then one may turn to consider the text in 17:55-18:30, which is of an entirely different character. It is the complete mixing of these issues in the past, because of the minuses in LXX, which have caused so much confusion.

Stephen Pisano

A serious case, however, can be made for the view that the long text represents the original version and that the shorter text of LXX is based on a Hebrew abridgement of the text. While this view has been advocated by a number of scholars in the past, only a few of the more recent presentations will be reviewed here. Two scholars who have dealt primarily with the text-critical aspects of the case for the longer text are S. Pisano and D. Barthé-lemy.[50] Pisano points out that, though the longer text of the MT clearly has a number of contradictions that reflect more than one tradition, this problem is only partly solved by the shorter text, and contradictions with its larger context still occur.[51] David, in 17:38-40 (part of the shorter text) "is portrayed as being unused to the soldier's armor although in 16:18 he is called a 'man of war.'"[52] In addition, "it is precisely at those points in the text which are problematic that LXX registers a 'minus' (e.g., 17:12 and

---

49. See above, pp. 121-123.

50. S. Pisano, *Additions or Omissions in the Books of Samuel* (OBO 57. Freiburg: Universitätsverlag, 1984), 78-86. On Barthélemy, see below, pp. 149-150.

51. See also S. R. Driver, *Notes on the Hebrew Text of the Books of Samuel* (Oxford: Clarendon, 1913), 150.

52. Pisano, *Additions*, 80.

17:55), thus indicating an attempt at harmonization and coherence in the narrative on the part of LXX."[53] Pisano also makes clear that the introduction of David in 17:12, while it has the appearance of being a new section, cannot do without the preceding introduction of Goliath so that David's appearance at this point is appropriate to the larger story.

An important issue in the discussion is the text of 17:36 in the LXX, because in this case the text of the LXX appears to have a plus in comparison with the MT. Moreover, this plus resembles closely the parallel text in 17:26, part of the longer MT. This can be seen by setting down the two texts side by side, using McCarter's translation,[54] with the parallel text in italics:

> 17:26 (MT) But David had been speaking to the men who were standing with him. So he said, "What will be done for the man who *strikes down that Philistine and takes [this] reproach away from Israel? For who is this uncircumcised Philistine that he should defy the ranks of the Living God?*"

> 17:36b (LXX[B]) So the uncircumcised Philistine will be like one of them: shall I not go and *strike him down and remove the reproach from Israel today? For who is that uncircumcised fellow that he should defy the ranks of the Living God?*

With this, compare the shorter MT text:

> 17:36b (MT) So the uncircumcised Philistine will be like one of them. *For he has defied the ranks of the Living God.*

Those like McCarter who maintain that the LXX text of 17:36 is original must assume that the text of 17:26 (MT) was an interpolation into the text modeled on 17:36. This would then require an explanation for the shorter text of 17:36 in the MT, and here McCarter, following earlier scholars, suggests that the MT has suffered from haplography because of the repetition of הערל הזה, which then required the restoration of כאחד מהם, "as one of them," to make sense of the text. But if part of the longer text was restored by a scribe collating the text, then why not the whole text? Pisano, however, asserts that the motivation for elimination of the insult to Israel has been deliberately added to 17:36 in the LXX once the earlier text was omitted. He concludes: "No apparent reason may be adduced to show that MT's shorter form in v. 36 is not original. If such was the case, then it is difficult to maintain that the earliest Greek text had no knowledge of vv. 11–31."[55] Pisano

---

53. Ibid.
54. McCarter, *I Samuel*, 283, 300.
55. Pisano, *Additions*, 83.

also makes reference to the fact that 1 Sam 20:8 (which is common to both the MT and the LXX) refers to an earlier covenant that had been made between David and Jonathan, and this can only refer to the one in 18:3, which is mentioned only in the longer text. As we have seen, this text causes considerable difficulties for those who advocate the shorter text of LXX as the original.

What also appears quite clear is that whatever text is original, there is no smooth transition between the story of David and Goliath and what follows in 18:6-30. David's remarkable feat is never mentioned again in this group of texts. The transition of 18:5 to the unit in vv. 6b-9, which is made in v. 6a (MT), "As they were coming home, when David came from killing the Philistine," is quite awkward, but the complete lack of any transition between 17:54 and 18:6b seems even more difficult, and 18:5 + 6b may simply go back to 16:23, where David is a regular member of Saul's military entourage. Pisano also points out that Josephus was well aware of the inconsistencies in the text and attempted to harmonize the contradictions in his own history. Pisano sums up his view:

> What was originally a conglomerate of two or more independent traditions concerning David's youth and early association with Saul was amputated by LXX in order to present one more or less unified story. It was cut up in such a way, however, that the particulars of the once-separate traditions were not respected, as their concatenation in the primitive text was seen by the LXX editors, looking at a coherent flow of narrative, simply as a series of contradictions which had to be rectified.[56]

Dominique Barthélemy and D. W. Gooding

D. Barthélemy gives primary attention to the literary criticism of the David and Goliath story, perhaps because his student, Pisano, has dealt so thoroughly with the text-critical issues.[57] He seeks to define the problem by understanding the nature of the relationship between the narrative within 1 Sam 17 and what comes before and after it, the extent to which it represents a continuity or discontinuity, and the internal relationship between the supposed pluses of the MT and the shorter text of the LXX. Concerning the two accounts in chap. 16, it is 16:1-13 that has a number of connections with chap. 17, in both the shorter and longer accounts. Thus,

---

56. Ibid., 86.

57. D. Barthélemy, "Trois niveaux d'analyse," in *The Story of David and Goliath: Textual and Literary Criticism* (by D. Barthélemy et al.; OBO 73; Göttingen: Vandenhoeck & Ruprecht / Freiburg: Éditions Universitaires, 1986), 47-54.

the description of David in 16:12 as "ruddy with beautiful eyes, and hand-some," אדמוני עם־יפה עינים וטוב ראי, is similar to 17:42: "ruddy with good looks," אדמוני עם־יפה מראה. The description of Jesse's sons, with Eliab as the eldest and David the youngest and the description of David as shepherd all correspond closely. Barthélemy is of the view that 16:1–13 is later that the story in chap. 17 and drew its description from this story. Yet he must ad-mit that some of the features in 17:12–16, such as the number of Jesses's sons being eight, are more appropriate to the account in 16:1–13, so that he must assume some additions by an "editor."

Barthélemy disputes the thesis of McCarter that in the text of the *Vorlage* of the LXX, the description of David and his place in court in 16:14–23 was fully integrated with the account in 17:32–54 before the later addition of 17:12–31. Barthélemy points out that the David that is presented as a young lad who keeps sheep in 17:12–31 is much more consistent with the accomplished warrior in 16:18. Likewise, the song of the women in 18:7 does not fit after 17:54 but must presuppose the transition in 18:5. As in the case of Pisano, Barthélemy points to the reference in 20:8 to the prior covenant in 18:3 and the fact that the LXX in 17:36 seems to have been modified by an addition to conform with the parallel text in 17:26, which suggests knowledge of the longer version.

D. W. Gooding likewise advocates the view that the story of David and Goliath is a unity, but he goes much beyond this and attempts to defend the thesis that the whole of 1 Sam 16–18 is a unity and belongs to a larger complex in Samuel that is all of one piece.[58] In this respect, Gooding com-pares himself with those Homeric scholars who identify themselves as "unitarians," namely, those who advocate the complete unity of Homer against the critics or "analyists."[59] This is an unfortunate attempt to paint the two approaches to the problem of the story of David and Goliath in an extreme way. Let me offer just one telling comment from the respected clas-sicist E. R. Dodd on the unitarians: "The 'naïve unitarians' . . . held a fun-damentalist faith in the integrity of the Homeric Scriptures; their religion forbade them to make any concession whatever to the infidel, although it compelled them at times to fall back on arguments as unconvincing as the

---

58. D. W. Gooding, "An Approach to the Literary and Textual Problems in the David-Goliath Story," *The Story of David and Goliath: Textual and Literary Criticism* (by D. Barthélemy et al.; OBO 73; Göttingen: Vandenhoeck & Ruprecht / Freiburg: Éditions Universitaires, 1986), 55–86.

59. On this development in Homeric scholarship, see my *Edited Bible*, 158.

worst efforts of the analysts."[60] By means of this unfortunate comparison, Gooding presents himself as just such a "fundamentalist" who must demonstrate at all cost the complete unity of the text, and much of his argumentation bears the same quality of exaggeration and caricature that is common among his classicist counterparts.

This approach allows Gooding to view the narrative with which he is dealing not just as a piece of literature but also as a report about actual events so that he can reconstruct what was likely to have taken place and greatly augment the material that is actually given in the story. Thus, when he is faced with the obvious contradiction between 17:55-58 in which Saul inquires about who is David's father and the prior introduction of David into Saul's court in 16:14-23 in which he has been told by members of the court that David is the son of Jesse, Gooding dismisses this problem. He explains:

> This discrepancy depends on the insistence that 16,18-22 must mean nothing less than that Saul informed himself fully on everything to do with David's father, and on a similar insistence that 17,55-58 must not mean anything more than that Saul was interested to know the *name* of David's father. Neither insistence is necessary, nor, in the light of the narrative thought-flow, reasonable. Having been supplied by his servants with an acceptable harpist, it was natural for Saul to "request" (i.e. command) his father to let the young man stay at the royal house. It is not true to life to imagine that Saul thereafter necessarily remembered the name of David's father, or cared twopence about him, let alone investigated his background, family and all about him. Similarly, it is not true to life to imagine that in 17,55-58 Saul is simply concerned to know the name of David's father. Saul has just promised to give his daughter in marriage to the man who kills Goliath, and to make his father's house free in Israel (17,25). Naturally, when Saul sees David actually going out to meet Goliath, and even more so when he sees him returning triumphant, Saul will be concerned to know not just the name of, but everything about, David's father and the family which, if he keeps his promise, is now to be allied by marriage to the royal family.[61]

This style of argumentation is typical of "unitarian" or "fundamentalistic" treatment of the text and is only one of many such examples throughout Gooding's treatment of the David and Goliath story. It assumes that the

---

60. E. R. Dodd, "Homer," in *Fifty Years of Classical Scholarship* (ed. M. Platnauer; New York: Barnes & Noble, 1954), 11.
61. Gooding, "An Approach," 79-80.

episodes in question are actual reports of past events, not just story narratives, and therefore he can fill in all the necessary details not in the story that are "true to life," which can easily reconcile the seemingly contradictory episodes. Thus, for Gooding Saul conveniently forgets David's patronymic, "son of Jesse," even though in later episodes he often uses it instead of his name David.[62] And all of the court, who recommended David as the son of Jesse, suffers from the same forgetfulness. Thus David, who becomes Saul's close aid-de-camp and whom Saul loves, remains almost a complete stranger to him, although he was also hired as a "man of war." Gooding further connects the request for the name of Jesse to the reward that has been offered, but we hear nothing of the granting of this reward; the subsequent offers of marriage are made for quite-different reasons and nothing is said about any connection to the slaying of Goliath. One could go on at great length about what is or is not "true to life," and little within the David and Goliath story seems to me remotely "true to life." But one must remain within the parameters of the story, because a vivid imagination could make any set of problematic texts work. This is the antithesis to literary criticism and has always been the case since the rise of historical criticism. It does not help in arriving at a solution here.

Alexander Rofé

Another example of the case for the longer text, based on its literary characteristics, has been set forth by Alexander Rofé,[63] and it is to this consideration that we will now turn. Rofé points out that at the base of the entire text is a folktale about how a mere shepherd boy is able to overcome a foreign champion, in spite of the great disparity in size, military experience and fighting equipment and as a result he becomes a national hero and the future king. Furthermore, everything is at stake in this struggle because the side that loses must submit in servitude to the other. For the champion who represents the Israelite side, the king promises wealth, his daughter's hand in marriage, and a special status for his family, free from obligations of royal tax and service. The facts that he is the youngest son of Jesse, that he is disparaged by his brothers, who are real soldiers, that he must make his case before the king by citing his prior victories over lion and bear in

---

62. See 1 Sam 20:27, 30–31; 22:7–9, 13; 25:10. More on this below.

63. A. Rofé, "The Battle of David and Goliath: Folktale, Theology, Eschatology," in *Judaic Perspectives on Ancient Israel* (ed. J. Neusner et al.; Philadelphia: Fortress, 1987), 117–51.

order to become the people's champion without the royal equipment, and that he carries off the severed head of the giant as his trophy all point to the totally unrealistic world of the fairy tale. The folkloristic features of the story are evenly distributed throughout the whole work and argue for its original unity.

Furthermore, it is into this folktale that the author has built his own theological elements, which are set alongside the folktale elements and even in some tension with them. As Rofé explains, this theological theme, which is interwoven with the folktale, "comprises the contrast between the uncircumcised Philistine, who 'has taunted the armies of the living God' (vv. 26, 36) and 'the Lord of Hosts, the God of the armies of Israel, whom you have taunted' (v. 45). Thus, the defeat of the Philistine testifies not to the superiority of shepherds' slingshots over battle armor but to David's faith. David fights and will win 'that all the earth might know that Israel has a God and that all who are here might know that God does not save through the sword and the spear—the war is the Lord's' (vv. 46-47)."[64] It is this theme that runs through both the part of the story preserved in the LXX and the pluses in the MT, and in both cases it represents an addition to the folkloristic theme.

This thesis may be demonstrated in the following way. The challenge of the Philistine champion is presented in great detail in 17:4-9 as a formidable foe and the basis for the folktale. However, to his speech there is added a second remark in v. 10: "And the Philistine said, 'I defy [חרף] the ranks of Israel this day. Give me a man and let us fight it out.'" This becomes the basic motif for the theological second theme as a supplement to the folkloristic first theme, and this combination is already present within "version 1" of Tov, in the LXX. After David is appropriately introduced and he arrives at the scene of battle in vv. 12-22, we are told that he heard the challenge of the Philistine, who "spoke the same words as previously" (v. 23), which are not repeated but refer back to the earlier remarks in vv. 8-10, especially v. 10. In v. 25, the Israelites are discussing among themselves this challenge by Goliath the Philistine: "Have you seen this fellow who comes forward? It is in order to taunt [חרף] Israel that he comes forward." This is followed by the description of the reward that will be made to the one who kills him: wealth, the daughter of the king in marriage, and special status for his family, the folkloristic theme. David then makes them repeat what has just been said, v. 26: "What will be done for the one who kills this Philistine and

---

64. Ibid., 118.

removes this disgrace [חרפה] hanging over Israel? Who is this uncircumcised Philistine that he taunts [חרף] the ranks of the living God?" The soldiers repeat the reward that was mentioned earlier in answer to the first
question, but David's second question is rhetorical and is meant to interpret the whole contest now as being between the uncircumcised, that is,
godless, foreigner and the true God of Israel. The taunting [חרף] has become an act of sacrilege. As Rofé further points out, this combination of the
folktale and the theological themes appears again in the dialogue between
David and Saul. David makes his case before Saul, based on the fact that he
has been able to kill a lion and a bear single-handed to defend his sheep,
and he can do the same against this uncircumcised Philistine.[65] To this,
David adds the theological reason for the anticipated defeat of Goliath: "because he has taunted [חרף] the ranks of the living God" (v. 36). To this, he
further adds the pious statement that the victory belongs ultimately to the
deity, "Yahweh . . . will also save me from the hand of this Philistine," to
which Saul replies, "Go and may Yahweh be with you" (v. 37).

At the climax of the battle scene, after Goliath taunts David and curses
him by his gods (vv. 41–44), we expect in the folktale that he would advance toward David to attack him while David responds and defeats him
(vv. 48–51). However, between these two points in the action is a long
speech by David that is full of references to the theological theme in which
David comes against this well-armed champion "in the name of Yahweh of
hosts, the God of the ranks of Israel whom you have taunted [חרף]" (v. 45).
In the language of holy war, it is Yahweh "who will deliver you into my
hand" so that both Goliath and all the forces of the Philistines will be killed
and become food for wild birds and animals in order that "all the earth will
know that there is a [true] God in Israel" (v. 46). And through this event
"the whole religious community (קהל) will know that Yahweh saves not by
sword or spear for the battle is Yahweh's and he will give you into our
hand" (v. 47). Rofé is certainly correct in asserting that the folkloristic motif of the great warrior against the shepherd boy is completely transformed
by the theological theme.

Now it seems to me that Rofé is quite justified in setting this analysis of
the two levels corresponding to the two themes, the folkloristic and the
theological, against the text-critical analysis of two sources or versions corresponding to the story in the LXX and the pluses of the MT. There is sim-

---

65. There is a close association in Near Eastern royal ideology between the heroic hunter and the victorious King. See Gen 10:8–12.

ply no correlation between these two approaches so that a choice must be made between them. Once one is convinced that the story of David and Goliath is a unity, at least within 17:1–54, in style, language, and themes, then there is no other option but to argue for the view that the Hebrew *Vorlage* of the LXX is indeed an abridgement, and Rofé offers a number of arguments in support of this view.[66] I will not repeat these but will simply point to one other example in 1 Samuel in which a Hebrew text of Qumran, 4QSam[a], also contains a plus of five lines in 1 Sam 11:1, against all the other known witnesses to Samuel (but not Josephus), and it is very widely accepted that in this case the longer text is the more original.[67] It must also be observed that in this case there is no obvious text-critical reason, such as haplography or other scribal mistake, so it could just as easily be a case of scribal abridgement. Now, as Rofé points out, there is evidence of harmonization between the story of David and Goliath in both its longer and shorter versions, the one by additions and the other by deletions. In neither case, however, has the process been very successful, and 1 Samuel is notorious for the number of doublets and contradictions that it contains. So, ancient scribes and authors seem less concerned about those matters than modern scholars.

Nevertheless, this still leaves open the question of the relationship between the story of David and Goliath and its larger context. If one adopts the view that the shorter version is original, then one must assume that the pluses in the MT that one finds in 1 Sam 18 also belong to this same source and are part of the same story as the rest. But in this case they are integrally related to the larger story of David in a way that the story of David and Goliath is not. However, if the MT is the original, then there is no need to make any such assumptions, and one must treat the literary analysis of chap. 18 in a quite-different way. This also raises very different questions about the nature of the possible harmonization within story of David and Goliath. It seems to me that at this point Rofé has not taken his own analysis seriously enough and has not worked out the nature of the relationship between chap. 17 with what precedes it in chap. 16 and what follows in chap. 18.

Another important issue that is dealt with in Rofé's study is his dating of the David and Goliath story. Rofé strongly criticizes the scholarly consensus that assigns an early date to the story, largely based on the notion that

---

66. See ibid., 119–23.
67. E. Tov, *Textual Criticism of the Hebrew Bible* (Minneapolis: Fortress, 1992), 342–44.

it constitutes a source for the story of David's rise, which itself is dated to the Davidic period. Instead of this approach, his method is to examine in detail the story itself with respect to its size and style of presentation, its distinctive vocabulary, its special idioms, the morphology of grammatical forms, and its syntax and features that reflect its social and historical environment.[68] On all of these matters, Rofé provides a massive amount of evidence with meticulous documentation to suggest that the work is a product of the late Persian period. This evidence extends quite uniformly throughout the whole of the longer version and cannot be explained away by the use of ascribing it to "redactional" additions. The implications of his analysis and conclusions as to the story's dating are very significant because they mean that the story must be viewed as later that Dtr, as well as later than any early account of David's rise. Indeed, it calls into question all of the usual schemes used for reconstructing the account of David's rise from 1 Sam 16–2 Sam 5. For the purpose of this present study it means that we must look again at the difficult problem of the relationship of the story of David and Goliath to its immediate context in 1 Sam 16 and 18, as well as some of its wider connections in the larger story of David.

Before turning to this task, I want to look at a recent criticism by Auld and Ho of Rofé's treatment of the story. They suggest that

> the complexity and ad hoc nature of Rofé's solution is thus easy to see. It says (1) that the original is not consistent and the contradictory parts are removed by the *Vorlage* of LXX, and (2) that those parts within the MT pluses . . . that tend to minimize the inconsistency are not original. One needs only to make a slight change to the literary criticism part of Rofé's paper to support an opposite hypothesis with the same theoretical strength as his: (a) the inconsistency detected by Rofé is traceable to interpolation, and (b) those elements taken by Rofé to be MT's attempt at harmonization are in fact evidence of an attempt to smooth out the inconsistency created by the interpolation of a large amount of parallel foreign materials.[69]

Does this way of solving the problem actually help? I think not. First, we are to attribute the pluses in MT to a skilful editor (and not a separate source) who created the materials in the additions by means of imitating features in the story of Saul that were all part of a larger corpus of texts. In doing so, he sometimes changed the whole character of the text imitated so that it resembled entirely the style, language, and perspective of the unit into which

---

68. Ibid., 123–34.
69. Auld and Ho, "The Making of David and Goliath," 23.

it was placed, as in the case of 17:12-31, but at other times he chose to retain the wording and style of the texts imitated, as in the case of 18:10-12, 30. Then, after this very skilful editor had done considerable damage to the consistency of the narrative, either he or a later editor tried to undo the damage by some rather unskillful additions in 17:15 and in shorter additions in other passages. However, the position that the LXX represents the shorter original text only has credibility if it is clear that the pluses of the MT all belong to the same hand, whether the author of a parallel account or a "skilful editor." In my view, this does not seem to me to be the case. The presentation in 17:1-54 seems to be so completely different from the rest in 17:55-18:30 that it is highly likely that there is more than one hand involved in the text, and the differences do not correspond in the least with the differences between the texts of the LXX and the MT. Furthermore, if one is not persuaded by the examples of imitation in the Saul story, then the so-called foreign material used by an editor to create the inconsistency in the David and Goliath story disappears, along with the editor.

Consequently, following the suggestions of Rofé, I accept the view that the story of David and Goliath, within the limits of 17:1-54, was an independent tale that developed in two stages. The first was a popular folk tale about David, the shepherd boy who defeated Goliath and thereby won the hand of the king's daughter and the other rewards promised by the king, eventually succeeding Saul on the throne in Jerusalem. This story was modified by a theological revision that played down the reward motive and gave to David a strong religious motive, making him a champion of the god of Israel against the uncircumcised infidel. It is this pious tale that was later incorporated into the larger story of David and Saul. All of this simply returns us to the central problem of the story, namely, what is the relationship of the story of David and Goliath to what precedes it and follows it? The answer to this question is altogether different if one views the LXX version of the story as the original and all the pluses as additions by a single later interpolator unrelated to what comes before or after chaps. 17-18, or if one views the MT as the original and then proceeds to a literary analysis without regard for the shorter text of LXX. So much focus has been given to the text-critical problem that this second alternative has not really been attempted.

The Story of David and Goliath within
Its Literary Context

The first question that must be asked is the relationship of 1 Sam 17:55-18:5 to the preceding story in 17:1-54. It should be fairly obvious that as soon as we move from the story of David's defeat of Goliath to the sequel in 17:55–18:5, we encounter some problems, not just the contradiction with 16:14–23, which everybody notes, but also with the immediately preceding unit. The ending in 17:54, "David took the head of the Philistine and brought it to Jerusalem, but his weapons he put in his own tent," does not fit well with the sequel in 17:55–18:5, even though the latter begins with a temporal return to the point in the story when David has left Saul to go and fight with Goliath. Immediately after David's killing the Philistine, he is brought by Abner to Saul "with the head of the Philistine still in his hand" (v. 57). He was presumably also loaded down with all of the weapons of Goliath as his spoils of war, but there is no appropriate opportunity, in what follows, for him to dispose of all these objects as indicated in v. 54. Furthermore, the gesture by Jonathan of equipping David with his armor seems a little superfluous if David has already acquired Goliath's armor and is still carrying it from the battle field. If the author of 17:1–54 is the same as 17:55–18:5, then he would certainly not have included the remark in 17:54, which is quite unnecessary and contradicts what follows. Consequently, we will interpret 17:55–18:5 as the work of a later author.

In this supplement to the story, we are introduced to two new characters who play an important role in the subsequent narratives. The first of these is Abner, the commander of the army, who will be mentioned again in 1 Sam 20:25 and 26:5, 7, 14–15 as being closely associated with Saul. In the first of these (1 Sam 20:25), his identity is assumed, but in the second he is identified both by his patronymic and by his rank, "Abner son of Ner, commander of his army" (1 Sam 26:5). He also plays an important role in the struggle of the Saulides against David in 2 Sam 2:8–4:12, and again he is introduced with both patronymic and rank, "Abner son of Ner, commander of Saul's army" (2 Sam 2:8). This suggests a close association with all of these texts. The other new personage in 1 Sam 17:55–18:5 is Jonathan, and he appears quite abruptly, without any identification, which is simply assumed. This is in contrast to the unit in 1 Sam 19:1–7, where Jonathan is clearly and repeatedly identified as Saul's son, and we are informed as if for the first time of Jonathan's close association with David. In 1 Sam 20, which is an extended parallel to 19:1–7, David meets with Jonathan to speak of Saul's threat on his life. The close relationship between David and Jonathan is assumed, as well as the fact that Jonathan is Saul's son, and a direct connection is made in 20:8 to the earlier covenant between David and Jonathan in 18:3. It is here in 20:25 that we also find both Abner and Jonathan in close regular attendance to Saul, which is precisely what must be assumed in 17:55–18:4. So there can be little doubt that 1 Sam 20 belongs to the same source as 17:55–18:4.[70]

Now scholars have all taken notice of the fact that the suggested ignorance of Saul as to David's identity in 17:55–58 contradicts the clear introduction in 16:18–22, where Saul refers to David by name and knows that he is the son of Jesse, the Bethlehemite. However, what is curious is that Saul asks Abner not for David's name but who his father is, and when David appears, needs to inform Saul not of his name but only who his father is: "I am the son of your servant Jesse, the Bethlehemite" (v. 58). What is significant is that in some episodes Saul deliberately refers to David by his patronymic, "son of Jesse," in a derogatory sense (1 Sam 20:27, 30–31; 22:7–9, 13; see also 25:10). As we shall see, all of these texts belong together to a restrictive group, whereas, with the exception of these texts, the patronymic does not continue in any of the other texts after 1 Sam 17. So the point of the unit is not to identify David for the first time—his name is not used in direct speech in the whole unit—but to highlight this patronymic, "son of Jesse," and its future use by Saul.

The unit in 18:1–5 also deserves closer scrutiny. Jonathan's initial encounter with David is directly linked to the preceding unit by the initial temporal clause: "When he [David] had finished speaking to Saul" (v. 1). However, after Jonathan's love for David is declared by the narrator at precisely that moment, one would expect its continuation in vv. 3–4, which speak of a covenant, "because he [Jonathan] loved him [David] as his own person," followed by Jonathan's giving David his personal armor. Instead, this scene is interrupted in v. 2: "Saul took him that day and would not let him return to his father's house," which recapitulates the statement in 16:22. This provides the necessary transition from the story of David and Goliath to the larger story of David and Saul. Nevertheless, the verse breaks the temporal continuity between v. 1 and v. 3, even though it provides the necessary condition under which the actions in vv. 3–4 make sense. It cannot be eliminated as merely "redactional." At the same time, it has its natural continuation in v. 5. What all of this suggests is that the unit in 17:55–18:4(5) is a highly artificial literary construction made up of components that use, or depend on, elements in the larger David and Saul story.

The limits of this unit in 17:55–18:4(5) also constitute a problem because they have been largely dictated by the notions that the shorter LXX is

---

70. Further discussion of the David-Jonathan episodes will be taken up below.

the original and that the pluses of the MT all belong to an alternate source or addition. This would mean that the unit extends to 18:6a. However, if we reject this assumption and analyze the MT as the original text, then there is no need to follow a source division of this sort. The statement in 18:6, as it stands, is obviously confused because it is made to serve two different purposes. On the one hand, it seems clearly to continue the statement in v. 5, which refers to various military campaigns in which David served under Saul. On the other hand, it makes reference specifically to David's feat in slaying the Philistine, which does not easily fit the song of the women. There are, however, obvious syntactical problems with the opening clauses, "When they were coming back, *when David returned*, from fighting the Philistine," in which two temporal infinitive clauses are set next to each other. It seems clear that the second one is an interpolation into the first; indeed one would simply expect the statement: "when they were coming back from fighting the Philistines" [הפלשתי]ם ויהי בבואם מהכות את־הפלשתי]ם (omitting בשוב דוד). This would follow directly from v. 5 and suggest that it was part of the older story and originally continued from 16:21–23, before the story of David and Goliath was added to the text.

There are only a limited number of references to David's killing of "the Philistine" in the subsequent narratives (1 Sam 19:5, 21:10, 22:10). Two of these (21:10, 22:10) occur in the account of the massacre of the priests of Nob, which also contains references to the patronymic "son of Jesse," as we saw above. Because the reference to "the Philistine" is secondary in 18:6, this looks like another clue to isolating this secondary stratum in the David and Saul story. Consequently, I would limit the preceding unit to 17:55–18:4 and regard it as an addition to the story of David and Goliath, which used the gloss about David's killing Goliath in v. 6a to integrate the story into the older David and Saul story. This unit in 17:55–18:4 is part of a larger complex of additions that have been inserted into the older narrative at various points.

This brings us to the observations made by a number of the scholars above that there are some instances within the David and Goliath story that betray the activity of a "redactor" attempting to connect this story with the preceding narrative. The most notable instance is in the scene that introduces Jesse's family and hence David himself into the story. As noted above, Lust has observed that there are some obvious interconnections between the unit in 17:12–15 and 16:1–13.[71] We have, first of all, in 17:12 the very

---

71. Lust, "The Story of David and Goliath," 90–91.

awkward introduction "Now David was the son of an Ephrathite, this very one from Bethlehem in Judah, named Jesse, who had eight sons."[72] The syntax of the whole sentence is very unusual, as S. R. Driver observed.[73] Lust shows from a number of examples that, if a hero is introduced at the outset of a story, it follows a clear pattern: name, patronymic, place of origin or tribal identity.[74] However, in all these instances, this is immediately followed by an account of the hero's deed. Thus, Lust concludes that the original text "has been tampered with," and on the basis of Judg 13:2ff., 1 Sam 1:1ff., and 1 Sam 9:1ff. they yield this pattern:

(wife/son) ולו ... (name) ושמו ... (locality) ויהי איש מן

In these cases, the father was introduced first and then the wife, who subsequently bears a child (the hero) or names the son directly. When applied to this case, it would yield this text: "There was an Ephrathite from Bethlehem of Judah and his name was Jesse, and he had eight [four] sons" (17:12*). It is only subsequent to this that the sons are introduced and David is identified as the youngest. It also seems clear that originally the story indicated that Jesse had only four sons, which necessitated his sending David to the front because the three eldest were there in service with Saul.

What this suggests is that the text has been deliberately modified to make a connection with the story in 16:1–13. In the earlier story, it is important that David is seen as the youngest of eight sons. The first three are specifically named in chronological order, just as they are in 17:13b, but in the latter case there is no need to know the names and order of the second and third sons as there is in 16:8-9. The repetition of 17:13a in v. 14b strongly suggests a textual expansion. The awkward insertion of "this very one" הזה into the text also looks like a conscious reference back to the mention of Jesse in chap. 16. In addition, it has frequently been noted that 17:15 is yet another effort to connect the story with 16:14-23, in which David has already entered Saul's service, and to suggest by the addition that David traveled back and forth between his home and Saul's camp as needed. In this regard, Saul's rather polite request in 16:22 that David remain in his service is greatly strengthened in 18:2, in which it is asserted that Saul would no longer permit David to return home.

---

72. This translation follows McCarter, *I Samuel*, 299.
73. See S. R. Driver, *Notes on the Hebrew Text of the Books of Samuel*, 140.
74. 1 Kgs 11:26; 2 Sam 17:25, 21:20.

What all of this suggests is that the quite-independent story about David's heroic slaying of Goliath has been made a part of the larger story of David and Saul by the addition of 17:55–18:4 and the insertion of a few additional interconnections. These have all been done not by an editor but by an author who is likewise responsible for a much larger corpus within the David and Saul complex. It is this larger supplementary composition that will need to be explored.

Chapter 5

David's Life in Saul's Court and David as an Outlaw: 1 Samuel 18-31

In my analysis of the block of material in 1 Sam 18-31, which scholars identify as HDR or the story of David and Saul, I will attempt to distinguish two strata that for convenience I will label *account A* and *account B*, the first being identified as the base account and the second as a later supplement. Only after examining a number of cases within this block of texts will we be able to define more precisely the nature and identity of these two accounts and their relationship to the story of David as a whole. As we have already seen in chap. 4 above, the initial introduction of David to the reader and his first appearance in the court of Saul in 1 Sam 16:14-23 belongs to the base text and therefore to *account A*, and this becomes the point of departure for the analysis that follows.

David as a Member of Saul's Court

In the present text of the David story, David is first introduced to Saul and made a part of his entourage in 1 Sam 16:14-23. In addition to David and Saul, we have references only to Jesse, who sends David to Saul with a gift of food, and Saul's "servants" (עבדי־שאול), as well as "messengers" (מלאכים). As we shall see throughout *account A*, the author uses the greatest economy of style in identifying individuals within the story; most of the figures remain anonymous. David joins Saul's forces as a "valiant champion" (גבור חיל) and a "warrior" (איש מלחמה),[1] who becomes Saul's armor-bearer and his musician to sooth his troubled mind. It is also said that Saul loved David dearly. The unit in 1 Sam 16:14-23, therefore, introduces a number of themes that are repeated in what follows: (1) David has exceptional qualities, including his military prowess; (2) David can play the lyre and sooth Saul's evil spirit; (3) it is also said of David that "Yahweh is with him"; (4) when David joins Saul, it is stated that Saul loves him greatly. David's

---

1. Cf. 1 Sam 14:52.

skill with the lyre is related to the two episodes in which David plays for
Saul and Saul tries to kill him with his spear (18:10-11, 19:9-10). David's
martial qualities are related to his many military exploits (18:5, 12-16, 27,
30; 19:8). The statement that Yahweh is with David but has departed from
Saul is also a constant theme (16:18; 18:12, 14, 28; 2 Sam 5:10), to which
his military success is directly related (18:17).[2]

In spite of this evidence of literary continuity, however, the narrative
that covers the time that David spent in the court of Saul, in 1 Sam 18:10-
19:17, has the appearance of being a mosaic of small units, with a number
of repetitions and doublets. This has led scholars to try to reconstruct parallel sources or an early source and a later supplement, supported also by
the fact that many of the doublets are lacking in the LXX. However, unlike
other doublets and expansions that we will encounter later, these sus-
pected additions are very short, and their language and style is so close to
the parallel units that it is difficult to decide whether or not they are additions to the text.

There are three texts that deal with the theme of David's playing the lyre
before Saul. They may be set down in a series:

> 1 Sam 16:23 (RSV): And whenever the evil spirit from God was upon Saul,
> David took the lyre and played it with his hand; so Saul was refreshed,
> and was well, and the evil spirit departed from him.

> 1 Sam 18:10-11 (RSV): And on the morrow an evil spirit from God
> rushed upon Saul, and he raved within his house, while David was play-
> ing the lyre, as he did day by day. Saul had his spear in his hand; and
> Saul cast the spear, for he thought, "I will pin David to the wall." But Da-
> vid evaded him twice.

> 1 Sam 19:9-10 (RSV): Then an evil spirit from the Lord came upon Saul,
> as he sat in his house with his spear in his hand; and David was playing
> the lyre. And Saul sought to pin David to the wall with the spear; but he
> eluded Saul, so that he struck the spear into the wall. And David fled, and
> escaped.

The language and outlook of the three texts are so similar that if 1 Sam
18:10-11 is by a different hand, the author of this piece has taken considerable pains to imitate the other two texts closely. The only points of discrepancy seem to be (1) that he has compared the coming of the evil spirit
to ecstatic prophecy, which does not seem entirely appropriate to the scene,

---

2. See my *In Search of History*, 265-67.

and (2) that he refers to the threat as having occurred "twice," which seems to anticipate the second event. It is also curious that David does not react to the event or take it to be a personal threat on the first occasion as he does on the second. It is quite possible that a scribe has embellished the account at this point, but little more can be said about it. Contrary to the parallel unit in 1 Sam 19:9-10, the text in 18:10-11 has no clear connection to what follows.

There are also a number of texts that deal with the theme of David's military success as a warrior, a theme first suggested in 16:18. In addition to 18:5-9, where David's success first raises Saul's fear and suspicion of David, the theme is continued in 18:12-16, 28-30, and 19:8 and frames the smaller units where David's military prowess serves as an explanation for Saul's fear of David and his increasing animosity. Scholars have argued that some of these may be secondary, but there is little way of knowing with any certainty. They do serve a thematic function within the narrative and constitute a very important theme within the larger Dtr history of David, as can be seen in 2 Sam 5:2, 10, 12, and 7:8-9. This does not mean that one can simply construe all of these texts as merely the work of a Dtr "redactor" or label them "pre-Deuteronomistic."[3] On the contrary, they identify the basic narrative in *account A* as the work of Dtr and part of DtrH. It is precisely David's military success and his role as leader of the people in the wars of Yahweh, because "Yahweh was with him," that legitimates his choice as the future monarch, in contrast to Saul, who no longer has this divine presence and who thus fears the loss of the monarchy. This theme underlies the basic story of David and Saul. This leaves us to consider the stories about David's relationships with Jonathan and Michal. In both cases there are narrative units dealing with these themes beyond the period covered by David's time in Saul's court, and we will need to extend our coverage to include these as well.

Before we proceed with our examination of the episodes in which Jonathan and Michal appear, it is appropriate to comment on the view of Willi-Plein, who uses these two figures as decisive in her analysis of the David narrative.[4] In her reconstruction of a primitive document, *die Davidshausgeschichte* (DHG), which, for her, extends throughout the whole of the

---

3. T. Veijola (*Die ewige Dynastie*, 99) considers the texts in 1 Sam 16:18 and 18:12, 14, 16, 28, which all use the *Beistandsformel*, to be *vordtr*. This is merely a way of avoiding the obvious.

4. See I. Willi-Plein, "1 Sam 18-19 und die Davidshausgeschichte," 138-77.

David story as far as 1 Kgs 4:6, the work begins in 1 Sam 14:47-52 and has its direct continuation in 17:55-58, followed by 18:2, 5-9, 16-30; 19:8-17.[5] This source division is problematic for a number of reasons. She has chosen 14:47-52 as her beginning because it contains the names of some key figures in her source, namely the daughters of Saul, Merab and Michal, and the commander of Saul's army, Abner. However, she excludes from DHG any episodes that include Jonathan, because he belongs to an alternate source, ignoring the fact that 14:47-52 also contains the name of Jonathan. Now the small unit in 14:47-51 is surely meant to summarize the reign of Saul and hardly constitutes a very suitable introduction to David. This seems to me to be a very late composition to include principle figures in the Saul story and suggest accomplishments in imitation of the David story. It is only v. 52 that supplies the link between the Saul and David stories. Furthermore, the application of this principle of selection of texts is inconsistent because Abner appears in 1 Sam 20:23 in close association with Jonathan, in the middle of a larger unit in which Jonathan plays a primary role, and therefore she must exclude it from DGH. Again, Abner is important in the second account of David's sparing Saul's life, in 1 Sam 26 (vv. 7, 14-16), but Willi-Plein seems uncertain about whether or not to include this episode.

Willi-Plein finds the continuation of 14:47-52 in 17:55-58, which she takes as the first reference to David, and so she does not include 16:14-23 in her early source or in any of the texts, such as 18:10-15, that directly depend on it, although she does include 19:9-10 (!), which also depends on 16:14-23. However, 17:55-58 must depend directly on the story of David and Goliath that precedes it and is tied to it in the closest way. It also presumes that David has already been introduced into the story in some way and can hardly serve as an introduction to the David story. Furthermore, the description that Saul gives of David as a "youth" and a "young man" do not agree with Saul's search for warriors and aristocrats in 14:52. This verse would agree much more closely with the description of David in 16:18. Given these serious problems with Willi-Plein's thesis, it remains for us to examine the narrative in 1 Sam 18-19 and the units that deal with David's relationship to Jonathan and Michal without prejudice to the source division suggested by Willi-Plein.

---

5. For the full list of texts belonging to DHG, see ibid., 166-68.

David and Jonathan

The first encounter between David and Jonathan in *account A* is in 1 Sam 19:1–7, and here the introduction makes clear in v. 1, as though for the first time in the David story, that Jonathan is the son of Saul. It also states that Jonathan is very fond of David and for this reason seeks to protect him from his father's intentions to kill David. Jonathan's affection for David corresponds to Saul's own initial strong approval of David (16:21) and to Michal's love for David (18:20, 28), as well as the affection of all Saul's servants and soldiers. This love and affection from Saul's family and servants constitutes an important theme throughout this source. It is this love that motivates Jonathan to intervene on his behalf, and through his intervention he is able to persuade his father to change his mind and to restore David to the court. There are, however, a couple of points in the account that seem to integrate it within a later version of events. The first is the reference to the dialogue between Jonathan and Saul taking place in a field where David is hiding (1 Sam 19:3aα), which seems to have no connection with what follows in vv. 4–6.[6] However, it anticipates a later episode in 1 Sam 20, in which the motif of the field plays a central role and was probably added for this purpose. The second addition is in v. 5a with its reference to the story of Goliath, which is not in the basic *account A*, as we have seen, and which is not the basis for Saul's jealousy and hatred. It appears to be a later attempt to tie the David and Goliath story more closely into the whole.

Furthermore, this episode regarding David and Jonathan knows nothing about the bond established between the two in 18:1–4. It is only much later (1 Sam 23:16–18), when David is on the run from Saul, that Jonathan comes to David, not only to encourage David but now to affirm that David will be the next king and that Jonathan is content to be second in command. Only then do David and Jonathan make a covenant "before Yahweh," which must mean that they swore an oath of loyalty to each other with this understanding in mind. These two passages belong together as the *only* treatment of the relationship of Jonathan to David in *account A*. As

---

6. Hertzberg (*I & II Samuel*, 163–64), followed by McCarter (*I Samuel*, 321–22), regards the reference in v. 3aα as an alternate parallel tradition that has been combined with the first one. I would view it as a scribal gloss. The repetition of ואני in v. 3, "*as for me,* I will go out" and "*as for me* I will speak," is a fairly clear marker that the first clause has been added by a scribe under the influence of the second incident.

in the earlier episode, Jonathan is again identified by his patronymic as the "son of Saul." The statement of Jonathan's recognition of David as the future king and the remark that his father also knows that this will happen (v. 17) anticipates the following encounter between David and Saul in chap. 24, in which Saul also acknowledges that David will be the future king (24:20). At this point, Saul extracts from David a different kind of oath, that David would not exterminate all Saul's descendents when he becomes king.

In *account B*, which is a supplement to the earlier story of David and Saul, the first encounter between David and Jonathan is in 1 Sam 18:1–4, and it is presented as a direct continuation of the previous David and Goliath story in chap. 17. Jonathan seems to appear on the scene out of the blue with no introduction, so it is assumed that we know him to be the son of Saul from the earlier story of Saul's and Jonathan's exploits. This unit expresses Jonathan's great love for David (vv. 1, 3) and also affirms that this is the point in time when David entered Saul's service on a permanent basis (v. 2). It also speaks about Jonathan's making a "covenant" with David but does not say what the content of this covenant was, although it may be suggested by the action of Jonathan in giving his own armor to David, which can be interpreted as symbolic of his commitment to David's right to kingship and succession in his place. This would also suggest an implicit connection with David's anointing in 16:1–13. As we have suggested above, the unit consisting of 17:55–18:4 is a secondary stratum in the story of Saul and David and serves as a transition between the David and Goliath story and the older version of the narrative in 1 Sam 18.

Likewise belonging to *account B* is the rather drawn-out unit in 1 Sam 20:1–42, which is a parallel to the earlier episode in *account A*, 19:1–7, but unlike the earlier one, this one presupposes that there is already a strong relationship between David and Jonathan on which David can depend. In the previous unit in *A*, Saul confides in Jonathan about his intentions because there is not yet a bond such as this between David and Jonathan. Consequently, 1 Sam 20:1–42 is well aware of both 18:1–4 and 19:1–7. Unlike the previous incident when Saul discloses his plans to Jonathan, however, there must now be a reason given why Saul's present plans are concealed from him. The simple plan of Jonathan's gaining information from his father while David is in hiding (19:2) is now turned into an elaborate scheme. In place of Jonathan's persuasive plea in David's favor, there is the breech between father and son that leads to a threat on Jonathan's life, with the same spear with which David was threatened, and the final parting of David and Jonathan. Embedded within this scheme, in 20:8, is a reference to a prior "covenant of Yahweh," which refers back to the earlier covenant in 18:3, but 20:8 also understands this loyalty oath as a sacred covenant, a "covenant before Yahweh" (ברית לפני יהוה) as in 23:18. Both texts are clearly presupposed in this remark in 20:8, but only 18:3 belongs to the same source, while the unit in 23:16–18, which is often regarded as Dtr, must be earlier than *account B* because it knows nothing of a prior sacred covenant. Furthermore, it only becomes clear in 23:17–18 that the covenant between David and Jonathan has to do with David's right to the throne and Jonathan's absolute oath of fealty to David. It is precisely this understanding of the covenant that is assumed in 18:3–4 in the actions of Jonathan simulating David's investiture with the use of Jonathan's own robes and weapons.

Likewise embedded in *account B* is a longer oath in 20:12–17, which expands the loyalty oath to include a lasting commitment to Jonathan's offspring in a way that is paralleled in David's oath to Saul in 24:20–22. The purpose of this expansion is to narrow this commitment from Saul's house in general to Jonathan only and to anticipate the dealings that David has with Mephibosheth in 2 Sam 9, which is directly linked to this oath. This combination of a general oath to Saul and a specific one to Jonathan is suggested in David's remarks: "Is there still anyone left of the house of Saul, to whom I may show kindness *for Jonathan's sake*?" (2 Sam 9:1). This connection between 1 Sam 20 and 2 Sam 9 would strongly suggest common authorship. What seems clear from this comparison is that the very simple and rather flat treatment of the relationship between David and Jonathan in the earlier *account A* has received great elaboration by this second *account B*. This later account also appears to be closely associated with the unit in 17:55–18:4 as part of the same supplementary layer, which, in turn, has a strong connection with CH.

David and Michal

The marriage of David to Michal in 1 Sam 18:20–27 is often represented as an example of another doublet to the proposed marriage to the eldest daughter Merab in 1 Sam 18:17–19. However, I doubt that this is the case and it makes better sense to read them both as part of the same pericope. In both cases, Saul seeks to use his daughters as bait in order to have David die as a casualty of war. In the first case, the vague promise of marriage to Merab has only moral force but no legal claim, and so Saul reneges on it.

In the second case, there are two important differences. The first is the fact that Michal loves David (v. 20), and it is this that initiates Saul's offer to David to give her to him as his wife. The second is that David negotiates with Saul to get a binding legal arrangement, a *mohar*, "bride price" (v. 25). Because David is relatively poor, Saul suggests the price of a hundred foreskins of the Philistines, so David delivers this price in double measure. Now Saul is *legally* obligated to give Michal to David. Saul's efforts in both cases have failed and he would now need to resort to other methods to get rid of David.

The reasons that are offered for regarding the story of David's marriage to Merab as a doublet are twofold. The first is the text-critical argument that the episode does not appear in the shorter text of the LXX, but, as indicated above, we have argued that the longer text of the MT is the original, so this argument does not have any force in the present discussion. The second argument is that it agrees with the statement in the David and Goliath story regarding the reward of marriage that King Saul will give to the one who defeats Goliath (1 Sam 17:25–again in the MT "pluses"). It should be clear, however, that the offer of marriage to Merab knows nothing about the previous story because in the Goliath story he has already earned the right to marry the king's daughter and has proven himself a valiant warrior (בֶּן־חַיִל), so that Saul's remarks would be quite inappropriate. It is significant that in 16:18 he is likewise praised as having the qualities of being a valiant champion and warrior, which fits well with Saul's statement to "be a valiant warrior *for me*" (18:17), that is, prove your reputation. The reward in the Goliath story also included the promise of wealth and special status for the victor's family, but in the marriage stories of 18:17–27 David claims that he has neither of these. If there was a common source for the offer of marriage to Merab (18:17–19) and the Goliath story, then one could certainly expect a clearer indication of this in the narrative.

The theme of Michal's love for David, mentioned both at the beginning of the account of David's marriage (1 Sam 18:20) and at the end (v. 28), is part of an underlying motif of this source, which emphasizes how Saul's family, both Michal and Jonathan, as well as all of Saul's servants, love David, as did Saul himself before he became so jealous of him and saw him as a risk to his dynasty. Michal's love for David is demonstrated in her actions to save him from the murderous intentions of her father (19:11–17). She takes the initiative to warn him and to plan the ruse that saves his life, at great risk to herself. This source suggests nothing further about the fate of

Michal.[7] In 1 Sam 25:44, in connection with David's later marriages to Abigail and Ahinoam, there is a remark that Saul gave Michal, David's wife, to Palti son of Laish, and this anticipates the episode in 2 Sam 3:12–16, in which David reclaims his wife Michal. Here, however, she becomes little more that a member of his growing harem, and she is used as a mere bargaining chip in negotiations with Abner for his own political ambitions. There is a direct reference back to the *mohar* of one hundred foreskins as David's right to have her, indicating that the later account is fully familiar with the earlier source. However, nothing is said about any love between Michal and David. Instead, it is the second husband, Paltiel, who is brokenhearted at his loss. The complete reversal of feeling between Michal and David is reflected in 2 Sam 6:16, 20–23, in which she now despises David for his actions and David expresses similar contempt for her. The contrast between the two sources could not be more strongly drawn.

David's Flight from Saul

After David's escape and flight from his home with Michal's help, the next episode in the extant text (1 Sam 19:18–24) presents David's arrival in Ramah, where David reports to Samuel what Saul has done to him and they both go to Samuel's dwelling in Naioth, within Ramah. This seems to assume that David has a prior relationship with Samuel, as reflected in 1 Sam 16:1–13, which also locates Samuel at Ramah. That, however, belongs to a later, post-Dtr source.[8] The story in 19:18–24 is a doublet of 1 Sam 10:9–13, which is part of a larger Dtr account of Saul's anointing and endowment of the spirit. This later story in 19:18–24 suggests that the effect of the spirit of Yahweh on Saul now leads only to his complete disgrace. There can be little doubt that this account in 19:18–24 is a later version and a caricature of the other. All these indicators point to this episode as belonging to *account B*. In my view, it is quite unlikely that this episode is a part of the early account of David's flight. It makes little sense for David to flee to some place further north in Israel a short distance from Gibeah. His destination was certainly back to Judah, where so much of Saul's later pursuit of David

---

7. Cf. I. Willi-Plein, "Michal und die Anfänge des Königtums in Israel," 401–19. Willi-Plein regards all of the references to Michal in 1 and 2 Samuel as belonging to the same source. I have offered reasons above for my disagreement with this view.

8. See my *In Search of History*, 260–64.

takes place. This episode is also linked to David's return from Ramah to meet with Jonathan in Gibeah (1 Sam 20:1), which likewise makes no sense as a flight from Saul. As we have seen above, however, this long meeting with Jonathan in the immediate vicinity of his greatest threat is a later composition (*account B*) and therefore not part of the early flight narrative.

The next stage in David's flight moves him from Gibeah to Nob, which is still in the heart of Benjamin, where he visits the leading priest of the sanctuary there (1 Sam 21:2–10, 22:6–23). Now we are expected to believe that this little village in Benjamin is the main cult place for the whole of the region, or indeed the whole state of Israel, and that it was a sacred city with a large priestly establishment of 85 priests of the first rank, as well as many other cult personnel. Furthermore, the story assumes familiarity with certain cultic procedures, such as the display of the bread of the presence. All of this seems quite anachronistic as an imitation of the Second Temple in the Persian period. Now within this temple one finds an Edomite who is a major official in Saul's entourage and who is also a worshiper of Yahweh, not his own deity, although as we later learn, he has no qualms about murdering all the priests of Yahweh. What is this sort of person doing in Saul's entourage? This makes no historical sense whatsoever for the 10th century. By the Persian period, however, there were a large number of Edomites living within the region of Jehud and its environs, and some were undoubtedly worshipers of Yahweh and given access to the temple.

The sanctuary at Nob was also the place where David could find the sword of Goliath, which means that the author is quite familiar with the story of David and Goliath. Yet it is clear that this is not the same source as in 17:54, which speaks of Jerusalem as though it were the capital and of David himself being in possession of Goliath's weapons. Above, I offered other reasons for seeing this story as part of the same source (*account B*) as in 17:55–18:4. Taken together with the anachronistic indicators in the text, everything points to a Persian date for this supplement to the David story.

In the sequel to David's appearance at Nob, in 1 Sam 22:6–23, a number of features are present that indicate the relationship of this unit to the larger narrative. From the lone fugitive in 1 Sam 21:2–10, David has now become a band of "David and his men" in 22:6, which means that the creation of this band in 22:1–2 is known and assumed. Saul also sits with his "spear in his hand," which seems to be the mark of his office in this source (see also 26:7). Saul makes an accusation of disloyalty against his Benjaminite followers that includes the charge that they have not disclosed to him the covenant between his son Jonathan and David, "the son of Jesse" (v. 8). This strongly suggests the secret encounter between David and Jonathan that is presented in chap. 20, although if it was secret, then it is not clear how Saul knew about it. Perhaps the accusation reflects Saul's suspicion of what is going on between the two as reflected in his outburst in 20:30-34. In both places, David is referred to as "the son of Jesse." There can be little doubt that the two episodes belong to the same source (*account B*).

In what follows, Doeg the Edomite makes his report on David's visit to Nob and his meeting with Ahimelech, the priest (vv. 9-10). However, he embellishes the encounter by adding the false but damning detail that the priest had consulted Yahweh on David's behalf. If that were so, then the priest would need to be party to what David was up to and thus culpable. In what follows, Ahimelech denies any such knowledge of David's flight or intentions and indicates that what he did was no different from the many times that he has aided David in the king's service (vv. 14-15). Ahimelech's description of David's status as son-in-law and as leader of Saul's personal forces seems to reflect knowledge of all the material in the older source. In what follows, we have the massacre of the priests of Nob, all their families, all the inhabitants of the sacred city, and even the animals carried out by Doeg the Edomite. This is an ironic travesty of the deuteronomic principle of the *ḥērem* carried out by an Edomite on orders from an anointed Israelite king.

David and Abiathar

Abiathar, one of Ahimelech's sons, escapes the slaughter and goes to join David (1 Sam 22:20-23). When David hears the report of what had happened, he is well aware that he is the cause of the massacre and gives Abiathar protection. Abiathar also comes to David with an ephod with which David could consult the deity (23:6). There were apparently 85 priests at Nob who could have preformed this function, but now only one remains, and he is in David's entourage. Did this mean that Saul no longer has this means of consultation? In the earlier source there is no mention of a priest such as this, so placing the arrival of Abiathar before the episode in 23:1-5 and the remark about the ephod in 23:6 is intended to suggest that the references to David's consultation of the deity in 23:1-5 was done through the medium of Abiathar's ephod. This makes it quite clear that this later source was a deliberate addition to the earlier source in 23:1-5.

Abiathar likewise plays an important role in CH alongside Zadok and then as a rival in the final episodes in 1 Kgs 1-2, so it is important that we understand the relationship between the references to Abiathar in CH and in the so-called HDR. In the scene in 1 Kgs 2:26-27 in which Solomon deals with Abiathar as a member of the rival party to the throne, Solomon commands Abiathar: "Go to Anathoth, to your estate; for you deserve death. But I will not at this time put you to death, because you carried the ark of [the covenant] of (the Lord) Yahweh before David my father and because you shared in all the hardships that my father endured." The remark about carrying the ark refers to the incident during the revolt of Absalom when Abiathar and Zadok with the Levites carry the ark of the covenant down to the Kidron river as David is leaving the city and then carry it back again (2 Sam 15:24-29). The further remark about sharing in David's hardships, however, cannot refer to the time of the Absalom revolt because Abiathar and Zadok remained in Jerusalem during this period, so it could only be a reference to the period of David's flight from Saul in 1 Sam 22:20-23; 23:6, 9; 30:7. This establishes a close connection between CH and this set of texts.

The fact that Abiathar is expelled to Anathoth, which is a Benjaminite town in the immediate neighborhood of Nob, further links this episode to the slaughter of the priests of Nob. This is confirmed by the remark in 1 Kgs 2:27 about the fulfillment of the prophecy against the house of Eli in 1 Sam 2:30-36, so CH must be familiar with this part of DtrH. One cannot dismiss this interconnection by proposing to make 1 Kgs 2:27b a Dtr addition because the original intention of the prophecy in 1 Sam 2:30-36 is clearly something quite different from what happened at Nob. What is required by the author to justify this remark is to make a genealogical link between Abiathar and the ancestor Eli. This link is found in 1 Sam 14:3, in which a priestly genealogy is quite artificially inserted into the narrative: "Ahijah the son of Ahitub, *the brother of Ichabod, son of Phinehas, son of Eli, the priest of Yahweh in Shiloh,* was carrying the ephod." That the connection between Ahitub and Eli is entirely artificial is revealed by the fact that he is made the *brother* of Ichabod and thus given a connection with the story of Eli and his sons and their fate in 1 Sam 4. The story tells us that when Ichabod was born his mother died in childbirth and the father Phinehas was also dead, 4:19-22. If Ichabod had an older brother, which is certainly not suggested by the story, then why does the genealogy not simply state Ahitub, son of Phinehas? The only point in this genealogical notation is to establish a link between Abiathar and Eli by this indirect reference to the story in 1 Sam 4.

This observation further suggests that all of the references to Abiathar, both in the David and Saul story and in CH belong to a common source.

Furthermore, within the story of David and Saul, they are integral to the narratives of both 23:6-13 (vv. 6, 8) and 30:1-31 (vv. 7-8), and these are in continuity with the whole narrative of the massacre of the priests of Nob. Consequently, this entire narrative corpus belongs to *account B*, which was written by the author of CH.

The episodes relating David's visit to Nob in 1 Sam 21:2-10 and the sequel in 22:6-23 are built around the two short units of *account A* concerned with David's flight in 21:11-16 and 22:1-5. In the first of these, David, as a lone fugitive, flees to Gath of the Philistines to find asylum there, but he discovers that he is known and must leave. This episode is a doublet to the later migration to Gath in chap. 27, so a comparison with this unit will be taken up below. The second has to do with David's assembling a group of misfits and malcontents and making them into a fighting force of 400 men. It is this force of men that he uses to fight the Philistines in 23:1-5. The unit in 22:3-4 also relates his concern to find protection for his family in the land of Moab.

The narrative in 1 Sam 23 is a patchwork of stories, much like 1 Sam 18, but these deal with episodes during David's efforts to elude capture by Saul. It is not so easy to identify which are primary, belonging to the early *account A*, and which are additions. We have already had reason to identify 23:1-5, 14-18 as part of the primary *account A* and 23:6-13 as secondary, *account B*. The following unit in 23:19-28 looks overloaded, with the first half, vv. 19-24a, somewhat suspect. Given the fact that in the earlier part of *account A* all of the people love David and some are willing to risk their lives for him, it is surprising that a group, the Ziphites, in southern Judah are anxious to help Saul find David to kill him. Their attitude seems similar to that of the inhabitants of Keilah, who even after being rescued from the Philistines were quite prepared to hand him over to Saul. We also find the Ziphites again offering their assistance to Saul, in 26:1-2, which introduces the second episode in which David spares Saul's life. All of this suggests that 23:19-24a does not belong to the early *account A* but is the later supplement, *account B*. For the rest, 23:24b-28 is part of the early *account A* and sets up the episode in 24:1-23[23:29-24:22] in which David spares Saul's life.

David Spares Saul's Life Twice

The two accounts of how David spared the life of Saul (1 Sam 24 and 26), when he had the opportunity to kill Saul in an unguarded moment during Saul's pursuit of him, is the most striking example of a doublet in 1 Samuel. It is often compared with similar examples of literary parallels in Genesis and is considered a classic instance of this literary phenomenon, resulting in quite similar kinds of critical conclusions as to the relationship between the two stories. The older approach, as reflected in the work of Julius Wellhausen, is similar to the Documentary Hypothesis, in which two independent versions of the story, an older and more original one (1 Sam 26) and a later version (1 Sam 24), were inserted by an editor into an older account about David's days as a freebooter.[9] His arguments are primarily based on his understanding of the development of Israel's religion, for example, the supposed more primitive remark about being forced to leave the land of Yahweh and thus to serve other gods in a foreign land (26:19–20). This approach is still followed by McCarter, which he regards "23:14– 24:23 as a tendentiously fashioned equivalent to 26:1–25,"[10] and part of a larger expansion of the story of David's rise.

A quite-different approach has been taken by Klaus Koch, influenced by the rise of form-criticism, with different results. His views have been quite influential and still underlie many of the current treatments of these texts, and so call for more detailed discussion. Koch's form-critical treatment of these two accounts contains many problematic assumptions that go back to Gunkel and the role of "sagas" in the rise of early historiography.[11] Thus, he regards the two accounts as originally independent oral versions of the same historical event, which he calls "heroic sagas" (*Heldensagen*) based on the analogy of the heroic tales in German folklore, and, using this analogy, he goes to great lengths to identify the characteristics in these stories that correspond to this genre. There is much that is problematic in this whole development in biblical criticism, and the present approach to explaining the relationship of these two accounts to each other is still dependent on this problematic foundation.[12] Koch's anaylsis of the twice-told tale in Genesis and Samuel is based entirely on his notions of patriarchal sagas in Genesis and heroic sagas in Samuel and his understanding of their form-

---

9. J. Wellhausen, *Prolegomena*, 264–65.

10. McCarter, *I Samuel*, 387.

11. K. Koch, *The Growth of the Biblical Tradition*, 132–48.

12. For a detailed critique of the literary development from "saga" to historiography as advocated by Gunkel and von Rad and followed here by Koch, see my *In Search of History*, 209–48. The rendering of "saga" for the German *Sage* in the English translation of Koch's work leads to confusion because Koch does not mean to refer to the Icelandic sagas, which are of quite a different character.

critical characteristics without any broader literary considerations. His form-critical assumptions cannot survive close scrutiny.

Once Koch identifies the genre as an independent tale, then anything that points to the larger context "outside the saga itself" or reflects a more advanced theological perspective and level of piety beyond that of "a rugged heroic saga" is relegated to a later stage in the tradition's development.[13] For Koch, this includes a gradual accumulation of other small units, such as those in 1 Sam 23 attached to *account A* in chap. 24 or the "elaborations" he finds in *account B*, chap. 26, perhaps still on the oral level. Unlike Wellhausen, he regards chap. 24 as the earlier version of the story.

From this "transmission history," Koch then moves to the "redaction history," which deals with the written record of the stories, and here he asserts that "it is easy to see that A and B could scarcely have been taken out of the oral tradition and written down by the same writer at the same time."[14] His primary argument for this is that "chapter xxiv ends with such a formal, sworn, peace agreement, that if chapter xxvi came from the same source Saul's breaking the peace would have been at least briefly mentioned."[15] Koch points to other literary disparities in the framework and interconnections of the stories with their contexts, particularly the confused geographical notations. From this, he concludes that, at least for *account A*, it became part of the story of David's rise extending to 2 Sam 5 and perhaps even including the succession of Solomon. This leads him to declare, "The complex literary type to which A belongs is therefore *historical writing*, for only a writer of history has as his theme the rise of the monarch's power over a particular nation and its persistence in the face of external and internal danger. Thus the writer is proved by this example to have incorporated heroic sagas into his work."[16] The fact that ancient historians made use of "sagas" is supported by reference to Herodotus and Thucydides, who did the same. However, what Koch fails to mention is that, for all the large amount of this sort of folklore that is present in Herodotus, there is no evidence that his history passed through the same elaborate tradition-historical and redaction-critical processes that Koch reconstructs for the biblical history.[17]

---

13. *Growth of the Biblical Tradition*, 143.
14. Ibid., 144.
15. Ibid.
16. Ibid., 145 (Koch's emphasis).
17. See W. Aly, *Volkmärchen, Sage und Novelle bei Herodot und seinen Zeitgenossen: Eine Untersuchung über die volkstümlichen Elemente der altgriechischen Prosaerzählung* (Göttingen: Vandenhoeck & Ruprecht, 1921).

In fact, Herodotus's rather free use of material such as this only demonstrates that Koch's hypothetical reconstruction is quite unnecessary.

Likewise basic to Koch's reconstruction of the compositional process is the assumption that it all took place within David's own lifetime, so that the stories reflect a process by which these "heroic sagas" about David formed, accumulated into collections by circulating orally, and then were transformed into primitive written historiography, all in one generation. It is the conviction that these stories must be early and based on true reminiscences of events that provide the foundation for the whole scheme. However, there are increasing doubts that a course of events such as this is the least bit likely. If one calls into question the very idea that the kingdoms of Judah and Israel had a common origin in a "United Monarchy," then the stories about this rivalry between the northerner Saul and the Judean David must be a rather late invention, perhaps no earlier than the end of the monarchy. As Herodotus vividly demonstrates, folktales about famous figures of the past can tell us nothing about when tales of this sort arose or the date of the literary work in which they are found. It is just as likely that there were popular stories about David at the end of the monarchy as at the beginning, whether favorable or unfavorable, and form-criticism can do little to help us in establishing the relative dating of these stories.

Though Koch is able to integrate *account A* into his developmental scheme, he has considerable difficulty with the redaction history of *account B*. He simply states, "It is more difficult to discover the present meaning of B as its wider context is unknown. The links with the material before and after are much less satisfactory than those of A."[18] As a consequence, he gives up entirely on trying to account for its presence in the text. That cannot be a very satisfactory solution to the literary history of these two units and to the corpus of stories as a whole. In fact, *account B* has far more connection to its context than Koch has recognized or is willing to admit.

I have taken this amount of space to outline Koch's views because one still meets the same basic assumptions about the two accounts as originating in two independent oral versions of the same story that were somehow incorporated into the present literary work from the time of the early monarchy. Thus, Klein follows Koch's tradition-historical and redaction-critical approaches in the same tight time frame, with *account A* being the more primitive (historical) version. He concludes, "We have little doubt that one event has come down through the tradition in a double form, and we also

---

18. *Growth of the Biblical Tradition*, 147.

believe that the writer of HDR himself incorporated both accounts to strengthen his defense of David and his critique of Saul (contra McCarter)." Klein thereby simplifies Koch's redaction history by attributing the presence of the two versions in the text to the same writer, the likelihood of which Koch denied.

Consequently, in what follows we will proceed on the basis of a quite-different form of literary analysis. Without denying that there may well be a body of folklore about David behind one or the other of the two accounts, we will assume that the author (or authors) made use of it for his own purposes and will endeavor to uncover the literary interconnections of the two accounts with each other and within their broader literary contexts. The assumption will be to go against the use of editors to solve literary problems or to finesse tradition-historical reconstructions. It seems more likely, according to what we have seen thus far, that we have to do with a base text, to which one of the versions belongs, and a secondary supplement, which also belongs to a larger literary addition.

There are so many similarities between the two stories that most scholars consider it unlikely that the same author was responsible for both. The usual explanation is to understand that both go back to a common oral source. Koch lists the similarities as follows:

> On both occasions David is in the wilderness of Judah fleeing from Saul. On both occasions he has the opportunity to kill the king. On both occasions there is the suggestion that it has been ordained by God, but though he is tempted to murder Saul, David strongly resists the impulse: he cannot violate the sanctity of the Lord's Anointed. But on both occasions he takes some material evidence with him. In the conversation which follows Saul recognises David's superiority, and departs as he came.

For Koch, these strong similarities lead him to conclude "that it must be two versions of the same story, both of which developed in oral form quite independently of each other."[19] However, in my view, this is not the only or even the most likely possibility. The differences between the two accounts are very important and they suggest a deliberate transformation in the story by one or the other version, depending on which is regarded as the more primitive. Those who chose Koch's option of two versions derived from oral tradition must then interpose an "editor" into the transmission process to account for some of these striking differences. But is an editor necessary? I think not.

---

19. Ibid., 142–43.

An alternative is to suggest that a later writer (not an "editor") added a second occasion in which he deliberately offered a quite-different version of an encounter such as this between David and Saul from his own revisionist perspective. We have already seen this to be the case with other double treatments of the earlier source document, and we therefore have reason to suspect that the same hand is at work in this instance also. The second author sticks to the same basic outline, as we have seen above, but he changes the location and the chronology, as well as some significant features in the story, to make it clear that this is a second occasion. This allows him to modify the story for his own purposes.

According to my literary analysis, given above, the episodes in 1 Sam 23:14-18, 24b-28 lead directly into 1 Sam 24, and this literary connection is generally accepted by most scholars, although 23:16-18 is often regarded as a Dtr addition.[20] However, because I regard the whole of the basic text as part of the DtrH, this does not constitute a problem for my view. At any rate, I have tried to show that the encounter between David and Jonathan in 23:16-18 is part of the earlier version of the relationship between these two, in which Jonathan recognizes David's right to the crown and directly anticipates the same acknowledgement by Saul in 24:21[20], which is equally Dtr. It is special pleading simply to eliminate this evidence by appealing to a hypothetical "editor." Consequently, for the sake of the subsequent discussion, I will assume that 1 Sam 24 is the earlier version of the story and that 1 Sam 26 is the later addition.

Important for our study of these two episodes within the context of our larger investigation are the distinctive features of each story in comparison with the other. In the first story in 1 Sam 24, *account A*, the only two named characters are David and Saul, but the second story, *account B*, introduces three new characters: Abner, son of Ner and commander of the army, who is placed alongside Saul, Abishai son of Zeruiah and brother of Joab, who is a foil for David, and Ahimelech the Hittite. These three additions are quite significant. We have already encountered Abner in previous episodes that we have clear reason to believe are also additions to the base text, and Abner plays an important role in CH, not least of which is his position as a counterpart to Joab and the other sons of Zeruiah. The mention of Abishai, Joab's brother, tells us that these accomplished warriors who are prominent figures in the later career of David were already part of the 600 men with David in the wilderness, so this is not just a rag-tag bunch of men but

---

20. See McCarter, *I Samuel*, 16–17; Klein, *1 Samuel*, 231.

a professional fighting force. Furthermore, Abishai plays the same role as a foil for David in CH in 2 Sam 16:9-12 and again in 19:21-23 in connection with Shimei, a member of Saul's family, whom Abishai wishes to kill. This establishes a strong connection between this unit and CH.

The third figure, Ahimelech the Hittite, is the most curious of all, for he is only mentioned in 26:6 alongside Abishai as one who might accompany David on his mission into the enemy camp and therefore of high rank in David's force, but he says and does nothing. Some have made much of the presence of this "Hittite" in David's entourage as evidence of remnants of this ethnic group from the Hittite empire of the second millennium B.C.E. still present among the population of Judah in David's day and therefore a witness to an early source. There is, however, no justification for any such suggestion. The Hittite realm never extended to the region of Palestine, which was firmly under Egyptian control during the period of the Hittite Empire. The explanation for the term is much simpler. By the Neo-Assyrian period, the term *Hittite* had lost its earlier ethnic connotation as a reference to a people of Anatolia and had become a general term for the people of Syria-Palestine. It is from this usage that the biblical writers picked up the term and used it as one of the designations for the aboriginal, non-Israelite population. Its use cannot be dated before the 7th century, and it simply means a foreigner.[21] This is precisely the same use that we find in connection with Uriah the Hittite, husband of Bathsheba (2 Sam 11). In both cases, they are high-ranking foreigners in David's entourage. This is in direct violation of the deuteronomic principles of war (Deut 20). Again, it is very likely that both references to Hittites in David's fighting force belong to the same late source. This source is suggesting that the kind of personal army that David had during his period in the wilderness is much the same as what he used later in his career.

This observation about the nature of David's army in 1 Sam 26 agrees with the general characterization of David and his men in this story, which is altogether different from that of the earlier story. In *account A* (1 Sam 22:1-2, 23:24b-28), David and his men are a rather rough collection of desperate individuals who are constantly on the run from Saul and are very fearful of being caught. By contrast, in *account B* they are no longer fugitives but a serious military force who are confident that on their own terrain they can outsmart the enemy, and they plan an action to demonstrate

---

21. J. Van Seters, "The Terms 'Amorite' and 'Hittite' in the Old Testament," *VT* 22 (1972): 64-81.

that they are a serious threat to Saul. David sends out scouts to learn of the location of the enemy like a military leader and then takes the initiative in the action that follows. And at the conclusion of the episode, David does not so much plead his case as negotiate terms, which Saul accepts.

Careful attention should be given to the differences in the scene in which David has the opportunity to kill Saul but refrains from doing so. In 24:4–8[3–7], Saul enters a cave to relieve himself, and it just happens that David and his men are hiding deep in the same cave. This episode is interpreted by his men as an act of God in which the enemy is given by the deity into David's hands. (The reference to a supposed oracle should not be taken too literally.) David, instead of killing Saul, merely cuts off part of his garment as proof that he could have killed him, but even this troubles him because Saul is Yahweh's anointed. It should also be remembered that, in our analysis, this source knows nothing of David's own anointing in 16:1–13, which is a later addition. All of David's actions were done in stealth, so Saul leaves the cave without knowing what David has done to him. Much is also made of the symbolism of the act of cutting the skirt of Saul, but again, this source knows nothing of 1 Sam 15 and the symbolic tearing of robes, which in any event has to do with the robe of Samuel, not of Saul.

The portrayal of this moment in *account B* is altogether different. It is now David who takes the initiative to penetrate to the heart of the enemy camp and to the highly guarded tent of Saul. How has this security perimeter been so easily violated? The answer is that the whole army of Saul has been completely incapacitated by the *tardēmâ* of Yahweh (26:12), but does not the *tardēmâ* trivialize the whole event? With this kind of divine intervention, even a child could have done what David did. It makes entirely hollow David's rebuke of Abner, because Abner and his men could hardly have been responsible for their actions. There was no breech of security in this episode as there was in the first one. It is equally miraculous that no sooner had David returned (in the middle of the night?) than the effect of the *tardēmâ* wore off, because they could all hear David call to Abner, which woke everybody up, even though David was quite a distance away![22]

In the second story, the spear, along with the water-jug, replaces the piece of skirt as evidence of David's presence in Saul's tent. But why the spear? It is, of course, the same spear with which Saul threatened David earlier, so the story is intended to recall the other episodes in which this spear plays a role. These also include 1 Sam 20:33, when Jonathan is also

---

22. Cf. Hertzberg, *I & II Samuel*, 210.

threatened by the same spear, and 22:6, in which the spear has become symbolic of Saul's royal power. Both of these references clearly belong to the secondary expansion. In this story, David returns Saul's spear to him, the symbol of his power as a defiant rebuke, because against David it is useless. Furthermore, when Abishai states (26:8) that "God has given your enemy into your hand today," he repeats the same theme as in *account A*, but now he volunteers to pin Saul to the ground with his own spear, ועתה אכנו נא בחנית ובארץ פעם אחת, just as Saul attempted to do to David, and Abishai adds, "I will not strike him twice" (ולא אשנה לו), which seems to allude to the two unsuccessful attempts on David's life.[23] The whole point of the foray into the camp of Saul is to obtain the spear.

Furthermore, in the earlier story David had some grave misgivings about cutting a piece from the royal robe of Saul, as if even this was a violation of "Yahweh's anointed," which in the earlier story can only refer to Saul. In the second story, however, there is some ambivalence to David's statement, "Do not destroy him; for who can put forth his hand against Yahweh's anointed and be guiltless" (v. 9). This later version knows the account of David's anointing so that the inviolability of Yahweh's anointed is now fraught with much self interest in his own inviolability. Thus, Abishai's suggestion about killing Saul with the spear is just an excuse for a little lecture by David about the inviolability of Yahweh's anointed. This remark, repeated in v. 11 may be compared with David's remarks about Saul's death in 2 Sam 1:14–16 and the death of Ishbosheth in 2 Sam 4:8–12. If David himself violates this principle, he can hardly expect others to respect it when he becomes king. Moreover, what could David gain in killing Saul? Nothing! He would merely have replaced Saul with Jonathan as his sworn enemy instead of an ally and friend, and he would have lost all hope of gaining the Israelites. At least that is the logic of the story. And because it is a story, it is perhaps best to refrain from speculations about purely political considerations as motivation for David's actions. What is primary is what the author wishes to say about David and his actions as reflective of the monarchy's origins.

Careful attention must be given to David's speeches to Abner and Saul, and to Saul's response. The speech to Abner (26:14–16) accuses him and his men of great negligence that is worthy of death because they have not

---

23. The language looks particularly reminiscent of 1 Sam 18:11, which speaks of pinning David *to the wall* with the spear and of David eluding him *twice* (ויטל שאול את־החנית ואמר אכה בדוד ובקיר ויסב דוד מפניו פעמים).

properly protected "Yahweh's anointed." The speech is a piece of mockery in which David, with quite false humility describes himself and his military aid as merely "one of the people," and again the focus is on "Yahweh's anointed," who must be kept inviolate. The charge against Abner and his men we know to be false because the narrator has clearly absolved them of responsibility. The ease with which David and Abishai walked through the whole camp without anyone stirring must have made this obvious. Furthermore, if this account knows of the secret anointing of David, then once again all his talk about not violating Yahweh's anointed is hypocrisy. There is, of course, no counterpart to this speech in the first episode, in which this sort of negligence of security would be much more to the point.

In the speech to Saul in *account A* (24:10–16[9–15]), David addresses Saul directly, at close range and only after prostrating himself before the king. In addition to the formal title of address, "my lord, the king," he dares to use the very intimate designation, "my father." The whole speech is framed as an argument of his innocence and against all charges of disloyalty. The main point of his case here is that the completely fortuitous circumstance in which Saul alone and without protection ends up in the same cave as David and his men, while David does not take advantage of the occasion to kill him, proves that those who have spoken of treachery are lying. They can point to no action of his to the contrary. Furthermore, he is hardly a significant adversary and no threat to the king. As evidence of what he could have done, he has the piece of Saul's cloak. David's remarks about the inviolability of Yahweh's anointed do not belong to an account that includes 1 Sam 16:1–13, so there is no duplicity in his words. The response by Saul in 24:17–23[16–22] is given in kind by the statement "Is this your voice, my son David?" corresponding to David's "my father," and it is followed by the remark "Saul lifted up his voice and wept." This, in turn, is followed by the complete and heart-felt acknowledgement that David is in the right and by Saul's gratitude that David has spared his life. More importantly, Saul now fully acknowledges that David will succeed him as king. This agrees closely with the remarks of Jonathan in 23:17 and belongs to the same source. Consequently, Saul extracts from David a solemn oath that he will not exterminate his descendants when he comes to power. David agrees to make this oath, and they then part company.

In the second account, 26:17–25, it is Saul who makes the opening speech to David, with the personal address, "Is this your voice, my son David?" (v. 17), in imitation of the first account, but now David speaks to the king at a great distance, he makes no act of obeisance, and he uses only the

formal title "my lord the king," thus flatly rejecting Saul's overture of personal address. The first of two speeches (vv. 17-20) focus entirely on his
pursuit and his banishment to a foreign power outside Israelite territory,
where he will be forced to worship other gods. This is quite a different argument from that used in the first account and clearly the central point of
this speech. Now up to this point David has not been driven from the "heritage of Yahweh," but, with the exception of one brief interlude (1 Sam
21:11-16[10-15]), all of David's time has been in Judah. So behind this pious talk is the threat of his defection to the Philistines. Even when he does
defect to the Philistines, he hardly spends any time at Gath in the court of
Achish but manages to spend most of his time in Judah and is not obliged
to worship any foreign gods.

In Saul's response, he acknowledges that he was in the wrong and he invites David back to the court. He can see that he has acted foolishly, because clearly this hint of David's defection to the Philistines is a serious
threat to his rule. Thus, Saul is quite willing to come to terms with David.
There is no such invitation in the first account to return to Saul's court because the relationship between David and Saul has formally ended. In
26:22-23, David, for his part, returns the spear but now makes the pious
claim that "Yahweh who rewards uprightness and loyalty will reward the
man [i.e., himself] into whose power he put you today, for I refused to lift
my hand against Yahweh's anointed. Just as your life was precious to me today so may my life be precious to Yahweh and rescue me from every adver-
sity" (vv. 23-24). David again lays emphasis on the theme of Yahweh's
anointed, but now he makes his own life as the new anointed the equivalent
of Saul's, the old anointed. David's approach is to set himself up as Saul's
equivalent, indeed, his better. What is particularly noteworthy is that, in the
previous account in 24:18-22[17-21], it is Saul, not David, who acknowledges that David is the righteous one because he spared Saul's life, and then
Saul expresses the prayer "May Yahweh repay you well for what you have
done to me today." This reward is to be David's rule of the kingdom in place
of his own. In the second account, it is David who declares himself to be the
righteous one, and in so doing he is throwing Saul's own words back at him
and expects nothing more from him. David is left with nothing but a rather
weak platitude in place of the statement about David's right to the throne.
"Blessings on you, my boy. You will go a long way" (26:25).

This second version of David's sparing Saul's life has the markings of a
revision of the earlier episode by the author of *account B*. The whole encounter between David and Saul is carefully staged by David to put Saul

and his men in the wrong and to justify his future action, which was to take up residence in the land of the Philistines. David could not return to Saul's court because he would lose control of his personal force of 600 men and would be under Saul's complete control. He has nothing to gain by reconciliation and everything to lose. Thus, he formulates his own destiny in the south in cooperation with the Philistines. It was Saul's mistake, his own foolishness as he admits, to be misled and allow David to create this sort of power base in the marginal region of Judah where Saul could never track him down.

Finally, the expectations that one has beyond these two contrasting episodes is entirely different. At the conclusion of *account A*, the story of David and Saul has come to an end as well. Saul's words recognizing David as his successor and extracting an oath about the fate of his own family reflects a foreboding about his own demise, so that the final showdown in 1 Sam 31 will quickly follow. *Account B* ends the relationship between David and Saul in a quite-different way, because even though David's flight from Saul comes to an end, the words of David clearly anticipate his subsequent service among the Philistines. In this respect, it is an introduction to what follows in chaps. 27–30, with this link in 27:1: "David thought to himself, 'One day I shall fall at the hands of Saul; there is nothing better for me than to make my escape to the land of the Philistines. Then Saul will give up looking for me any longer within the borders of Israel, and I shall escape from his grasp.'" While scholars have recognized this connection they have been reluctant about attributing all of the material to a supplementary status, so they either regard 27:1 as redactional or they find arguments for viewing chap. 26 as the earlier version. The task, therefore, remains for us to test this thesis by looking at chaps. 27–30 to see how it fits with the later supplementary material in *account B* that has been isolated thus far. But first one must consider chap. 25, which has been placed between the two parallel accounts, to understand its relationship with chap. 26 and what follows.

David and Abigail

Once it becomes clear that the second account of David sparing Saul's life is an artful imitation of the first, created by an author who has greatly amplified the story of David, then the story of David and Abigail can be seen as a convenient way of separating the two narratives from one another. It also presents a description of the activity of David and his men as a band of "brigands"[24] who live off the wealthy land-owners by providing "protection," whether they want it or not. It is clearly not a very complementary portrait and quite different from the one presented in 23:1–5, where David and his men intervene against a robbing band of Philistines. David's threat to massacre the household of Nabal for defying him, which is only narrowly averted by the intervention of Abigail, also does not flatter David's image. It is clearly similar to the image of the David in chap. 26 rather than chap. 24, and it is this connection with the later source that needs to be explored.

The story of David's dealings with Nabal and the timely intervention of Abigail have a number of similarities and close associations with CH. These may be listed as the following.

1. The sheep shearing at Carmel by the servants of Nabal that includes a great feast with lots of wine that almost ends in a catastrophe, but ends only in the death of Nabal, is parallel to the sheep shearing of Absalom on mount Baal-hazor, which also includes a great feast by David's sons that results in the death of Amnon, although it is falsely represented at first as a great slaughter of the sons of David.

2. When Abigail intervenes to save her household, she does so by taking a gift of food to David and his men. It is described as consisting of 200 loaves, 2 skins of wine, 5 sheep ready dressed, 5 measures of parched grain, 100 clusters of raisins, and 200 cakes of figs, which were borne on asses. When Ziba, the servant of Mephibosheth, meets David at the beginning of his flight from Absalom (2 Sam 16:1), he comes with asses bearing 200 loaves of bread, 100 bunches of raisins, 100 summer fruits, and a skin of wine. The similarity can hardly be fortuitous.[25]

---

24. See McKenzie, *King David*, 96–101; J. D. Levenson, "1 Samuel 25 as Literature and History," *CBQ* 40 (1978): 11–28. However, both McKenzie and Levenson regard this story as an early narrative reflective of actual historical events, and this colors their interpretation of it.

25. This is an example of what Gunn calls "oral patterns" in the David and Saul stories. See his discussion of these in a series of articles: D. M. Gunn, "Narrative Patterns and Oral Tradition in Judges and Samuel," *VT* 24 (1974): 286–317; idem, "David and the Gift of the Kingdom," *Semeia* 3 (1975): 14–45; idem, "Traditional Composition in the 'Succession Narrative,'" *VT* 26 (1976): 214–29. I responded to these in "Oral Patterns or Literary Conventions in Biblical Narrative," *Semeia* 5 (1976): 139–54; idem, "Problems in the Literary Analysis of the Court History if David," *JSOT* 1 (1976): 22–29. Cf. D. M. Gunn, "On Oral Tradition: A Response to John Van Seters," *Semeia* 5 (1976): 155–61.

3. Abigail is represented as a woman of good sense (טובת־שכל), 1 Sam
25:3, and this reminds one of the wise woman (אשה חכמה) of Tekoa (2 Sam
14:4-20). In both cases, the women appear before David to make a solemn
appeal, and they behave very similarly. When Abigail approaches David
(1 Sam 25:23-24), she quickly dismounts from her ass "and she fell before
David upon her face and did obeisance to the ground" (ותפל לפני דוד על פניה
[ותשתחו ארצ]ה, v. 23) and pleads "On me alone, my lord, be the blame" (אדני
בי־אני העון), "let your handmaid speak in your hearing and listen to the
words of your handmaid" (ותדבר־נא אמתך באזניך ושמע את דברי אמתך). This
same self-deprecating style of address occurs in the speech of the woman of
Tekoa (2 Sam 14:4-20), using the same language, but in different parts of
the speech so that it is not simply a matter of one scene imitating another.
The woman approaches the king in the same way: "she fell upon her face
to the ground and did obeisance" (ותפל על־אפיה ארצה ותשתחו, v. 4). After
she tells the king of her plight, the king promises to address her problems,
but then she begins a new appeal: "On me, my lord the king, be the blame"
(העון עלי אדני המלך, v. 9). When the woman finally ends her fabricated tale
and turns to the real issue of her request, she begins her plea with the
words "Let your handmaid speak to my lord the king a word" (תדבר־נא
שפחתך אל־אדני המלך דבר, v. 12). Though the woman's preferred term of self-
deprecation is שפחה, there is a shift to אמה in vv. 15-16 for no obvious reason. Just as in the story of Abigail, the term she uses for herself is אמה, but
in 1 Sam 25:27 and 41 she shifts to the more demeaning term, שפחה. Furthermore, in both stories the object of the women's speeches is to change
the mind of David by persuasive rhetoric for the betterment of his present
or future rule of his people. To my mind, there can be little doubt that both
episodes are constructed by the same author.

Besides these obvious parallels, there are some important ideological
connections with both Dtr and CH. Within the speech of Abigail, there is
a shift in vv. 28-31 in which she plays on David's aspirations to greatness,
which may be jeopardized by a rash vendetta against Nabal and his household. Here, the language clearly imitates themes that derive from Dtr, that
Yahweh will give to him a "sure house" (בית נאמן), that is, a dynasty, "because my lord has fought the wars of Yahweh, and no evil (moral? or material calamity?) will be found in you as long as you live." This obviously has
reference to the Davidic promise in 2 Sam 7. In addition, Abigail refers to
a previous promise that was made concerning David: "It will happen that
when Yahweh has made good to you all that he has promised and in-

stalled you as *nāgîd* (נגיד) over Israel. . . ." This refers back to the rather specific language of 1 Sam 13:14b: "Yahweh has search for a man after his own heart and Yahweh has appointed him as leader (*nāgîd*) over his people." The statement of Abigail also corresponds closely with the remarks in 2 Sam 5:1-2, 3b: "Then all the tribes of Israel came to David in Hebron and said to him, 'We are your bone and flesh. In the past, when Saul was king over us, it was you who led Israel in campaign. And Yahweh said to you, "you it is who shepherd my people Israel and you will become leader (*nāgîd*) over Israel."' And there they anointed David as king over Israel" (see also 2 Sam 7:8). This passage seems to point to some past revelation that was given to David, just as we have it in Abigail's remarks, even though no such direct promise is given in the text. This anointing as *nāgîd* is parallel to the anointing of Saul as *nāgîd* over Israel in 1 Sam 10:1, so that the theme of the deity's election of the *nāgîd* clearly belongs to DtrH.

Consequently, there can be no question about the fact that the passage in 1 Sam 25:38-31 is either by Dtr or is dependent on DtrH and imitates it. Likewise, Abigail's words anticipate the anointing in 2 Sam 5:1-3; however, they are not just a Dtr gloss on the text, for they clearly constitute the decisive argument that prevents David from carrying out his sworn actions. Yet how does Abigail know about the earlier prophecy (v. 30), and where is it specifically announced to David prior to his coronation? It cannot refer to the secret anointing of David by Samuel in 1 Sam 16:1-13 because the terminology used throughout is quite different; David is anointed as king, not *nāgîd*, and there is reason to believe that the second account of the rejection of Saul in 1 Sam 15:1-16:13 is a later addition to DtrH.

There is, however, another use of the same theme within the context of CH, in 2 Sam 6:21, in which David, in response to the criticism of his behavior by Michal, his wife, states, "It was in the presence of Yahweh, who chose me in place of your father and his entire household to appoint me as leader (*nāgîd*) over Israel, the people of Yahweh, and in his presence I will dance for joy." There can be no question of the close imitation of the theme of Saul's rejection and David's election of *nāgîd* in DtrH, but here the theme is used in quite an ironic sense. David invokes the theme in order to belittle the criticism of Michal and to justify his sexually provocative actions in the present and future promiscuous activity with the slave-girls. This suggests that the author of CH viewed the theme of God's election of David as *nāgîd* in place of Saul as simply a piece of religious propaganda to justify the abuse of power and privilege by the royal house.

When we turn back to the story of Abigail and consider the many indications within the story that point to an authorship that is shared with CH, then this casts the speech of Abigail in a quite-different light. David is the leader of a large armed band of brigands who may be employed as mercenaries or who demand protection payment for not stealing goods from land owners. He is hardly fighting the "wars of Yahweh." So like the woman of Tekoa, Abigail flatters David with the myth of his divine election as *nāgîd* and future greatness in order to keep his hands clean from unnecessary bloodshed. Why jeopardize this future when she has already given him what he would have otherwise demanded? It is of no concern to the author how Abigail could have known about this promise to David of kingship. As in the case of the encounter between Michal and David, the author merely wishes to cast doubt on its value as a means to justify the Davidic monarchy. As circumstances would have it, the convenient death of Nabal leads quickly to David's acquiring Abigail as his wife along with a second wife, Ahinoam of Jezreel. It is noteworthy that these two wives are continuously referred to together until the time of David's installation in Hebron, and then Abigail is regularly identified as the "wife of Nabal." If the story of Abigail does belong to the author of CH, then all of these references to the two wives likewise belong to this same literary work. The unit ends in v. 46 with a remark that Saul gave his daughter Michal to another man. This anticipates the episode in 2 Sam 3:12–16 (CH) in which Michal is returned to David as another member of his harem.

David among the Philistines:
Observations on 1 Samuel 27–31

This section deals with a series of events that lead up to the final defeat of Saul by the Philistines. While each individual unit within this section is tied to this theme, they are not all of one piece or authorship. One significant clue here is what appears to be a resumptive repetition in 1 Sam 28:3 that repeats the same wording of 1 Sam 25:1 in a shorter form. The translations usually differentiate between the two references by rendering the second one in the pluperfect, "Samuel had died." This might suggest that all the narrative between these two points is a later addition. We have already demonstrated that chaps. 25 and 26 are later additions. So this raises the further possibility that chap. 27 is also part of the later expansion. It follows rather directly on chap. 26. I have also demonstrated elsewhere that 1 Sam 28:3–24, along with 1 Sam 15:1–16:13, is a later supplement to

DtrH and is not entirely consistent with its context.[26] The text in 1 Sam 28:4 indicates that the Philistines mustered their forces and were encamped at Shunem in the Jezreel valley while Saul's forces were encamped opposite them on the slopes of Mount Gilboa. But at the end of Saul's encounter with the medium of Endor in the same region, the Philistines in 29:1 were still mustering their forces at Aphek, many miles south of Jezreel, and it is only later that they proceed to Jezreel. This would suggest that 29:1 is a continuation of 28:1-2, but 29:1 reads like a recapitulation of 28:1 as though to accommodate the unit in 28:3-24. There is also no question that 27:1-28:2 belongs to what follows in 29:1-31:13. One further indication of the continuity of chap. 25 with this later corpus is the repeated reference to the two wives of David, Abigail and Ahinoam (1 Sam 25:43, 27:3, 30:5; 2 Sam 2:2).

There is, of course, the obvious problem of the doublet in 21:11-16[10-15] with David's relations with the same king in 27:1-28:2, 29:1-11. In the earlier episode, David appears alone at the court of Achish of Gath to seek asylum as a fugitive, similar to Rehoboam's seeking asylum in Egypt as a fugitive from Solomon (1 Kgs 11:40). It is clear that this story knows nothing of the story about David's triumph over Goliath, the champion of Gath, but it does know of the song of the women who praise his great military exploits. However, the servants of Achish mistake the comparison with Saul to mean that David is now king of the land of Israel. When David's identity is discovered, he feigns madness and is dismissed. There is no reason, it seems to me, to question that this little scene belongs to *account A* of the David and Saul story. This makes it hard to reconcile it with David's later appearance in Gath with his men where he becomes a vassal to this same king. It is clear that they cannot belong to the same "source." At the same time, this episode in 21:11-16[10-15] can hardly follow from the previous one in 21:2-10[1-9] in which David acquires the sword of Goliath, the former champion of Gath. One would expect that Gath is the last place in which David would seek refuge. And David's defeat of the Philistines at Keilah (1 Sam 23:1-5) also makes it rather difficult to see him in the ranks of the Philistines at a later date.

The presentation of David in chap. 27 is not a very praiseworthy one. He is the leader of a mercenary band of 600 armed warriors who offers his services to Achish, king of Gath, in the land of the Philistines and thus out of Saul's reach. Here he plays the very dangerous and deceptive game of

---

26. See my *In Search of History*, 261-64.

removing himself from the king's immediate control by becoming a client ruler over Ziklag, conducting raids on the aboriginal peoples of the region, including the Amalekites, massacring the inhabitants. This *ḥerem*-like operation is not for any religious reasons, as in the case of Saul in 1 Sam 15, but is merely to David's own advantage so that no one may report his activities to Achish, who is given the impression that he has been raiding the inhabitants of Judah. The goods and animals are not placed under the ban but used as booty to please the pagan king and to win support in Judah. Diana Edelman makes much of the comparison between Saul's campaign against the Amalekites in 1 Sam 15 and that of David, pointing out the similarity in the territory covered by the raids (1 Sam 15:7; cf. 27:9), and suggests that the comparison "indicates that David was picking up where Saul left off, eliminating Yahweh's sworn enemy from the region."[27] This statement, however, is quite misleading. The earlier account in 1 Sam 15 suggests that the Amalekites were completely destroyed, including the king, who survived the raid itself. There was nothing more for David to do! Furthermore, there is no suggestion in chap. 27 of any religious motive for David's actions, no divine consultation, and he included non-Amalekites as well. The comparison is indeed deliberate but only to emphasize that David's actions were done entirely for his own self-interest and that of his band of men. Though David is thus deceiving Achish, the latter places great trust in David and wishes to make him his bodyguard for life. This is, of course, a complete reversal of the roles of both Achish and David as presented in 21:11–16[10–15]. Also unlike the earlier account, in this later version no one in Gath seems to have ever heard of David and his earlier exploits. Furthermore, for the purposes of this narrative, the author completely ignores the Goliath story.

Among all of the discussion of parallels and doublets, there is a striking parallel to David's role in Gath that has generally been overlooked. In CH, during the recounting of the revolt of Absalom, we are confronted with the fact that David's bodyguard consists of a large group of mercenaries, the Cherethites and Pelethites, and "all the six hundred Gittites who had followed him [Ittai] from Gath" (2 Sam 15:18). At the head of this group is the Philistine Ittai the Gittite, who is clearly one of the most senior and most trusted of David's commanders. This band of mercenaries seems to be cast in a role very similar to that of David in Gath. Indeed, at this all-important mustering of his forces David suggests to Ittai not to participate in the civil

---

27. Edelman, *King Saul*, 235.

war: "Why should you also go with us? Return and be with the [new] king, for you are a foreigner and you too are in exile from your homeland. You came only recently and shall I now make you travel about with us, and I do not even know where I am going." Ittai protests against this suggestion and swears his absolute loyalty to David, to share in his hardships and even to die for him. With this he is invited to join the ranks, with all of his men and their families who have been living in exile with them.

Such an explicit description of Ittai and his followers is surely intended to draw a parallel with David's own exile in Gath; both have the same number of men and both are in exile with all of their families. It is even suggested in 1 Kgs 2:39 that the king of Gath was still Achish at this time. The irony is obvious. Whereas David was quite disloyal and deceitful and served Achish out of his own self-interest, Ittai shows himself to be completely loyal. In the final battle in 2 Sam 18:2–5, Ittai ranks as the third commander of the forces alongside Joab and Abishai. David, in the final showdown between the Philistines and the forces of Saul (1 Sam 29), is judged to be untrustworthy by the other commanders of the Philistines, and in spite of all his protestations of honesty and loyalty, which we know to be false, he does not take part in the final battle. In the Absalom revolt, however, most of the Israelite forces have deserted David and he is now heavily dependent on his mercenaries, so he has little choice but to trust Ittai. With all of the similarities drawn between Ittai and David, and the very strong emphasis on the theme of trust and loyalty, there can be little doubt that the two narratives belong to the same hand.

In 1 Sam 30 David and his men have returned from Gath to Ziklag only to find it in ruins with their families taken. The Amalekites apparently did not massacre the women and children of their enemies as David and his men did. The story of David's pursuit and victory have many interconnections with what has gone before, as we have noted above, so there is no question that it belongs to this same late author. The whole episode is skillfully developed. The mustering of the Philistine forces so far north has left the southern regions vulnerable to attack by marauding Amalekites, and with David's complete force at Aphek, his home base in Ziklag is sacked. The men return to find the place in ruins and their wives and children gone. In their distress, they blame David for leaving their families defenseless and threaten revolt. David, however, gets himself out of this difficulty by using Abiathar and the ephod to get his men into action in pursuit of the Amelekites. It is their good fortune that they find an Egyptian slave of one of the Amalekites who was left behind to die because he was sick and who is able to give David directions as to how to find the Amalekites. It is again fortunate that they catch the Amalekites off guard, celebrating their victories, and are able to defeat them. It is, of course, quite miraculous that they were able to recover all of the wives and children from Ziklag and all the booty as well as what was taken from the other places raided by the Amalekites. David and his men did not suffer a single casualty, but this is the nature of fiction. On his return with this vast booty, David is able to use it for political purposes among the elders of Judah, calling the gifts a present "from the spoils of the enemies of Yahweh," which suggests a comparison with 1 Sam 15. The spoil that was taken from the land of the Philistines (v. 16) was, of course, not returned. So much for David's loyalty to his overlord. This circumstance now prepares for the defeat of Saul and David's ascent to the throne of Judah.

This brings us to the decisive battle between Saul and the Philistines in 1 Sam 31. There can be no doubt that this unit belongs to *account A* of the David-Saul story and provides the transition to David's reign. It constitutes yet another doublet with 2 Sam 1 on just how Saul died. However, before we address this issue we must first ask how we are to get from the last episode in *account A*, namely, 1 Sam 24 and this ending in chap. 31. It is obvious that 31:1 is not the beginning of the narrative of the final battle; it lacks the appropriate introduction. There are a number of references to the initial mustering of the Philistines and the Israelites in preparation for this battle that have become separated from it by various additions:

1 Sam 28:1a ויהי בימים ההם ויקבצו פלשתים את־מחניהם לצבא להלחם בישראל

Now it happened at that time that the Philistines mustered their forces for war to fight with Israel.

1 Sam 28:4 ויקבצו פלשתים ויבאו ויחנו בשונם ויקבץ שאול את־כל־ישראל ויחני בגלבע

The Philistines mustered and came and encamped in Shunem while Saul mustered all Israel and encamped at Gilboa.

1 Sam 29:1 ויקבצו פלשתים את־כל־מחניהם אפקה וישראל חנים בעין אשר ביזרעאל

The Philistines mustered all the forces at Aphek while Israel was encamped at the spring in Jezreel.

1 Sam 29:11b ופלשתים עלו יזרעאל

Then the Philistines went up to Jezreel.

1 Sam 31:1 ופלשתים נלחמים בישראל וינסו אנשי ישראל מפני פלשתים ויפלו
חללים בהר הגלבע

The Philistines fought against Israel and the men of Israel were routed before Philistines and the corpses fell on Mount Gilboa.

It seems to me that among these various texts, the original combination is reflected in 1 Sam 28:1a, 4aβ, b; 31:1 (see the underlined portions), which clearly reflects the beginning of hostilities, the assembling of the two forces and their location, and their engagement in combat with the rout of the Israelites. While 1 Sam 29:1 repeats the mustering of the Philistines from 28:1a and 4, it changes the location of the two camps from Shunem to Aphek for the Philistines and from Gilboa to the spring of Jezreel for the Israelites. However, 1 Sam 31:1 retains the reference to Gilboa. The statement in 29:11 that the Philistines moved on up to Jezreel, at the same time that David went back south to Ziklag, was necessary because Aphek was a long distance from Jezreel. But this makes the location quite inappropriate for the events in 28:5–25, where Saul seems to have a clear view of the Philistine camp from the slopes of Gilboa. Thus, the text would read "Now it happened at that time that the Philistines mustered their forces for war to fight against Israel. . . . They came and encamped in Shunem and Saul mustered all Israel and encamped at Gilboa. The Philistines fought against Israel and the Israelite forces were routed before the Philistines and the corpses fell on Mount Gilboa." This sequence was broken up twice; once by the inclusion of the episode of Saul and the medium of Endor (1 Sam 28:3, 5–25), with resumptive repetition in 28:4aα, and a second time by the narrative about David and Achish in 28:1b–2, 29:1–11 and David's return to Ziklag in chap. 30. This has involved a good deal of resumptive repetition in 1 Sam 29:1. In addition, there is the adjustment of geographic details, not all of it entirely satisfactory. Consequently, the seams in the narrative are still evident.

Competing Ideologies in the Story of David and Saul

What has evolved from this study of the story of David and Saul is a development scenario that is quite different from the one usually put forward. As we have seen in our earlier review of scholarship on the David story, attempts have been made to reconstruct an independent History of David's Rise, alongside another independent Succession Narrative, as the two major sources for DtrH. Attempts such as these largely faltered on the recognition that there were many interconnections between these two bodies of text, and the thesis of a History of David's Rise could not adequately deal with all the doublets within it that suggested a plurality of sources. In place of attempts to find an early account of David's rise, we have suggested that the oldest form of the story of David and Saul in *account A* was that constructed by the Dtr Historian.[28] This narrative was only a fraction of the final form, the larger portion consisting of later supplementation, *account B*, which was not an independent source.[29] It is the combination of these two accounts, *A* and *B*, that has produced the *David Saga* as we have it today (minus the additional texts in 2 Sam 21–24). And because the second account has been added to the older Dtr version, the author of the *David Saga* is also the author of *account B* in the David and Saul story, as well as what I formerly referred to as the Court History. Consequently, from this point on, we may conveniently distinguish between Dtr and the author of the *David Saga*.

The narrative in Dtr's *account A* is a very straightforward presentation of David's rise to power that is entirely positive. David is guileless, transparently honest, loyal to Saul, and upright in all his actions. This portrayal of David is in complete agreement with Dtr's general presentation of David, as we shall see below. All the people, the servants and warriors of Saul and his own family love and admire David and recognize that Yahweh is with him. This is the basis of his great success against the Philistines and confirmation of his divine election. Only Saul is opposed to David because he represents a threat of the ultimate loss of his dynasty, but even he in the end is won over to accepting David as his successor. It is this presentation that dovetails so closely with the Dtr climax of David's reign in the divine promise to David concerning the establishment of his dynasty in 2 Sam 7. The Dtr Historian may have had access to some older traditions about David, particularly about his skirmishes with the Philistines, but no earlier narrative about David's rise to power can be reconstructed. It seems to me that the connection between David with his band in Judah and Saul, an early king of Benjamin, is a product of Dtr's own literary construction, and this

---

28. The outline of Dtr's story of David and Saul in *account A* can be seen in the following components: 1 Sam 16:14–23; 18:5–9*, (10–11), 12–16, 17–30; 19:1–17; 21:11–16; 22:1–5; 23:1–5, 15–18, 24b–28; 24:1–23; 28:1a, 4αβ, b; 31:1–13.

29. The following components belong to *account B*: 1 Sam 17:1–18:4, 6a*; 19:18–21:10; 22:6–23; 23:6–14, 19–24a; 25:1–44; 26:1–25; 27:1–28:2; 29:1–11; 30:1–31.

link continues Dtr's earlier presentation of the reign of Saul and his account of the origin of the monarchy in Israel.

To Dtr's modest corpus of the David and Saul story has been added a larger body of texts, much of which is reflected in double and even triple accounts. It is this large body of material, so un-Deuteronomistic in character, that has misled so many scholars who regarded it as early sources that were simply incorporated by Dtr largely unchanged into his work. This gave the impression that the books of Samuel were quite different from Kings and made it hard to integrate them into a larger DtrH. The problem, however, is quite otherwise. As we have argued, a very large portion of the David story is a much later fictional addition that is completely at odds with the earlier Dtr presentation. It is not so much anti-Saul or anti-David or anti-Solomon as it is *antimonarchy*. This major revision, the *David Saga*, is not just a matter of numerous "editorial" glosses and alterations. It is primarily an extensive literary creation that has been built into the earlier Dtr narrative with minimal change to this work that forms its framework.

Any treatment of the story of David and Saul must take seriously the problem of the doublets, and this has lead scholars to fall back on the method used in pentateuchal criticism, in which doublets are understood as parallel sources or older oral traditions that have been combined by editors, who are likewise responsible for many "creative" additions. By contrast, our analysis has found that all the doublets and evidence of different sources reflects deliberate extensive additions made to the Dtr account, in two stages. The first is a new introduction of David and his secret anointing by Samuel in 1 Sam 16:1–13 that is part of a larger addition in 1 Sam 15:1– 16:13; 28:3, 5–25.

The second expansion of Dtr's *account A* is an extensive addition, *account B*, which runs through the whole of the Dtr narrative and uses the older *account A* as its framework. Our analysis identified the author of *account B* as the same author who wrote CH, and therefore they should be considered part of the same literary work. It is a finely crafted literary work that is much larger than Dtr's own account of David's reign, and the literary additions consist of a number of extended literary blocks, some of which are doublets of episodes in Dtr and others whose subject matter is quite original to the author. The intent of the work is to offer a revision of Dtr's work by way of supplementation, to call into question the institution of the monarchy in general and the Davidic dynasty in particular, and to question the theological legitimacy that has been used to support it.

As we saw above, the story of David and Goliath in 1 Sam 17:1–54 orig-inated as an independent heroic tale about David that was given a strong theological interpretation and then incorporated into the larger context by the addition of 17:55–18:4, as part of *account B*. The final author uses the narrative in 16:1–13 concerning David's family to expand the remarks about David and his brothers in 17:12–16. In the addition, the important figures of Jonathan and Abner are introduced alongside Saul, and both play an important role in his later work. However, it is especially the close rela-tionship of Jonathan to David that is greatly developed in a new way in this source. The covenant between David and Jonathan, which occurs in Dtr at the end of David's relations with Jonathan and Saul, in which David's right to the succession is acknowledged (23:16–18) is transplanted to the very first encounter that Jonathan has with David when he enters Saul's service. It is based entirely on Jonathan's affection for David and his willing sub-mission to David "because he loved him as his very self" and for no other reason. From this point onward, Jonathan, the heir to the throne, is under the complete control of David. Finally, the later author has also added the phrase "when David returned (from slaying the Philistine)" (18:6), to make the connection of the story of David and Goliath with the later context.

The large block of narrative in 19:18–21:10, 22:6–23 dealing with Da-vid's flight is linked with what precedes and what follows. David first flees to Samuel, who provides a curious kind of protection by which first Saul's servants and then Saul himself are incapacitated by coming under the influ-ence of prophetic ecstasy. This episode serves as a doublet to the earlier one in 1 Sam 10:5–13, in which Saul's prophetic experience of ecstasy receives a very positive interpretation. It is by means of this possession of the spirit that he is victorious in the battles of Yahweh. Here the fit of ecstasy is com-pletely degrading and leaves him helpless. This cannot be merely attributed to the "evil spirit" as proposed by Dtr (16:14) that is said to possess him from time to time. Here it is attributed to the influence of Samuel who is the leader of a band of ecstatics at Ramah, and it is just this sort of person who is responsible for the anointing of kings. This makes the whole religious le-gitimacy of kingship suspect. Furthermore, because this source knows of the surreptitious anointing of David by Samuel, the close association of Da-vid with Samuel points directly back to that rather treasonous act against Saul. Nothing is said here about David's "prophesying," although he is also in the presence of the ecstatics. He seems curiously immune.

From Samuel in Ramah, David returns in his flight to the court of Saul in order to meet with Jonathan and confront him with the threat by his father on his life (20:1-42). Contrary to the prior instance in which it is Jonathan who informs David of Saul's intentions and takes the initiative to protect David, here it is David who sets out an elaborate plan of deception that needlessly puts Jonathan in mortal danger (20:30-34). After renewing their solemn pledge to each other, the plan is formed by which Jonathan will learn of his father's intentions and inform David. Saul's strong desire to kill David becomes entirely clear to Jonathan, and this leads to a tender scene of parting and to the renewed flight of David. Because it is obvious that this episode is tied closely to those that precede it in chaps. 18 and 19, David's return to the court and Jonathan's ignorance of his father's intentions make no sense in terms of the story's plot. The purpose of the episode is intended solely as a revision of the parallel scenes in order to flesh out the characters of David and Jonathan and to set a context for the oath between them concerning Jonathan's descendants that will play a role in a later part of the *David Saga* (2 Sam 9).

The next episode having to do with David's visit to Nob (21:2-10, 22:6-23) is constructed in two parts around the Dtr units in 21:11-22:5. David's flight from the court takes him to Nob, which is still in Benjamin, close to Gibeah, and there he receives the aid of the priest of the holy city of Nob. Again, there seems to be no particular reason for David to visit this place except to obtain a little food and a weapon by deceit,[30] thereby placing the priests of this sanctuary in great jeopardy, an act that he later regrets. The sequel in 22:6-23 reveals the disastrous consequences for the priests with their massacre by Saul. The point of the story centers both on the character of David, whose actions and ambitions needlessly place the lives of others in jeopardy, and the nature of Saul's monarchy. In the latter case, Saul, out of fear and jealousy, engages in an act of *ḥerem* on the sacred city of Nob and all the priests of Yahweh, using an unscrupulous Edomite for this purpose. If the king's own kin and countrymen will not carry out his murderous intentions, then he can always employ foreign mercenaries who have no such scruples.[31] Abiathar, the one priest who escapes, joins David's

---

30. There is no logic in this choice of aid such as this for either food or weapons. Did not David already have Goliath's sword (17:54)? And why did not Jonathan arrange to supply David with these necessities, a much more likely source?

31. One cannot ask questions about the historical probability of the account, such as whether there ever was a sacred city such as this, presumably the successor of Shiloh and its priesthood, and whether one man could carry out the massacre of the whole city by himself with no protest and only one survivor.

entourage and plays an important role in the later narrative of the *David Saga*.[32]

David and his men take up residence in Keilah in Judah (23:6–14), and this follows directly on the previous episode in Dtr (23:1–5) in which David rescued Keilah from the hands of the Philistines. However, in the sequel in 23:6–14, the people of Keilah are quite prepared to give David into the hands of Saul. The author has attempted to build the arrival of Abiathar in 22:20–23, 23:6 around the deliverance of Keilah by David in 23:1–5 by suggesting that Abiathar fled directly to Keilah with the ephod so that he was the one through whom David consulted the deity. However, it is clear that David was not yet in Keilah when the Philistines were attacking the city and only went to the city's rescue after consulting the deity. It is only in the second episode in 23:6–14 that Abiathar and the ephod now function directly as the means of divine consultation. David's forces have now increased to six hundred men (23:13), the figure that is consistently used in this source.[33] As in the case of the men of Keilah, so also in 23:19–24a the Ziphites of Judah are eager to help Saul in his attempt to find and kill David. The author suggests that in both of these instances there is no loyalty or love for David in Judah in preference to Saul; they are both treated as a menace. This is entirely the opposite attitude of those with whom David served in Israel and who all love him in Dtr's narrative.

After Dtr's episode in *account A* in chap. 24 concerning David's sparing Saul's life, the *David Saga* in *account B* incorporates a large section in 25:1–28:2, 29:1–30:31. It begins in 25:1a with a remark about the death, mourning, and burial of Samuel that has nothing to do with what comes before or after it. However, the statement is repeated in almost the same language in 28:3 as a resumptive repetition, where it is very closely associated with the following narrative about Saul and the medium of Endor, and this leads us to conclude that everything from 25:1–28:2 belongs to *account B*. This narrative, in turn, is continued in 29:1 by recapitulating 28:1a, and it extends to 30:31. As I have pointed out above, numerous interconnections throughout this corpus make its literary unity quite secure.

---

32. Abiathar has no place whatsoever in DtrH.

33. See 1 Sam 27:2, 30:9. It is also used of the Gittite mercenaries under Ittai in 2 Sam 15:18. This was the size of the fighting force that Saul used in 1 Sam 13:15, 14:2 to fight the Philistines! It seems to be a fairly standard military unit as compared with the 400 men that followed David in the earlier source.

Nevertheless, within this complex source are a number of individual episodes with their own theme and plot, the first of which is the story of David and Abigail in 25:1–44. Our earlier analysis of this story revealed a very close similarity with episodes in CH, especially those having to do with the wise woman of Tekoa and with David's wife Michal. This leads us to conclude that the characterization of David in this story must be understood within this larger context. Thus, in contrast to Dtr's view in which David and his men protect the towns of Judah against the marauding Philistines (23:1–5), this author presents David and his men as engaged in extortion from wealthy landowners for their "protection," and David and his band are only diverted from a massacre by the wise action of the landowner's wife, who is able to dissuade David by showing him that it is for his own good not to engage in this kind of slaughter. She also becomes one of David's many wives, while Michal, his former wife who has not joined him in his flight, is temporarily given to another husband.

It is within this context that one must understand the pious speech of Abigail in 25:28–31. While this certainly picks up the Dtr theme about David's election as *nāgîd* over Israel, it is not a "redactional" addition, as some suppose, but a rather satirical play on this theme of royal ideology that contrasts the ideal with the reality. Her statement "For Yahweh will indeed establish for my lord a secure dynasty, seeing that my lord has been fighting the battles of Yahweh, and nothing wrong will happen to you [or be discovered against you?] as long as you live" can be read as heavily ironic. The prediction of a "secure dynasty" that points to the promise in 2 Sam 7:11–16 also points beyond it to the very insecure and troubled house of David in the later narrative. Under Saul, David was certainly fighting the "battles of Yahweh" against the Philistines, but in this source since his flight he has not been so engaged and he will soon be employed as a mercenary for the Philistines. Nowhere in this source is there any suggestion that any of David's military activity is motivated by or conducted according to the principles of holy war. As for the final ambiguous statement about "harm" or "wrong" being "found" in him for the rest of his life, this remains true only to the extent that he survives to old age, but for all his cunning he certainly does not go undiscovered in his offenses. What Abigail's statement seems to suggest is that the ideology of David's election with all its pious language may be used for important political ends without corresponding to the actual facts of royal behavior. Indeed, this same Dtr ideology of kingship is used in just this way by David against the criticism of Michal in 2 Sam 6:21–22 to justify his rather promiscuous behavior.

The unit in 26:1–25 presents a second occasion of David sparing the life of Saul, and it is a parallel to the episode in chap. 24, as we have seen. Its purpose is to revise our understanding of a final encounter between David and Saul such as this. This is done in several ways. First, as we have seen above, David's rather motley group has become a serious fighting force of 600 men that includes the future commanders of his army, such as Joab and Abishai, whereas Saul's commander is Abner. These are the same protagonists that will appear later in CH. As in 23:19–24, the Ziphites are again offering aid to Saul as his spies in Judah. David is not on the run but has his own spies reconnoiter the enemy camp, and he takes the initiative. Even though Saul outnumbers David, he is vulnerable when not on his own turf. Also in David's force are foreign mercenaries—Hittites (i.e., Syrians)— who attain to high rank, just as they do when he becomes king. This account mentions Ahimelech the Hittite alongside Abishai, and later in the *David Saga* we also encounter Uriah the Hittite. A role of this sort for *Hittites* within the army of Yahweh and under anyone who is said to be fighting the battles of Yahweh (25:28) is in strict violation of deuteronomic law and is hardly tolerable for a Deuteronomist. There seems to me to be no other point in referring to Ahimelech *the Hittite* than to draw attention to this fact. Throughout this work, David's actions are a parody on Dtr ideology.

The scene in which David spares Saul's life is no longer a matter of a fortuitous circumstance in which Saul alone comes under David's control, as in *account A*, but is a carefully devised plan to penetrate the very center of Saul's army with the help of a divine *tardēmâ*, which makes the whole army quite helpless. Thus, David's rebuke of Abner is just pious posturing. The removal of both Saul's spear, which is used in this source as symbolic of Saul's royal authority, and his water jug, a basic necessity of travel in the desert, becomes the means for public humiliation before Saul's entire army. David has not physically violated the person of Yahweh's anointed, but symbolically he has stripped him of his inviolability, which he now claims for himself. In this source, David is greatly concerned with the defense of the inviolability of the anointed because he is so vulnerable himself. (To the issue of Yahweh's messiah we will return.)

As we saw in our earlier analysis, David's speech to Saul is quite different from that in *account A*. In 26:18–20, he spends little time on the defense of his innocence and in its place gives a pious speech about being driven out from the presence of Yahweh to serve other gods in foreign territory. This, however, is just a thinly veiled threat that he will serve other rulers in Philistine territory with his band of mercenaries. Saul recognizes this threat, admits his serious mistake, and invites David back into his service, but it is too late. David is disdainful of the offer, justifies his future action by his own "righteousness" toward Saul, and claims to owe him no further loyalty. That this is precisely David's intention is immediately confirmed in the sequel in chap. 27. There is no hint in what follows that David did in fact serve the "gods" of the Philistines or even spend much time in the royal court of Achish.

In contrast to the Dtr version in *account A* (21:11-16[10-15]) in which David is merely an individual asylum seeker in the court of Achish, attempting to escape from Saul and finding himself quite unwelcome there, the *David Saga* in *account B* (27:1-28:2) presents David as the head of an alienated band of mercenaries, ready to sell their services to the Philistine king, who is all too happy to receive them. Mercenaries, historically, have no fixed loyalties and will fight for anyone who pays and feeds them. Here, David quite deceitfully and with little sense of loyalty to his new master carries out a brutal campaign against the aboriginal inhabitants of the southern region to further his own interests. This, of course, makes a complete mockery of the earlier remarks of Abigail, in which she speaks about David's fighting the battles of Yahweh and of not spilling innocent blood. This *ḥerem* against the ancient inhabitants had no religious motivation but was a surreptitious massacre to keep the true nature of his activity hidden from his lord, while retaining all of the spoils of war and sharing them with Achish. He also misrepresents his raids as activity against his own people to further ingratiate himself with his lord to win his approval. It is quite remarkable how scholars can construe this presentation as a pro-Davidic apologetic or wonder at the wisdom and cunning of David's deeds or even view David's actions and words as humorous.[34] Some even suggest that it is unlikely that the author could have possessed any moral scruples about David's actions.[35]

Contrary to the claims of modern commentators, however, it is this narrator who created this portrait of David to make the point that David rose to power over Judah and Israel by just this kind of ruthless method over an extended period of time. One cannot miss the comparison with the actions of the Amalekites, who have the worst reputation among the aboriginal peoples of the region. In chap. 30, the Amalekites have made a raid on

---

34. McCarter, *I Samuel*, 416; Hertzberg, *I & II Samuel*, 214-15. Klein, *1 Samuel*, 265-66; Edelman, *King Saul*, 235-37.

35. J. Mauchline, *1 and 2 Samuel* (NCB; London: Oliphants, 1971), 179-80.

Ziklag in David's absence, destroyed the city, and "taken the women and
[all] who were in it, both small and great; *they killed no one*, but carried
them off, and went their way." Given the relentless slaughter by David of
the Amalekites and their neighbors, one might have expected a similar
kind of slaughter. Instead, David and his men pursue the Amalekites and
are able to recover everyone alive as well as all of the spoil. Both David's
company and the Amalekites are marauding bands who raid each other's
communities and live off the spoil, but the Amalekites seem to be more
scrupulous in their treatment of captives. There is nothing "apologetic"
about this portrait of David. It is, indeed, a damning moral critique that is
entirely in keeping with so much of the rest of the author's treatment of David and his monarchy.

The highly questionable nature of David's character comes out in the episode in 28:1-2, 29:1-11, in which Achish shows his complete confidence
in David's loyalty, which the reader knows to be quite unjustified, by inviting David to participate with his troops in the final showdown with Israel.
The other commanders are not so easily duped and regard David, quite jus-
tifiably, with deep suspicion. Their remarks about David's possible defection during the decisive battle are so convincing that the reader cannot be
sure whether or not David would have chosen this course of action to finally gain his end or stayed loyal to the Philistines and gained more control
over the Philistine hinterland in that way. David, however, does not need to
make that choice because Achish sends him back to David's base in Ziklag.
Even after the gullible Achish expresses full confidence in David's loyalty,
David protests too much against his dismissal: "What have I done? What
wrong have you found in your servant from the day that I entered your service until today, that I may not go out and fight the enemies of my lord the
king?" (29:8). The language that he uses here is very similar to that used
before Saul in 26:18 and before Jonathan in 20:1. The reader knows that a
protest such as this to Achish is quite deceitful, and thus the same words
used before Saul are no more trustworthy.[36]

The answer that Achish gives to David's protest, "I know that you are
blameless in my sight as an angel of God" (29:9), may be compared with
two other instances in the *David Saga* (2 Sam 14:17, 19:28[27]), in which
David is likewise compared with "an/the angel of God." We have also seen
in our earlier analysis that the role of David and his men as foreign merce-

---

36. Recall also the remark of Abigail in 1 Sam 25:28 and comments above,
pp. 188-190.

naries is very similar to that of Ittai the Gittite and his 600 men from Gath who served in the army of David. In contrast to David, however, these mercenaries are completely loyal and play a major role in David's ultimate victory over the superior forces of Absalom. All of these interconnections within the *David Saga* indicate that they belong to the same corpus, and therefore it is entirely appropriate to make comparisons with David in the earlier part of the story and to draw conclusions about David's character in the light of these comparisons.

In the unit 1 Sam 30:1–31, David and his men return to Ziklag "on the third day" after a long journey from Aphek to find that the Amalekites have made a raid on the region, including Ziklag, which was left quite defenseless in their absence, and have burned down the city and taken all the wives and children captive. His men hold him responsible because he led all of them so far afield for a military adventure, leaving their families without protection, so that they now threaten mutiny. In this crisis, David finds aid in his religion (even in Philistine territory!) and uses the priest Abiathar and the ephod to consult the deity and thereby to spur his men into action. The question put to the deity, "Shall I pursue after this band? Shall I overtake them?" and the reply, "Pursue, for you shall certainly overtake them and rescue" (30:8), hardly requires special divine guidance, but this use of religion reinforces David's leadership in the crisis. It is not, however, by any obvious divine direction but by fortuitous circumstances that David and his men find an Egyptian slave, left behind by the Amalekites, who is able to lead them to the Amalekite camp. They make a surprise attack on the encampment, defeat the Amalekites with a great victory, and recover all the captives alive, along with a great mass of booty that was taken not only from the Judean region and from Ziklag but from the other southern communities as well. All of it becomes "David's spoil."

The story allows the reader to take one of two quite-different attitudes and perspectives toward these events. On the one hand, they could be viewed as a miraculous intervention by the deity in that there was not a single casualty and nothing missing that was taken in the raids. How anyone could know this is, of course, beside the point. This author deals with the manifestations of divine intervention in a way quite different from that of Dtr, who can signal the moment of divine deliverance quite explicitly. Here, it is to be seen in the seeming fortuitous circumstances of finding the Egyptian slave and in their arrival at the camp of the Amalekites when they are inebriated from their victory celebrations and unfit for the surprise attack by David's men. In a similar fashion, when David is fleeing from

Absalom and is most vulnerable to attack and then hears that Ahithophel, his wisest counselor, is among the conspirators, David utters a prayer in desperation: "O Lord, I pray, turn the counsel of Ahithophel into foolishness" (2 Sam 16:31). Almost immediately, David encounters Hushai, who then becomes the means by which this prayer is answered. One could therefore interpret the story of the Amalekite pursuit and rescue as a theological narrative about divine guidance and interaction in the affairs of men and nations.

A more cynical reading of the narrative, and the one that seems to come closer to the relentless drive of the narrative itself, is to see in David one who is able to manipulate events, with a certain amount of pious legitimization, in such a way as to bring him to his goal in the accession of power. Thus, it is that he takes some of the spoil and distributes it "to his friends, the elders of Judah, saying, 'Here is a present for you from the spoil of the enemies of Yahweh'" (30:26). This is the kind of political gift that will encourage this same group to come to Hebron and make him king of Judah there. Nothing is said about any restitution of the great quantity of spoil that had been taken from the land of the Philistines (30:17), even though David is a vassal of a Philistine king. What looks like a calamity becomes an occasion by which he can consolidate his position within Judah and make his move out of Philistine territory back into Judah. But first he must wait for the results of the Philistine campaign against Saul.

Chapter 6

David Becomes King of Israel:
Dtr's View

The Death of Saul in DtrH and in the David Saga

In this chapter, our concern will be to present Dtr's view of the reign of David, from its inception to the final succession by Solomon. In doing so, we will need to disentangle it from the larger *David Saga*, especially where the later author has attempted to dovetail the two versions together. Once the parts have been clearly identified, then we will be able to delineate Dtr's presentation of David and its place within the larger perspective of his work. This will further clarify Dtr's ideology of the Israelite monarchy, both with respect to what has preceded in 1 Samuel and what follows in 1 Kings, a continuity that in the past has been greatly obscured by prior literary analysis.

We begin with the account of Saul's death in 1 Sam 31. Even though this concludes the previous discussion about the David and Saul story, it is intimately related to the events that follow and the relationship of Dtr's presentation of these events to the larger *David Saga*. This is because the account of Saul's death in this chapter is one of two versions of the event; the other is in 2 Sam 1:1–16, and these differ so radically from each other that scholars are divided as to how to deal with them. There has been a strong tendency in the past to view the two accounts as derived from independent alternative traditions or parallel documents that have been conflated in the present text. A counter approach to these views is to take the whole of 2 Sam 1 as a unity by the same hand as 1 Sam 31 and to interpret the Amalekite's speech as a lie, for which he pays with his life.[1] This solution, however, does not square with the details of the text itself in 2 Sam 1 and must make large assumptions about what constitutes the primitive story of David and Saul in the preceding corpus of 1 Samuel. What one finds lacking in any of the earlier analyses of these parallels is a view that

---

1. McCarter, *II Samuel*, 62–64.

sees the second account of the death of Saul as part of a quite-deliberate addition to the earlier narrative. I have tried to demonstrate this sort of approach in my analysis of the David and Saul story up to this point and will
now show its usefulness for solving this problem as well.

The account of the battle against the Philistines and Israel's defeat in
1 Sam 31 describes first how the three sons of Saul, Jonathan, Abinadab
and Malchishua, were all killed. There is no hint in this account that any
other sons or Saul's general, Abner, survived the battle. It is curious that the
second son, Abinadab, is called Ishvi in 1 Sam 14:49, but this does not justify identifying Ishvi with Ishbosheth in 2 Sam 2-4, as a fourth son who
survived the battle.[2] Dtr makes it clear that all of the sons of Saul were
killed, and this cleared the way for David to become king in Saul's place.
The battle account also makes clear that Saul died by his own hand (v. 4),
in contradiction to the version in 2 Sam 1:5-10. To this we will return below. Finally, there is the account of how the Philistines took the bodies of
Saul and his sons and hung them on the wall of Bethshan and, subsequently, how the men of Jabesh-Gilead came by night and recovered the
bodies in order to give them a proper burial. This recalls the earlier rescue
of Jabesh-Gilead by Saul in 1 Sam 11 and appears to anticipate the remarks
of David in 2 Sam 2:4b-7. Consequently, this rather short account of the final battle sets up a number of literary issues that need to be resolved, and
to these we will now turn.

The account of David's response to the deaths of Saul and Jonathan is
given in 2 Sam 1. The older analysis of this chapter is that 2 Sam 1 consists
of two sources, and this, in my view, has considerable merit.[3] It isolates the
older source as consisting of 1:1-4, 11-12, 17-27, with the later source interrupting this sequence by the revelation of the Amalekite as to how Saul
died, vv. 5-10, and the execution of the Amalekite for his slaying of Saul,
vv. 13-16. Both of these units are an awkward fit in their present context.
One expects that, as soon as David hears the bad news about both Saul and
Jonathan, he would express his grief at that point and not engage in some
interrogation. When David asks for evidence of the deaths of both Saul and
Jonathan, he receives information only about Saul. Yet his grief is as much

---

2. Cf. Klein, *1 Samuel*, 141-42. Contra Klein, it is the Chronicler (1 Chr 8:33;
9:39) who consistently has Jonathan, Abinadab and Malchishua (and adds Esh-
baal). It is Ishvi that is suspect.

3. See Smith, *Samuel*, 254-55. The problem with the older views is that they
treated the two sources as parallel accounts, which will not work.

about Jonathan as it is about Saul. So the information he receives is quite unrelated to the response of grief. Furthermore, the rites of mourning go on for some time, presumably the whole day, because "they mourned and wept and fasted until evening" (v. 12). Yet David's interrogation of the messenger continues in v. 13 without interruption, leading to an execution that is hardly appropriate for the circumstances described in vv. 11-12. The lament in vv. 17-27 seems much more suitable to the context after v. 12 than following v. 16.

Further light can be cast on this problem by considering some parallel examples of messenger scenes. The scene of the messenger bringing bad news in 2 Sam 1 has often been compared with a similar scene in 1 Sam 4:12-18, with even some striking similarity in language, most notably the description of the messenger "with his clothes torn and dirt upon his head." There is the same pattern of inquiry, the delivery of the bad news and the same immediate reaction of grief. However, in the case of the Eli story, there is no parallel for any interrogation about how the two sons of Eli died, so the units in 2 Sam 1:5-10 and 13-16 have no equivalence in the messenger pattern. Even in the much more elaborate messenger scene in 2 Sam 18:19-19:1, which consists of news of the victory of David's forces, David's primary concern is about his son Absalom, and when he makes repeated inquiry from two messengers and finally receives the bad news, he makes no further investigation about how the death happened but immediately engages in mourning for his son.

There are some notable features within the two supplements (1 Sam 1:5-10 and 13-16) that suggest their connection with a larger source. First, in his speech the messenger describes Saul as leaning on his spear. This close association of Saul with his spear to the bitter end is quite characteristic of *account B* in the *David Saga*. Second, the messenger is identified as an Amalekite both to Saul and to David. This cannot be accidental, for in two different episodes the Amalekites are the sworn enemies of both Saul and David. However, both of these episodes (1 Sam 15 and 30) are not part of the earlier source, which makes no mention of these people, and both are part of the larger corpus of the *David Saga*. Identifying the messenger as an Amalekite is therefore quite deliberate. Indeed, David's inquiry (v. 13) as to where he comes from is quite redundant because the messenger has already recounted to David that he is an Amalekite (v. 8). The identification must therefore be important to this author. In addition, the Amalekite also identifies himself as the son of a *ger*, a "resident alien," but this status for an Amalekite within the people of Israel is hardly conceivable for Dtr. Third, the Amalekite gives to David the crown and the armlet that were taken from Saul and he brings them to David. This seems a rather ironic gesture to have an Amalekite giving to David the symbols of Saul's kingship. David, in the *David Saga*, seems to be a collector of objects of this sort (cf. 2 Sam 12:30). Fourth, David's reason for slaying the Amalekite is that he has violated the person of Yahweh's anointed. We have already seen that this is a principle theme in this source and is always ironic. Furthermore, the incident is closely tied to the slaying of Ishbosheth (2 Sam 4), in which David makes a direct comparison between the deaths of Saul and Ishbosheth (vv. 9–12), thus justifying his execution of the assassins for similar reasons. It is clear that both texts belong to the same source, the *David Saga*.

There is one other piece of this late supplement that is not so easily detected. In 1:1–2a we have this statement: "After the death of Saul, when David had returned from slaying the Amalekites, David stayed two days in Ziklag. On the third day a man came from Saul's camp, with his clothes torn and dirt upon his head." This introduction connects two events that are construed as parallel in time, the death of Saul in 1 Sam 31 and the campaign of David against the Amalekites in 1 Sam 30. However, the remark in v. 2 beginning "on the third day" creates a problem because what follows makes this time marker refer to the death of Saul and the time that it took to travel from the battle field in the north to wherever David was in the south. Yet the remark that David stayed in Ziklag two days now connects it with this second event, but nothing in what follows relates to this quite-different event. There are two observations that make the reference to David's return to Ziklag suspect. First, the expression "on the third day" is very common in Hebrew prose and refers generally to something that takes place after a major event to which it is related. There is no other instance where it is preceded by a remark about the previous two days. The remark about David's stay in Ziklag does not fit this pattern. Second, there is a quite-similar instance of two events being combined in this same way, and that is in 1 Sam 18:6, where both the homecoming of the army and the return of David from slaying the Philistine are combined, but the sequel of the women coming out to meet them clearly relates to the first and not the second. As we saw above,[4] the second remark about David is a later addition; in a similar fashion, that is what has happened here. The author of the story about David's campaign against the Amalekites has used the same literary device to dovetail his account with the older narrative as he did in the

---

4. P. 160.

earlier case in 1 Sam 18:6. All of these additions belong to the author of the *David Saga.*

This analysis of 2 Sam 1:1–2a would yield this combination:

‫ויהי אחרי מות שאול . . . (ויהי)ביום השלישי והנה איש בא מן־המחנה מעם שאול . . .‬

"After the death of Saul . . . on the third day a man came from the camp of Saul . . ."

The repetition of ‫ויהי‬ may have been used to tie the two clauses closely together, the second as a resumption of the first,[5] although it is also quite likely that the second ‫ויהי‬ is included here to accommodate the addition of the phrase about David's return to Ziklag. It is clear that the first phrase is necessary because the end of the account of Saul's death in 1 Sam 31 mentions that the inhabitants of Jabesh-Gilead fasted seven days.[6] One would perhaps expect some reference to the place where David was staying. The last mention in 1 Sam 24:22 is the "stronghold" at Adullam, and it may be that a reference to Adullam has been replaced by the reference to Ziklag. For the rest, the short text works very well as a transition from the story of David and Saul to that of David's accession to the throne in Hebron and eventually in Jerusalem.

David's Accession to the Throne: Competing Accounts

The unit in 2 Sam 2:1–7 has a number of interconnections with the earlier story of David and Saul. The method used by David to consult the deity (without the mention of Abiathar and the ephod) is the same as the method used in 1 Sam 23:1–5 and will again be used in the war with the Philistines in 2 Sam 5:17–25. All of these belong to the same source, Dtr. The reference to David's two wives, in v. 2b, is a secondary insertion by the later version, so the text originally read "So David went up there and his men who were with him (David brought up), every one with his household, and they settled in (the towns of) Hebron" (2:2a, 3).[7] Whether what follows in 2:4–7

---

5. See Driver, *Notes on Samuel*, 231.

6. It is also possible that 1 Sam 31:8–13 is a later addition, in which case the opening phrase "after the death of Saul" in 2 Sam 1:1 would also be a later addition to accommodate it.

7. "David brought up": see McCarter, *II Samuel*, 81. He regards this phrase as textually doubtful. The scribal addition may be the result of the earlier insertion of the reference to David's wives in v. 2b. McCarter (ibid.) also views the references to "the towns" (‫ערי‬) as dubious and a later addition.

belongs to the early source is more difficult to decide. The reference to the actions of the men of Jabesh Gilead in 2:4b–7 certainly depends on 1 Sam 31:11–13 and speaks for the early source. Yet, if 2 Sam 2:8–4:12 all belongs to the *David Saga* (i.e., CH), then the invitation to one small part of the "house of Israel" does not seem to lead so easily to the full delegation of all the tribes of Israel in 5:1. On the other hand, it is also quite possible that 1 Sam 31:8–13 is a later addition, because the temporal link "on the morrow" (v. 8) with the preceding remarks in v. 7 is very weak.

After David and his men settled in Hebron we are told that "the men of Judah came and anointed David king there over the house of Judah" (2:4). There is some confusion in the text of Samuel–Kings about whether David reigned over Judah in Hebron for 7 years (and 6 months) and then over both Judah and Israel in Jerusalem for 33 years (2:11, 5:5) or whether he reigned over all Israel for 40 years, 7 in Hebron and 33 in Jerusalem (1 Kgs 2:11). In support of the latter is the statement in 2 Sam 5:1 that *all* the tribes of Israel came to Hebron and anointed him as king there. Because the whole account of the separate reigns of Ishbosheth and David is the invention of the author of the *David Saga*, Dtr knows nothing of this long gap and struggle between the two regions and the invitation of the tribes of Israel to David reads as something that takes place very shortly after Saul's death. This would mean that the separate anointing of David by *the house of Judah* (2:4) is an addition by the *David Saga* to accommodate its story of the conflict between the two regions, and with this anointing by Judah one would have to add David's message to Jabesh-Gilead to defect from the northern ranks, in 2:4b–7. The delegation of all Israel to Hebron would fit quite well with 2:3. The term *house of Judah* is obviously an anachronism before the rise of the southern state of Judah centuries later so that no such entity could have anointed David king. Dtr seems to have used only the designation *the house of Israel* to represent the people belonging to David's realm[8] and makes the distinction between the house of Israel and the house of Judah only after the revolt of Jeroboam in 1 Kgs 12:21. It is the *David Saga* that makes the distinction between these two entities in 2 Sam 12:8 and consistently in 2 Sam 2:4, 7, 10–11. For this author it is important that David's reign represented a dual monarchy of two distinct realms.

---

8. See 2 Sam 1:12; 6:5, 15. See also 1 Sam 7:2–3. P also uses it quite anachronistically for the whole people in Exod 16:31, 40:38; Lev 10:6; Num 20:29; and in other late texts: Josh 21:45, Ruth 4:11.

Nevertheless, what remains a puzzle is how the author of the *David Saga* views the reign of David in Hebron after the two-year reign of Ishbosheth comes to an end and before David takes up residence in Jerusalem five and a half years later. His chronology suggests a reign over Judah alone for seven and a half years in Hebron and yet he adopts as his framework the earlier Dtr text in which "all the tribes of Israel" came to Hebron to anoint David as king (5:1). Does he mean to suggest that Israel still remained without any king for five and a half years until just before David's move to Jerusalem?[9] A suggestion such as this rather undermines the great enthusiasm for David's reign by the Israelite tribes that is clearly indicated in 5:1-2, which is Dtr's view of the Davidic kingship.

Furthermore, there are some curious features evident in 5:3a that call for discussion. The text states, "Now all the elders of Israel came to the king in Hebron and King David made a covenant with them in Hebron before Yahweh." The first thing to observe is that the statement about the *elders of Israel* coming to David in Hebron is quite redundant following the remark about *all the tribes of Israel* coming and speaking with David in Hebron in vv. 1-2. This makes it a doublet, but as in the case of so many of the other doublets that we have observed, it is not part of an independent source because it is fully dependent on its larger context. Second, the opening statement in vv. 1-2 indicates that the Israelites approached David with the intent of making him their king, but v. 3 has the elders coming to *King* David, so that he is already a king. The difference in terminology is quite significant. Third, the purpose of the *elders of Israel* is to negotiate a covenant agreement with one who is already king of Judah. This is the same kind of arrangement that is reflected in 2 Sam 3:20-21 in which Abner had intended to negotiate this sort of covenantal agreement with David on behalf of the *elders of Israel*, a deal that was foiled by Joab's murder of Abner. There can be little doubt that this is a text by the same hand. Dtr certainly does not understand the basis of David's kingship as an agreement between the elders of Israel and the king. In v. 3b, David becomes king by means of the tribes of Israel's anointing him. The statement "and they anointed David as king over Israel" is a direct continuation of v. 2 with the same subject, the *tribes of Israel*.

From all of these observations, I conclude that the earlier Dtr text simply recorded that David and his men moved to Hebron (2:1-2aα, 3),

---

9. Are the additional six months intended to suggest the period of overlap in Hebron of David's reign over both Judah and Israel?

and immediately following this all the tribes of Israel, including Judah, came to Hebron and anointed David as their king (5:1-2, 3b). Dtr may have included a remark about David's age when he began to reign and the total duration of his reign (v. 4),[10] but the statement about the periods of David's reign in Hebron and in Jerusalem (v. 5) represents a revision of Dtr's original summary in 1 Kgs 2:11. Therefore, the rest of the narrative in 2 Sam 2:2aβb, 4–4:12, and 5:3a, (4), 5 all belongs to the author of the *David Saga*.

David and His Wars
(2 Samuel 5:6-12, 17–25; 8:1-14; 10:15-19)

This collection of texts has to do with a number of loosely connected units and topics that do not fit into any clear chronological development and feature a number of difficult, if not insoluble, problems. These have to do with David's capture of Jerusalem and his building of a palace in 2 Sam 5:6-12, his wars against the Philistines in 5:17-25, 8:1, and his wars against other neighboring peoples, 8:2-14, 10:15-19. There are two different kinds of problems here. The one has to do with understanding the various units and their possible relationship to older sources, and the second is the relationship of these units to the larger literary composition. We will deal with each of these units in turn with respect to these questions.

David's Capture of Jerusalem (2 Samuel 5:6-12)
There are many enigmatic elements within this short unit that have elicited a great amount of speculation and debate. This has to do primarily with the meaning of some of the terms and how they might relate to some of the archaeological features unearthed in the region of the Ophel, the southeastern hill of the ancient city-site that constitutes the City of David, mentioned in this text. In addition, the description in the text of exactly how the city was captured likewise remains a puzzle with various suggested solutions. Elaborating on all the details of this debate does not serve the purposes of this study, so I will only briefly summarize the main points of the discussion.

The description of the capture of Jerusalem in 2 Sam 5:6-8 is very brief. David and his men go to Jerusalem to make war against its inhabitants. It is not clear what the text means by "his men," but many speculate that this was his own professional elite force. The inhabitants of Jerusalem are iden-

---

10. See 1 Sam 13:1. However, no age is given for Solomon in 1 Kgs 2:12 or 11:42, so it must remain doubtful.

tified as Jebusites, so that Jerusalem is understood as belonging to neither Judah nor Israel. Consequently, the object of David's campaign is understood to be an attempt to take this city as his own personal property and make it his capital, which was strategically located between Judah and Israel.[11] This scenario, which is widely followed, builds an elaborate hypothesis on very little evidence. The notion that there was a clearly delineated Kingdom of Judah in the south and a Kingdom of Israel in the north, in the time of David, is an anachronism, based on texts that reflect a much later history of these kingdoms. As we have seen above, there are many archaeological reasons for questioning whether David even controlled any extensive region north of his rather small city in Jerusalem. Even the very designation of Judah as encompassing a particular people who understood themselves as Judeans living in a particular region is quite debatable for this period. Such an understanding of identity follows a long period of political domination and shaping by a central authority.

If, however, there were no Judeans in this later political sense, then who were the Jebusites? The text merely identifies them as "the inhabitants of the land," which in the terminology of Dtr regularly refers to one of the aboriginal inhabitants of the land. It seems to me highly doubtful that the name derives from an earlier name for Jerusalem (Jebus), because Jerusalem is already the name of the city in the Amarna age. What is more likely is that Dtr merely meant to signify a non-Israelite enclave because David can hardly be presented as making war against his own people. Thus, in actual fact we can say virtually nothing about the circumstances of how David came into possession of Jerusalem, or even if he actually did do so.

The details of how the city was captured are strange and difficult to reconstruct. The description suggests the Jebusites were so confident in their defenses that they made use of only blind and lame guards as a taunt to David and his men but that David managed to find a route into the city through a shaft that led down to the city's water source, the Gihon spring (?) and so presumably were able to climb up into the city by this means. If this is what the text means, then the account has no plausibility and is the figment of someone's imagination. No fortified city under enemy attack would defend itself in this way, and anyone who had access to the water shaft would already be inside the defensive perimeter of the city. The

---

11. See Alt, "The Formation of the Israelite State," 217; idem, "The Monarchy in the Kingdoms of Israel and Judah," in *Essays on Old Testament History and Religion* (Oxford: Blackwell, 1966), 248.

mouth of the water shaft would be the most defensible point of access into the city. The account, however, never actually says that they did use the water shaft to take the city. It is clear that the Chronicler (1 Chr 11:4–9) did not understand the account and so modified it by dropping any reference to the taunt of the lame and the blind, as well as the water shaft, and simply has David promise that the one who first strikes the Jerusites will become the commander of the army. But Joab was already the commander of the army before they ever got to Jerusalem. Chronicles does nothing to solve the problems of this text.

Furthermore, the whole incident about the blind and the lame is given a curious etiological connection to a common saying, "The blind and the lame shall not come into the house" (v. 8), referring to some future practice. The blind and lame in this saying, however, refer no longer to Jebusites but to the population in general, and the "house" can only mean the temple. This means that a common prohibition having to do with ritual impurity in the temple is given a completely fanciful and legendary etiology relating to the time of David and the beginnings of Jerusalem as a Judean city. This hardly helps to establish any primitive context for the account.

The text also seems to be at pains to identify Jerusalem as a "stronghold," מצודה (5:7, 9), specifically associating it with with the "City of David."[12] This is the only place where Jerusalem or a part of it is characterized in this way, and it hardly seems appropriate. The term denotes a place that is geographically difficult to access and is used in the stories of David's flight from Saul or his encounters with the Philistines in which the location offers him protection from attack by a superior force (1 Sam 22:4–5, 24:23; 2 Sam 5:17; cf. also 1 Sam 23:14, 19). All the references to David's being in the "stronghold," apart from the capture of Jerusalem, are associated with the early period of David's military activity and the region of Adullam, with the exception of 2 Sam 5:17, which is placed after he captures Jerusalem. However, if Jerusalem is itself a "stronghold," then why must David go to the stronghold, as though it is some other well-known place from which he is accustomed to conducting his military activity? It seems to me that the identification of the City of David with his stronghold is an effort to place his struggles with the Philistines *after* he became king in Jerusalem. The accounts of these skirmishes with the Philistines do not suggest any connection with Jerusalem.

---

12. See also 1 Chr 11:7, which uses the alternate form מצד.

David is said to have extended the city from the Millo inward, as though the Millo was a well-known and clearly recognizable structure. Archaeologists have frequently attempted to identify this Millo in the region of the City of David. In 1 Kgs 9:15, 24, and 11:27, Solomon is also said to have built the Millo, which presents a contradiction, unless one assumes that Jerusalem had more than one Millo. The term very likely refers to a major fill or platform that was made in preparation for the construction of a large public building such as a palace or temple.[13] One frequently encounters references to large-scale operations of this sort in Assyrian inscriptions, such as in Sennacherib's building of the "palace without rival."[14] It seems to me that the remark about the Millo is just an anticipation of the later statement about David's construction of a palace (v. 11). The remark about David's increasing greatness in v. 10, "David became increasingly great and Yahweh of Hosts was with him," seems to interrupt the description of David's building activity, but it is deemed necessary to account for the fact that Hiram dispatches a delegation to him and supplies him with material to build a palace. This sort of undertaking is entirely implausible, given the modest dimensions of David's domain with no access to the sea and the fact that David is subsequently engaged in defensive actions with the Philistines in the region that lies directly west of Jerusalem.

From this brief examination it becomes clear that this unit is not based on some archival fragment; instead, it is a short ideological statement constructed by Dtr to account for the origin of David's rule in Jerusalem and to connect it with subsequent themes that were important in his work. David's capture of Jerusalem from the aboriginal population of the land inaugurates the final phase of the conquest begun by Joshua. Only with this capture of the city will the ark find it resting place. The remarks about the blind and lame are very confused and have suggested that some of these are later additions. The concluding etiological explanation about handicapped persons such as these being excluded from the holy city may reflect a later ideological modification of the account. The remarks are not found in Chronicles, but this fact is not very conclusive. However, as noted above, the identification of the City of David with David's stronghold in his activity

---

13. For a discussion about identifying the stepped embankment of stones with the Millo, see Steiner, *Excavations by K. M. Kenyon*, 52 (§5.2.2); see also Na'aman, "The Rise of Jerusalem," 43–44.

14. D. D. Luckenbill, *Ancient Records of Assyria and Babylonia* (vol. 2; Chicago: University of Chicago Press, 1926–27), 160–79.

against the Philistines suggests that Dtr has deliberately placed all of his struggles against the Philistines after the capture of Jerusalem.

David's building activity in Jerusalem is obviously modeled on that of Solomon, with the construction of the Millo and his palace in the City of David. It receives little elaboration because it will be completely superseded by Solomon's building activity. Nothing is said about any temple being built because at a later stage David will bring back the ark and place it in a tent. Only later after all his wars are over and his palace is completed will David think about building an actual temple. The ordering of these events is purely ideological. David's association with Hiram, king of Tyre, early in David's reign anticipates Hiram's willingness to assist Solomon in his building activities out of Hiram's long-standing friendship with David; 1 Kgs 5:15[1]. The remarks about David's increasing greatness and the fact that Yahweh was with him is language familiar from Dtr's earlier treatment of David's rise and success under Saul.

The Philistine Wars
(2 Samuel 5:17-25, 8:1)

The description of David's wars with the Philistines give us only a few details regarding the time and place of the offensives against David by the Philistines, and scholars often resort to making use of information from the larger narrative, most notably the later *David Saga*. This, as we have argued above, is quite unreliable and leads to a mistaken understanding of these texts. In particular, Albrecht Alt's whole presentation of the formation of the monarchy is predicated on these very assumptions.[15] Thus, building on the notion that David was a mercenary leader under the Philistines as portrayed in 1 Sam 27-30 and that he continued to be their vassal while king over Judah in Hebron, as set out in 2 Sam 2-4, he assumes that it was only when David became king over Israel as a whole and moved to Jerusalem that the Philistines took action against him. All of this depends on these late narrative additions, with the result that we must look at the account of these wars without this kind of prejudice. According to Dtr, as we have reconstructed it, David became king of all Israel in Hebron immediately after Saul's death. This means that David inherited the prior enmity that existed between the Philistines and the Israelites when he became king. With this perspective in mind, let us look at the text.

---

15. A. Alt, "The Formation of the Israelite State," 171-237.

The account of the Philistine war begins with the statement "As soon as the Philistines heard that David had been anointed king over Israel, all the Philistines went up to search for David; and when David heard this he retreated to the stronghold." This relates directly to the account of David's anointing by Israel in 2 Sam 5:1-2, 3b in *Hebron*. Thus, the Philistines come looking for David in the region of Judah in much the same way that Saul did, and David also responds in a similar fashion by retreating to the "stronghold," probably in the region of Adullam. The Philistines are described not in an encampment ready for action but spread out in the Valley of Rephaim and therefore vulnerable to attack (cf. 1 Sam 30:16). It is just this sort of situation that allows David to engage in a sudden charge and win the day, just as the pun on the place name Baal-perazim suggests. The location of this encounter is quite obscure. The assumption that the Valley of Rephaim is southwest of Jerusalem seems to be dependent entirely on the connection made between these episodes and the prior unit on David's capture of Jerusalem, and this is then reflected in the late texts of Josh 15:8, 18:16. This makes very little sense, and one would expect a location closer to Adullam. The Philistines in their flight abandoned their gods, characterized as "idols," which then become booty for David and his men.

The second battle (2 Sam 5:22-25) takes place in the same location, with the Philistines "spread out in the Valley of Rephaim," as if they learned nothing new from the first time. It strongly suggests that it is merely two episodes of the same battle. In this case, the maneuver is to attack them by surprise in the rear. This stage of the encounter is viewed as decisive for expelling the Philistines from the region. We are not concerned here with the logistics of these battles, which can only be guesswork. What is noteworthy is that in both cases David consults the deity before battle and gets a response that begins the battle. This is very similar to the logistics of David's earlier attack on the Philistines in 1 Sam 23:1-5, before he became king. The language of inquiry and response is the same and must belong to the same source. Nothing is said in any of these cases about Abiathar and the ephod as the means by which the inquiry was made. It may be that all three belonged to an old collection of stories about David and his men and their struggles against the Philistines in the region of Judah. Dtr, however, has fitted them into his narrative for his own particular purposes.

These very limited skirmishes against the Philistines do not seem to reflect any decisive battles, any capture of their cities, or any control of the region. Nevertheless, 2 Sam 8:1 states categorically that "David defeated the Philistines and subdued them" and that he "took *Metheghammah* out of the control of the Philistines." If the untranslated term is a place-name, it is so obscure as to have no significance and hardly reflects an appropriate complement to the opening remark. The Chronicler, in 1 Chr 18:1 construes it to mean "Gath and its villages," גת ובנתיה, which seems to represent an interpretation of an original גת האמה, "Gath the mother-city," in which אמה is a variant of אם, understood as the "leading city" or "capital" of a region (see also 2 Sam 20:19).[16] While all reconstructions are conjectural and require some emendation, this at least has the following points in its favor. The capture and control of Gath, understood as the leading city of the Philistines in the time of David, would at least compliment the statement that David subdued the Philistines. It would also parallel the following events in chap. 8 in which David successively defeated the other major powers in the surrounding region. As we will see, these military exploits seem to imitate events that took place in the 9th century, at which time the Arameans defeated and put an end to the prominence of Gath among the Philistine cities, a feat that is perhaps here being attributed to David. At any rate, 2 Sam 8:1 stands in marked contrast to the modest successes of David against the Philistines in 5:17–25 and clearly belongs to Dtr's attempt to portray David's military prowess and political control of the whole region into a Levantine empire.

Wars against Moab, Edom, the Arameans,
and the Ammonites

Before we begin to deal in detail with the individual accounts of these wars, I would like to make some general comments on the nature of the accounts and their various limits. The reports of the wars against the Moabites (8:2) and the Edomites (8:13–14) are very short, and each one highlights only one distinctive incident. In the case of Moab, it is an atrocity carried out by David after the defeat of Moab in which two-thirds of the male population are arbitrarily slaughtered. In the Edomite war, one battle in the Valley of Salt is mentioned, in which a very large number are killed and the rest put into servitude. The war against the Arameans (8:3–8) is dealt with in much greater detail and in various stages. The first stage is the war against Hadadezer, son of Rehob, king of Zobah, with a battle in Syria that results in the defeat and capture of Damascus and much booty. This leads to a further alliance with the king of Hamath (vv. 9–10). There seems to be a second stage and sequel to this in 10:15–19 in which a wider circle

---

16. Driver, *Notes on Samuel*, 279–80.

of Aramean coalition forces or vassals are drawn into the conflict by Hadadezer from "beyond the Euphrates" and they too are defeated by David so
that David's power and control is extended to a considerable empire. Nevertheless, for all the differences that these Aramean wars have with the others
of chap. 8, they also share some important literary features in the framing
of the events and in terminology that point to a common source or author.

By contrast, David's war with the Ammonites (10:1–14, 11:1–12:31) is
embedded in a long narrative, which is of an entirely different character,
and even the details of the war itself have little in common with the other
war accounts. As we shall see, it is integrally related to the *David Saga*, with
the result that one must treat it in quite a different fashion. Efforts in the
past to isolate a primitive document within this narrative are not convincing. Consequently, we will look at the first group of texts in 8:2–14 and
10:15–19 and then consider their relationship to the account of the Ammonite wars.

Until recently, the general tendency in biblical scholarship was to understand these accounts of David's foreign wars as historical records preserved from the royal archives of David's court and therefore reflective of
politics of the United Monarchy and its "empire." The most recent archaeological appraisal of Jerusalem and Judah in Iron I and early Iron II, as well
as the social history of the period, however, has greatly modified this picture. As we have seen above, the archaeological evidence suggests that the
very modest city of Jerusalem together with the largely rural region of Judah could not possibly sustain the kind of Levantine state with vassals and
dependencies as portrayed in these texts. Judah was, in fact, much later in
its development than the Northern Kingdom of Israel and there is little reason to believe that a united kingdom of Judah and Israel under a Judean
king of the 10th century was a reality. Nor could the bureaucracy of this
little polity have had such extensive archives of official documents and
records that it could furnish the accounts of royal activities for future historians. Consequently, a different explanation must be sought for the various battle reports that one finds in 2 Sam 8:2–14, 10:15–19.

To my mind, the most persuasive suggestion for understanding these
texts has come from Nadav Naʾaman.[17] He argues that there are many

---

17. N. Naʾaman, "Hazael of ʿAmqi and Hadadezer of Beth-rehob," *UF* 27 (1995):
381–94; idem, "Sources and Composition in the History of David," in *The Origins of
Ancient Israelite States* (ed. V. Fritz and P. R. Davies; JSOTSup 228; Sheffield: Sheffield Academic Press, 1997), 170–86; idem, "In Search of Reality behind the Account of David's Wars with Israel's Neighbours," *IEJ* 52 (2002): 200–224.

striking parallels between the description of events in the Aramean wars and the time Hazael and Benhadad, kings of Damascus at the height of Aramean control of most of Syria, the Levant, and Transjordan in the mid-9th to early 8th centuries B.C.E. It is these correspondences that lead him to propose that it is this period of Aramean dominance and not the earlier period of the 10th century that is being used to portray David's military exploits in the region. Until the time of Hazael, there was no state that dominated the region west of the Euphrates. Instead, there were a number of Neo-Hittite states in the region from Karateppe and Karkamish in the north to Hamath in the south. These were heirs of the old Hittite Empire.[18] In addition, there was a growing number of Aramean kingdoms that developed in Upper Mesopotamia and in the region from the Euphrates to Damascus and the borders of Israel.[19] The Assyrian kings who campaigned in the west in the mid-9th century, such as Ashur-nasir-apli II and Shalmaneser III, give us a good impression of the political development of the region in this period leading up to the time of Hazael. Thus, in the account of Shalmaneser's battle of Qarqar (853 B.C.E.), the opposing forces included a coalition consisting of Ahab of Israel, Adad-idri (Hadadezer) of Aram, and Urhuleni of Hamath. These were the principle leaders, and among the several other contributors was a certain Ba'asa, king of Beth-Rehob and Amana (Zobah) in the Beqa valley and the Anti-Lebanon Mountains. This corresponds to the region of which Hadadezer is said to be king in 2 Sam 8:3, 5, 12.

This coalition of states held together against the Assyrians for over a decade until Hazael gained the throne of Damascus, at which point the rulers of Damascus became bitter enemies of both Israel and Hamath. After the demise of Shalmaneser III, the Assyrians went into a period of decline in the west and Hazael was able to gain control over most of the region from the Euphrates to the border of Egypt, including the Philistines, and the Transjordanian region as far as the Arnon. The Assyrian and Aramaic inscriptions as well as the biblical texts give ample testimony to the power of the realm established by Hazael and his successor, Benhadad, and the lasting impression that it left on the Israelites as subjects and vassals.

---

18. J. D. Hawkins, "Karkamish and Karatepe: Neo-Hittite City States in North Syria," in *CANE* 2:1295–1307.

19. In addition to Na'aman, "Hazael of ʿAmqi," see also P.-E. Dion, "Aramean Tribes and Nations of First Millennium Western Asia," *CANE* 2:1281–94 and literature cited there.

As Na'aman has argued most persuasively, it is this period of Aramean domination under Hazael that offers the only appropriate context for the portrayal of the Davidic wars in 2 Sam 8 and 10. Neither the period before Hazael, in which there was no one state that dominated the region, nor the period following the demise of the power of Damascus furnishes a picture of the times that matches the one that is presented as backdrop for David's victories. The author of these accounts uses what he knows from his sources about this period as a model for recreating the time of David. Na'aman states:

> It seems to me that the figure of Hadadezer "*ben* Rehob, king of Zobah" was modelled upon the figure of Hazael, king of Aram. The author built up the early, vague figure of Hadadezer along the lines of the better-known king of Damascus. By borrowing outlines from concrete events that had taken place in later times he was able to add a sense of authenticity to the narratives. The selection of Hazael as a model for David's adversary is not accidental. He was the most powerful and successful king in the history of Aram-Damascus; defeating such a powerful king as Hazael portrays David in the light that suited the historiographical objectives of the author.[20]

In support of this thesis, Na'aman offers many detailed comparisons with parallels from inscriptions and other data from the 9th century. We will go through David's wars with the Arameans in 2 Sam 8:3–12 and 10:15–19 and note some of the important correspondences with the period of Hazael's domination.

In David's wars with the Arameans, the major protagonist opposing David is Hadadezer *ben* Rehob, king of Zobah. The name "*ben* Rehob" is of interest because in this case it does not mean that Rehob was his father but has the meaning of being a scion of the house of Rehob, as reflected in the Assyrian equivalent *mar Ruhubi*. This region, also known as ʿAmqi in Assyrian texts, consisted of the Beqaʿ valley of Lebanon, north of the Israelite city of Dan. In addition, Hadadezer was also designated as king of Zobah (Assyrian Ṣubite/Ṣubat), which is the region of the Anti-Lebanon north of Damascus, also known as Mount Amana. As we have seen above, this kingdom with just this double designation is known from Shalmaneser III's inscription, which includes Baʾasa, son of (Bit)-rehob and Mount Amana. As Na'aman has argued, it also appears to be the case that Hazael was likewise king of Beth-rehob and Zobah, probably as the son of Baʾasa, and that he

---

20. Na'aman, "In Search of Reality," 209.

gained control of Damascus as a usurper to the throne after Adadidri (Hadadezer), who is mentioned in the Shalmaneser inscriptions as king of Aram (Damascus).[21] It is Hazael, as king of Beth-rehob and Zobah, as well as ruler of Damascus, who became the major antagonist to the Assyrians for control of the west, and with the Assyrian's decline, the imperial ruler of the whole region west of the Euphrates and the Syrian desert. This portrayal of Hazael from the historical and biblical sources corresponds so closely to the Hadadezer presented in David's Aramean wars that it seems highly likely, as Na'aman argues, that Hadadezer is being modeled on Hazael.

There has been considerable discussion about what 2 Sam 8:3 means when it says that David defeated Hadadezer "when he was on his way to set up his monument at the Euphrates," בלכתו להציב ידו בנהר.[22] The act of setting up a monument implies that the whole region from one's home base to the location of the marker has already been brought under military or political control.[23] That would hardly be appropriate if David were understood as the subject of the infinitive phrase בלכתו. There is now inscriptional evidence to suggest that Hazael actually campaigned on the far side of the Euphrates,[24] so that it is entirely likely that he set up a monument at the Euphrates to commemorate the event, and, as Na'aman has suggested, Hadadezer is represented in this verse as doing the same. This would mean that David made an attack on his territory while he was preoccupied with actions in the north. Where the first battle took place is not specified, only that he captured 1,700 horsemen and 20,000 infantry (2 Sam 8:4). This differs from the account in 1 Chr 18:4, which mentions the capture of 1,000 chariots, 7000 horsemen, and 20,000 infantry. The fact that both Samuel and Chronicles mention hamstringing all but 100 of the chariot horses strongly suggests that the original text may have included 1000 chariots, 700 horsemen, and 20,000 infantry. It is interesting to note that the Assyrian accounts of their wars against coalition forces and against Hazael mention very similar numbers of troops with the same general

---

21. See esp. Na'aman, "Hazael of ʿAmqi," 381–94.

22. The verb להשיב (MT) is curious here, and Driver (*Notes on Samuel*, 281) proposes to read להציב, based on 1 Chr 18:3 and the parallel texts in 1 Sam 15:12 and 2 Sam 18:18.

23. The Assyrians frequently speak of setting up their monuments in foreign territories at the conclusion of a successful campaign.

24. Na'aman, "Hazael of ʿAmqi," 382–84.

breakdown into chariots, cavalry, and infantry. Thus, in Shalmaneser III's victory over Hazael, he claims to have captured 1,121 chariots and 470 cavalry and to have killed 16,000 infantry.[25]

The second phase of the war mentions that when Arameans from Damascus came to the relief of the Hadadezer's forces, David killed 22,000 men of this force (v. 5). No attempt is made here to break them down into specific groups. Such exaggerated numbers of war dead are quite typical of Assyrian royal annals.[26] The consequence of this victory was that David occupied Damascus and installed garrisons within the region to control it and to make it pay tribute to him (v. 6). He also took valuable booty in the form of golden shields and brought them to Jerusalem, as well as bronze objects from various towns of the region (vv. 7-8). Again, it is typical of Assyrian inscriptions to list valuable booty as well as the reception of tribute at the end of the battle account.

The result of these victories is that David receives a delegation from Toi, king of Hamath, with congratulations and gifts (2 Sam 8:9-10). This reaction to David's success is quite understandable within the context of the 9th and early 8th centuries. Israel and Hamath were longstanding coalition partners against Assyria in the 9th century, and when Hazael left this coalition he became a serious adversary to both Israel and Hamath. This situation extended well into the 8th century. Consequently, it is not hard to imagine that a victory by either Israel or Hamath over their arch rival in Damascus would have been most welcome to the other alliance partner. This defeat of the Arameans finally came from the Assyrians under Tiglath-pileser III in 732 B.C.E. The dedication of gifts and booty, such as are mentioned in 8:10-12, to the deity's temple is also typical of royal inscriptions of all periods, even though in this case David does not yet have a sanctuary in which to place them.[27]

A second war with Hadadezer is set out in 2 Sam 10:15-19. It is likely that this account originally followed either 8:8 or 8:12 and was removed to its present location by the author of the *David Saga* in 10:1-14 and 11:1, with the very weak link at 10:19b. The Ammonites play no role whatsoever

25. Idem, "In Search of Reality," 209.

26. Ibid. On the totally unrealistic nature of such high percentages of casualties in ancient warfare, see R. Waterfield, *Xenophon's Retreat*, 11-12.

27. Chronicles gets around this problem by suggesting that all the precious booty of David's wars was dedicated for the future temple of Solomon, 1 Chr 18:8, 26:26-28.

in the battle described in 10:15-19a, although they have a major role in what precedes in 10:1-14 and what follows in 11:1. In the second Aramean war, Hadadezer enlists the aid of the Arameans who were from the region "Beyond the River" עבר הנהר. From the point of view of the Israelites, this might suggest the region east of the Euphrates, but as Na'aman points out, this terminology imitates the technical Assyrian term for the Aramean region on the *west* side of the Euphrates, including a number of Aramean states, which in the time of Hazael were vassal states under his authority.[28] The battle takes place at Helam, the location of which is uncertain. Some scholars want to locate it somewhere in northern Transjordan in order to make the battle more relevant to the Ammonite war, but as we have suggested, the battle has nothing to do with that war. A more likely possibility is some point north of Damascus, between Damascus and the region west of the Euphrates. The number of casualties suffered by the Arameans in the one battle, 700 charioteers and 40,000 horsemen, with no mention of the infantry, seems to reflect some corruption in the text.[29] The result of this battle is that the kings who had been vassals of Hadadezer now became vassals of David, which suggests that his imperial reach extended all the way to the Euphrates and that at the height of his power, David's western empire corresponded in extent to that of the later, much dreaded Hazael, ruler of Damascus. This complete subjugation of the whole Aramean state from the Euphrates to the frontiers of Israel does not reflect the time of David. That fact is now widely recognized, and Na'aman's suggestion, namely, that a later writer has imitated information from older accounts of hostilities in the region from the 9th to early 8th centuries to reconstruct an imperial realm for the time of David as founder of the dynasty corresponding to that of Hazael as founder of the "house of Hazael," is entirely plausible. This, of course, makes wars of this sort a complete fiction.

The wars against Moab (2 Sam 8:2) and Edom (vv. 13-14) may be dealt with more briefly. Na'aman also regards both of these wars as imitations of similar events that took place in the 9th and early 8th centuries. In the case of Moab, the atrocity committed by David recalls the massacre of Israelites by Mesha, king of Moab, as celebrated on his famous stele. As Na'aman says of these late 9th-century wars between Israel and Moab, "these wars were

---

28. Na'aman, "Sources," 174-75.

29. See McCarter, *II Samuel*, 269, for the textual variants. It is significant that whereas David often fights against large forces of chariots and cavalry, he is never represented as having any of these in his own army.

the bloodiest and most destructive in the course of Israelite-Moabite relations. . . . Israel was defeated and never recovered its lost territories." This would constitute a kind of literary reprisal for that event, set in the time of David.[30] In the case of Edom, the victory over the Edomites in the Valley of Salt strongly resembles Amaziah's victory at the same place in 2 Kgs 14:7, so that David's victory of over Edom imitates that of the later Judean king. This leads Na'aman to set the dating of the source that contained the accounts of David's wars to the early to mid-8th century.[31] In a similar fashion, the remark about David's conquest of Gath in 2 Sam 8:1, if we have reconstructed this verse correctly, would fit with the devastation of this city by Hazael in his conquest of the region (2 Kgs 12:17, Amos 6:2), and again the victory of David would represent an imitation of the later event.[32] Thus, all of these foreign wars are literary inventions for the ideological enhancement of David's reign.

This brings us to a consideration of the Ammonite wars in 2 Sam 10:1–14, 11:1, 12:26–31. The presentation of these wars is of an entirely different character from the others and must be recognized as such in order to properly appraise the relationship between the two literary works in which the wars of David are embedded. Let us look at a number of these differences:

1. The Ammonite wars are an integral part of a larger narrative in a way that is not the case with the other wars. Thus, the first Ammonite war begins with a narrative episode in 2 Sam 10:1–5 that presents the *casus belli* for the war that follows in vv. 6–14. There is nothing comparable in any of the other wars that we have reviewed. In the second Ammonite war, the events of the war are intermingled with an extended narrative about David's affair with Bathsheba that takes place during the course of the war. This leads to the curious situation in which the war becomes protracted over a long period of time (ca. 2 years), unlike the single battles of all the previous wars.

2. The presentation of the opening battle in 2 Sam 10:6–14 has the Ammonites begin the hostilities by hiring Aramean mercenaries from four distinct regions, 20,000 infantry from Beth-rehob and Zobah, a thousand from Maacah, led by its king, and 12,000 from Tob. This contrasts with all the other accounts dealt with above in which nothing is said about any

---

30. Na'aman, "In Search of Reality," 212–13.
31. Ibid., 214.
32. On the fate of Gath in the 9th century, see ibid, 210–12.

mercenaries. These would appear to constitute the largest part of the forces, together with the Ammonites. Nothing is said about the Aramean forces being under the joint command of Hadadezer, whose name does not appear anywhere in this unit. The large-scale use of mercenaries is typical of the other military accounts within the *David Saga*, as we have seen, but is entirely missing from DtrH. Furthermore, the description of the battle with different units of the Israelites taking on the different elements of the mercenaries and the local conscripts is typical of warfare in the Persian period as described by Xenophon in his *Anabasis*, whereas in 10:15–19 (Dtr) Hadadezer's allies are vassal states, not mercenaries. The nature of the battle in 10:6–14 does not fit any description of warfare in the 9th or 8th century, but it is very characteristic of the late Persian period and must be a later addition to the Aramean wars.

3. In the previous accounts of the wars in 2 Sam 5:6–10, 17–25; 8:1–14; and 10:15–19, David is always involved in the battles and there is no mention of any of his commanders. In 10:6–14 and in chaps. 11–12, David is not involved in the action, but in his place we have Joab and Abishai. Only at the end of the Ammonite war when the issue has been largely decided does David make a show of taking the city of Rabbah. It is characteristic of the *David Saga* that David does not lead his troops in battle but has his professional army under the command of the sons of Zeruiah take the lead of the campaign on his behalf.

4. The Aramean wars of 8:3–14 and 10:15–19 distinguish among the various types of troops, charioteers, cavalry, and infantry and give the number of those killed in each group. The accounts in 10:6–14, 11:1, and 12:26–31 make no distinction between types of troops, and while they mention the numbers of mercenaries (but not the number of local conscripts), they do not indicate how many were killed. The style of presentation is fundamentally different.

5. In contrast to all the other battles mentioned in the earlier account of the wars, the battle against the Arameans and Ammonites in 10:6–14 is inconclusive. The Arameans simply flee (with no apparent casualties) and the Ammonites retreat into the fortified city so that the troops under Joab simply return to Jerusalem. This sets up the situation for the subsequent campaign against Rabbah, which consists of a long siege that takes up to two years. In the earlier accounts, much is also made of the booty taken and dedicated to Yahweh, whereas in 12:30 there is only a very perfunctory remark about spoil taken from the cities of the Ammonites, while much is made of the precious crown set on David's own head.

From all of these observations, it is reasonable to conclude that the Ammonite wars derive from an entirely different literary work than the corpus belonging to Dtr, and they share little with any older 9th-century models or Assyrian inscriptions. Their distinctive character strongly suggests that they are the creation of the author of the *David Saga* in which they are embedded and belong to the late Persian period.

Perhaps the most difficult question to answer about the primary account of the wars of David has to do with the nature of the sources that the author used and at what stage in the compositional history of the David legend they were put together in their present form. Na'aman's thesis is that there was a "chronicle of early Israelite kings" written in the first half of the 8th century because his sources were so consistently drawn from this period. It was this early "chronicle" that was later used by Dtr for his larger history.[33] This thesis is very attractive, but in chapter three above I expressed reservations about his early date for a chronicle such as this. Furthermore, there is still a question about how to interpret the individual sources on which a chronicle such as this was based. It is not enough to invent a corpus of *quasi* historical documents and annals stored within royal and temple archives.

With respect to David's wars against the Philistines, there seems to have been a body of legends about numerous skirmishes, most of them of a very limited and defensive nature, with their own particular characteristics quite distinct from the other wars. This corpus had its own development, extending over a long period of time, as seen above in the case of the David and Goliath story. The war against Moab does not require a documentary source but only the memory of a bitter struggle to produce the account of David's atrocity as suggested above. By contrast, the victory of David over Edom suggests the use of a specific source used by Dtr in his history of the later Judean kings. It could have been derived from a royal monument.

It is only in the wars of the Arameans that we encounter so many specific details that seem to correspond to information contained on Aramean and Assyrian monuments and in a style that imitates some of the features of these monuments. Now it would seem to me that the Northern Kingdom of Israel was much more involved with the Arameans and Assyrians in the 9th century, as is clearly indicated in the biblical tradition, and even though Judah was sometimes a junior partner in some of the hostilities against Aram and Moab, the place where one might expect "sources" about this

---

33. Na'aman, "Sources and Composition," 173–79.

early period is in the Northern capital of Samaria. It is here that one might find Aramean and Assyrian monuments, such as those similar to the Tel Dan inscription or a stele of Shalmaneser III regarding his final campaigns in the region.[34] It is possible that the content of inscriptions such as these became part of a scribal collection in Samaria and at a later date this came into Judah along with many other northern traditions and so was accessible to Dtr. This is all quite speculative, but a scenario of this sort seems more likely than one that suggests a southern scribe in Jerusalem could have composed a "chronicle of early kings" in the early 8th century with apparently a lot of access to what must have been distinctly northern sources. Because a northern scribe would not likely compose a chronicle of early kings that featured David and Solomon as heroes, I therefore suggest that it was Dtr who used these sorts of sources to shape his early history of David, and these wars are very much a part of his work.[35]

Literary Observations on the Wars of David

The question that I want to address under this heading is the literary relationship of the accounts of David's wars to each other and to the larger literary context. We have already argued that the primary account of David's wars is separate and distinct from those having to do with the Ammonite wars and that the latter belong to the *David Saga* as an addition to the former corpus. From our previous literary study, we may safely assume for the purposes of analysis that the primary account is that of Dtr. Let us look at the interconnections with that corpus of texts.

The story of David's capture of Jerusalem (2 Sam 5:6–12) presents the etiology of the origin of the "City of David," which is a favorite designation of Dtr and some later texts directly dependent on DtrH.[36] David's building

---

34. See A. Biram and J. Naveh, "An Aramaic Stele Fragment from Tel Dan," *IEJ* 43 (1993): 81–98; idem, "The Tel Dan Inscription: A New Fragment," *IEJ* 45 (1995): 1–18; N. Na'aman, "Three Notes on the Aramaic Inscription from Tel Dan," *IEJ* 50 (2000): 92–104. Note that Shalmaneser III set up a stele at Ba'li-ra'si, "a headland of the sea," where he received tribute from Tyre, Sidon, and Jehu of Israel. Some would identify Ba'li-ra'si with Mt. Carmel. See Luckenbill, *Ancient Records of Assyria and Babylonia*, 1:243.

35. We may quickly dismiss the proposal by Halpern (*David's Secret Demons*, 107–226) that 2 Sam 8 was the product of David's own scribes, based on David's actual conquests, set down in the style of Assyrian annals. As indicated in the above discussion, all the indications of a later fictitious composition make this approach to the David story quite unacceptable.

36. 2 Sam 6:10, 12, 16; 1 Kgs 3:1; 8:1; 9:24; 11:27; Isa 22:9.

activity in the City of David, with the Millo and palace, also anticipates the account of Solomon's later building activity, except that David builds no temple. This is left entirely to Solomon. The building of David's house of cedar with Hiram's aid directly anticipates the remark about David's living in a house of cedar in 7:1-2. The remark about David's increase in strength and renown and the fact that Yahweh was with him (5:10) is a theme that we have seen in the story of David's dealings with Saul (1 Sam 18:5, 12, 15, 28, 30). This goes closely with the concluding statement in 5:12, which reads, "David recognized that Yahweh had set him up as king over Israel and that he had raised to eminence his kingdom for the sake of his people Israel." This statement harks back to the remarks of the tribal representatives at the time of David's enthronement in 5:1-2 and it anticipates David's prayer in 7:18-29, which elaborates this same theme. Thus, David's capture of Jerusalem and his building activity, as well as the accompanying remarks, all tie the unit very tightly into DtrH.

The Philistine wars seem to make use of some older traditions that have been tied into the present narrative context only rather loosely, as we have suggested above. In 2 Sam 5:17 the attack of the Philistines is connected with the occasion of David's anointing in 5:1-2, 3b, which, however, happened at Hebron before David's capture of Jerusalem. This would make the stronghold more likely a reference to the earlier activity of David in the south, such as at Keilah (1 Sam 23:1-5) with the stronghold at Adullam. The identity of the stronghold with the City of David is an attempt to displace these events to a time after the capture of Jerusalem. The capture of the "idols" of the Philistines as war booty is a common motif in accounts of battle and is not necessarily a reference to the Philistines' capture of the ark as booty in 1 Sam 4. The concluding remark in 2 Sam 5:25 that David defeated the Philistines "from Gibeon as far as the approach to Gezer" is used as a summing up of the wars but it does not make much sense in the present context. Some have tried to suggest that this was the route of the Philistines' flight,[37] but nothing in the account suggests the enemy's flight and Israel's pursuit, and the supposed route seems quite unrelated to the prior battles. The region in question is that of Benjamin, and it would be a fitting summary for the wars of Saul against the Philistines as reflected in 1 Sam 14, which in v. 31 includes a very similar summary in which Saul's forces "defeated the Philistines from Michmash to Aijalon." This summary is in fact very closely related to the action that has preceded it. It looks,

---

37. McCarter, *II Samuel*, 157-60, and map 4.

therefore, as though the summary has been imitated as a conclusion to David's campaigns. Gibeon is merely substituted for Michmash as a more prominent site in the region and "the approach to Gezer" is equivalent to Aijalon, since it stands at the head of that approach. Thus, there is some reason to suspect that Dtr has transferred some of Saul's success against the Philistines in the region of Benjamin to David.

The wars of David in 2 Sam 8:1–14 and 10:15–19 exhibit a number of similar patterns and clichés. The wars against the various nations begin with similar statements: "After this David defeated the Philistines and subdued them" (2 Sam 8:1a); "and he [David] defeated Moab" (8:2); "and David defeated Hadadezer son of Rehob, king of Zobah" (8:3a); "when he returned from defeating the Arameans [he defeated Edom] in the Valley of Salt, 18,000 men" (v. 13). The Moabites become "servants of David" and pay tribute 8:2); David puts garrisons in Damascus, and the Arameans become "servants of David" and pay tribute (8:6); David puts garrisons in Edom and they become "servants of David"; the kings who had been "servants of Hadadezer" make peace with David and they are made subservient to Israel (10:19). In both the Aramean and the Edomite wars, it is said that "Yahweh gave David victory wherever he went" (8:6b, 14b). This general uniformity in style, even when the sources of information or models used were different, as we have shown above, suggest that it is a common author who has attempted to unify and integrate this corpus into his larger work, DtrH. In my view, all of the wars originally stood before the account of the restoration of the ark and the statement in 2 Sam 7:1 that Yahweh had given David rest from all his enemies that surrounded him. The remark about Yahweh granting David victory also corresponds with the statements in 5:10, 12 about Yahweh making David great and his kingdom preeminent.

It is these artificially reconstructed wars of David by Dtr that have resulted in the myth of the Davidic empire as reflected in 1 Kgs 5:1[4:21], which includes everything "from the Euphrates to the land of the Philistines and to the border of Egypt." Yet there are many contradictions to a scheme in which the cities of the Philistines are not subdued, with the possible exception of Gath, and that does not include any of the other coastal cities of the Levant or the cities of the Orontes, such as Hamath and the other so-called neo-Hittite cities. There are also some late attempts to modify the extent of David's kingdom, as in the story of the census in 2 Sam 24 with its very vague northern border in vv. 6–7. Hiram of Tyre is scarcely considered as a vassal of either David or Solomon. Nevertheless, there seems to be some correspondence with the myth of the Davidic empire and "the land of the Hittites" promised to Joshua (Josh 1:4) in the Dtr ideology but never realized until David. This "land of the Hittites," which covered the whole territory from the Euphrates to the border of Egypt, reflects the terminology of the late Neo-Assyrian Empire.[38] It would appear that the closest that Dtr could come to a model for this was in the various sources dealing with Hazael's Aramean kingdom, which, under the guise of the imagined realm of Hadadezer, David conquered.

David and the Ark (2 Samuel 6)

The common approach to David's bringing up the ark to Jerusalem in 2 Sam 6 is to follow the lead of Rost, in principle if not in detail, and to see it as the climax of the larger Ark Narrative (AN) in 1 Sam 4:1–7:2 and 2 Sam 6, which Rost believed to be an independent literary composition.[39] Rost regarded it as a source that was used by the author of SN, based on the fact that this author had added the episode of David's encounter with Michal in 2 Sam 6:16, 20–23, which was built into and made a part of AN. For Rost, this meant dating AN to the time of David and interpreting it as a legitimization of David's choice of Jerusalem as capital and religious center of the realm. Much of the analysis and interpretation of AN as a whole and this episode in 2 Sam 6 in particular is governed by fitting the details of the story into the social and religious context of an early dating scheme such as this, and no other alternative is considered.

Once the scholarly guild was convinced that AN was of an early date, as early as the time of David's reign, and that it reflected a set of events that stretched from the use of the ark in Israelite religion in premonarchic times to its restoration as a central object in the cultus of Jerusalem, scholars offered numerous speculative suggestions about its origins and original religious significance.[40] These include the notions of a portable shrine such as are found among the Bedouin or the ark as a war palladium or as an object related to the theme of Yahweh's enthronement, because of statements relating the ark to the deity "enthroned on the cherubim" (2 Sam 6:2).[41] In

---

38. Van Seters, "The Terms 'Amorite' and 'Hittite' in the Old Testament," *VT* 22 (1972): 64–81.

39. Rost, *Succession*, 6–34.

40. See the review of suggestions such as this with bibliography by H.-J. Zobel, "aron," *TDOT* 1:363–74; also T. N. D. Mettinger, *The Dethronement of Sabaoth* (CBOT 18; Lund: Gleerup, 1982).

41. This is the view especially championed in ibid.

this last case, the ark is then identified with the throne of the deity, based on the iconography that presents the deity sitting on a throne or the footstool on which the god rests his feet.[42] The objections to these suggestions are obvious. The cherubim in the iconography are an integral part of the throne, but the throne itself is never identified as an ark. Von Rad's attempt to identify the throne in Isa 6:1 with the ark begs the question.[43] With respect to the footstool, the case is even weaker because the cherubim are never associated with it in the iconography of the divine throne. Furthermore, the term *aron* means a "chest" or "container," and there is no evidence that either the throne or the footstool ever served as such. The fundamental meaning of the ark as a container of objects likewise argues against all of the other notions suggested above.

This is not the place for an elaborate critique of all the proposals about the origin and meaning of the ark. I will simply set forth my view on how the biblical evidence can be understood and all of the elements accommodated to it. First, there seems to me little reason to doubt that within the Jerusalem-Zion theology Yahweh was viewed as an enthroned deity, much like other Near Eastern deities, and that much of the cultus as reflected in the psalms of enthronement was centered on this theme. The visions of Isaiah in Isa 6:1 and of Ezekiel in Ezek 1:26 may even suggest that the temple had a throne (with or without an image) as its central object and with which "heavenly" beings, such as seraphim and cherubim, were associated. However, nothing in all of this suggests any need for an ark. The deuteronomic reform presents an entirely different and competing focus for Judean religion, centered on obedience to the law, and this became epitomized in the Decalogue. The Dtr authors also created a special box, the ark, which contained the Decalogue—the covenant of Horeb—inscribed by Yahweh and bearing his sacred name (Deut 10:1–5). It is this ark with the Decalogue and the inscribed *name* that was now to be the central representation of the deity's presence in the temple and nothing else (1 Kgs 8:6, 9). Yet some accommodation to the prior Zion theology was made by the assimilation of some of its elements, with cherubim now placed on either side of the ark, and the older language of Yahweh as exalted king "enthroned on the cherubim" now became associated with it. The ark, which was originally con-

---

42. G. von Rad, "The Tent and the Ark (1931)," *The Problem of the Hexateuch and Other Essays* (Edinburgh: Oliver & Boyd, 1966), 103–24; Mettinger, *Dethronement*, 19–24.

43. Von Rad, "Tent," 121 n. 54.

ceived as just a simple wooden box, increasingly became a sacred object in its own right. This reaches its apex in the Priestly Writer's imagination, in which the simple wooden box is covered with gold, and the cherubim are mounted on a "covering" that fits on top of the ark. It is this covering that now becomes the throne of the deity (Exod 25:10–22).

Here I must make a few brief remarks about Mettinger's thesis in his book *The Dethronement of Sabaoth*.[44] I am in essential agreement with him that the deuteronomic *šem* theology, which spoke of the presence of Yahweh in terms of his "name," was an attempt to replace the Zion-throne theology as a result of the disastrous destruction of the temple and the sack of the city. I also agree that the *kabod* theology of the priestly tradition as reflected in both P and Ezekiel was in essential continuity with the prior Zion theology and that both of these theologies represented responses to the destruction of the temple. Where I have serious disagreement with Mettinger is in his understanding of the ark as originating in the divine-throne theology. On the contrary, the ark belongs to the Dtr theology and is closely associated with the "name" of the deity.[45] The "name" is present in the ark because the inscribed name is part of the Decalogue. Thus, when God chooses Jerusalem as a place in which to set his *name*, the city is the resting place for the ark, which is housed in the temple, built by Solomon specifically for the ark of the covenant.

It must be emphasized that the ark is an invention of an author of the exilic period. *There never was an ark in the temple of Jerusalem.* Not even in Ezekiel in the visions of the temple's destruction and renewal is there any hint of the ark. His imagery is still within the tradition of the Zion divine-throne theology. The theology of the ark represents a radical restructuring of Israel's memory of its early history, and all the stories about the ark are part of this ideological fabrication. The absence of references in the prophets and the Psalter is deafening.[46] Consequently, if the *David Saga*, which includes CH, belongs to the Persian period, then the whole question of AN's dating and interpretation is cast in a quite-different light. There seems to me little point in reviewing in detail all of the various proposals that begin with the assumption of an early date and a hypothetical understanding

---

44. Mettinger, *Dethronement*, 19–24.

45. See my discussion in "The Formula *lešakken šemo šam* and the Centralization of Worship in Deuteronomy and DH," *JNSL* 30 (2004): 1–18.

46. The exception, Ps 132, is merely a late messianic psalm that is built on the story of David and hardly an independent tradition as some suggest.

of the place of the ark in the primitive premonarchic religion of Israel. Instead, I will follow a literary analysis that seeks to understand the unit in
2 Sam 6 in relation to the earlier references to the ark in 1 Sam 4:1–7:2 as
well as to the broader understanding of the ark in DtrH and other related
texts.

The initial verses in 2 Sam 6:1–2 present a number of problems, which
have received a variety of solutions. The opening in v. 1 states "David again
assembled the whole of the elite corps in Israel, thirty thousand strong."
This suggests a massive military operation that is a continuation of those
that had preceded it against the Philistines in 5:17–25. However, nothing
in the largely defensive actions against the Philistines resembles a muster
of troops like this, and the language used throughout is quite different. Furthermore, even in the rest of the accounts of David's wars in Dtr, as discussed above, there is never any mention of the size of David's own forces,
only those of his enemies. The specific terminology used in 6:1, כל־בחור
בישראל, reflects a rather late usage that is not typical of Dtr. The closest
parallel is 2 Sam 10:9: מכל־בחור בישראל.[47] Similar also is the statement in
1 Sam 23:2 in which Saul is accompanied by 3,000 men, the elite of Israel
(בחורי ישראל). This rather strongly suggests that this introductory verse in
2 Sam 6:1 is actually an addition or rewrite by the author of the *David Saga*
and serves as a parallel to v. 2a.

Verse 2 also has its problems. It begins with the statement "David arose
and went, along with all the people who were with him from Baʿale-Judah,
to bring up from there the ark of God." The difficulty with this rendering is
that if one takes מבעלי יהודה as a place name, then the preposition מן seems
to be pointing in the wrong direction because the phrase "from there"
(משם) suggests the destination to which David and his group are heading,
not from which they are departing. However, there is no other reference to
a place such as Baʿale-Judah, and 1 Chr 13:6 renders the parallel text as "to
Baʿalah, to Kiriath-jearim, which belongs to Judah." This seems to be a "correction" based on a reference to Baʿalah in the lists of Judean towns in Josh
15:9, in which it is also identified with Kiriath-jearim. The further qualifier,
"which belongs to Judah," probably reflects the reference to Judah in the
phrase Baʿale-Judah in 2 Sam 6:2. However, in 1 Chr 13:5 the Chronicler
has already understood the reference in his source "from there" (משם) to
mean "from Kiriath-jearim," which makes further clarification of the place
name in v. 6 quite redundant.

---

47. For this reading of the defective text, see 1 Chr 19:10.

There is another way of interpreting the phrase יהודה מבעלי in 2 Sam 6:2, and this is to interpret it as "from the citizens/inhabitants of Judah." A very similar use of this terminology can be found in Judg 9, which speaks repeatedly of the "citizens of Shechem" (שכם בעלי). This would mean that in contrast to v. 1 it was a group of people from Judah that accompanied him. This would still leave the problem of the place reference intended in the phrase "from there" (משם), which would require the place-name Kiriath-jearim, as we have it in Chronicles. One would have to believe that it fell out of the text, but no solution to the problem is foolproof.

Much more important for our present study, however, is the description of the ark in 2 Sam 6:2: "the ark of God, which is called by the name of the name of Yahweh of hosts who is enthroned on the cherubim" (האלהים ארון עליו הכרבים ישב צבאות יהוה שם שם נקרא אשר). This is paralleled by a very similar description of the ark at the beginning of the AN in 1 Sam 4:4: "the ark of the covenant of Yahweh of hosts who is enthroned on the cherubim" (הכרבים ישב צבאות יהוה־ברית ארון). The ark in the latter example is clearly the Dtr ark of the covenant that contains the Decalogue, as described in Deut 10:1–5. The divine epithet, "enthroned upon the cherubim," does not mean that the cherubim are part of the construction of the ark itself, such as one finds in the elaboration of the Priestly Writer of the Pentateuch. It merely alludes to the deity's heavenly enthronement. The terminology in 2 Sam 6:2, while showing a very close relationship to that of 1 Sam 4:4, expresses the same thought in a somewhat different form. It attaches the divine epithet "Yahweh of hosts who is enthroned on the cherubim" to the ark by the phrase (literally) "over which the name . . . is called." This expression, to call the name of the deity over something, is used by Dtr with reference to the temple in Jerusalem. Thus, in 1 Kgs 8:43, "your name is called over this house that I have built," בניתי אשר הזה הבית על נקרא שמך, is directly related to the thematic phrase used throughout Solomon's prayer, "to build a house for the name of Yahweh" יהוה לשם בית לבנות (8:17; see also vv. 18–20, 44, 48). This suggests that the *šem* theology of the Deuteronomist is tied in the closest way to the ark.

The phrase "ark of God" (האלהים ארון) is used regularly (6×) in this unit, where it sometimes alternates with "the ark of Yahweh" (יהוה ארון) (6×) so that Elohim with the article is clearly synonymous with Yahweh as "the (one and only) God." This same fluctuation occurs elsewhere in AN in 1 Sam 4–6, but "ark of God" (האלהים ארון) is not used in the story of the crossing of the Jordan (Josh 3–4) or in the circumambulation of Jericho (Josh 6) or in the dedication of the temple in 1 Kgs 8:1–9. In these places, it is called "the ark of Yahweh" (ארון יהוה) or, in the longer form, "the ark of the covenant of Yahweh" (ארון ברית־יהוה) or is abbreviated to "the ark of the covenant" (ארון הברית).These are the typical terms for the ark in Dtr.[48] There may also be epithets attached to the name of the deity.

The terminology within AN begins with the standard Dtr form, "the ark of the covenant of Yahweh" (ארון ברית־ יהוה) in 2 Sam 4:3-6, where it alternates in v. 4 with the phrase "the ark of the covenant of God" (ארון ברית האלהים).[49] After the ark falls into the hands of the Philistines, it then is referred to as "the ark of God" or "the ark of the god of Israel." However, in chap. 6, when the ark is in the process of being returned to Israel, the story then reverts to the alternative phrase "the ark of Yahweh." Two things are clear from the account of the ark in 1 Sam 4-6. The ark is understood as the repository of the covenant, namely, the Decalogue, as understood in Deuteronomy, and it is also the only symbol of the divine presence, the Israelite counterpart to the iconic gods of the Philistines. This is completely in keeping with the perspective of DtrH as reflected in 1 Kgs 8:1-11. There is no justification for trying to eliminate all traces of Dtr terminology in order to reconstruct a more primitive notion of the ark, as so many scholars have done.

The rather remarkable feature of the story about the ark's "return" to Jerusalem is the incident in 2 Sam 6:6-14, in which the one responsible for the care of the ark is killed, resulting in a long delay. The ark is temporarily placed in the house of a Philistine, Obededom, the Gittite, until a more favorable time is found to continue its trip to Jerusalem. Scholars account for this strange incident in what is otherwise an event of great celebration by assuming that it records an actual series of events related to the restoration of the ark. Yet this kind of explanation seems to me quite unacceptable for a number of reasons. First, if the ark is indeed an exilic invention of Dtr and never was a real object, then the episode is also a literary invention. It is unlikely, however, that this incident is the product of Dtr. In AN, there seems to be no difficulty in the mere transport of the ark from place to place (1 Sam 7:1-2), although there was a different fate for the curious who looked into the ark and thereby violated its sanctity (1 Sam 6:19-21). Once it is placed in the house of Abinadab (1 Sam 7:1-2), Eleazar, his son, is consecrated to take care of the ark, and thus presumably he was able to handle it. The period of time that the ark was in Kiriath-jearim is said to be

48. See also the terminology in Deut 31:25-26.
49. This phrase may be defective. See the BHS.

a long time, 20 years. However, it would have to cover the whole period of Samuel as judge, the reign of Saul, and much of David's reign, certainly more than 20 years. In 2 Sam 6:3–4, we are introduced to two new sons of Abinadab, Uzzah and his brother, in place of Eleazar, who was consecrated, and it was one of these sons, Uzzah, who, in reaching out to steady the ark, was killed as a result. One has the impression that this is a parody on the incident in 1 Sam 6:19–21 involving the death of the curious peeking into the ark. Why, in this later episode, were these two sons of Abinadab not also consecrated and therefore immune to this disaster?

David, we are told, becomes both annoyed with the deity and afraid, and so he places the ark in the house of a *Philistine*, Obededom the Gittite, because he does not want to run the risk of having such a dangerous object in his own residence. It is difficult to understand how anyone can fail to see how ridiculous this makes the whole project of the ark's restoration. After AN tells us that the ark spent seven months among the Philistines (1 Sam 6:1), causing them great mischief, now David places this most sacred object once again in a Philistine household! But instead of causing this Philistine any trouble, it has the opposite effect, so that David wants to take it back for himself. Presumably, in order to appease the deity, David offers sacrifices every six paces on the journey from the house of Obededom to Jerusalem. One must ask how it is possible, after David's prolonged struggle against the Philistines (2 Sam 5:17–25), that there is one of them with a landed estate near Jerusalem, whom he now entrusts with the ark? I find it difficult to imagine how any of this could be the work of Dtr, much less reflect any historical reality. The Chronicler has considerable trouble with this incident, which he cannot avoid including in his work (1 Chr 13). However, he does his best to turn Obededom into a Levite and has the Levites carry the ark from Obededom's house to its proper place in Jerusalem.

It seems to me that the identification of Obededom as a Gittite[50] reflects the author of the *David Saga*, who likewise has David employ a band of mercenaries from Gath in 2 Sam 15:19–23. McCarter wants to associate both Obededom and the Gittite mercenaries under Ittai with the time that David spent in Gath and Ziklag,[51] but there is much in the text that speaks against this. David, while in Ziklag, was careful to have no Gittites in his group who could report back to the king of Gath what David was actually

---

50. The name Obededom is actually Edomite and probably reflects the large number of Edomites in the region in the Persian period.
51. McCarter, *II Samuel*, 170.

doing. And David's remarks to Ittai in 2 Sam 15:20 suggest that Ittai and his men only joined David's service recently before the Absalom revolt. According to the author of the *David Saga*, David's realm comprised both Israelites and non-Israelites without any distinction or discrimination so long as they were loyal and submissive to him. In this, the *David Saga* is altogether different from Dtr. This unit in 2 Sam 6:6–14 has all of the features of this post-Dtr author. This would mean that Dtr recorded the restoration of the ark from the house of Abinadab in 2 Sam 6:3a, and the procession of rejoicing in v. 5, followed by v. 15. The remark about David's dancing in v. 14 anticipates v. 16 and belongs to the *David Saga*. In vv. 17–19 (Dtr), David places the ark in the tent that he has set up for it, offers sacrifices before it, and then gives a festal meal to all the people before they depart, very similar to Solomon's great festival at the conclusion of the dedication of the temple in 1 Kgs 8:62–66.

Thus, Dtr's restoration of the ark, which consists of 2 Sam 6:2–3a, 5, 15, 17–19 is an uninterrupted occasion of joy and celebration. It may be rendered as follows:

> Then David and all the people who were with him from the citizens of Judah arose and went to bring up from [Kiriath-jearim][52] the ark of God, which is called by the name of Yahweh of hosts who is enthroned upon the cherubim. They carried the ark of God upon a new cart, and they brought it from the house of Abinadab which is on the hill. And David and all the house of Israel were making merry before Yahweh with all their might to the sound of songs, lyres, lutes, tambourines, castanets, and cymbals. Thus David and all the house of Israel were bringing up the ark of Yahweh with cheers and with the blast of the ram's horn. And they brought in the ark of Yahweh and set it down in its place within the tent that David had set up for it. Then David offered burnt offerings and wellness offerings before Yahweh. When David had finished offering the burnt offerings and the wellness offerings, he blessed the people in the name of Yahweh of hosts, and he distributed among all the people, the entire mass, to each man and woman a loaf of bread, a portion of meat and a cake of raisins. Then all the people went home.

This event constitutes the climax of David's career and leads directly into the episode that follows in chap. 7.

It is the author of *account B* (the *David Saga*) who completely undermines this occasion by interrupting the festivities with the Uzzah incident

---

52. See 1 Chr 13:5.

and the sojourn of the ark for a further three months on a Philistine estate. Even the joyful procession is soured by characterizing David's behavior during the event as morally questionable in 6:20–23. This last unit also breaks the continuity between the end of the restoration in 6:17–19 and the opening remarks in 7:1–3 about David's desire to build a "house of cedar" for the ark. The scene in 6:20–23 also anticipates the theme and the language of David's election by God in 7:8–9 and David's prayer in 7:18–29, but it does so in a way that undermines both the theme of divine election and David's humility reflected in his prayer. If this interpretation of David's restoration of the ark in chap. 6 is correct, then it radically changes the nature of the discussion of chap. 7 that has dominated the scholarly debate for many years. To this subject we will now turn.

The Divine Promise to David (2 Samuel 7): A Retrospective Survey

The interpretation of 2 Sam 7 is so fraught with controversy and difference of opinion that it is scarcely possible to give a complete summary of all views. Nevertheless, it is useful to sketch out the main lines of development in the discussion, to understand where the difficulties of the chapter lie and how to address them. This I will attempt to do before I present my own discussion of the chapter. While much was written about this chapter by older scholars of the 19th and early 20th centuries, the contemporary discussion may be said to have its origin in the important proposals and interpretation of Leonhard Rost.

The promise to David in 2 Sam 7 plays a central role for Rost within his larger scheme of SN, which also included the HDR, because in his view both these literary works make direct references to the promises to David as contained in 2 Sam 7.[53] Given the fact that both these literary works are viewed by Rost as dating close to the time of David and reflecting historical realities of that period, he has little choice but to discover within this unit in 2 Sam 7 some historical oracles that date to the time of David himself. Rost acknowledges, in his study of this chapter, that earlier scholarship viewed the text as a later literary work and that there was at least some late "reworking" of the text. Nevertheless, he argues for evidence, however fragmentary, of ancient Davidic oracles.

---

53. L. Rost, *The Succession to the Throne of David*, 35–56.

Rost begins with what he regards as his strongest argument, the prayer of David in 2 Sam 7:18–29. This was usually regarded as a late pious addition, but Rost identifies only vv. 22–24 as a Dtr embellishment and the rest as a literary work based on a tradition of an actual prayer by David given on the occasion of his reception of a personal revelation about his future dynasty. This personal direct revelation, as reflected in v. 27, is set in contrast to the oracle mediated though Nathan in the previous unit in vv. 4–17. Apart from attestations that the prayer must be old, the only concrete evidence for its authenticity is its similarity to the prayer of Jacob in Gen 32:10–13, which also makes reference to the personal revelation to Jacob at Bethel (Gen 28:10–22), and Rost attributes Jacob's prayer to the Yahwist, which for him is Davidic in date. The weakness of this argument should be obvious. Few scholars today would date the Yahwist's work in general or Jacob's prayer in particular to Davidic times, and they see it rather as dating close to the time of Dtr or later, suggesting that David's prayer as a whole is likewise a Dtr literary construction. The reference to divine revelation in 2 Sam 7:27 as "uncovering the ear" is merely a poetic way of speaking about the prior event of hearing Nathan's oracle and nothing more.

The prayer of David, excluding vv. 22–24, deals only with the theme of the Divine promise of a dynasty. This leads Rost to isolate such a precise oracle in the previous unit in vv. 8–17, and he finds it in vv. 11b, 16: "And Yahweh declares to you that Yahweh will make for you a house, . . . and your house and your kingdom will be secure forever before me, your throne will endure for all time." The problem for Rost is that the form of this oracle suggests that it was mediated through the prophet, Nathan, and would appear to contradict his prior conclusion about v. 27. That does not bother him so long as the subject of the oracle is the same. He simply asserts that "the content of this oracle of Yahweh [vv. 11b, 16] holds out the prospect of the enduring continuation of David's dynasty. That such an oracle can be ascribed to the time of David has already been shown when we were dealing with David's prayer."[54] The fact that the early dating of the prayer of David may be in serious doubt, however, removes any support for the antiquity of the oracle in vv. 11b, 16, which he has reconstructed. Rost sees this oracle as embedded in a literary stratum in vv. 8–17, dating to the late 8th century, with v. 13 being an even later interpolation.

The unit in vv. 1–7 has a quite-separate literary origin in a distinct oracle against the building of a temple, vv. 4b–7, with a later literary introduction

---

54. Ibid., 47.

in vv. 1–4a, whose relationship with vv. 4b–7 is confused because it is interpreted as contradictory. Although there is mention of the ark in v. 2, Rost does not see any original connection with the AN. Because Rost strongly maintains the view that vv. 8–17 have no original connection with vv. 18–29, he must decide whether vv. 1–7 are originally connected with what follows, as seems most obvious, or belongs with 18–29 as a second oracle spoken by the deity directly to David (making vv. 4b–5aα secondary?). Rost chooses this second option, but he then allows for the author of the "second stratum" in vv. 8–17 to incorporate vv. 1–7, making both oracles the words of Nathan, which leaves vv. 18–29 in limbo. The whole literary reconstruction becomes so baffling and implausible that it is simply given up in later scholarship. Nevertheless, it had one important consequence, and that was for scholars to try to find alternative ancient oracles and an alternative way to preserve the notion that there was an ancient basis to the account of the divine promise to David in 2 Sam 7, because this chapter remained a keystone in the edifice supporting the early story of David.

A different attempt to find an ancient source behind 2 Sam 7 is to be seen in the study of S. Herrmann.[55] He interprets the chapter as a whole in terms of the literary genre of the so-called *Königsnovelle* of Egypt that in his view may be dated to the United Monarchy. On the basis of this study, A. Weiser made use of Herrmann's work to argue for the existence of a royal document that was used as the basis not only for 2 Sam 7 but for HDR as a whole, which only reached its climax in this chapter.[56] The view that a *Königsnovelle* such as this provides an appropriate parallel or adequate explanation for 2 Sam 7 has received sharp criticism from a number of quarters.[57] In the past, I have seriously questioned the notion of a genre that includes such a wide range of historiographic and fictitious texts, which cannot be adequately reflected in a simple schematization.[58] This position also assumes that there was rather active cultural interchange between Egypt and a large and prosperous united kingdom, a view that I have challenged as quite unlikely in other parts of this study. Consequently, any interpretation that rests

---

55. S. Herrmann, "Die Königsnovelle in Ägypten und in Israel," *WZK-MUL* 3/1 (1953–54): 51–62.

56. A. Weiser, "Die Templebaukrise unter David," *ZAW* 77 (1965): 153–68; idem, "Die Legitimation des Königs David: Zur Eigenart und Entstehung der sogen. Geschichte von Davids Aufsteig," *VT* 16 (1966): 325–54.

57. See F. M. Cross, *Canaanite Myth and Hebrew Epic*, 247–49; T. Veijola, *Die ewige Dynastie*, 70–72.

58. J. Van Seters, *In Search of History*, 160–64, 271–72.

on the thesis of an original *Königsnovelle* behind the text of 2 Sam 7 must be viewed with grave suspicion.

Martin Noth, likewise, adopts the position that 2 Sam 7 is an ancient text of the Davidic period and that it is a unified composition.[59] Although he accepts Herrmann's form-critical argument for the shape of the text as a *Königsnovelle*, his understanding of the nature of that unity is quite different. His method is tradition-historical in the sense that he sees in the various components of the chapter certain themes that originally belonged in different worlds or social contexts—those having to do with the old amphictyonic league and those connected with the Jerusalem monarchy and temple cultus—that have been deliberately brought together for ideological purposes at the inauguration of the monarchy. Thus, he insists that literary-critical analysis alone, as reflected in Rost, does not adequately address the unity of this chapter; it is primarily a matter of content.

Thus, Noth sets out the issues in the following way:

> The subject-matter of the chapter is threefold: the building of a temple for the Ark, the divine steering of the history of Israel, and the promise of lasting rule for the House of David. It is not certain whether these matters were originally related to one another, or whether they were only put together more or less by chance within the framework of a divine message from the prophet Nathan to David.[60]

Noth does not see the unity of the chapter in the literary juxtaposition of the statement of v. 5, "Will *you* build me a *house* to dwell in?" with the statement in v. 11b, "Yahweh will make you a *house*," or with the statement in v. 13a, "*He* will build a house for my name." Noth objects to the first option because "house" has two different meanings in these cases: in the one it is a "building," and in the other it is a "dynasty." But if word-play is intended, then this is not a serious objection. The second option is rejected because the statement in v. 5 is interpreted as a rejection of temple building so that this would also include David's successor in v. 13a. Furthermore, Noth regards v. 13a as a Dtr addition. Consequently, he looks for the basis of the chapter's unity in a quite-different direction.

Noth sees the underlying unity of the chapter in the juxtaposition of the theme of a dynastic promise to David with the theme of the past history of the people of Israel, "my people Israel," in which David is understood as

---

59. M. Noth, "David and Israel in II Samuel VII," *The Laws of the Pentateuch and Other Essays* (Edinburgh: Oliver & Boyd, 1966), 250–59.
60. Ibid., 250.

the divinely chosen *nāgîd* over God's people (vv. 8–10). By means of this combination, Noth suggests that "a function is assigned to David in Israel as the ancient sacral tribal confederacy."[61] Noth, following A. Alt, takes the earlier story of David, which he views as basically historical, and he suggests that David's establishment of the monarchy in Jerusalem was without any connection to Israel's earlier sacred amphictyonic traditions but that this connection was made by means of the "transfer of the Ark, the ancient shrine of the tribes, into his royal city of Jerusalem."[62] Indeed, Noth makes the "Ark-shrine" the setting for the dynastic promise and the reference to the ark in v. 1 as integral to the whole unit. Thus, Noth concludes, "The unity of content in II Sam. vii lies in the fact that everything in the chapter is seen from the standpoint of the shrine of the Ark in Jerusalem."[63]

In order to bolster this thematic unity, as Noth understands it, he adopts Herrmann's form-critical discussion of the *Königsnovelle*, or "King's Letter," as Noth prefers to call it, and sees it as the literary form in which the chapter was cast as a self-contained unit. He acknowledges minor additions by Dtr in vv. 1b, 12b, 13a, 22–24 but retains the rest except for minor possible corruptions. He concludes:

> In the "King's Letter" in *II Sam.* vii, questions are decided which must have arisen as a result of transporting the tribal shrine of the Ark to Jerusalem. The question of building a temple for this shrine in Jerusalem is decided, as is the question of the position of the kingdom of David with regard to the traditions of ancient Israel represented by the Ark. Both questions are decided permanently. For the rejection of the plan to build a temple is certainly meant as fundamental; and the position of David within "Israel" is clarified with regard not only to David's person but also his whole dynasty after him. Not only is the duration of the dynasty in itself dealt with, but also the relationship of the reigning Davidic monarch to the God of Israel (vv. 14–16).[64]

Noth's position has become problematic for a number of reasons, not merely because of his use of Herrmann's *Königsnovelle*, which does not really touch the heart of his position. First, he depends heavily on his thesis of the existence of a premonarchic amphictyonic league of all Israel with a central ark-shrine, which was also the bearer of the pentateuchal tradition,

---

61. Ibid., 254.
62. Ibid., 255.
63. Ibid.
64. Ibid., 258–59.

as well as the pre-Dtr traditions of the period of the judges. This viewpoint
has come in for much criticism and receives little support today.[65] Indeed,
the whole notion that the premonarchic twelve-tribe league was an amphictyony centered on the ark-shrine that moved from place to place is supported by Noth entirely on the basis of 2 Sam 7:6.[66] In the book of Judges
there is no hint anywhere of the ark or its movement from one location to
another. The story of the ark in 1 Sam 1–6 places it in a temple in Shiloh,
and the Priestly Writer assumes that it was there since the days of Joshua.
So any appeal to the social setting of an amphictyony amounts to a completely circular argument.

Second, Noth puts far too much confidence in what can actually be accepted as historical events and conditions in the time of David, based on the
account of his reign in 1 and 2 Samuel. His explanation of 2 Sam 7 is therefore proposed as a historical document put forward in response to a set of
actual contemporary events that he can reconstruct from the biblical texts.
This is because Noth has accepted the view of Rost that the story of David's
rise in 1 Sam 16:14–2 Sam 5:25 and SN in 2 Sam 6–7, 9–20, 1 Kgs 1–2 are
sources dating from the period of David and Solomon and one can reconstruct a history of David's reign on the basis of these texts.[67] In his earlier
work, *Überlieferungsgeschichtliche Studien*, Noth actually places 2 Sam 7
within the limits of SN. In this later study, however, Noth ends with a question about what the relationship of this chapter might be to the larger story
of David in which he admits there are a number of references to this text.
That, it seems to me, is certainly important to its interpretation, as scholars,
both before and after his own study, have indicated.

Third, even if one were willing to grant some plausibility to his thesis,
Noth does not explain how the terms of the document in 2 Sam 7, which
Noth says were "decided permanently," were completely reversed in the
next generation with Solomon's construction of the temple for the ark. Nor
does he explain how the document itself could have survived such a radical religious transformation, resulting in a house of cedar being built for
the ark. Noth's reconstruction of historical events behind 2 Sam 7 would

---

65. R. de Vaux, *Histoire ancienne d'Israël*, vol. 2: *La période des Juges* (Paris:
Gabalda, 1973), 67–86; C. H. J. de Geus, *The Tribes of Israel: An Investigation into
Some of the Presuppositions of Martin Noth's Amphictyony Hypothesis* (Assen: Van
Gorcum, 1976).

66. M. Noth, *A History of Israel* (2nd ed.; New York: Harper, 1958), 91 n. 3.

67. Idem, *The Deuteronomistic History* (JSOTSup 15; Sheffield: JSOT Press, 1981),
54–57.

encounter great skepticism today, and it is certainly not supported by this study up to this point.

Nevertheless, Noth's study has highlighted two important elements that will be taken up below. The first is that it is quite possible to read the chapter as a unity, depending on the perspective from which one starts. Conversely, those who do not do so also come to it with certain assumptions that virtually demand its fragmentation. The second important feature of Noth's position is that Noth has placed the ark and David's relationship to it, as set forth in 2 Sam 6, at the heart of the discussion. Of course, he did so in terms of his understanding of a particular historical event, the integration of the Israelite ark-shrine into the completely non-Israelite capital city of Jerusalem. However, even if one rejects this historical interpretation of events, the connection between 2 Sam 6 and 7 could also be viewed in a purely literary way and have a considerable impact on the understanding of the whole text. This connection with the ark was neglected before Noth and has been largely ignored since. We will also take up this matter below.

In 1965, Dennis McCarthy published a short-but-important article on 2 Sam 7.[68] Most of the earlier studies on this chapter had recognized the fact that there was evidence of some Dtr language and clichés within 2 Sam 7, but they treated these as disruptive glosses and interpolations that had little significance in the understanding of the text as a whole. Even Noth did not give much attention to this aspect of the chapter. By contrast, McCarthy recognized that the chapter was a programmatic text along with a number of these texts that gave shape to the whole of the DtrH. In this, he was following Noth's lead in his *Überlieferungsgeschichtliche Studien* in which Noth had identified a number of such texts reflecting Dtr's special ideology at turning points in history. To Noth's list of texts McCarthy now added 2 Sam 7. Its purpose was to mark the Davidic monarchy as an important era and turning point in the history of the people as a whole. This is especially reflected in the contrast between the past period of the judges and the founding of David's dynasty, which begins a new departure. In this connection, there is also the pattern of promise and fulfillment with the prediction of the temple construction that is completed by Solomon and also recognized as such by Solomon's programmatic speech in 1 Kgs 8:14–21.[69] Thus, the language and themes of Dtr were much more pervasive and

---

68. D. J. McCarthy, "II Samuel 7 and the Structure of the Deuteronomistic History," *JBL* 84 (1965): 131–38.

69. More attention to the specific themes will be given below.

important to the shaping and interpretation of the whole than earlier scholars had recognized. Consequently, in subsequent studies, this Dtr aspect of the text had to be taken much more seriously. Nevertheless, McCarthy did not address what exactly was the relationship of this text to the rest of the story of David, although he recognized that parts of this larger context seem to be cognizant of some of the themes within 2 Sam 7.

Frank Cross took up McCarthy's suggestion and affirmed the great importance of 2 Sam 7 for the DtrH, and he went on to compile a very detailed list of all the Dtr terminology supported by textual documentation from the Dtr corpus. One can be in no doubt about the fact that Dtr's hand permeates the whole chapter and not just a few incidental passages. Nevertheless, in spite of this affirmation, Cross attempted to find evidence for fragments of two archaic oracles which he believed went back to the time of David. He suggested that poetic elements of these original oracles could be extracted from the prose narrative that embodied them. The basic clue that Cross uses to discover these poetic elements is parallelism, the hallmark of Hebrew poetry. Thus, as an example, he reconstructs the following bicolon in 2 Sam 7:2:

אנכי ישב בבית ארזים
וארון ישב בתוך יריעה

> I dwell in a house of cedar,
> But the ark dwells in the midst of curtains.

This is the only bit of poetry that is recovered from the first oracle. To do so, Cross has to eliminate the introductory phrase "See now" (ראה נא) from the beginning of line one and "God" (האלהים) from the phrase "ark of God" in the second line. Of course, the lines are attributed to David and belong to a description that creates the occasion for the oracle that follows, so strictly speaking they are not oracular at all. Furthermore, the poetry here is rather bland by comparison with the regular features of Hebrew poetry, which loves inversion and variation of parallel verbs, and so on. Prose imitation of oracles, hymns, and prayers in DtrH are full of such simple elements of parallelisms, as the rest of the oracular speech in vv. 4–16 and the prayer in vv. 18–29 make clear. The same can be said for the very Deuteronomistic prayer of Solomon in 1 Kgs 8:22–53. Selecting a few examples of parallel phrases out of many in 2 Sam 7 and then modifying them by deletions and additions to improve their poetic quality in order to reconstruct archaic oracular fragments is not convincing. Furthermore, Cross's appeal to Pss 89 and 132 or 2 Sam 23:1–7 to support the antiquity of oracles such as these is likewise unconvincing because, as L. Perlit has argued, these examples are all late and directly dependent on 2 Sam 7.[70]

The methodological approach of Timo Veijola to 2 Sam 7 represents a return to the position of Rost, with important modifications, in his search to uncover two primitive oracles within 7:1-7 and vv. 8-17, which he believes have been comprehensively reworked by two Dtr redactions (DtrG and DtrN).[71] This Dtr *Bearbeitungsschicht* is much more extensive than in Rost, following the earlier work of McCarthy and Cross, and includes now the whole of the prayer of David in vv. 18-29, as well as additions to the two oracles in vv. 1b, 6, 8b, 11, 13, 16. What is clear from this is that the theme of the dynastic promise, so important to Rost, and its relationship to SN has now become part of the Dtr revision.[72] Eliminating these Dtr elements leaves Veijola with a first oracle in vv. 1a, 2-5, 7 and a second in vv. 8a, 9-10, 12, 14-15, 17. To a large extent these two oracles are the product of a process of elimination, by removing what must belong to the later Dtr stratum, with little discussion about their character as self-contained texts. Let us look at each in turn.

The first oracle, as identified by Veijola in vv. 1a, 2-5, 7 is not in the usual form of a poetic prophetic oracle but a piece of prose that is part of a larger story. Cross, at least, could recognize the fact that, in its present form, vv. 1-7 could not be an ancient oracle, hence his efforts to find evidence of an older form. The setting in v. 1 and the proposal in v. 2 make no sense without the earlier references to David's construction of his palace in Jerusalem, his victories over his enemies, and his restoration of the ark, which he has placed in a tent in the city. The oracle itself in vv. 5-7 is merely a long question, interpreted as rhetorical with no need for reply and implying a negative judgment on David's plan. Yet this is certainly a very strange way to formulate an entire oracle. Surely something else is expected. There has been a serious lack of any form-critical discussion about the nature of oracles of this sort involving questions and answers, apart from the attempt of Herrmann, which Veijola rightly rejects. To this we will return below. Veijola rejects v. 6 as Deuteronomistic, but according to the documentation of Cross, mentioned above, vv. 5 and 7 also have clear evidence of Dtr terminology.

---

70. L. Perlit, *Bundestheologie im Alten Testament* (WMANT 36; Neukirchen-Vluyn: Neukirchener Verlag, 1969), 50-52.

71. T. Veijola, *Die ewige Dynastie*, 68-79.

72. This means that the many allusions to this theme in the HDR and in SN are treated by Veijola as Dtr redaction.

The very subject matter of these verses also presupposes the construction of a history from the exodus and wilderness period through the judges to the rise of the monarchy and this history is Dtr's own creation. Furthermore, if there did exist an oracle from the time of David condemning the building of a temple, then how was this oracle preserved and transmitted to a later age, and why would Dtr have felt the slightest obligation to pay any attention to it when his view of the temple so completely contradicted it?

The second oracle in vv. 8a, 9–10, 12, 14–15, 17, as identified by Veijola after it has been cleansed of some of its more obvious Dtr elements, nevertheless still retains several of these elements in vv. 9–10, according to Cross's list.[73] This leaves the dynastic promise in vv. 12, 13b, 14–16, from which Veijola has tried to eliminate the most obvious Dtr language in vv. 13 and 16, but the whole of the dynastic promise is basic to the Dtr outlook. And v. 15 refers back to the earlier history that deals with the divine rejection of Saul and the rise of David in his place, which is assumed, so that it is embedded within this larger narrative context. If, as Veijola understands the limits of this oracle, it refers only to the immediate successor of David and not to a future dynasty, then there is no need for an oracle of this sort to have been preserved and transmitted beyond the succession of Solomon. Does Veijola believe that these oracles were somehow kept as archival relics until they were discovered centuries later and reinterpreted by Dtr? This scenario is completely implausible, but no other is offered.

In his study of 2 Sam 7 in *King and Messiah*,[74] Tryggve Mettinger, much like Veijola, reverts to a position similar to that of Rost, although he too admits to more Dtr influence on the text, under the influence of McCarthy, Cross, Veijola, and others. He now speaks of a Dtr redaction, but only in vv. 1b, 10–11a, and 22b–26, and some alteration in v. 13. In what remains he distinguishes two distinct layers, or *skopoi*, one having to do with the establishment of David's "house" or dynasty, found in vv. 8–11, 16, and the other found in vv. 12–15, which has to do with Solomon's construction of the temple. These two *skopoi* overlap in the ambiguous use of the word "house," *bayit*, and this means that both have an important connection with vv. 1–7. As a consequence, the two literary layers cannot be viewed as separate sources; instead, one must be an expansion or "redaction" of the other.

---

73. Cross, *Canaanite Myth*, 253–54.
74. Mettinger, *King and Messiah*, 48–79.

The oldest layer has to do with the theme about David's building a house for the ark and the divine response to this (understood as negative) in vv. 1-7, followed by the promise that David's offspring would succeed him, in vv. 12-15. Of particular importance for Mettinger is the parallelism between v. 5 and v. 13, which he gives as follows:

v. 5: האתה תבנה לי בית לשבתי

Will *you* build for me a house to dwell in?

v. 13: הוא יבנה |לי| בית לשמי

He will build [for me] a house for my name.

The problem with this view is that v. 13a as it stands is widely regarded as Dtr, and even Mettinger concedes that at the very least לשמי must be a Dtr addition,[75] but without it the parallel is seriously diminished. Furthermore, if v. 5 is understood as negative, then לשמי is necessary as a correction to לשבתי, otherwise the statement "he will build a house for me" reflects no opposition to the building of a temple. In addition, the statement in v. 13b, "I shall establish his royal throne in perpetuity," certainly suggests that the author has in mind more than the immediate successor to David; rather it suggests a continuous dynastic succession. If one eliminates v. 13 as a later addition, then the connection with vv. 1-7 is broken, and what remains in vv. 12 and 14-15 is just an isolated fragment with no context. Mettinger likewise needs v. 13 to date this oldest layer to the time of Solomon and the construction of the temple. Yet the account of the temple construction in 1 Kgs 5:15-8:66 is thoroughly Deuteronomistic, and in it this same language of v. 13a appears and, indeed, much of the rest of the promise to David as well.

The second layer Mettinger identifies as the "dynastic redaction" and dates it to the end of the Solomonic era and closely associates it with HDR. Indeed, he sees it as the conclusion to HDR and regards it as an account legitimizing the dynastic succession after the death of Solomon. To this layer belong vv. 8, 9, 11b, 16, 18-22a, and 27-29, which have been added to the earlier text.[76] The argument that this is a distinctive layer is based on the contrast between the term *house* in the sense of *dynasty* in vv. 11b and 16 and the term *seed* (*zeraᶜ*) in vv. 12-15, understood by Mettinger as referring only to Solomon, the immediate successor. This distinction, however,

---

75. See idem, *The Dethronement of Sabaoth*, 49.
76. Mettinger fails to indicate to which stratum 7:17 belongs.

seems much too forced. The use of the term *zeraʿ* in the patriarchal stories of Genesis suggests that it regularly has in mind the continuous succession of generations. It also seems very doubtful that the remarks concerning the deity's relationship with David's offspring have to do only with a single individual person, Solomon. Indeed, according to SN, which Mettinger views as closely related to this source, David already had many sons. The remarks about the deity's relationship to David's offspring have to do with all of the future kings of the dynasty and not just the first. What the deity says about establishing David's "house," kingdom, and throne forever, in v. 16, is the same as what is said about his "seed" in v. 13b. Mettinger has not made the case for the diversity of strata that he proposes.

Following the lead of so many earlier scholars, Kyle McCarter understands the text of 2 Sam 7 to consist of three different layers.[77] He sees the evidence for this above all in the fact that, within vv. 5-16, "the incongruous ideas—the refusal of a temple (vv. 5b-7) and the promise of a dynasty (vv. 11b-16)—are joined together in a precarious unity by v. 13a, 'He [the scion of the dynasty] will build a house for my name. . . .' This half-verse, then, is the linchpin of the passage."[78] Because there is no other reference to the temple in vv. 11b-16 and no reference to David's offspring in vv. 5b-7, v. 13a must be judged as editorial in combining the two, and because so many scholars regard v. 13a as Dtr, with its reference to building "a house for my name," the combination must be the work of Dtr. He concludes from this that "we may therefore conclude with some confidence that v. 13a is . . . a Deuteronomistic plus, forging a tenuous link between the incongruous oracular motifs of temple refusal and dynastic promise."[79]

No sooner does McCarter make this assertion than he muddies the water by recognizing that there are strong assertions for Dtr phraseology throughout the whole of vv. 5-16 and not just in this one half verse (v. 13a). He argues that much of this supposed Dtr language in vv. 5-7 belongs to an older "prophetic source" that he has identified throughout 1 Samuel, which belongs to the 8th century, and it was this prophetic source that introduced the theme of disapproval of a temple implied in 7:5b-7 into an earlier oracle of dynastic promise. The task of Dtr was to resolve the contradiction that now existed within this earlier prophetic history of the early monarchy

77. McCarter, *II Samuel*, 209-31.
78. Ibid., 222.
79. Ibid.

so as to suggest that David's good intentions were carried out by Solomon. McCarter sums up his views on the stratification of 7:1-17 thus:

> For all these reasons, therefore, we conclude that the earliest form of Nathan's oracle was a promise of dynasty to David made in connection with his declared intention to build a temple for Yahweh. This ancient document was expanded by a writer with a less favorable view towards the temple and towards David himself. The final form of the passage was the work of a Deuteronomistic editor who further amended it to express his own point of view.[80]

Needless to say, faith in the existence of a pre-Dtr prophetic source such as this is necessary to make this scheme work, and I do not share this faith.[81] Nevertheless, it may be instructive to look at his understanding of the oldest source in 2 Sam 7, which differs considerably from the earlier studies we have reviewed. The oldest document is identified in 7:1a, 2-3, 11b-12, and 13b-15a, and in this unit the intention to build a temple and its approval vv. 2-3 is linked with the dynastic promise. On the basis of a number of comparative studies that closely link the activity of kings with temple construction, McCarter makes this statement: "There was, in other words, an ancient and widely understood association between a king's erection of a temple to a particular god (or gods) and the hope for divine sanction of the continuing rule of the king and his descendants. In the present case we may speak of a connection between the establishment of a royal dynasty and the provision of a temple for the dynastic god."[82]

In my view, this statement goes way beyond the evidence and suggests something quite different from what the Assyrian and Babylonian texts state. It was, of course, expected that Near Eastern kings were responsible for the housing, care, and feeding of the state gods and could expect in return divine blessing on their domains and families, including the continuation of their dynasties. One frequently finds in inscriptions that mention the royal construction of a temple a prayer of dedication *after* the temple has been built, in which the king expresses the hope that the god will reward this good deed with prosperity and offspring and the continuation of the dynasty. But this is far different from saying that these texts contain oracles from court prophets suggesting that the *founding* of a dynasty is

---

80. Ibid., 223-24.

81. A full critique of McCarter's prophetic history of the monarchy can be found above, pp. 21-23.

82. Ibid., 224.

directly related to the building of a temple, much less to the mere intention of doing so. What is much more pertinent in a comparison between 2 Sam 7 and Assyrian royal inscriptions is the connection between a cessation of military activity and the subsequent construction of temples, which is so common in the Assyrian texts and is also featured in this biblical text. However, because McCarter relegates the remark about David finally having "rest" from all his enemies to a scribal mistake, this observation can have no relevance for his reconstruction. We will return to this comparison again below.

With respect to the reconstructed text, vv. 1a, 2–3, 11b, 12, and 13b–15a, McCarter has ingeniously turned Nathan's reply in v. 3 and what follows in v. 11b into a single oracle, with a little careful pruning of Dtr elements in vv. 1b, 13a, and 15b, although the Dtr terminology in v. 3b, "for Yahweh is with you," still remains. But what is curious is that there should be no formal introduction in v. 3, identifying it as an oracle, and most scholars do not understand it this way, whereas the second part of the reconstructed oracle in v. 11b receives a much more formal introduction. Mc-Carter's reconstruction seems too contrived. The form of the oracle is given in reported prose with narrative introduction, although nothing is said about the fact that David's intentions were never fulfilled by him. McCarter suggests that the theme of the oracle is "You promised to build me a house. Therefore I shall build you a house."[83] However, David's remarks to the prophet seem more like a request for approval than a promise, and if the "promise" was never kept by David, then how can the promise of a dynasty be understood as conditional on David's intention?

The second prophetic source is found in 7:4–9a and 15b and seems to me to be carved out of the larger collection of Dtr texts as others have identified them. There is little similarity to Mettinger's second stratum. McCarter regards the prophetic source as both anti-temple and anti-monarchy. Yet it is hard to see how vv. 8–9a can possibly be interpreted as anti-David, although McCarter conveniently omits v. 9b, "and I shall make [have made?] for you a great name, like the names of the famous who are on the earth," which certainly points to the glories of royal greatness. McCarter also identifies this same source with that of the story of David and Bathsheba, but this seems to me very unlikely.[84] In my own analysis, this latter story be-

---

83. Ibid., 225.

84. Does this mean that 1 Kgs 1–2, in which both Nathan and Bathsheba also play prominent roles, also belongs to this prophetic source?

longs to the *David Saga* and is post-Dtr in date. The bits and pieces that are left in vv. 1b, 9b–11a, 13a, and 16–17 are attributed to Dtr. They need no further comment here. The prayer of David in vv. 18–29 is similarly carved up, but it adds nothing new to the discussion. There is little agreement about a division such as this.

Just for the sake of comparison with McCarter, one may observe that Walter Dietrich attributes to the Deuteronomists 7:1–11a, 13, 16, 17a, and 18–29, divided between two editions, and this leaves only the theme of vv. 11b, 12, 14–15, and 17b, dealing with the theme of dynastic succession, and nothing about the temple.[85] With so much of the chapter viewed as the work of the Deuteronomists, the sole purpose of salvaging an ancient nucleus is that it is necessary if one is to maintain the existence of an early pre-Dtr SN, because SN requires the knowledge of a dynastic promise such as what Rost argued. Given the use of the dynastic promise elsewhere by Dtr, there seems to be no other reason that these few verses along with all the rest could not be the work of Dtr. Furthermore, the treatment of Dtr within 2 Sam 7 by Veijola, Mettinger, McCarter, and Dietrich, has been altogether different from that of McCarthy. The former group have all treated Dtr as an "editorial" process of incidental ideological additions in one or two stages, while McCarthy regarded 2 Sam 7 as a deliberate composition by Dtr to produce a central interpretive text for his whole history.

In contrast to the previous scholars, we have reviewed who seek to find the remnants of earlier sources in the text, my own earlier study in *In Search of History* followed the lead of McCarthy, as well as the study of Dtr phraseology by Cross, in support of the notion that 2 Sam 7 represented a unified composition of Dtr.[86] I also argued that 2 Sam 7 showed a number of interconnections with Dtr's treatment of the earlier history of Israel, including the stories of Saul and David. More recently, Steven McKenzie has likewise followed McCarthy, Cross (in his study of Dtr language), and my earlier study, and simply asserts that "2 Samuel 7 is best read as a Dtr unit."[87] The mere fact that Dtr inherited the tradition that it was Solomon

---

85. W. Dietrich, *David, Saul und die Propheten: Das Verhaltnis von Religion und Politik nach den prophetischen Überlieferungen vom frühesten Königtum in Israel* (BWANT 122; 2nd ed.; Stuttgart: Kohlhammer, 1992), 114–36.

86. Van Seters, *In Search of History,* 271–77.

87. S. L. McKenzie, "Why Didn't God Let David Build the Temple? The History of a Biblical Tradition," in *Worship and the Hebrew Bible: Essays in Honour of John T. Willis* (ed. M. P. Graham, R. R. Marrs, and S. L. McKenzie; JSOTSup 284; Sheffield: Sheffield Academic Press, 1999), 208.

and not David the dynastic founder who built the temple is, for McKenzie, enough to account for his particular treatment of this theme. He goes on to state that

> the connection between temple and dynasty was well established in the ancient Near East, and the tie between David and Jerusalem specifically was extremely important to Dtr. But it is no longer possible to determine what these sources were much less to restore actual documents. Dtr's work in 2 Samuel 7, in short, was that of an author creating something new rather than that of an editor supplementing an inherited document.[88]

While there is strong general agreement between McKenzie and me regarding the unity of 2 Sam 7 and its Dtr character, there are still a number of points of disagreement on the interpretation of particular texts. Therefore, in my analysis that follows it will be useful to engage in a dialogue with him and other scholars on these matters.

2 Samuel 7 within the David Story and the Larger DtrH

The difficulties with understanding 2 Sam 7 arise already in v. 1. McKenzie follows McCarter and others in seeing v. 1a as the key to understanding the chapter as a whole, because v. 1a introduces the theme of *house*: "It happened that when the king dwelt in his house" (ויהי כי־ישב המלך בביתו). It is true that this relates back to the end of the episode in 6:19[89] and the theme of *house* is picked up again in the rest of chap. 7, but it is a little misleading to put so much on this half verse. This is because McKenzie and McCarter regard v. 1b as a textual corruption, as we shall see. The real theme is expressed in 7:2: "The king said to Nathan the prophet, 'Look here, I am living in a cedar house, while the ark of God is sitting in a tent.'" This, of course, relates back to the episode in chap. 6[90] about the bringing of the ark to Jerusalem and David's placing the ark in a tent, v. 17. It expresses the wish that David build a more permanent "house" for the ark of God as the symbolic presence of the deity. It is this theme about building permanent houses that is central to the whole chapter. David wishes to build a permanent house (a temple) for Yahweh, and Yahweh will build a permanent house (a dynasty) for David.

---

88. Ibid., 208–9.
89. Not 6:20a as McCarter suggests (*II Samuel*, 195).
90. In the Dtr version without the later additions, as discussed above.

Before we begin to tackle the major problem of how the deity responds to this intention of David, we must address the statement in 7:1b that "Yahweh had given him [David] rest from all his enemies on all sides." This statement is directly contradicted by what follows in the texts from 2 Sam 8-20 and in the suggestion in 7:11a that a "rest" of this sort is in the future. Consequently, some would remove it as redactional, a Dtr gloss on an earlier text. McCarter explains it as a marginal correction that was made originally on the text in v. 11a to change "and I will give *you* (לך) rest" to "and I will give *them* (לו) rest," referring to the people instead of David, as in v. 10, and this correction was somehow transferred to v. 1, which also resulted in the change from future to past.[91] McKenzie likewise follows McCarter in this explanation, but it is entirely too farfetched to be plausible. A marginal correction would have contained only the one word with suffix (לו) and not the whole sentence, and its shift to an entirely different location is hardly convincing. The argument by McCarter that v. 1b is missing from the more "original" version in Chronicles carries no weight, as McKenzie admits,[92] because the parallel sentence in v. 11a is also missing in Chronicles. The reason that Chronicles deleted these references is obvious. He had a text that included all of 2 Sam 8-20, and his understanding of the reign of David was entirely different from that of Dtr. Consequently, I reject any such emendation of v. 1b, and I will deal with the apparent contradiction with v. 11a in its place.

In fact, the statement in v. 1b that "Yahweh had given him rest from all his enemies on all sides" is a most appropriate introduction for what follows. As I have pointed out in an earlier treatment of this text, it is a convention of Assyrian annals that the inscriptions always give a long recitation of the king's military victories before it recounts the building of any temple, leaving the impression that this building activity occurred only at the conclusion of all such military activity.[93] Regarding the problem of the references to later wars against Israel's neighbors, we must distinguish between those within the *David Saga* in chaps. 9-20 and those in chap. 8 (+ 10:15-19a).[94] Because we have argued that the *David Saga* is a later addition to DtrH, these references do not come into consideration here. This leaves only 2 Sam 8:1-14. Now it should be obvious that 8:1, which is a

---

91. McCarter, *II Samuel*, 191.
92. McKenzie, "Why Didn't God Let David Build the Temple?" 217.
93. See my *In Search of History*, 272.
94. See above, pp. 220-221.

summation of David's victory over the Philistines, is actually a continuation of the wars against the Philistines in 5:17-25 and not an introduction
to a new series of wars. The block of texts in 8:1-14 (+ 10:15-19a) was
shifted to its location after chap. 7 in order to provide a closer transition to
the *David Saga* and its wars against the Ammonites in chap. 10. This means
that 8:15 was the summing up of David's career after the final episodes related in chaps. 6-7. One must therefore consider chap. 7 as representing
an event that took place at the *end* of David's career and not at a time early
in his reign as the addition of the *David Saga* suggests. This means that the
statement by Dtr in 1 Kgs 5:17-18[3-4], which suggests that David spent
his whole life battling his enemies until they were finally defeated, with the
result that he was not able to built the temple, does not contradict 1 Sam
7:1b but rather confirms our reconstruction of the Dtr text. David's intention to build the temple comes at the end of his life and it is for this reason
that the era of peace that Solomon's reign inaugurates provides the appropriate context for building the temple.

There are a number of observations that support this interpretation.
First, the Dtr theme of Yahweh giving rest (הניח) from one's enemies has its
most obvious parallel in the case of Joshua. In Josh 1:13, 15; 21:44; 22:4;
and 23:1, the theme of Yahweh's giving rest to Israel is directly related to
the cessation of conflict after the wars of conquest by Joshua and is closely
tied to the end of Joshua's career. All these texts belong to Dtr and provide
a structural balance between the divine promise of rest in 1:13-15 and its
completion in 21:44, 22:4, and 23:1.[95] Consequently, the pattern of God's
giving rest to his people following the conquest and then Joshua's making
his final speech as a major piece of Dtr ideology parallels the same situation with David, in which David's wars are finally over and he receives
these divine promises at the end of his life. Second, as I have argued previously, the whole pattern of Joshua's conquest of the land is based on that
found in Assyrian royal inscriptions,[96] so it would not be surprising to find
the same dependence on a motif from these inscriptions in the case of David, namely, that of temple construction following the cessation of warfare.

---

95. Ibid., 331-37. McKenzie seeks to discount some of these references as not
Dtr, but I cannot accept his analysis of these texts.

96. J. Van Seters, "Joshua's Campaign of Canaan and Near Eastern Historiography," *SJOT* 2 (1990): 1-12; also N. Na'aman, "The 'Conquest of Canaan' in the Book
of Joshua and in History," in *From Nomadism to Monarchy: Archaeological and Historical Aspects of Early Israel* (ed. I. Finkelstein and N. Na'aman; Jerusalem: Israel
Exploration Society, 1994), 218-81.

Third, Deut 12:10–11 links the theme of Yahweh's giving rest to his people with the choosing of a place to set his name there, and it is clear that both 2 Sam 7:1 and 1 Kgs 5:17–19 identify the end of David's reign as the time when the promise in Deuteronomy is to be fulfilled.

This still leaves the contradiction between 7:1b and vv. 10–11a. Verses 8–9 begin with the formal introduction "And now, thus says Yahweh" followed by a series of statements about what the deity has done for David in the past.[97] This is continued in v. 11b with another introductory phrase, "Yahweh has announced to you," followed by the future action of securing David's dynasty. This sequence is interrupted by a promise directed to the people as a whole, vv. 10–11aα, and not to David. This promise to David seems to be construed as a promise to the people in exile: "I shall assign a place for my people Israel, and plant them and they will settle in their own place, and they will never again be disturbed and never again will violent men oppress them as previously from the days when I appointed judges over my people Israel." Now v. 11aβ curiously shifts back to a statement addressed to David, "I will give you rest from all your enemies," and this is regularly emended by scholars to a statement addressed to the people, "I will give *them* rest from all their enemies," as in the former statements, but without textual support.

There is likewise the problem of how to understand the references to the future in v. 10a: "I shall assign a place for my people Israel, and plant them and they will settle in their own place." A statement such as this would make sense as a promise before the conquest of the land, but it is totally inappropriate for the time of David.[98] It is possible to construe the verbs as perfects with the conjunctive *waw* and render them in the past tense: "I have assigned . . . I have planted . . . they have settled," but this does not completely resolve the issue. If it refers to a past event, then it is out of historical sequence, and the remarks in vv. 10b–11aα must still refer to the period after David. The text seems clearly to suggest a comparison between a former settling and planting by Joshua, which was followed by a long period of disturbance and oppression "as previously," and a new planting and settling that will not be subject to circumstances of this sort. Likewise, the sudden shift

---

97. With the LXX, I would read the final verb in v. 9 as a past tense, "and I have made," וְעָשִׂיתִי.

98. McCarter's attempt to overcome this problem by understanding the reference to "place" as referring not to the land but to the temple seems to me a little desperate. Even so, the ark is already sitting in its "place" in Jerusalem. However, the metaphor of planting always refers to the land. It is quite unambiguous.

to the people and then back again to David is awkward, as many have noticed, and suggests a deliberate insertion in the text.

Thus, it seems to me more likely that v. 11aβ was part of the original
statement to David in vv. 8–9, which was split apart by the interpolation
(vv. 10b–11aα), and as such it was another act of Yahweh in the past parallel to the statement about Yahweh's cutting off all of David's enemies, v.
9aβ.[99] The statement to David could then be reconstructed as:

> And now, thus you are to say to my servant David: 'thus says Yahweh of
> Hosts, I took you from the pasture and from following the sheep to be a
> leader over my people Israel. I was with you wherever you went and have
> eliminated all your enemies who opposed you, and *have given* you fame
> like the most famous who are on the earth and I *have given* you rest from
> all your enemies. (2 Sam 7:8–9, 11aβ)[100]

This would bring it into complete harmony with 7:1b. This leads right into
the promise of a sure dynasty that follows.

In order to support this reconstruction, it remains for us to prove that
1 Sam 7:10–11aα is a later addition to the text. This is to be seen in the expression of a hope, which, as noted above, seems quite inappropriate at the
climax of David's career when the people already have achieved a place in
their own land and are apparently flourishing. The language of this expression of hope, however, makes its origin quite clear. In several instances in
Jeremiah there are repeated references to the people of Israel as the object
of Yahweh's planting, and most of the texts have to do with a future hope
of restoration.[101] Thus, in Jer 24:6 in a prose oracle addressed to the exiles
in Babylon, the deity states, "I will look upon them favorably and return
them to this land, I will build them up and not tear them down; I will plant
them and not uproot them." This image is again picked up in the salvation
oracle at the end of the book of Amos (9:11–15), which speaks of the restoration of the "booth of David" and ends with this statement: "I will plant
them upon their land and they will never again be uprooted from their land
which I have given to them, says Yahweh their God" (v. 15). It is not diffi-

---

99. Efforts to limit v. 9aβ only to the opposition of Saul and others to his becoming king are forced and carry even less weight in our analysis of the earlier
texts, which does not include 2 Sam 2:8–4:12 within the DtrH.

100. I have construed the perfects in vv. 9b and 11aβ as past tenses; this is the
sense of the passage. The same is true for והגיד in v. 11b, which must also be a perfect with conjuctive *waw* and is therefore past tense.

101. Jer 1:10, 2:21, 18:9, 24:6, 31:28, 32:41, 42:10, 45:4.

cult to see how this theme has been shaped to its present context with a repetition to the time of the judges in 2 Sam 7:11aα borrowed from v. 7, even when it is not entirely appropriate. Consequently, I would argue that 7:10–11aα is a salvation oracle that has been inserted into this promise to David in order to make it applicable to the hope of restoration in the Post-exilic Period. There can be little doubt that the promise to David in 2 Sam 7 was interpreted in the Postexilic Period in a messianic sense and could have attracted to it a more explicit reference to this sort of hope.

This brings us back to the most important problem of the entire unit, the rhetorical question in 7:5, which has given rise to so many theories about an original negative oracle rejecting David's proposal in v. 2. The text in v. 5 states, "Go and say to my servant David, 'Thus says Yahweh, Will you build me a house to live in?'" and this is interpreted as a rejection of the notion that the deity lives (ישׁב) in a temple comparable to the king's liv-ing (ישׁב) in a palace. The problem is that such a negative evaluation of this rhetorical question contradicts Nathan's apparent approval of David's in-tentions in v. 3, and there is nothing particularly negative in any of the rest of the oracle. It is further suggested that Dtr overcame this problem by in-troducing the "name" theology, which suggests that the future temple will be not the *residence* of the deity but only the place where the deity "sets" his name (v. 13a). This seems to me to be an entirely forced and unjustified in-terpretation of the question in v. 5 and its larger context. Thus, we will have to work through the text step by step.

First, the account begins by David's drawing attention to the fact that he "sits/dwells" (ישׁב) in a house of cedar while the ark of God "sits/dwells" (ישׁב) in a tent. The latter presumably was the appropriate type of shrine in which to deposit the ark up to this point. There is nothing to suggest that it is inappropriate to speak of the ark as "sitting" (ישׁב) in the tent. Now all that David proposes is that instead of the ark "sitting" in a mere tent it should be housed in a more permanent and appropriate structure, that is, "sitting" in a cedar house. David is not making a grand promise or laying out his plans for a royal chapel. He is merely hinting at what he has in mind and seeking divine direction from the prophet. The whole issue is about what sort of structure should house the ark and nothing more than this. To this proposal Nathan gives ready approval. When the deity there-fore raises the question "Will you build me a house in which to dwell (ישׁב)?" he is still speaking about David's proposal for housing the ark, so that the ark is understood as symbolic of the divine presence. The deity then goes on to recount the fact that he (i.e., the ark) has been traveling about in a tent from the days in the wilderness and through the time of the judges until the ark's present location in a tent that now sits in Jerusalem.[102] Up to the present time it was inappropriate for the ark to be in any other form of living quarters because it had no permanent resting place. From Dtr's perspective, this is obvious because only under David would the ark finally come to Jerusalem. There can be no dispute, therefore, over the appropriateness of the use of the verb יָשַׁב, "to dwell," because it applies just as much to the ark in a tent as it does to the ark in a temple. The distinction between the ark's sitting in a tent or in a temple must rest entirely on the difference between the time of the judges and the rise of the monarchy under David and the new capital in Jerusalem. Is the ark to be permanently resident in Jerusalem, the royal capital? If it is, then it needs a permanent house.

Furthermore, Dtr associates the divine "name" of Deut 12:5, 10-11, which Yahweh will deposit in the place of his choosing, in the closest possible way with the ark. The statement about David's son's building a house for the "name" in 7:13a means the same thing as building a temple for the ark. This becomes very clear in the account of the temple construction in 1 Kgs 6:14-28, in which the *debir* is specially constructed and adorned to house the ark, and this is the whole focus of the procession of dedication in 1 Kgs 8:1-13. In Solomon's blessing on the people in 8:14-21, there is a constant movement back and forth between the "name" and the ark. Solomon begins by stating that during the period of time from the exodus to the rise of David Yahweh chose no city in which to build a house for his name (8:16), and this is made to parallel the deity's past statement in 2 Sam 7:6-7 about the period of time during which the deity traveled about in the tent. Solomon continues by saying that it was David's intention to build a house for the "name" (1 Kgs 8:17), which apparently means the same thing as David's desire to build a house for the ark in 2 Sam 7:2. Solomon then declares that this intention of David was met with divine *approval*, and this is parallel both to Nathan's immediate agreement with the plan in 2 Sam 7:3 and to

---

102. G. von Rad ("The Tent and the Ark," *The Problem of the Hexateuch and Other Essays* [Edinburgh: Oliver & Boyd, 1965], 103-24) argues for separate traditions for tent and ark, based on the fact that the ark is not associated with the "tent of meeting" in Exod 33:7-11, so that he rejects any connection between the ark in the tent in 2 Sam 7:2 and Yahweh's abode in a tent in vv. 5-7. However, I have argued that Exod 33:7 is directly dependent on the reference to David's setting up a tent for the ark in 2 Sam 6:17. See my *Life of Moses*, 322, 341-44.

the rhetorical question in v. 5, which so many scholars insist on interpreting as disapproval. Finally, Solomon identifies the fulfillment of the divine promise that David's son would build a house for the "name" is realized in Solomon's building a place for the ark (1 Kgs 8:20-21).

The interplay between David's building a house (temple) for the deity and the deity's building a house (dynasty) for David is certainly intended to tie the foundations of monarchy and temple together in the closest way. The fact that two quite-different themes are being combined is indisputable, but this does not justify trying to find a literary basis for this distinction in separate sources. Both the election of David and the temple as a repository for the ark of the covenant are very important to Dtr, and this was his way of literarily binding them together. The same combination permeates the blessing of Solomon in 1 Kgs 8:14-21. Indeed, the building of the temple is understood as the confirmation of the election of David.

Nevertheless, it seems clear to me that there is some justification for scholars who sense a polemical element in Dtr's construction of the events in 2 Sam 7. However, it is not a primitive polemic against the building of the temple by the Davidic dynasty but part of the deuteronomic reform, which endeavored to reconceptualize the nature of the temple and the monarchy. There is reason to believe from other biblical evidence that prior to Deuteronomy there was a temple theology that viewed the deity as enthroned in the *debir* of the temple, from which he ruled the nations and the world.[103] This temple cultus had no original connection with the exodus-wilderness traditions, which were probably a late northern Israelite import. This applies also to the period of the judges, who are all northern heroes.[104] It is the ark of the covenant of Yahweh that symbolizes the exodus and Horeb traditions of covenant and thus establishes the continuity between those traditions and the Jerusalem temple cultus. In this way, the ark becomes the symbolic presence of the deity. The pair of guardian cherubim, formerly flanking the deity's throne, now becomes associated with the ark of the covenant, which is placed between the cherubim, replacing the divine throne.

There is no reason to suppose that the ark of the covenant ever represented a historical reality during the period of the first temple. It is a com-

---

103. See Mettinger, *The Dethronement of Sabaoth*, 19-37, for a useful collection of the evidence. For my earlier discussion of Mettinger, see pp. 235-236 above.

104. The story of Othniel, the only representative from Judah, is an obvious artificial construction and does not belong to the rest.

plete ideological construction of Dtr that was invented as a way of replacing the divine throne and its seated deity in the inner sanctum of the temple with the ark containing the deuteronomic law, especially the Decalogue, and thus placing this ark of the covenant at the heart of Israel's religion and worship in the Exilic Period. For Dtr, it was important that this deuteronomic law be tied in the closest way with both David and Solomon, but not with Saul, and with the founding of the Davidic dynasty in Jerusalem.

In a similar fashion, the monarchy of Jerusalem was a typical Near Eastern institution that considered the king as the divine offspring of the deity who reigned in perpetuity by virtue of this ancestry. Deuteronomy, in 17:14-20, rejects this ideology of kingship and places the king under great restrictions, including his obligation to the deuteronomic laws. Dtr represents a compromise in that the Davidic kingship is chosen by Yahweh to reign in perpetuity, and his offspring are to be considered the deity's sons, in a metaphoric sense, and subject to his discipline. This monarchy is construed as being in continuity with the past, as reconstructed by Dtr, and at the same time as a new era in that history. For this monarchy, David becomes the righteous ideal. At the same time, Dtr establishes the connection between David's monarchy and that of Saul (v. 15). David is the successor of Saul and therefore the king of all Israel, but he is also his replacement. Unlike Saul, however, David's dynasty will survive in perpetuity. This brief remark about Saul both assumes the prior story of David and Saul and sums it up within this important ideological statement.

The primary attention given by scholars to the prayer of David in 2 Sam 7:18-29 has been to try to salvage a pre-Dtr or even Davidic period stratum distinct from a Dtr "editing" of the text. However, if we accept the position that the whole account of the preceding narrative in 7:1-17 belongs to Dtr, then there is no longer any need to debate this issue in detail. More recent studies may wish to relegate the whole or part of it to a later "edition" of DtrH, but I see no convincing argument for doing so. There are also a number of textual difficulties in this unit that have led to a number of conjectures as to how to emend the text, but these have resulted in little general agreement. Appeal to the parallel text in 1 Chr 17:16-27 or to the LXX does not always help. In spite of these difficulties, however, the general sense of the text seems fairly clear.

The content of the unit may be set forth as follows. In response to the preceding revelation by Nathan, David (v. 18) enters into "the presence of Yahweh," which must refer to the tent containing the ark of the covenant in v. 1, and he takes his seat there. It is clear that sitting "before Yahweh" means before the ark, which is symbolic of the divine presence. David then offers his prayer.

> Who am I, lord Yahweh, and what is my house that you have brought me so far. Yet, to you this seems but a trifle, lord Yahweh, for you have made promises to the house of your servant concerning the distant future, and you have revealed to me generations to come, lord Yahweh.[105] And what more can David say to you; you yourself know your servant, lord Yahweh. For the sake of your promise, and in accordance with your intention you have done this great thing by revealing it to your servant. (vv. 18b-21)

This unit must refer directly back to the revelation by Nathan of the divine promises concerning David's offspring and the secure dynasty that will follow him into the distant future.

The next unit makes a shift back to Yahweh's incomparable deeds in the past. David states:

> Therefore you are great, lord Yahweh, for there is none like you; there is no god besides you according to everything we have heard with our ears. What other nation on earth is like your people Israel, whose god went[106] to redeem [them] as a people for himself and to make a name for himself, and doing for them great and wondrous things, by driving out from before his people, whom he redeemed for himself from Egypt, nations and their gods. Then you established your own people Israel for yourself as a people forever, and you Yahweh became their god. (vv. 22-24)

There seems to be little dispute that this unit represents a thoroughgoing Dtr perspective (see Deut 26:16-19), and for this reason it is sometimes regarded as a late secondary addition by those who would date the rest of the prayer to an earlier period. The only reason, apart from the language, for seeing this as a later addition is the shift from the focus on the king and his family to the people as a whole. However, the central point of the author (Dtr) is to integrate the divine election of the Davidic dynasty into the larger sacred history of deliverance from Egypt and conquest of the land. This parallels the unit in 7:6-9, which seeks to integrate the theme of the ark in its travels from Egypt down to the establishment of the Davidic monarchy

---

105. There is a difference of opinion as to whether למרחוק refers to the past (so McCarter) or has reference to the future. I take this phrase as parallel to what follows, but that is also somewhat corrupt. "Generation to come" follows Wellhausen's reconstruction, based partly on 1 Chr 17:17.

106. "Other": most scholars read אחר (LXX) for אחד (MT). "Whose God went": see Driver, *Samuel*, 278.

and the temple in Jerusalem. The etiology of monarchy and temple are both embedded within the Dtr ideology of *Israelite* history.

With the final unit of the prayer (vv. 25-29), the subject returns to the theme of the establishment of the house of David. It is this theme that will now dominate the rest of the treatment of the monarchy in DtrH. The perspective uttered here deals not just with the promise of succession by a son of David but rather with the whole of the dynastic history that is to follow in this literary work. There is another theme in v. 26 that is missed or lightly passed over by most scholars, but that is quite central to the whole chapter and to Dtr's thought as a whole. The text states, "May your name be famous forever, whenever people say, 'Yahweh of Hosts is god over Israel,' and may the house of your servant be permanent before you [for ever]." As we have seen throughout Dtr's treatment in chap. 7, the "name" of the deity has been tied inextricably with the temple as well as with the ark, and in 6:2 the title *Yahweh of Hosts* is likewise associated with the ark, which means that the fame of Yahweh is tied to the temple in Jerusalem. Furthermore, the destiny of the temple of Jerusalem and of the Davidic dynasty in this place ("before you") are being bound together in the closest way. That connection later becomes clear again in the prayer of Solomon in 1 Kgs 8. Consequently, the prayer as a whole is a programmatic statement like so many that are uttered by the leaders who have gone before—Joshua in Josh 23 and Samuel in 1 Sam 12—with both a retrospective and a prospective view. This is usually presented by Dtr as a kind of swan-song, so that the placement of David's prayer in the present story of David has obscured this character of the prayer. However, in Dtr's treatment of David, as I have tried to reconstruct it, the prayer comes precisely where one would expect it, at the end of his life and just before the transition of the rule from David to Solomon.

This would mean that following the prayer we originally had the statement in 1 Sam 8:15: "So David ruled over all Israel maintaining the law and acting justly towards all his people." This, in turn, was followed by the unit in 1 Kgs 2:1-4, 10-12. The whole point of the prayer of David in 1 Sam 7:18-29 anticipates this transition to Solomon and leads directly into the final remarks at the end of David's life. It is the radical rearrangement that places 2 Sam 8:1-14 + 10:15-19a after chaps. 6-7 and then the major addition of the *David Saga* of 2 Sam 9-20 and 1 Kgs 1, between 1 Sam 7 and its proper ending that trivializes the real significance of the prayer in the overall structure of Dtr's work. However, given the fact that Dtr frequently makes reference to David as the ideal monarch for all the future kings of Israel and Judah, it is precisely the kind of statement that one would expect Dtr's David to make at what is both the highpoint and end of his career.

David's Final Admonition to Solomon
and the Succession

We turn now to the last unit in Dtr's story of David in 1 Kgs 2:1–4 and 10–12. This is embedded within the *David Saga*, and we will leave to the next chapter the problems of the relationship of this unit to that larger context. Our primary concern here is to understand this brief account of the transition between the two reigns of David and Solomon within the context of DtrH. The text states:

> As the time of David's death approached, he gave orders to Solomon his son, saying, "I am about to part this earthly life, but be strong and be a man. Be sure to keep your obligation towards Yahweh your God, by walking in his ways and keeping his statutes, his commandments, his laws, and his precepts, according to what is written in the law of Moses, in order that you might succeed in all that you do and wherever you turn; in order that Yahweh may confirm his promise, which he spoke to me, saying, 'If your descendants carefully direct their ways by proceeding faithfully before me with all their heart and all their soul, you will never lack a man upon the throne of Israel.'" . . . Thus David slept with his fathers and was buried in the city of David. The period of time that David reigned over Israel was forty years; he reigned seven years in Hebron and thirty-three years in Jerusalem. Then Solomon sat upon the throne of David, his father, and his kingdom was firmly established.

These verses are so clearly in the form, style and language of Dtr that they cannot be denied to this author. The primary argument that the whole of 1 Kgs 2:1–4 belongs to Dtr rests on the structure of the scene in 2:1–4 as it relates to similar scenes in DtrH (Deut 3:28, 31:1–8; Josh 23:1–16). This consists of the following components: (1) the divinely designated leader (Moses, Joshua) at the end of his life (2) gives a solemn charge (צוה) to his successor[107] (3) to be strong and courageous and (4) to keep the laws and commandments of God as reflected in the laws of Moses. A slight variation

---

107. In the case of Joshua 23, the charge is addressed to all the people, but the effect is the same.

on the model is when God encourages Joshua after the death of Moses in the same way as Moses himself had done (Josh 1:1-9).[108] All other examples of the form directly depend on Dtr. Because 1 Kgs 2:1-4 fits all of the basic elements and shares much of the terminology of Dtr, there can be no doubt that the whole is Dtr's work.[109]

This structural similarity between the transition from Moses to Joshua and from David to Solomon, what McCarthy calls "an installation genre,"[110] together with David's remarks about the need for obedience to all of Yahweh's laws as set down in the laws of Moses, reinforces the unity between the Moses tradition and that of the monarchy. It is a deliberate attempt to reshape the ideology of kingship to accommodate the Deuteronomic reform. Much is made of the fact that the supposed reference in v. 4 back to the promise in 2 Sam 7:14-15 does not exactly correspond with this one in 1 Kgs 2:4, presenting a more conditional promise, based on obedience to the law. This has led to assigning this text to a later nomistic Dtr "editor."[111] This does not seem to me to be necessary. The remarks in 2 Sam 7:14-15, which uses the imagery of the father disciplining his son for disobedience certainly implies obedience to Yahweh's law, which for Dtr was the Law of Moses. This exhortation of David is intended as a further elaboration on the same theme.

Summary

As we have seen in this chapter, Dtr's presentation of David's reign is rather brief compared with the elaborate expansion by the *David Saga*. Dtr

---

108. There is also the post-Dtr example of induction in Deut 31:14-15, 23, but this is built so clearly on the prior Dtr speech in 31:7-8 that it is hardly an independent example of the form.

109. The only example outside Dtr that is remotely similar is that of Joseph's exhortation to his brothers just before his death, in Gen 50:22-26. But, as I have shown elsewhere (*Life of Moses* [Louisville: Westminster John Knox, 1994], 16-19), this is part of a larger unit including Exod 1:6, 8 that is directly modeled on Josh 23 + Judg 2:6-10 and belongs to a post-Dtr Yahwist. To this same late source also belong the remarks in Gen 50:16-17 about Jacob's prior "charge" (סוה) to his sons. The content of the charge, however, is quite different from those in Dtr. The deathbed command of Jacob in Gen 49:29-33 is from P and hardly comes into consideration here.

110. D. J. McCarthy, "An Installation Genre?" *JBL* 90 (1971): 31-41.

111. T. Römer, *The So-Called Deuteronomistic History: A Sociological, Historical and Literary Introduction* (London: T. & T. Clark, 2005), 30; cf. p. 147.

states that after Saul's death David immediately becomes king of all Israel in Hebron as successor to Saul and from there he conquers Jerusalem, which becomes the future capital of the realm. David then engages in a career of conquest by first liberating Israel from the Philistines. He then conquers the neighboring nations until he is ruler of an empire from the Euphrates to the borders of Egypt. Having accomplished all this he then restores the ark to its rightful place in Jerusalem and plans to build a proper temple for it. While the deity acknowledges his desire for this to be done, he promises to David instead a perpetual dynasty, so that it will be David's son who will build the temple. The transition from David's reign to that of Solomon follows quickly. The traditions behind Dtr's brief historical sketch are few. It seems likely that some old tradition linked the house of David with Hebron as well as Jerusalem and that David as a Judean chieftain engaged in hostilities with the Philistines in the southern highlands region from his stronghold there. The wars with the other states are probably all fictional constructions. I have also argued that there are no old traditions behind the story of the ark's restoration or the promise to David. The two episodes in 2 Sam 6 and 7 are entirely ideological constructs.

This presentation of David's reign is linked in the closest way with the previous story of Saul through Dtr's *account A* of David's rise to power as Saul's divinely chosen successor. The ideological purpose of this link is to make David the founder of the greater state of Israel inclusive of Judah and therefore the house of David the legitimate heir of the whole "people of Israel." In addition, along with the people of Israel, the house of David is also heir to the sacred traditions of Israel from Moses to Saul as reflected in DtrH and symbolized in the ark of the covenant. The account of the Davidic promises of dynasty and the future temple establishes the closest link with Solomon and the building of the temple. This revolutionizes the ideological understanding of the monarchy and Dtr's presentation of the Mosaic law in the king's relationship to the deity and the Jerusalem temple as the true center of religion for the whole people of Israel. Once the true dimensions of Dtr's David story are understood, it becomes clear that it has a central and indispensable place in the DtrH as a whole.

Chapter 7

A Portrayal of Life in the Court of David: *The* David Saga

As we saw in the story of David and Saul in 1 Sam 16-31,[1] there are two quite-different strata throughout, *account A (Dtr)* and *account B (David Saga)*. These are two different treatments to the story of David, and the second account, the *David Saga*, is built directly into Dtr and cannot be understood as an independent narrative. Though part of the *David Saga* is interwoven with Dtr in 1 Sam 18-24,[2] there is a large block of the *David Saga* text inserted between 1 Sam 24 and 31. When we come to the account of David's reign, we find the same literary phenomenon. We have already seen that there are several interconnections between the *David Saga* in the story of David's rise and what scholars previously called the Court History, which leads us to believe that the Court History is part of the larger *David Saga*. Consequently, it has the same relationship of dependence on Dtr's account of David's reign (chap. 6) that we found in the story of David and Saul. Most of the *David Saga* is contained in the large block of material in 2 Sam 9-20, but the treatment of David's reign in Hebron as king of Judah (2 Sam 2:8-4:12) and the last days of David and Solomon's succession (1 Kgs 1-2) are fitted into the Dtr narrative and create a completely different and rival account of these events. We begin, therefore, with David's conflict with Ishbosheth in 2 Sam 2:8-4:12.

David's Conflict with Ishbosheth for Control of Israel

Let me begin by recapitulating Dtr's account of David's ascent to the throne. After the death of Saul and all his sons in the battle with the Philistines (1 Sam 31) and a period of mourning over the death of Saul and Jonathan (2 Sam 1:1a?, 2-4, 11-12, 17-27), David and his men move to Hebron (2:1-2a, 3) where all of the tribes of Israel (including Judah) make David

---

1. See above, chap. 5, pp. 163-206.
2. See the appendix, pp. 361-363.

king as successor to Saul (5:1–2, 3b), there being *no* survivors among the
sons of Saul. This transition of power is radically altered by the additions of
the *David Saga*, which sees David as anointed king of Judah first (2:2b, 4),
quite distinct from the rest of Israel. In the *David Saga*, Judah and Israel are
treated as two distinct political entities. The *David Saga* then invents a surviving son of Saul, Ishbosheth, against whom David carries on a civil war by
an invasion into Benjaminite territory, and this war goes on until Abner is
murdered and Ishbosheth assassinated, all of which happens in two years
(2:10). Yet it is only after another five years, according to the *David Saga,*
that the elders of Israel finally enter into an agreement (*bĕrît*) with David,
and he now becomes king of the region of Israel as well (5:3a). In this radical modification of Dtr's "historical" framework, the *David Saga* presents his
version of David's reign in Hebron and his war with Ishbosheth.

After David is made king of Judah, there is a rather curious episode in
which David sends envoys to Jabesh-Gilead, acknowledging their courageous act in burying Saul and then asking them to recognize him as king,
just as Judah had done (2 Sam 2:4b–7). What makes this invitation odd is
that there is no response from the people of Jabesh-Gilead to David's overture. Two observations may be made about this episode. First, the staunch
loyalty of Jabesh-Gilead to the house of Saul would, of course, lead one to
believe that they would pledge their loyalty to Saul's son, Ishbosheth. This
would therefore appear to be an attempt through flattery and diplomacy to
win some of the Israelites to David's side in the coming conflict. Second, it
becomes apparent at a later point in the story that David, during this period, had a close friendship (a treaty?) with Nahash, king of Ammon, who
was the archenemy of Jabesh-Gidead and the one from whom Saul had rescued Jabesh-Gilead. Is this episode in 2:4b–7 intended to be deliberately
ironic?

The *David Saga* begins its account of the war between David and Ishbosheth by establishing certain "historical facts" as the necessary background to the events (2 Sam 2:8–11). Abner, the commander of Saul's army,
had apparently escaped the disastrous defeat of Saul's forces, and he now
becomes the kingmaker of Saul's son, Ishbosheth. We have encountered
Abner frequently in the earlier part of the *David Saga*, so it is not surprising
to find him in this part too. However, the author seems to have no concern
for Abner's age because he is identified in 1 Sam 14:50–51 as Saul's uncle
or cousin.[3] Because Ishbosheth was 40 years old, Abner was Ishbosheth's

---

3. The ambiguity is discussed in McCarter, *I Samuel*, 256.

senior by several years, and yet the rest of the account does not seem to recognize this fact. Ishbosheth is set up as king in Mahanaim, as though to put him well out of harm's way for the coming conflict in which he takes no direct part. In the list of regions over which he is set as king by Abner, the first mentioned is Gilead, as though completely to contradict David's earlier intentions. The Ashurites or "Assyrians" are then mentioned, and this has puzzled scholars as an obvious anachronism. It refers to the population that was transferred to the region of Israel by the Assyrians after the fall of Samaria, similar to the Aramean regions further north, and eventually they gave the name of (As)syria to the whole region. It is not surprising that in the Persian period a significant element of the population would be known by this term. Jezreel is also included in this region, ignoring the fact that this whole region had fallen into the hands of the Philistines after Saul's defeat. Indeed, the Philistine threat is completely ignored throughout this period of civil war. Finally, the territories of Ephraim, Benjamin, and all Israel are intended to suggest both the heartland and the periphery of the state of Israel distinct from Judah, which was under David. These supposed historical "facts" are a completely artificial reconstruction by the author of the *David Saga* to create a verisimilitude to a historical account of this conflict between the two regions. All efforts to make historical sense out of this background piece are futile.

The hostilities between the forces of David and the forces of Ishbosheth begin in Benjamin, the homeland of Saul. The two armies, the one led by Abner and the other by Joab, meet as though by prearrangement at Gibeon at the pool or waterworks in the middle of the city. This is the first introduction to Joab, who is merely identified as son of Zeruiah, which hardly seems adequate, given his significance in the rest of the *David Saga*. Nevertheless, he is presented as the one in charge of David's army and Abner's counterpart. What is remarkable is that David is not in command of his own forces, and indeed, within the *David Saga* he never leads his troops in battle, as distinct from his involvement in Dtr, but always remains behind at the home base. The two generals begin the hostilities by arranging a contest of arms between the two battle groups, consisting of twelve men from each side. The objective of this contest is never indicated. Perhaps it was intended that the winner would settle the dispute between them and the loser would have to agree to the terms of the victor. This sort of limited contest of arms is typical of sagas in settling a feud or grievance, but it hardly works in the case of hostilities between two states. At any rate, the contest ends in a *dead* draw, because all 12 of each side kill each other simultaneously, resulting in a larger battle between the two forces. It is also interesting that the event gives rise to an etiology, which is another standard device in sagas linking a place-name with this sort of contest of arms.

The central element in the battle account is the rout of the Israelites and the pursuit of Abner by Asahel, the brother of Joab (2:18–23). One cannot read this as a realistic episode with the young and swift Asahel chasing the old man Abner, loaded down with weapons and with a dialogue carrying on between the pursuer and the pursued. The scene is purely for dramatic effect, in which Asahel's death, the result of his brash behavior, leads to a deadly feud between the two generals, Joab and Abner. As noted earlier, feuds of this sort are one of the most basic features of sagas and a key literary devise used for dramatic continuity. The author makes clear certain "facts" about this situation. First, Asahel's death occurred during a battle in which there was no personal animosity on Abner's part to motivate him to kill Joab's brother. Quite the opposite: he was reluctant to do so and only did it when his own life was threatened. Second, it was, after all, Asahel who was the pursuer, whose aim was personal fame. He could have taken on lesser men and been amply rewarded with the spoils of war. He was warned but paid no heed. All of these considerations are important to the later scene when Joab takes his revenge on Abner.[4]

The following scene suggests that Abner is able to regroup his forces on a hilltop, and he makes a persuasive speech that calls to Joab for a truce (vv. 24–28). That Joab yields to this, given what has just happened and that he appears to have the upper hand, is curious, but it also corresponds to a typical literary devise of the saga, a temporary truce in a feud. Yet the note of foreboding remains in the remark of Abner: "Do you not realize that the end will be bitter?" (v. 26). This looks ahead when the feud is taken up again. Abner's speech also construes the conflict as a civil war between "brothers," which puts the forces of David in the wrong. After all, the battle takes place within Israel in the very homeland of the house of Saul. The casualties are quite uneven, 360 to 20 in favor of Judah, all of whom are nameless, except Asahel, the brother of Joab, who is buried in the family tomb in Bethlehem.

The conflict between David and Ishbosheth is construed in 2 Sam 3:1 as a struggle not between two states but between two rival families, the "house of Saul" and the "house of David." This has nothing to do with holy war but involves personal ambition. What exactly is meant by David's getting stronger while the house of Saul gets weaker is not clear, because it can have

---

4. See Gunn, *The Story of David*, 77–81.

nothing to do with David's conquering territory from Israel. It must have to do with the fact that David in one way or other is gaining sympathy for his cause within Israel that threatens the loyalties of the Israelites toward the family of Saul. This is taken up in the sequel in 3:6–21 and the threatened defection of Abner.

Before this larger narrative episode is taken up, the action is interrupted with a list of David's sons, in the order of their birth, and the names of their mothers. As indicated earlier, this list has important connection with the larger *David Saga*, because three of the sons are later represented as being in the position of the crown prince, succeeding each other in the order of their birth. In addition, the first two wives, Ahinoam of Jezreel and Abigail the (former) wife of Nabal of Carmel, are paired in the earlier account as David's wives before David becomes king in Judah, and their mention re-calls the earlier part of David's career. On the other hand, the third wife and mother of Absalom, Maʿacah, is identified as the daughter of Talmai, king of Geshur, and in the later story Absalom spends time in exile in his grandfather's realm. There can be little doubt, therefore, that this unit be-longs to the *David Saga*. It may further be noted that the Icelandic sagas fre-quently interrupt the action of the saga by giving just this kind of list of family connections, which is vital for the understanding of individuals and their relationships to other persons in the narrative.

After this interlude of a list of David's sons, the action picks up again with the resumptive remark about the war between the rival courts, but now the shift of attention is to the "house of Saul," in which Abner is be-coming the more powerful figure at the expense of Ishbosheth, to the ex-tent that he even makes use of Saul's former concubine, Rizpah, for his sexual needs, much to the displeasure of Ishbosheth. Many speculate that this is a political action, even to the point of making a claim to the throne,[5] but this is quite unlikely; Abner's actions both before and after contradict this. It was Abner who made Ishbosheth king and it is Abner who will also offer the kingship of Israel to David. As is so typical in the case of the saga, a quarrel arises over "a fault concerning a woman" (v. 8), which Abner con-siders an insult to his pride and a lack of gratitude for his loyalty. Feuds such as this always have dire consequences. Abner utters a threat with an oath to transfer the rule over Israel to David so that he will become king of both Israel and Judah, and against this threat Ishbosheth is too weak to do anything.

---

5. See McCarter, *II Samuel*, 112–13.

What is most remarkable about Abner's threat is that it includes the religious confession that he now plans to be the agent of the will of Yahweh, who has also sworn in the past to make this transfer of power from Saul to David (vv. 9-10). The question, of course, is whether Abner actually believes this. If he does, then why did he make Ishbosheth king in the first place, and why carry on a protracted war against David? Where is there such a specific divine oath or promise, and how could Abner know anything about it? Abigail also claimed this (1 Sam 25:10), but in neither case can it be supported by any text that tells of such a direct promise. Furthermore, when Abner confers with the elders of Israel about making David king, he makes reference to another divine promise that Israel was to be saved from the power of the Philistines and other enemies by David (2 Sam 3:17-19), but this was actually said of Saul and not of David (1 Sam 9:15-17, 10:1). This seems to be a deliberate and ironic transfer of an oracle from Saul to David for obvious political purposes. In both cases, the author strongly suggests that religious claims of this sort about divine election and promises of victory and glory are nothing but crass politics in disguise.

No sooner has Abner made the threat to Ishbosheth than he proceeds to carry it out. He sends word to David that he is prepared to make a deal (a "covenant") with David by which he will deliver all Israel to David (2 Sam 3:12). There is no suggestion here that this is David's divine right. David, for his part, wants the return of Michal, Saul's daughter. The claim is based entirely on legal grounds that he paid for her and not because he cares for her. He has other wives in his growing harem. The move is entirely political, part of the deal with Abner. The claim had to be made through Ishbosheth, Michal's brother, but it is clear throughout that it was executed by Abner, who dismisses Michal's distraught husband. Michal, however, is not included in the list of queens and sons in 3:2-5, for reasons that become apparent later.

Abner is able to persuade the elders of Israel as well as the "entire house of Benjamin"—the home territory of the family of Saul, often viewed in the *David Saga* as a distinct entity—to joint his deal with David, using the language of divine election and holy war typical of Near Eastern monarchs (3:17-19). Abner and his close circle of twenty men arrive at Hebron to make the final arrangements with David, and they are received with a feast—a scene so characteristic of the sagas for sealing an important alliance of families. Abner assures David that he can deliver on their agreement, which of course would mean that Abner would replace Joab as the commander of the forces of both regions, the real power behind the throne. It was obviously good for both David and Abner, who departs in peace to carry out his part of the bargain.

Joab, who returns with David's men from a raiding expedition with much booty, discovers what has just happened and confronts David as though he has done something very foolish. He makes the visit of Abner appear as though it is nothing more than a spying operation, but this charge is merely to justify the subsequent action that he will take in killing Abner. Both David and Abner know better, but neither will admit the truth. Then, quite unknown to David, Joab sends messengers to Abner to return, and he does so to a designated place away from the court. This allows Joab to carry out his revenge for his brother's death, as well as save his own position. This will not be the last time that Joab does so. When David hears of the murder he disclaims all responsibility for it and lays a curse on the house of Joab. Thus, one feud ends but another begins—between David and his general, Joab—which is not resolved until the end of the *David Saga*, by another murder carried out by Solomon (3:26–30).

Much is made of David's great show of grief and protestation that he is innocent (vv. 31–39), which are certainly intended to persuade the Israelites, whose real leader had been Abner. Some scholars want to interpret this public demonstration by David as a cover-up for a crime that he himself instigated, and to read the account here as mere propaganda. However, as we saw above, this sort of "against-the-grain" reading of the text is only possible if it reflects an actual event that is deliberately being misrepresented for political purposes. As we have argued above, all of these episodes in the *David Saga* are fiction, so that whatever the author tells us about David's part in Abner's death we must accept as his story. The author himself may cast doubt on David's words and actions, but what he gives us as "facts" cannot be changed. David concludes by making the admission that the sons of Zeruiah are too difficult for him to handle, and this becomes confirmed throughout the rest of the *David Saga*. Only at the end when Joab makes the fatal choice of selecting the wrong contender to the throne does he meet his match in the form of another military leader who murders him. David's curses and prayers for revenge (vv. 29, 39) are a strange form of prophecy about Joab's ultimate end.[6]

With the death of Abner, the final demise of Ishbosheth and the triumph of David were only a matter of time. We are now introduced to two leaders

---

6. Prophetic curses and forebodings are very common to sagas.

of raiding gangs, who will be responsible for his death. However, before the author proceeds to recount these events, he interrupts the narrative, just as he had in chap. 3, and gives us a piece of information about Jonathan's son, Mephibosheth, and how he became lame (4:4). Thus, before the death of Ishbosheth we are informed that there is another Saulide who is a potential heir, albeit lame, and this we will need to know for a later part of the story. The author then returns to the main narrative in v. 5. The two opportunists decide to kill Ishbosheth during his afternoon siesta and have little trouble penetrating the royal quarters. After killing and decapitating him, they take his head to David in Hebron, hoping for great reward, because David, after all, is at war with this son of Saul. David, however, pretends to be outraged and decrees for them the same treatment that he gave to the Amalekite when he received news of Saul's death. While there is certainly no suggestion in the narrative that David was a party to their murder, the author, nevertheless, leaves the quite-distinct impression that all of this show of outrage and honor given to Ishbosheth is merely for political purposes.

The author of the David Saga ties all of these events into the prior account of Dtr, which, as I have said earlier, knows nothing of any conflict with the house of Saul. In sharp contrast to Dtr, who has all the tribes of Israel come to anoint David at Hebron immediately after Saul's death (5:1), it is the *elders* of Israel (v. 3a; see 3:17) who come to *King* David and make a covenant with him, an agreement that had been postponed for an indefinite period after the death of Abner. As though to emphasize this point, the *David Saga* has David reigning over Judah in Hebron for 7 and a half years and over Israel and Judah for only 33 years (v. 5), in contradiction to DtrH, which states that David reigned over Israel for 40 years (1 Kgs 2:11), with no distinction between Judah and Israel. This creates an entirely different conception of the Davidic kingship, in terms of both its legitimacy and its nature, between Dtr and the *David Saga*. The one rests on the divine right of kingship, the other on power and political arrangement.

David and the Return of the Ark

As I indicated in the previous chapter, Dtr's account of the return of the ark to Jerusalem in 2 Sam 6:2–3a, 5, 15, 17–19 is a very simple narration of the triumphal return without incident. This account, however, has been seriously compromised by the additions of the author of the *David Saga*. Rost had already recognized the addition's having to do with the scene between

David and Michal in 6:16, 20–23, but scholars have missed those that radically transformed the whole account into something quite different from its original. The author of the *David Saga* has turned the joyful occasion of Dtr into one that is fraught with death and ambiguity. The ark is treated as a sacred object that must be handled with the utmost care; it can cause grave problems not only to the Philistines but also to the Israelites themselves. The sudden death of Uzzah casts a pall over the event of the ark's return, and David gets angry at the deity's displeasure. He postpones the further procession of the ark from entering the City of David. Furthermore, without any consultation of the deity, as one would expect in this situation, David arbitrarily puts it into the house of a Philistine, Obededom, which happened to be just outside the city, to see what would happen. The deity, Yahweh, as though to spite David, blesses Obededom and his entire household during a three-month period (6:3b–4, 6–11).

David's response to the report of the divine blessing on Obededom's household because of the ark leads him to reclaim the ark from the Philistine so that he can get this benefit for himself. Again, there is no consulting the deity for a good omen; nor is there any use of special priestly personnel, such as the Levites. However, David does make excessive use of elaborate appeasement offerings every six paces from Obededom's place to his own set location in Jerusalem. The celebration is also resumed, with David's dancing, dressed in a linen ephod, the garment of a priest. It was this activity that so provoked Michal.

What can we make of this revised version of the return of the ark? It seems to me that this is constructed as a parody on the earlier version as well as the later version in which the ark is transferred from the City of David to the new temple built by Solomon in 1 Kgs 8:1–11. Processions in which the god is conducted to his temple, whether on the occasion of an annual festival with much celebration or with the building of a new temple, were a common practice throughout the Near East. Dtr had attempted to "demythologize" this practice by replacing the image of the deity with that of the ark of the covenant as a new symbol of the divine presence. The author of the *David Saga*, however, remythologizes the whole procedure again in a most crass and obvious fashion, making the ark a mere fetish, the effect of which is quite unpredictable. The whole point of the *David Saga's* intention is to subvert Dtr's scene of the ark's return by seriously distracting attention to the additional episodes. Furthermore, one will find other places in the *David Saga* in which the ark is made the object of parody, as we shall see below.

The scene between David and Michal, Saul's daughter in 6:20-23, is closely tied to this revision of the ark's procession and specifically to David's dancing before Yahweh (6:14, 16, 20). Michal's judgment of the whole religious display belittles it as an orgy. When Michal rebukes David for his provocative sexual behavior with his vulgar dance, he responds by stating that his merry-making was conducted before Yahweh, who chose him as *nāgîd* over Israel in place of her father and the rest of his family, and this gives him license to behave in any fashion he chooses (6:21-22). This speech deliberately anticipates the remarks in the following Nathan prophecy, which speaks about Yahweh choosing David to be *nāgîd* over his people Israel (7:8) and his rejection of Saul (7:15). David's response to these prophetic declarations in Dtr's version leads to his humble and self-effacing prayer (7:18-29), but in marked contrast to this in the *David Saga* the same statements are used as an arrogant boast that allows him to flaunt his behavior in front of Saul's daughter (6:21-22). This use of the Dtr theme of David's divine election completely undermines its use in the David oracle and turns David's humility into hypocrisy.

This brings us to a discussion of the place of 2 Sam 6 in a so-called Ark Narrative. Ever since Rost argued for the existence of a self-contained Ark Narrative that went back to the time of David and was used as a source for SN,[7] scholars have spoken of the close association of 2 Sam 6 and 1 Sam 4-6. This view has not gone un-contested, the argument against it being largely based on the difficulty of the awkward transition from 1 Sam 7:1 to 2 Sam 6:1, but the difficulty of the time gap between the two texts was entirely based on the assumption that AN was a self-contained independent source.[8] Earlier I argued that the continuities between the two parts of the so-called Ark Narrative were the work of Dtr because the ark was, in fact, his own invention. There never was a primitive tradition about the ark. Furthermore, it is clear that the story of the ark's travels was intended to give it great honor and prestige as the symbol of the divine presence among Yahweh's people and an object of dread among Israel's enemies. It is clear that, for Dtr, the end of those travels comes about not with the deposit of the ark in the tent in 2 Sam 6:17 but in the grand procession and the deposit of the ark in the temple in 1 Kgs 8:1-11. Indeed, one can suppose

---

7. Rost, *The Succession to the Throne of David*, 6-34.

8. P. D. Miller and J. J. M. Roberts, *The Hand of the Lord: A Reassessment of the "Ark Narrative" of 1 Samuel* (Baltimore: Johns Hopkins University Press, 1977), 22-26. Cf. my *In Search of History*, 349.

that the remark in 8:5 about Solomon and all the people who were gathered with him in front of the ark "were sacrificing so many sheep and oxen they were beyond count and number" is parodied in 2 Sam 6:13 by the suggestion that David and his group sacrificed two animals every six paces. This clearly makes the whole procession quite ludicrous.

Consequently, it is clear that so completely at odds with this story of the ark's return are the additions by the author of the *David Saga*. The account in 2 Sam 6 has become a complete parody of the earlier sojourn of the ark amongst the Philistines because the ark's presence now blesses a Philistine household (2 Sam 6:11-12), and David's provocative dancing is in stark contrast to the solemn priestly procession in 1 Kgs 8. Even the etiology created to commemorate the occasion remembers only the divine anger that kills Uzzah (6:7-8).[9] One cannot imagine anyone creating a narrative of this sort in order to honor the ark. On the contrary, the whole purpose of the narrative additions is to dismiss the ark as the relic of a bygone age that is of dubious benefit to anyone. It is simply another mark of the anti-Dtr character of the *David Saga*.

David and Mephibosheth

One of the remarkable features of the *David Saga* is the way in which the late revisionist author makes many interconnections between part one in David's rise to power and part two in the history of David's court, as well as within CH itself. An instance of this is in the introduction of Mephibosheth, son of Jonathan, into David's court in 2 Sam 9. The account begins when David expresses an interest in any survivors of the house of Saul so that he might show his loyalty (*ḥesed*), for Jonathan's sake. This reflects the knowledge of the close relationship of David to Jonathan in part one, but it is much more than an acknowledgement of friendship between the two in general. As we saw above, there are two versions of the close relationship between David and Jonathan, and it is within the later version, particularly in 1 Sam 20:12-17, that we have the closest link in language and content with this text. Thus, Jonathan states (vv. 14-16),

> As long as I live, show me the covenant loyalty made before Yahweh (חסד יהוה), but if I should die, do not cut off your loyalty (חסד) from my house forever. When Yahweh has eliminated the enemies of David from the face

---

9. It is a common feature of sagas to mark certain events, such as a violent death, with an etiology.

of the earth, if the name of Jonathan is eliminated from within the house of David, let Yahweh hold David to account.[10]

This is followed by a solemn oath that deals with this future contingency of what will happen after Jonathan's death. Only here is it clearly anticipated that Jonathan will predecease David and that Jonathan has some reason to be concerned about how David will treat the survivors of his household. First, Jonathan recalls the covenant made with David when they first met (1 Sam 18:3), and then he extends this to include his offspring as well. They are to be preserved "within the house of David," which can be construed as within the realm that David will rule or within his personal household. Thus, David is placed under oath by Jonathan to show *ḥesed* to his offspring.

This extension of David's oath toward Jonathan is picked up in the setting and language of 2 Sam 9. First, Jonathan anticipates his death on Mount Gilboa (1 Sam 31:2) and the fact that his son Mephibosheth will be a survivor (2 Sam 4:4). Jonathan's remark about Yahweh's eliminating David's enemies imitates a similar remark in 2 Sam 7:1 and anticipates David's victories in 2 Sam 5 and 8, so that it is appropriate that immediately after the account of these wars David then takes up his commitment to Jonathan in 2 Sam 9. The specific language used to reflect this obligation is "the *ḥesed* of Yahweh" (1 Sam 20:14) in the one case and the "*ḥesed* of God" (2 Sam 9:3) in the other. There can be little doubt that, in seeking out Mephibosheth and in bringing him under the protection of his "house," David is fulfilling this sworn obligation to Jonathan. Everything points to the closest connection between 1 Sam 20:12–17 and 2 Sam 9.[11]

Kaiser objects to this conclusion on two grounds. First, because there is no mention of a *běrît* in 2 Sam 9, the connection is not entirely necessary. But this is rather weak, because only David knows of the covenant, because it was made in private, so there is no need for him to mention it. David pretends to be more magnanimous than he really is. Kaiser's second point is that 1 Sam 20:12–17 is a redactional addition that interrupts the narrative flow between vv. 11 and 18. He therefore understands this text as a secondary expansion based on 2 Sam 9. This line of argument is very weak because

---

10. This is a difficult text, and various proposals have been suggested for its interpretation: McCarter, *I Samuel*, 336–37; Klein, *1 Samuel*, 203; Driver, *Notes on Samuel*, 164–66.

11. P. Ackroyd also notes the close connection between these texts ("The Succession Narrative [So-Called]," *Int* 35 [1981]: 390). For him, it is a problem of setting the limits of SN.

it does not explain why a redactor meddled with the text if by Kaiser's own judgment it was not necessary. In fact, the language of the two texts is so close that this seems to be another case in which the author of the *David Saga* has composed this unit in 1 Sam 20:12–17. He is the only one who has a motive for anticipating the later episode in a very precise and poignant way. As we have seen above, there is reason to believe that in fact the whole of 1 Sam 20 is the work of the author of the *David Saga*. Another similar anticipation of 2 Sam 9 is found in 2 Sam 4:4, which gives the explanation for Mephibosheth's disability. Again, there is no need to invoke a redactor for this addition. These anticipations of 2 Sam 9 reflect the author's technique of creating interconnections throughout his work, a feature that is noted in other cases by Rost.[12]

The narratives that deal with the relationship between David and Mephibosheth are instructive in what they say about David's perceived relationship to the house of Saul, and in this respect they must also be viewed in the light of the other episodes that include members of Saul's family. In our treatment of these narratives, however, we must be careful never to assume that we are reconstructing some historical reality but only that we are trying to understand how the author wishes us to view the behavior of David in these contexts. David appears, on the surface, to be magnanimous toward this grandson of Saul, who was only five years old when his father died and could know nothing of David's relationship with Jonathan. It would seem that a considerable length of time has passed before David thinks about his secret commitment to Jonathan, and when he does find Jonathan's son, he remains quite formal and shows none of that affection that one would expect at finding the sole offspring of one's dearest friend. Mephibosheth, a cripple, shows only a fearful obeisance because his life is under threat.

David takes two actions with respect to Mephibosheth. First, he commits to him all of the lands that belong to the estates of Saul, and he assigns to him a large body of retainers under Ziba who will serve him but who will also report directly to David. Second, while Mephibosheth and his family will be able to enjoy all of the benefits of this land grant, Mephibosheth will himself be present in Jerusalem at the king's table "like one of the king's sons." This seems quite similar to the position of Jehoiachin, the Judean king in exile (2 Kgs 25:29), whose place in the Babylonian court is akin to

---

12. It is also a common technique in sagas.

that of a hostage.[13] The point of this whole exercise seems to be remarkably political, namely, to neutralize the possible internal threat of the house of Saul by putting all the properties of Saul under one member of that family who had the strongest claim to succeed his grandfather and yet that person would be under direct control and observation in Jerusalem itself. Mephibosheth's movements are further hampered by the fact that he is crippled. The author makes two further points that enforce this interpretation. The first is that Mephibosheth is from the region of Lo-debar, which is east of the Jordan and a considerable distance from Jerusalem. This was the same region that Ishbosheth used as his power base. Second, the author indicates that in spite of Mephibosheth's physical condition he did have a son who would be his heir.

This episode is closely interconnected with a number of other episodes that follow. In the account of the rebellion of Absalom, during the rather lengthy retreat of David from Jerusalem, after David has passed the summit of the Mount of Olives, Ziba, Mephibosheth's majordomo, comes out to meet David with a large quantity of foodstuffs from his master's estates (2 Sam 16:1–4).[14] The absence of Mephibosheth is noted by David, and he calls for an explanation. The reason that Ziba offers is that Mephibosheth thought, "Today the house of Israel will restore to me the kingdom of my father" (v. 3). Of course, this reason does not make any sense, because there is no more prospect of his restoration under Absalom than under David, and the personal threat to Mephibosheth is, if anything, even greater. David immediately accepts this vilification at face value and rewards Ziba with the promise of all the lands of his master's estates. Ziba's clever calculation seems to have paid off.

Soon after this encounter with Ziba, who remains behind in his newly acquired estates, another member of the house of Saul, Shimei, came out to curse David and insult him with accusations that he is a "man of blood," that is, a murderer, and that David's troubles are the result of divine retribution: "Yahweh has requited you for all the murders of the house of Saul, in whose place you have reigned; and Yahweh has handed over the kingdom to your son, Absalom. Look at you in your misery, for you are a murderer." This accusation takes us back to the various episodes in the earlier

---

13. See Hertzberg, *I and II Samuel*, 300–301.

14. The similarity with the gift of food brought to David by Abigail in 1 Sam 25:18 is significant and points to a common source.

texts that have to do with the deaths of Saul, Abner, and Ishbosheth (2 Sam 1:1–16, 3:22–39, 4:1–12), and apparently the charge has merit. This is not a matter of reading the narrative "against the grain," because the doubts and suspicions of David's involvement in these events are precisely those that have been created by this brilliant writer.

This becomes all the more apparent when Abishai, Joab's brother, wants to go immediately and kill this Saulide who is making these charges, but the earlier narrative has clearly indicated that both Joab and Abishai were implicated in the death of Abner (2 Sam 3:30), and David's weak excuse is that he could not control them. So David's rebuke of the "sons of Zeruiah" is his acknowledgement that the cursing of Shimei is not unjustified and perhaps from Yahweh. He accepts it as a kind of sacred discipline for his past actions or inactions. Furthermore, what David does not reveal but what we know is that David is under oath to Saul that he will not harm anyone of the house of Saul (1 Sam 24:20–22). To do anything to Shimei would be to violate this oath, so he must take his lumps and endure the humiliation.

When the revolt of Absalom has come to an end with his death and David returns with his entourage to the Jordan, among the first to restore the king to his domain on the west side of the Jordan is Shimei, with a thousand Benjaminites and the men of Judah, and in his company is also Ziba and his family and servants. This creates a decisive moment that has very large consequences. Shimei pleads for forgiveness for the wrongs he committed against the king but also points out that he has brought a significant delegation from Benjamin as the first of the "house of Joseph" to invite the king back into his realm. In other words, Shimei's approach to David is accompanied by a political gesture that can hardly be refused. If it is, then the whole of Israel may be lost again. The hothead Abishai does not understand this and persists in seeking to kill Shimei: "Should not Shimei be put to death because he cursed Yahweh's anointed?" (2 Sam 19:22). Is not Abishai correct? Did not David lecture Abishai on an earlier occasion about the inviolability of Yahweh's anointed (1 Sam 26:8–11)? To curse the king is a capital offense.[15] What this rough mercenary leader does not understand, however, is that this is a political moment in which politics trumps any principles of law. It has nothing to do with mercy, as David makes quite clear in his response: "Shall anyone be put to death in Israel this day? For today I realize that I am to be king over Israel" (2 Sam 19:24). To kill Shimei, who is leader of this important delegation from Israel ("the House

---

15. Exod 22:27, 1 Kgs 21:10–13.

of Joseph") would immediately alienate the population that he is trying now to win over and perhaps precipitate another round of bloodshed at the very moment of his grand entrance into the land. Consequently, David not only announces a pardon but confirms it with an oath.

This does not mean that David has forgiven Shimei or is not vindictive, because he does not regard Solomon as bound by the same oath. This comes out in the deathbed scene when David recapitulates these events and holds Solomon to the obligation to find some excuse to do away with him (1 Kgs 2:8–9). This completely belies the appearance of piety that David expresses in 2 Sam 16:10–12 and reveals David's true sentiments and actions. In spite of the fact that Shimei was a supporter of Solomon's party, he was eventually to be rewarded by murder at the hands of a mercenary general (1 Kgs 2:36–46). More on this below.

At this point, Mephibosheth appears on the scene (2 Sam 19:25–31). Exactly where this happens is not clear, although from the context it seems to be in the region of the Jordan, and it is also not clear how he got there because he is a cripple and did not have the aid of his servant Ziba. What the narrator is at pains to make absolutely clear, however, is that what was previously reported by Ziba to David is a complete falsehood. Mephibosheth has been in a state of mourning and sympathy for David during the whole of David's ordeal, as the evidence of his appearance firmly attests: "He had neither cut his toenails[16] nor trimmed his beard, nor washed his clothes, from the time that the king left until the day that he safely returned" (2 Sam 19:25). It is the narrator who reports these facts, and this kind of evidence is obvious and indisputable. David, however, ignores it and asks Mephibosheth why he did not accompany him into exile, but such a question already implies an accusation of guilt. There are others that did not do so, including Ziba and all of his family and servants. Of what possible use could this cripple have been? If he had offered, he would also have been sent back anyway. However, Mephibosheth is well aware that he is under suspicion and gives his defense: it was his intention to go with the king, but his servant deceived him and then slandered him. He flatters David by comparing him with "the angel of God," a term used previously in the same way by the wise woman of Tekoa: "But my lord has wisdom like the wisdom of the angel of God to know all things that are on earth" (2 Sam 14:20). Mephibosheth's case is simply that, far from having any aspirations of regaining the crown, he is in a situation of grave risk and depends on

---

16. See McCarter's discussion of this phrase (*II Samuel*, 417, 421).

David's good will: "For all my father's house are doomed to die by my lord the king, but you have given me a place among those who eat at your table. What further right have I to utter a plea to the king?" David, however, sweeps aside both the physical evidence of Mephibosheth's present condition and the reasonable case that is set before him by refusing to make a judgment and simply divides the property between the two parties. In spite of this obvious injustice, Mephibosheth remains magnanimous by renouncing any claim to the property and utters his final pleasure that the king has now returned in safety.

Throughout this whole narrative of David's relationship with Mephibosheth, there is nothing in David's actions toward this crippled son of Jonathan, to whom he was so closely attached, that shows any emotion or tenderness. Everything is done under the obligation of an oath or dictated by political calculation. In spite of his flattery toward David, Mephibosheth seems totally unaware of David's former relationship with his father and all too aware that he lives a very precarious existence and that little prevents David from doing away with the family of Saul entirely. This portrayal is altogether consistent with what we have seen earlier and what will follow.

As we have noted earlier, a remarkable feature of this narrative source is its complex pattern in interconnections. This is not just a matter of the repetition of a particular theme as one might find in the DtrH or the Yahwist but has to do with the interaction of numerous characters in the plot in many different scenes and episodes and over an extended period of time. This can be seen in David's relationship with Mephibosheth that begins in the middle of David's reign but makes a connection with the events relating to Saul's defeat and Jonathan's death, as well as the accident that cripples Mephibosheth, and then to the earlier relationship between David and Jonathan that has to do with their oaths of loyalty and commitment to look out for Jonathan's family. The connections are picked up again at the beginning and at the end of the revolt of Absalom. At the same time, the affairs of Mephibosheth are closely interconnected with another Saulide, Shimei, who arises in close parallel with Mephibosheth in the Absalom revolt but carries into the final episodes of the palace intrigue and succession of Solomon. Within these episodes, there are many minor interconnections, such as the behavior of Abishai in the scenes that have to do with Shimei in the flight and return of David, which reflects back on the same rash behavior that is exhibited in Abishai's eagerness to kill Saul when he and David have penetrated the camp of Saul in 1 Sam 26:7–12. Again, the detail about Mephibosheth being from the house of Machir the son of Ammiel in Lo-debar (2 Sam

9:6) is picked up again in 2 Sam 17:27, where Machir of Lo-debar is one of those who bring food aid to David in his flight from Absalom. All of these details, and many more in language and plot, lead to only one reasonable conclusion, namely, that they point to the skilful literary craftsmanship of a single author.[17]

The Bathsheba Affair

David's illicit affair with Bathsheba, resulting in the murder of Uriah, is set within the context of David's war with the Ammonites,[18] so we will begin with a look at the conflict as set out in 2 Sam 10:1–14. As we saw earlier, the war against the Arameans in 10:15–19 originally had nothing to do with the Ammonites and was displaced from its original connection after 8:8 to its present position. This war against the Ammonites stands out from all the other foreign wars of David by the way in which it pays attention to particular details. First, it deals with the *casus belli* for the war in 10:1–5, something that in Dtr's treatment of foreign wars needs no such explanation. The occasion that gives rise to hostilities is the succession to the Ammonite throne by Hanun, the son of Nahash, the former king. David apparently had a solemn treaty of friendship (*ḥesed*) with the prior ruler Nahash and wished to extend this to his son. The acknowledgement of such a relationship between David and Nahash is quite remarkable because Nahash, in the days of Saul, had been a bitter enemy to the Israelites living east of the Jordan, and Saul's defeat of Nahash had been one of the great wars of Yahweh of that period and the event that brought Saul into the kingship (1 Sam 11). The great rescue of Jabesh-Gilead had endeared them to the house of Saul to the end of his reign (1 Sam 31:11–13). In the view of Dtr, the Ammonites were a bitter enemy of the Israelites from the time of the Judges onward, but most especially under the cruel king Nahash.

How is it, then, that David could have had a treaty of friendship with Nahash? Are we to suppose that this dates back to the time when Ishbosheth was encamped in Mahanaim? A treaty of friendship of this sort would have

---

17. One is also reminded of the same kind of interconnection made between episodes by the authors of the Icelandic sagas.

18. See Gressmann, "The Oldest History Writing in Israel," 23–25. Gressmann regards the whole of 2 Sam 10:1–11:1, 12:26–31 as belonging to an older military report into which the story of Bathsheba has been fitted. Many scholars have followed his lead.

been convenient to both. However, this kind of speculation does not correspond to real events because the relationship is a fiction of the author. What he clearly wants to suggest is that David's relations with the Ammonites were entirely a matter of personal loyalties and friendship and not based on any larger principle such as what Dtr articulates. It is hardly conceivable that Dtr would have approved of a friendship such as this between David and Nahash, which means that the author quite deliberately casts David in this negative role.

According to the narrator's account of events, the military leaders of the Ammonites are suspicious of David's intentions in sending mourners to express his condolences and advise the new king that David is engaging in espionage in preparation for a military attack. On the one hand, given David's longstanding cordial relations with the king's father, this does not seem reasonable, but on the other hand, the previous accounts of David's wars in the earlier source (Dtr) suggest that David had conquered all of the other nations on Israel's borders, so it was not unreasonable to expect that in time Ammon would be next. However, the deliberate humiliation of David's messengers by shaving their beards and cutting their robes to the buttocks and sending them back could only lead to serious reprisals. David's honor had been seriously violated.[19] The prolonged and costly war that followed between David and the Ammonites, therefore, was based not on some principle of "holy war" but on a matter of a foolish personal affront by one ruler toward another. David fights not "the wars of Yahweh," as Abigail suggested (1 Sam 25:28), but wars based on his own ambition or personal relations with other rulers. This is the reality of absolute monarchic rule.

The Ammonites, realizing that offensive action of this sort could only lead to war, set about enlisting mercenary armies from a number of Aramean states. As I pointed out above, this is not a matter of entering into an alliance with a central Aramean power under a single ruler, Hadadezer, as in the Aramean wars of DtrH, but it is a case of creating a viable military force by employing professional mercenaries under their own individual commands. As we have seen, this feature of warfare strongly reflects the pattern of military activity in the late Persian period. Thus, when the armies confront each other, the Ammonites are gathered in one place in front of the city, while the Aramean mercenaries are arrayed in the open field in their own ranks. Unlike the battles in Dtr, David does not himself engage in any military operation but leaves it entirely in the hands of his command-

---

19. Violations of honor such as this often led to feuds and serious reprisals in the Icelandic sagas.

ers, Joab and Abishai. It is these generals who develop the military strategy; Joab uses the elite force of professionals against the mercenaries, while his brother takes the rest of the citizen soldiers against the corresponding group of Ammonite conscripts. This is how one is to understand this arrangement. The advantage of the forces under Joab and Abishai is that there is a completely unified command with the one contingent supporting the other, while the Ammonites and their mercenaries are divided under multiple commands, and once one of these breaks rank and starts to flee because there are no loyalties between them, the panic spreads to the rest.[20] Thus, when the Aramean forces are routed by Joab, the Ammonites also panic and retreat into the city behind them. The result is a victory for David's side, but nothing is gained because no territory is captured and there is no account of any war dead. Perhaps to make up for this lack, the author has shifted Dtr's account of the Aramean defeat under Hadadezer in 10:15-19 from its original location, in order to supply the war with a huge toll of enemy casualties and the subjugation of new groups of Arameans. The tag at the end, "So the Arameans were afraid to help the Ammonites ever again" (v. 19b), ties this narrative unit into the larger context.

Nothing, however, has been resolved with respect to the Ammonites who are still in safe retreat in their city, having no part in the military encounter in 10:15-19, which, in its original form, had nothing to do with them. The next phase of the Ammonite war is covered by the whole of chaps. 11-12; and this means that it lasts as long as two years, all of it in the shadow of the city of Rabbah. There are a number of scholars who would attempt to extract a few verses from this account in order to reconstruct an original source, corresponding to the other wars of David,[21] but there is little to commend this approach. Even if one follows the lead of 1 Chr 20:1-3 and strips the account of all references to the Bathsheba affair,[22] one still ends up with features that are characteristic of the later source and not those of military accounts in Dtr. Thus, it is Joab and not David who is in complete command of the army, while David remains behind in Jerusalem, and only after Joab has taken the city does David come

---

20. See Waterfield, *Zenophon's Retreat*, 1-19, which gives a wonderful picture of this kind of warfare in the battle of Cunaxa.

21. McCarter, *II Samuel*, 275-76; Hertzberg, *I and II Samuel*, 317-20.

22. See A. G. Auld, "Prophets through the Looking Glass: A Response to Robert Carroll and Hugh Williamson," *JSOT* 27 (1983): 41-44. Cf. my "'Shared Text' of Samuel-Kings and Chronicles Re-examined," in *Reflections and Refractions: Studies in Biblical Historiography in Honour of A. Graeme Auld* (ed. R. Rezetko et al.; VTSup 113; Leiden: Brill, 2007), 503-15, esp. 505.

to claim the spoils. In my view, Joab appears nowhere in DtrH, whereas in DtrH David always leads the forces in battle. There is thus no reason to regard any of the narrative in chaps. 11-12 as belonging to a source that is earlier than or different from the larger *David Saga* corpus.

The military context that the narrator fashions as background for the Bathsheba affair begins with this opening statement (2 Sam 11:1):

> In the springtime, the time when kings go forth to battle, David sent Joab along with his other officers and all Israel, and they laid waste to Ammon and besieged Rabbah, but David remained in Jerusalem.

David's action against Ammon is clearly a continuation of the earlier war, which was left unresolved, but it is also construed as belonging to a regular pattern of kingship in the ancient Near East. Kings, particularly the great powers, go on campaign yearly to pillage enemy territory, to conquer cities, and to collect booty. This is the social reality and David is made to fit this pattern. He behaves just as any other Near Eastern despot. Furthermore, he has a professional army that can take charge of this activity, even if conscripts are also used on a seasonal basis. David, however, need not concern himself with this activity, so he remains in Jerusalem. The army ravages the countryside of Ammon, which means that the region will be stripped of its agricultural products and places of living, bringing grave hardship to the local people, but this is what armies do. The real object of the enterprise, however, is the siege of Rabbah, and this siege lasts for two years or more! The length of the siege is governed entirely by the needs of the story. Thus, when Uriah is killed, which must be within a fairly short time after Bathsheba learns that she is pregnant, David expresses some impatience with the siege and urges Joab to press on and take the city. Yet it is not until Bathsheba's second child is born that the city finally falls. It is futile, therefore, to attempt to reconstruct a primitive military account from bits and pieces of the Ammonite war. All of its features are shaped to the needs of the Bathsheba affair in which it is set, and the very presentation of the details helps to shape the character of David and the narrator's views on his reign. These will be taken up in the course of the exposition of these events.

Let me begin our close inspection of the Bathsheba affair by repeating the clearest and strongest argument against the use of this episode as a source for DtrH.[23] This is the fact that we have a basic contradiction be-

---

23. Van Seters, *In Search of History*, 277-91; idem, "The Court History and DtrH," 71-77.

tween the behavior of David in the *David Saga* and Dtr's judgment of David that he was the epitome of the just and righteous king who was completely obedient to Yahweh and who was the model for all the subsequent kings to follow.[24] There are a number of scholars who will go to any length to overcome this contradiction. In one critique of my view, Robert Gordon states, "Above all, we may ask whether there is any difficulty in the standard doctrine that the Deuteronomist(s) could have regarded David as a seriously flawed individual and yet as having satisfied the basic deuteronomistic requirement of eschewal of pagan cults and loyalty to Yahweh."[25] In this way, Gordon seems to limit Dtr's positive assessment of David and his positive or negative judgments of subsequent monarchs only to a narrow cultic criterion. But is this the case? The fact is that this cultic criterion is never directly applied to David. No specific cultic action, only the intention of building a temple for the ark, is singled out for approval.[26] For the rest, the emphasis is on David's complete obedience to *all* of the laws, statutes, and commandments, which means Deuteronomy, and this includes the Ten Commandments and not just the cultic regulations. Murder and adultery, such as are reflected in 2 Sam 11, cannot possibly be excluded from Dtr's understanding of obedience to the law or doing what is right in the eyes of Yahweh.

Furthermore, in 1 Kgs 21 we have a story within DtrH that focuses specifically on the king's (and queen's) abuse of royal power that leads to murder, the murder of Naboth.[27] Although Ahab is only indirectly involved in Naboth's death, it is this act that is cited as the reason for divine judgment on the house of Ahab, and it is considered just as evil as the cultic sins of Jeroboam. Indeed, the similarity of this episode in DtrH with the Bathsheba

---

24. The strength of this argument is now admitted by McKenzie (in "The So-Called Succession Narrative," 123–35), but he regards this episode as a later addition to CH, while the rest of CH he simply attributes to Dtr. This position, in my view, is untenable.

25. R. P. Gordon, "In Search of David: The David Tradition in Recent Study," in *Faith, Tradition and History: Old Testament Historiography in Its Near Eastern Context* (ed. A. P. Millard, J. K. Hoffmeier, and D. W. Baker; Winona Lake, IN: Eisenbrauns, 1994), 289.

26. Indeed, the implications of 1 Kgs 3:2–3, which mentions the use of high places at the beginning of Solomon's reign, is that they continued in existence from the time of David.

27. See Noth, *The Deuteronomistic History*, 71; S. L. McKenzie, *The Trouble with Kings* (VTSup 42; Leiden: Brill, 1991), 67–69.

affair calls for further consideration.[28] In the Ahab story, we have a king who desires to obtain some property in the vicinity of the palace, at first through legitimate, nonviolent means and then, when he is frustrated, through the surreptitious means of judicial murder. As soon as he lays claim to the property, God intervenes with his prophet, who confronts Ahab with his crime. The judgment that follows includes a historical ré-sumé, in which the punishment will fall on Ahab's entire household, and its execution will be made to fit the crime. When Ahab shows deep re-morse, there is a mitigation of the sentence in his own lifetime.[29]

Virtually every element of this story has its equivalent in the David-Bathsheba affair.[30] David too desires property in the vicinity of his palace, in this case another man's wife. When he does secretly take her and make her pregnant, he tries by nonviolent means to cover up his act. This fails, and so he decides by surreptitious means to murder the husband. After Da-vid takes possession of Uriah's wife, God intervenes by sending his prophet to confront him with his crime and, following a historical résumé, passes sentence in which the punishment is made to fit the crime, a pun-ishment that will include the whole household. When David admits his sin, God mitigates the punishment so that David himself does not die, but the rest of the sentence remains.

I am not overlooking the fact that there are important differences as well as similarities, and I do not think for a moment that they belong to the same author. But the similar structure of the two accounts speaks against

---

28. See now Marsha C. White, *The Elijah Legends and Jehu's Coup,* (Brown Judaic Studies 311; Atlanta: Scholars Press, 1997), 17–24. There is also a brief comment on the similarity in M. Garsiel, "The Story of David and Bathsheba: A Different Ap-proach," *CBQ* 55 (1993): 261.

29. For the purposes of the following comparison it makes no difference whether the whole of 1 Kgs 21 is considered the work of Dtr or only the additions in vv. 20b–29. The similarities encompass the whole unit.

30. See the recent works of G. H. Jones, *The Nathan Narratives* (JSOTSup 80; Sheffield: JSOT Press, 1990); R. C. Bailey, *David in Love and War: The Pursuit of Power in 2 Samuel 10–12* (JSOTSup 75; Sheffield: JSOT Press, 1990). Both ascribe a major role to Dtr in shaping older materials (not necessarily SN) to create the present narrative. Nevertheless, they do not compare it with parallel texts in DtrH. White (in *Elija Legends,* pp. 17–24) simply adopts the position of Rost on the com-position and dating of this unit and has no discussion on the Dtr character of Nathan's prophecy in 2 Sam 12. She also argues that 1 Kgs 21 is dependent on the Bathsheba-Nathan narrative of 2 Sam 11–12. This would result in a situation in which Dtr modeled the behavior of Ahab, the king that he viewed as the worst of all the Northern kings, on that of David, his royal ideal. This is simply not credible.

any attempt to make part of the Bathsheba story in 2 Sam 12 a later addition.[31] Furthermore, the similarity of the two stories goes beyond the matter of structure and plot and includes specific language. What David does is "evil in the sight of Yahweh" (11:26), a judgment that is repeated by Nathan as well: "Why have you despised the word of Yahweh to do what is evil in his sight?" This statement of judgment is very similar to that uttered by Elijah: "Because you have sold yourself to do what is evil in the sight of Yahweh."[32] Statements such as these are reserved by DtrH for the worst kings as the basis for the demise of their dynasties and ultimately the reason for the downfall of the two kingdoms. Ahab is considered by Dtr as the very worst of all, but how is he any different from David? They both receive the same kind of judgment. In David's case, this refers both to events during his reign, but also to later acts of violence during the entire period of his dynasty (viz., to the end of the Judean monarchy): "The sword shall not depart from your house (= dynasty) forever." This judgment is no less severe than that passed on Ahab.

The language used by the author of the *David Saga* has become an important issue in the analysis of this corpus and must be given some attention here. The fact that the language is similar to that used by Dtr has led many to the erroneous view that this is evidence of a Dtr redactor.[33] But we can say with certainty that it is not Dtr. It is simply not possible to believe that at one point David can be accused of being a king who, like Ahab, does evil in the sight of Yahweh and despises the "word of Yahweh" and at another point be heaped with praise for doing only what was right in the sight of Yahweh and for being completely obedient to all his laws. The use of the phrase דבר יהוה (12:9) is quite remarkable here. There is no good reason to prefer an emendation by omitting דבר and simply rendering the text "You have despised Yahweh."[34] This phraseology is not attested elsewhere, and even if it were possible it would mean that David was not a worshiper

---

31. The comparison with Dtr has usually been too narrowly restricted to terminology with unfortunate consequences.

32. White (*Elijah Legends*, p. 34), regards 1 Kgs 21:20b as a Dtr addition to the older narrative but says nothing about the parallel use of the same language in the Nathan prophecy.

33. See R. C. Bailey, *David in Love and War: Pursuit of Power in 2 Samuel 10–12*; W. Dietrich, *David, Saul und die Propheten*, 36–41; Jones, *The Nathan Oracles*, 93–117. See also Dietrich and Naumann, *Die Samuelbücher*, 233–56.

34. So H. P. Smith, *The Books of Samuel* (ICC; New York: Scribners, 1899), 324; also P. K. McCarter, *II Samuel*, 295.

of Yahweh but worshiped some other deity, which is not at issue in this text. The phrase "word of Yahweh" is consistently used in DtrH in this situation to mean a specific oracle from Yahweh given previously by a prophet. This is also its usual meaning in the prophetic literature. By extension, it can refer to a specific command given by God through Moses. But here it cannot have either of these meanings. It must refer in a more general way to the established written expression of the divine will as reflected in the Torah and specifically in the Decalogue.

Now precisely this phrase, "to despise the word of Yahweh" (בזה דבר יהוה), occurs in Num 15:31, a P text, where it refers to a deliberate sinful act against any commandment of God. It is this same general sense of the phrase that occurs in 2 Sam 12:9. This general sense of the phrase "word of Yahweh" is rather rare but seems to be reflected in 1 Chr 10:13, in which it describes Saul as "unfaithful" and one who did not keep the "word of Yahweh," which refers to his general behavior and not to a specific act or command. 2 Chronicles 34:21 includes the statement "because our fathers have not kept the word of Yahweh, to do according to all that is written in the book." This departs from its parallel in 2 Kgs 22:13: "because our fathers have not obeyed the words of this book, to do according to all that is written concerning us." It is clear that by the Chronicler's time the "word of Yahweh" is another way of speaking of the Torah in general, and it is this late post-Dtr use that is reflected in 2 Sam 12:9. In v. 14, the parallel to the phrase in v. 9, is "You have scorned Yahweh by this act."[35] The use of נאץ with Yahweh as its object occurs in a number of places with various meanings. It can refer to disloyalty to Yahweh by serving other gods (Deut 31:20) or to distrust and rebellion against Yahweh's promise of the land (Num 14:11, 23; 16:30 [J]) or to scorning the words of the prophets (Isa 1:4, Jer 23:17). In the case of 2 Sam 12:14, however, the nuance is somewhat different. Here, the scorning of Yahweh is done through murder and adultery, the deliberate violation of the laws of the Decalogue. The language, while similar to Dtr, is certainly later and postexilic in date.

Consequently, it will not do to ascribe this rebuke of Nathan in 12:7–12 to a "Prophetic History" prior to DtrH[36] that Dtr chose to use and then bla-

---

35. Omitting "enemies" with Smith, *Samuel*, 324–25.

36. So McCarter, *II Samuel*, 7–8, 304–9; cf. G. Keys, *The Wages of Sin: A Reappraisal of the Succession Narrative* (JSOTSup 221; Sheffield: JSOT Press, 1996). Keys regards 2 Sam 10–20 as a self-contained document by a prophetic writer prior to its use by Dtr and independent from the theme of succession in 1 Kgs 1–2.

tantly contradict. Nathan's historical résumé, likewise, makes the dating of the story clear. It refers to David's anointing by Samuel (1 Sam 16:1-13), which belongs to a post-Dtr addition to the David story.[37] Furthermore, David's anointing is part of a larger unit, 1 Sam 15:1-16:13, that includes an account of Saul's rejection by God, alluded to by Nathan (in 2 Sam 12:8) and a favorite theme within the *David Saga*. In this story of Saul's rejection, Saul is also accused of doing what is evil in the sight of Yahweh (15:19) and of rejecting the "word of Yahweh" (vv. 23, 26), which is very similar to Nathan's accusation of David.[38] Saul also admits his sin ("I have sinned") as David does but then pleads for forgiveness, which David does not do. But Saul receives no forgiveness, only a judgment on his future dynasty. It should also be noted that Samuel precedes his statement of judgment by a similar historical résumé of Saul's rise to power. The similarities, however, do not support the view that these texts belong to the same hand but only indicate that the narrator of the Bathsheba story was familiar with all of this literature and imitated it.

The motif of the child of the king that dies because of the sin of the father suggests yet another comparison with DtrH. In this case, it is the child of Jeroboam who becomes ill (1 Kgs 14). When his wife consults the prophet Ahijah about her child, he declares to her the divine judgment in a manner very similar to Nathan's, beginning with the historical résumé: "Because I raised you from among the people and made you leader over my people Israel, and tore the kingdom away from the house of David and gave it to you" (v. 8). However, Ahijah then continues with a comparison between Jeroboam and David: "And yet you have not been like my servant David, who kept my commandments, and followed me with all his heart, doing only what was right in my eyes, but you have done evil above all who were before you" (vv. 8-9). This speech is clearly not by the same hand as the Nathan reprimand. Ahijah continues with his judgment of Jeroboam in a manner similar to that of Ahab, which consists of punishment on the *house* of Jeroboam, including the sick child. Now regarding this sick child, a rather remarkable statement is made, that, in spite of his premature death, "something favorable to Yahweh the God of Israel was found in him among those of Jeroboam's household." Within the David story, a similar statement is made, not of the first child of Bathsheba but of the second,

---

37. Van Seters, *In Search of History*, 260-64. See also above, pp. 121-135.

38. But in 1 Sam 15:23, 26, the "word of Yahweh" refers specifically to the divine command given to Saul through Samuel.

Solomon: "Yahweh loved him." What the author means by this is not our concern here. We will return to this below. It is enough merely to note the remarkable coincidence of features between the Bathsheba story and the prophetic stories of judgment within an already "expanded" DtrH. The matter could, of course, be solved by relegating the whole of the Bathsheba-Uriah story to a late post-Dtr addition.[39] However, the interconnections between it and other episodes, such as the revolt of Absalom and the final succession to the throne, are too strong to permit such an easy solution.[40]

As I have argued consistently in the previous treatment of comparisons between the two accounts of David's career and as I hope has now become quite irrefutable, the author of the Bathsheba affair has consciously set out to revise and undermine the favorable view of David and his dynasty.[41] It now remains to look more closely at some of the particular details in the story in order to see how the narrator is attempting to shape our understanding of life in David's court. After introducing the beginning of the new campaign against the Ammonites—a major operation that includes "all Israel" as well as the professional corps—David himself does not lead the forces but stays at home in Jerusalem to enjoy the good life. It is under these circumstances that David, at his leisure on the roof of his palace, succumbs to the temptation of adultery at the sight of a woman bathing. It is not as though David does not already have a large harem to service his sexual needs, nor does he have the slightest thought for the consequences of his actions. He is informed that she is the wife of one of his trusted warriors, Uriah, who is with the army in the field, but engages in his act of adultery regardless. What David has not counted on is the fact that she becomes pregnant from this "one night stand."

When a man and a woman commit adultery in Israel it is a capital offense, but such laws do not apply to an absolute monarch, for he is above the law and there is no one who can prosecute him, except the deity. Thus, David acts from a position of blatant power, and the woman does not have much choice but to submit. It is idle to speculate about Bathsheba's collaboration in this affair—that is the stuff of novels. The author has only David's position and actions in view. Bathsheba's only decisive action is to inform the king of her pregnancy; the rest is left to David to decide. David's re-

---

39. See McKenzie, "The So-Called Succession Narrative."
40. See Bailey, *David in Love and War*; W. Dietrich, *David, Saul und die Propheten*, 36–41.
41. In addition to works cited earlier, see my "Court History and DtrH."

sponse is to bring her husband, Uriah, back from the front in order that he might engage in sex with his wife, so David's child would be attributed to Bathsheba's husband. It is clear, therefore, that David's interest in Bathsheba was purely based on lust without any further concern for the woman or her welfare, to say nothing of love or passion for her.[42]

The focal point of the narrative in 2 Sam 11 is not the relationship of David with Bathsheba but David's dealings with her husband, Uriah, which takes up most of the narrative space. There is an obvious contrast that is drawn between these two figures that goes beyond the limits of character portraits and speaks to the criteria to be used for interpretation of the narrative source as a whole. The most obvious point of comparison is the contemptible disloyalty and duplicity of David toward his faithful warrior Uriah, who is completely loyal to David and to the cause for which he is risking his life. Is Uriah aware of the court gossip about the affair? Does he suspect David and so resist being drawn into David's scheme of covering his guilt? These questions require idle speculation, based on the supposition that we are dealing with actual events. They miss the point of the narrator, who has created the episode; we must be careful to follow his lead.

The first major clue is that David's actions are being compared with those of Uriah the *Hittite*. The designation *Hittite* has nothing to do with the historic Hittites of the second millennium B.C.E., as is so often suggested. At the time of writing this term was the standard way of referring to a member of the non-Israelite primitive population, much like the terms *Canaanite* and *Amorite*, the population that should have been exterminated or at the very least expelled from the whole land of Israel. But here we have Hittites at the very heart of the empire as part of the elite professional forces. There is no reason to doubt that Bathsheba, the daughter of Eliam, is from an important Israelite family. So one can assume from the story that intermarriage of this sort was common and accepted in the Davidic realm, in sharp contrast to and in polemic against the strong taboos of the late Persian period in Judah.

Furthermore, this "Hittite" is also a very devout worshiper of Yahweh who has so many religious scruples, in contrast to David, that he causes

---

42. I do not find the suggestion of Gunn that Bathsheba reflects the common saga motif of the "woman who brings death" very convincing. See Gunn, *The Story of King David*, 43; cf. my "Love and Death in the Court History of David," in *Love and Death in the Ancient Near East: Essays in Honor of Marvin H. Pope* (ed. J. H. Marks and R. M. Good; Guildford, CT: Four Quarters, 1987), 121–24.

David no end of trouble with his piety. He treats the whole campaign against the Ammonites as though it were a holy war and not just a seasonal war for booty. When he does not go down to his house to sleep with his wife and David questions him about his activity, he lectures David about what is expected of him under the requirements of holy war: "The ark and Israel and Judah are living in booths (*sukkot*),[43] while my lord Joab and the servants of my lord are encamped in the open field. Am I then to go to my house and feast and have sex with my wife? By your life, I will not do such a thing." It is clear that the reference to the ark and the people living in booths (or temporary shelters; cf. 1 Kgs 20:12, 16) gives to the military enterprise a holy war character, but it is uncertain whether it has to do with the ark and the people being actually in the vicinity of the battlefield or whether it implies that all of the people are observing a kind of ritual abstinence while the army is engaged in holy war. In either case, this is in stark contrast to the king, who is feasting and engaging in sex with the wife of a brave and scrupulously religious soldier who is not even an Israelite! Even after this lecture by Uriah, David does not have the slightest qualms about violating these principles, but he forces Uriah also to break the rules by "inviting" him to feast and getting him drunk, with the intent that he will disregard the taboo on sex with his wife as well, but this Uriah does not do.

With his cover-up plans thwarted by this conscientious Hittite, David must now resort to a staged killing by the enemy, even if it also means that many others will die unnecessarily as well. Uriah faithfully bears the letter containing his own death warrant to Joab, who carries out David's orders. The complete callousness with which Joab and David carry out this murder, culminating in the good news to David, "Uriah the Hittite is dead" (11:21, 25), reminds us repeatedly of this contrast between these two men. The only one to lament this righteous "aboriginal"[44] is his wife, Bathsheba. After her period of mourning, David then takes her in and she becomes his wife, one more in a large harem, and she bares him an illegitimate son.

Up to this point there has been an implicit subversion of the older theological and ideological categories, in which David represents the divinely

43. McCarter (*II Samuel*, 287) interprets *sukkot* as the place name Succoth, but this seems quite unlikely. The city of Succoth is a considerable distance from Rabbah and there is no explanation for why all the people with the ark would be there while the army is encamped in the environs of Rabbah.
44. He is certainly not a *ger* as some have suggested. This is a quite different legal status.

chosen shepherd of Israel and Uriah the aboriginal population, those who would undermine the true faith and lead the people astray. Exactly the opposite has happened here, with the gravest injustice done by David, who is celebrated as the most just and righteous one. Now the author makes quite explicit use of Dtr language: "But Yahweh viewed what David did as quite wrong" (11:27b), and this remark always refers to the most serious offenses. As we have seen above, this suggests a deliberate comparison with all of those other kings of Israel and Judah who fall under this same judgment. Like the wicked Ahab, who murdered Naboth and was reprimanded by Elijah, Yahweh sends his prophet Nathan with a divine word of judgment, which is introduced by the famous parable (2 Sam 12:1-4). Here, as elsewhere in his work, the author makes little distinction between prophetic oracle and words of wisdom, when it comes to the medium of divine inspiration. The parable contains its own implicit word of judgment, which results in David's self-incrimination (vv. 5-6). The more direct prophetic word, in imitation of the prophetic models in Dtr, follows the parable and spells out the details of the charge (vv. 7-12).

I will not repeat the discussion of the literary qualities of the parable and its use as a self-judgment device.[45] It is not necessary, in my view, for all of the elements of the parable to correspond to David's actions—nothing is equal to David's murder of Uriah. It is only necessary that David recognizes in another a grave act of injustice, leaving himself vulnerable to the same charge, that is, "you are just this type of person." Nor should we take all the statements in Nathan's historical résumé as fact and assume that David actually took over Saul's harem. Nowhere is it suggested that Saul in fact had more than one wife, Ahinoam, who was the mother of all his children (1 Sam 14:49-50). The point is that David had everything he could possibly want, including a large harem of women, and he hardly needed to steal another man's wife for his own momentary pleasure. Unlike the poor man in the parable who could receive reparations, Uriah is dead and cannot be repaid for his loss. David is guilty of two capital offenses and will pay for them with the lives of his offspring. As indicated above, the "house of David" not only includes his immediate family, but, as in the other oracles of judgment against the kings of Israel, it extends to the whole dynasty. The downfall of the Davidic dynasty of Judah reaches back to its founder, David. Note also that it is specifically the injustice and murder done to Uriah the *Hittite* that calls for the same kind of action against David's house

---

45. See Gunn, *The Story of King David,* 40-42.

as a continuing nemesis. This deity has as much concern for the god-fearing Hittite as he does for the Israelite. It is the deity who appears to take the side of Uriah as his *go'el* in this endless feud for revenge on the house of David. This is a very anti-Dtr perspective, a revisionist theology.

The particular punishment that corresponds to David's act of adultery "in secret" is that the deity will take David's wives and give them to another, who will engage in sex with them quite publicly. This is in direct anticipation of the actions of Absalom, who, in keeping with the advice of Ahithophel, took the concubines that David had left behind in Jerusalem to keep his estate and had sex with them in a grand tent set up for the purpose on the roof of the palace in Jerusalem (2 Sam 16:20–23).[46] This advice is specifically described as being like "an oracle of God," which not only makes the connection with the earlier judgment obvious but suggests that this "inspired" advice was the means by which the deity fulfilled the judgment that he would give his wives to another. The reference to the roof of the palace as the place where this public action took place also connects it with the story of the adultery. There can be little doubt that the two stories are closely interconnected.[47]

Finally, there is the brief remark about the birth of Solomon, the second son of Bathsheba, which imitates a fairly standard pattern of the birth and naming of the child, in 2 Sam 12:24. David has many other children, so from his perspective there is nothing remarkable about this one. However, the notation on the birth receives the additional comment that "Yahweh loved him" (v. 24bβ), and this message was confirmed by the prophet Nathan, who gave him the name "Jedidiah, on behalf of Yahweh" (v. 25). There has been a great deal of speculation about the meaning and significance of these comments regarding Solomon's birth and naming. There is some connection between these comments and the account of the succession in 1 Kgs 1–2, in which Nathan and Bathsheba work together toward Solomon's enthronement. Yet it is too much to interpret the remarks in vv. 24bβ, 25 as suggesting that Solomon is the one chosen by Yahweh to succeed David. The name is never used again, and David apparently pays no attention to it at all. It is significant that Nathan does not address David and reveal to him the divine will or the requirement that Solomon is to be

---

46. Has the author of the *David Saga* consciously made Bathsheba the daughter of Eliam and therefore the granddaughter of Ahithophel? That would make Ahithophel's role in the revolt very ironic, but about this detail we cannot be sure.

47. Contra McKenzie, "The So-Called Succession Narrative," 133.

called Jedidiah. It merely establishes a close link between Solomon and the prophet, who apparently used the name "Jedidiah" as a term of affection for the child, and accounts for the fact that Nathan is a member of the Solomon party in the fight for succession.

The conclusion of the Ammonite war, which is the larger context for the Bathsheba affair, is set out in 2 Sam 12:26–31. Apparently, Joab was able to secure control of the water supply for the city of Rabbah, which meant its rapid capitulation. Joab informs David of these events and is summoned to make a final show of force and thus take credit for the city's capture and lay claim to its spoils. The author has David place the crown of the god Milcom on his head, its size, weight, and value greatly exaggerated perhaps to emphasize David's hubris. The primary object of the war is to collect booty and spoil and to use the population of Ammon as slave labor for David's own aggrandizement. The account leaves entirely vague where these laborers and craftsmen were used. For the author, this is unimportant; David is merely being portrayed as a conquering despot. Having completed his conquest, David returns to Jerusalem.

Rape and Murder in the Court of David

After David's sordid affair with Bathsheba and the murder of Uriah, the author returns to a presentation of life in the Davidic court among David's offspring; the picture does not improve but, if anything, grows darker (2 Sam 13–14). The sons prove to be no better than the father. We are introduced to the family members in a curious way. There is Absalom, a son of David, who has a beautiful sister, named Tamar, and another son of David, Amnon, who is in love with his sister Tamar, to whom Amnon refers as Absalom's sister. This could all be very confusing if we did not already have the important information given to us in 2 Sam 3:2–5. Amnon is the firstborn, whose mother is Ahinoam, whereas Absalom is third in line by a different mother, Maacah, who must be the mother of Tamar also, and thus Tamar is Amnon's half-sister. The author assumes this knowledge, so there is every reason to believe that he is responsible for the creation of this list. Furthermore, any author of the Persian period would have assumed the right of primogenitor as heir to the throne, and exceptions to this rule would have been dictated by special circumstances or the fact that the heir designate proved unworthy of this right.

Amnon falls in love with his beautiful sister Tamar and develops an obsession that makes him ill. His condition is noticed by his cousin and

friend, the very crafty (*ḥakam*) and devious Jonadab, who immediately de-
vises a plan by which Amnon can make his conquest of this young virgin.
This involves feigning illness, so that when his father, David, comes to visit
him, Amnon may persuade David to send Tamar to him to prepare some
food for him and personally to feed him as he lies in bed. This deception
merely allows Amnon to seize Tamar in the privacy of his bedroom and demand that she have sex with him. She protests that such an incestuous act
would be a scandal (*nĕbālâ*) that would cause her ruin and make him a
wanton fool. She also tries to reason with him and suggests that David, if
he asked, would permit his son to marry her. Amnon is not moved by any
consideration regarding the sexual taboo and its consequences, nor has he
any interest in marriage but only desires immediate sexual gratification,
and so he rapes her. After he has done so, his love turns to revulsion and
he kicks her out. She protests this vile treatment to no avail. She departs
sobbing and in a state of mourning, with robes torn and ashes on her head.
When Absalom discovers what has happened, he takes her into his care
and plots his future revenge for the deed. The *feud*, as a kind of divine nemesis, now enters the household of David and wreaks havoc to the very end
of his reign.[48]

This violation of Tamar is one of the most poignant narratives in the Hebrew Bible,[49] but we are concerned only with one aspect of it: what it says
about life in the royal court and David's place in these affairs. David is easily manipulated by a clever nephew and a favored firstborn son into becoming party to the whole affair. If our dating of the narrative is correct,
then there can be no doubt that the law regarding incest in the Holiness
Code (Lev 20:17) was familiar to the author and reflected the attitude of
the readers/audience. Nevertheless, in the view of the narrator the king
would still permit a marriage of this sort between brother and sister to take
place, perhaps reflecting the well-known practice of brother-sister marriages such as this within the Egyptian royal families. The standards of the
court are quite other than those that apply to the people in general. David's
response to these events is that he becomes very angry. But why? Is it that
he has been so easily duped? That his daughter has been violated? That his

---

48. As indicated above, this is a common theme of the Icelandic sagas.

49. For a study in the contrast between this narrative and the "rape" of Dinah in
Gen 34, see my "Silence of Dinah (Genesis 34)," in *Jacob: A Plural Commentary of
Gen. 25-36. Mélanges offerts à Albert de Pury* (ed. J.-D. Macchi and T. Römer; Geneva:
Labor et Fides, 2001), 239–47, and additional literature cited there.

son has shown himself to be so much like his father? The situation calls for some action, some justice, and consolation to the injured woman. But David "does nothing to upset Amnon his son because he loved him for he was his firstborn" (that is, the heir). David's indulgence leads to gross injustice concerning this crime and to negligence toward his daughter for what she has suffered, and this in turn leads to serious reprisals by her brother. Crimes such as this should have disqualified Amnon from his right to the throne, at the very least, but this did not happen. David is thus responsible for what happens in all of the events that follow. They make a complete mockery of Dtr's statement that David administered his realm "with justice and equity" (2 Sam 8:15).

Absalom is very careful to bide his time, and the occasion comes after two years, when Absalom was shearing his sheep at Baal-hazor, a festive occasion to which he invited the king and all of the royal sons, including Amnon.[50] The king declines, but Amnon and the rest of the royal party attend. Absalom informs his servants that they are to strike Amnon when he is drunk, and they do so, at which point the rest of the royal sons flee. The rumor that reaches David is that all the sons of the king have been massacred, but the crafty Jonadab informs the king that it is not as bad as that: only Amnon has been killed, as an act of revenge for what he did to his sister Tamar. The rest of the royal sons return, just as Jonadab has said; there is great mourning by the court and the king's own mourning for Amnon is prolonged. Meanwhile, Absalom takes flight and goes into exile in the residence of his maternal grandfather, king of Geshur, for three years. When David is finally consoled about the death of Amnon, he begins to long for Absalom.

Once again, the narrator makes clear that it is David's lack of attention to affairs in his own household that leads to another murder, one among his own sons. The remarks by Jonadab suggest that Absalom's determination to get revenge on Amnon was well known within the court. David therefore quite needlessly puts his own family at risk in this longstanding feud between brothers. It is also clear that Amnon, as the crown prince, is the leader of the delegation of royal sons in place of his father. His personal behavior is symptomatic of the rot within the court, and this is only made more evident when a rival son, Absalom, can make his own henchmen carry out the murder of the crown prince on his orders. Once David comes to

---

50. Feasts such as this are a common motif in sagas and often the occasion of violence.

terms with Amnon's death, his affections shift to the absent Absalom, who becomes the next contender for the throne, passing over Chileab, son of Abigail, David's second son, about whom nothing more is heard.

The change in David's affections toward Absalom leads to the extended narrative about Absalom's recall from exile and his restoration to a place of privilege within David's court (2 Sam 14). In this, Joab plays a major role, but the obvious question that arises is what does he have to gain by getting involved in this affair? Given the prior appearances of Joab in the narrative, we are well aware of his astute and Machiavellian character. If Absalom is now David's favorite and if Joab can bring about his restoration, then, as the likely heir to the throne, Absalom will be under some future obligation to Joab. In any event, Joab is seen as a powerful manipulator of policy in the court and of David's actions and decisions in particular. The method that Joab uses to persuade the king is to resort to the services of a wise woman of Tekoa. Joab instructs the woman as to what he wants her to do and "puts the words into her mouth" (vv. 2–3), but we are probably to assume that the skilful presentation is hers. Throughout the extended dialogue between the woman and the king there are numerous parallels to and reminiscences of other biblical texts. First, the story that the woman invents is similar to the story told by Nathan in extracting from David a self-judgment in 2 Sam 12:1–6, with just enough similarity to David's own situation to make him take action regarding Absalom. Second, the woman's behavior in her approach to the king is very similar to that of Abigail, with a number of verbal correspondences.[51] Third, in her story, the fratricide that takes place in the open field is similar to Cain's murder of Abel, which suggests dependence on this source. Thus, the scene is built into the fabric of the larger narrative, with the intent of expanding on the character of David and his role in the rule of his people.

The story of fratricide that the woman invents has a rather obvious weakness in that she and her husband have only two children, whereas the king has many children, and therefore the death of the murderer would not result in the same dilemma of leaving no heir. Yet she gives the story in this form in order to accomplish two purposes. First, when she extracts from the king a perfunctory judgment that he will deal with her situation, she wants the additional assurance of complete immunity from any reprisals for speaking out, and she wants her son also to be safe. Second, she moves on to the more dangerous ground of drawing a parallel to the king's situa-

---

51. See above, pp. 187–188.

tion of his son's banishment. She forces the analogy between the two stories by making the demand that of the general populous, which is clearly not the case, and by suggesting that it is the will of the deity to have Absalom return. Here, she comes very close to acting in the role of a prophetess, but using wisdom and ratiocination instead of prophetic oracle. She then flatters David by suggesting that he has the angelic power to discern right from wrong, which we know to be hardly the case.

By this time, David has finally understood that someone else is behind this attempt to persuade him to restore Absalom and demands that the woman tell him who it is. She again flatters his perception and tells him that it is Joab. This constant insistence on David's divine wisdom is the clearest evidence that the woman "doth protest too much." David is, in fact, quite stupid and quite unjust in his actions. For David to refuse the woman's request and seriously engage her argument would be to reject her flattery. He is easily persuaded because he longs for Absalom's return, and the woman has given David an excuse to bring him back. Joab is then permitted to go and fetch Absalom, but David still hesitates to be completely reconciled to him, so Absalom must dwell in his own house without an audience. This half-hearted attempt at reconciliation only allows matters to fester. After two years, Absalom finally forces a showdown by provoking Joab into arranging an audience with the king, and he demands either that the king act according to the rule of law and take his life or accept him back. When he does come before the king, David is unable to do the former and receives him back with a kiss.

At this point, it would be useful to make a comparison between the household of David and the treatment of the household of Eli by Dtr. The sons of Eli are portrayed as immoral persons who abused their office as priests by their greed and sexual impropriety (1 Sam 2). Not only they were condemned but also the whole of the *house of Eli*, which means the line of priestly succession, even though Eli himself does nothing wrong. It is enough that he did not discipline his sons and so brought the institution of the temple cultus into disrepute. The pattern of divine rejection of Eli's house is the same as that used by Dtr for the later Israelite kings.[52] Thus, one would have expected a similar judgment on David for the sins of his two sons, Amnon and Absalom—one for rape and the other for murder. The portrayal of David as overly indulgent toward his bad offspring puts him in the same class with Eli and makes him equally culpable. Therefore, it is

---

52. See my *In Search of History*, 341–53, esp. p. 351.

quite clear that Dtr could not have known or made use of the *David Saga* or made additions to it without committing the most flagrant inconsistencies and producing a totally incoherent history of the monarchy as a whole. To permit this sort of inconsistency and incoherence within a literary work is to give up all hope of doing literary criticism.[53]

The Revolt of Absalom

Most commentators, having accepted an early date for the so-called Succession Narrative, are concerned with trying to uncover, within the story of Absalom's revolt, the underlying causes of the civil war. That there was a civil war led by David's son and pretender to the throne is taken as a historical fact, but the reasons given in the biblical account embedded in the personal affairs of the royal family or in the personality of Absalom are viewed with skepticism.[54] Nor does it seem reasonable that the whole of Israel and Judah should support Absalom while only David's personal guard in Jerusalem are supporters of the king, and yet the latter prevail over all of the others in a single battle. Consequently, a distinction is made between the event itself and a propagandistic presentation of the event by a supporter of David to put the latter in a more positive light. Thus, McKenzie asserts:

> While the outline of the story may be basically historical, the stress on David's gentleness is apologetic. It was designed to counter charges that he maintained ruthless control over his kingdom even to the point of killing his own sons. Violent deeds are consistently blamed on the "sons of Zeruiah," who are just too rough for gentle David. A modern historian evaluating these stories will doubt that a man with David's political savvy and longevity was quite so gentle with his enemies as the writer describes.[55]

---

53. To offset this contrast between CH and the DtrH, Gordon ("In Search of David," 290) points to an instance in DtrH in which David is less than perfect, namely, the episode in 1 Sam 21 in which David deceives Ahimelech, the priest of Nob, into giving him assistance. This in turn leads to the massacre of the priests by Saul. This is an important point. David's behavior in the earlier episodes in the story of David has been dealt with above (pp. 172–173) where it has been shown that they belong to the same source as episodes in the *David Saga*. Gordon further imputes to me the view (p. 291) that 2 Sam 21–24 belongs to DtrH, though I have never expressed this view, and then argues that David's behavior in this "appendix" is as problematic as in the *David Saga* (CH). However, within the texts usually ascribed to DtrH, he can find little to match the moral turpitude of David and his family in CH.

54. McCarter, *II Samuel*, 357–59, with earlier literature cited there.

55. McKenzie, *King David*, 165.

This view allows one to read the narrative "against the grain" as a political apology. As I have argued in the introduction to this volume, the *David Saga* is a late Persian literary work with no basis in any historical event, and it is therefore certainly not "apologetic." We have only the David that the author presents to us and the events as he chooses to create them, nothing else. Furthermore, as we shall see below, the adjective "gentle" is hardly the most appropriate description of David's actions in the episode.

The narrator tells us that, after Absalom is reconciled to his father David, he acquires a chariot and a personal guard of 50 men. This is the regalia of a crown prince.[56] What we have presented to us is not the portrait of a primitive Judean monarchy but something that more closely resembles the Persian court, in which the eldest surviving son was presumed to be the heir and was given royal status and prerogatives, second only to the king.[57] The narrator indicates that Absalom was not content with this exalted status but deliberately encouraged dissention throughout the tribes of Israel, based on grievances regarding the execution of justice and the courts to deal with claims and disputes. Absalom makes the charge that the king has deputized no one to take responsibility for social justice, and the narrator says nothing to dispute this charge. It is again a mockery of Dtr's presentation that David "administered justice and equity to all his people" (2 Sam 8:15). It was this grave social evil within the monarchy, as well as his pretense of accessibility, that allowed Absalom to win the favor of the common citizens. Like David, the Persian monarchs were also known for being inaccessible to the common people.

Absalom makes his move with the pretext of fulfilling a vow to sacrifice in Hebron, a request that David can hardly refuse. He sends messengers to all parts of Israel that he has won over and collects his supporters to Hebron, including the all-important royal counselor, Ahithophel. The insurrection is initially successful, with large numbers coming to his side. The ploy of using the need to offer a sacrifice to Yahweh in a location distant from the capital as the basis of political subversion seems to imitate Samuel's trip to Bethlehem to anoint David as the future king in 1 Sam 16:1–13.

---

56. It is quite misleading to suggest that the chariot and runners mean that Absalom has already assumed the role of a king; so McCarter, *II Samuel*, 356. While kings and tyrants certainly had bodyguards, the crown prince also had royal prerogatives commensurate with his position.

57. See A. T. Olmstead, *The History of the Persian Empire*, 214–20 ("Xerxes as Crown Prince"); J. M. Cook, *The Persian Empire*, 132–46 ("King and Court").

David also used a similar religious obligation as a pretext to explain his absence from Saul's court, but Saul was not so easily fooled (1 Sam 20:5–6, 28–31). The location of Hebron, as the heartland of Judah, is also significant as the place in which David himself was anointed as king of both Judah and Israel, and the narrator's choice of the location is deliberately ironic. It is here that all Israel anoints Absalom as king in place of David (cf. 2 Sam 19:10).

A messenger brings to David a report of the conspiracy, and the extent of the unrest clearly dictates flight from the capital. Given the urgency, one would expect this retreat to be reported quickly, but the narrative of David's flight is greatly prolonged, so that the whole process moves at a snail's pace with frequent interruptions. This allows the narrator to present a number of different scenes that reflect on the character of David and his reign. The first group to be mentioned is his household, including the families of his sons and daughters and all their servants, a very large group. But none of the other sons are mentioned by name, and they play no role in the whole account of the revolt. However, 10 concubines are considered expendable and left behind in charge of the palace, which seems rather foolish, as subsequent events prove. After this large group has moved out of the city, all of the military also passes by the king in review. Included within the military are "his servants," which presumably refers to the professional army, as well as the Greek mercenaries, the Cretans and the peltasts. In addition to these regulars are a distinct group of 600 mercenaries from Gath. As I have indicated above, mercenaries play an important role in David's army, and the Greek mercenaries, the Cretans and peltasts, appear here in the story for the first time. This reflects the late date for the whole account of the revolt.

The Philistine mercenaries from Gath, however, call for special attention. The text in 2 Sam 15:18 has become somewhat defective in the MT, and the Greek text does not offer much help.[58] The Hebrew text reads "And all the Gittites, six hundred men, who came in his entourage (ברגלוי) from Gath," and McCarter,[59] along with others, wants to interpret this to mean that the Gittites had originally joined David when he was a mercenary in Gath. This, however, goes against the general sense of the text and the former account of David's activity there. In 1 Sam 27, it is clear that David's

---

58. See Driver, *Notes to Samuel*, 312–13; also Hertzberg, *I and II Samuel*, 338 note g; cf. McCarter, *II Samuel*, 363–64.

59. McCarter, *II Samuel*, 370.

men were not Philistines, nor had they any connection with Gath, because persons such as these would betray his activities to the king as disloyal. The phrase "in his entourage" (ברגלוי) is used in the earlier part of the text and refers to David's larger entourage that included the Cretans and peltasts. It is quite likely, as Driver suggests, that the name of Itti the Gittite has fallen out of the text before the reference to "the Gittites," so that the suffix in ברגלוי refers to Ittai's entourage, not David's. This would agree with the fact that Ittai and his men had only recently come from Gath to join David (v. 20). So it is this Philistine mercenary leader and his 600 men who now appear in review before David.

This appearance of a band of 600 Philistine mercenaries sets up an interesting little vignette between David and Ittai (2 Sam 15:19–23). As I suggested above, it is no accident that this scene presents a close parallel between David and Ittai, only now it is Ittai and his 600 men from Gath who are serving as mercenaries under David instead of David and his 600 men who served as mercenaries under the king of Gath. Ittai is described as a foreigner and an exile who has been residing in Jerusalem with his men and their families. But why is he an exile from Gath? No explanation is given. There seems to be an obvious intent by the narrator to make Ittai's situation as close a parallel as possible to that of David, the mercenary. David raises the question about whether he should accompany him, because he has come into David's employment so recently, and David suggests that he should return and stay "with the king" (v. 19). If the intent is that his mercenary force is to join Absalom, then it appears almost suicidal on David's part. The reference to "the king" could hardly refer to Achish of Gath, because he is described as an exile from his homeland. It may be that this is just a way for David to test Ittai's loyalty and provoke a solemn oath from him. Ittai persuades David of his loyalty, that he will not change sides, and gives him an oath, which, as we have seen, is common in the case of arrangements between mercenaries and their royal employers. Ittai is then permitted to go with the rest of the entourage. This scene is remarkably similar to the military review before a battle between the Philistines and Israel in 1 Sam 29, in which a question is raised about David's loyalty. In his case, he is not permitted to go with the king of Gath. It seems clear that the later episode in the *David Saga* has been constructed in imitation of the earlier one, and both belong to the same source. Once David accepts Ittai and his men into his entourage, then the whole company, along with their families, also becomes part of the larger force and baggage train, so typical of mercenary armies.

The implied comparison between the Philistine mercenary Ittai and David as mercenary to the Philistines is transparent. As we saw earlier, David,
for all his protestations of loyalty to Achish in the face of suspicion by
other Philistine leaders, is quite untrustworthy, whereas Ittai the Philistine
is true to his vows and entirely loyal, and he receives a major position of
command alongside the sons of Zeruiah as their equal. Furthermore, it is
not this Philistine but Joab who violates the king's instructions regarding
Absalom, which were issued to the three commanders together. The Philistine Ittai even makes an oath to David in the name of Yahweh and not in
the name of one of his own gods. Thus, the foreign mercenaries, both the
Greeks and the Philistines, form a major part of David's army and are
largely responsible for saving his skin.

After this lengthy review of the troops by David, the people and the king
are in the act of crossing the brook Kidron (2 Sam 15:23), when who shows
up a little late but the two priests Abiathar and Zadok "with all the Levites,
bearing the ark of the Covenant of God. Then they set down the ark until
all the people passed over [Kidron] from the city" (v. 24). After the people
have crossed the stream, the two priests are told by David to return and to
take the ark back to Jerusalem. Of course, the mention of the Levites carrying the ark looks Deuteronomistic, and so it is attributed to a redactor. The
whole scene is reminiscent of the crossing of the Jordan and repeats almost
verbatim the phrase "as soon as all the people had passed over" (Josh
4:11). In this case, the assistance of the ark to help the people cross the
Kidron is imitation that borders on a monstrous parody of the conquest
theme. Instead of standing in the river bearing the ark while the people
pass over, the Levites set the ark down as though it were a burden. The
crossing of the Kidron is hardly the threat that the Jordan in flood is seen
to be in DtrH. Then, instead of the ark going before the people as a form of
divine guidance, it is returned with the two priests to its place.[60] David's
flight with all his foreign mercenaries is the reversal of Joshua's grand entrance into the land.

David now proceeds at a snail's pace up the Mount of Olives, as though
in a funeral cortege, with all the people following his rather pathetic lead
(2 Sam 15:30–31). He receives the news that the most revered counselor

---

60. The reference to נוהו, "its/his abode" (v. 25), is late usage for either the
temple or the holy city of Jerusalem (cf. Ps 79:7). This goes closely with the references to two distinct classes of priests, the priests and the Levites, which is clearly
post-Dtr.

Ahithophel has joined the conspiracy,[61] and he utters a desperate prayer: "O Yahweh, I pray, turn Ahithophel's counsel into foolishness" (v. 31). When David reaches the summit of the Mount of Olives "where one offers worship to God,"[62] he suddenly encounters Hushai the Archite as though in answer to his prayer. Hushai's appearance with torn garments and earth on his head immediately identifies him as sympathizing with the king, and this inspires a plan to overturn any advice that Ahithophel may offer to Absalom. At the same time, he can communicate through the sons of the two priests, Zadok and Abiathar, acting as spies, what is going on in the palace and any plans that Absalom may make. So Hushai returns to Jerusalem, "just as Absalom is entering the city." Absalom and his supporters have traveled all the way from Hebron, while David and his entourage have barely gotten beyond the crest of the Mount of Olives.

The next two episodes return to the theme of David's relations with the house of Saul. The first deals with David's encounter with Ziba (2 Sam 16:1–4) and the second with Shimei. These we have discussed earlier in connection with David's treatment of Mephibosheth, and my remarks need not be repeated here. Nevertheless, we must stop at this point and reflect on the temporal and special markers in the text. The first incident with Ziba takes place just beyond the summit of the Mount of Olives and the second with Shimei a short distance beyond that point in the descent to the Jordan. It should be obvious that these indications of time and place have nothing to do with the reality of the situation they describe and delimit, because if Absalom is just entering Jerusalem from the south with all his people, then someone in his party would certainly be aware of the fact that a very large group is on the move out of the city to the east. And why would David and all his entourage have made the totally unnecessary ascent up the mount in the first place, when they are in flight, and the most obvious route to the Jordan is on the valley road around the south end of the Mount of Olives. These temporal and special markers form a purely literary structure in which to place the individual scenes. It is as though the narrator is standing on the summit of the Mount of Olives and can witness the drama of

---

61. It is possible that the narrator is aware of the reference in the list of David's heroes to Ahithophel's being the father of Eliam (2 Sam 23:34), which would make him the grandfather of Bathsheba and add to the irony of the situation. But about this we cannot be sure.

62. This is a rather remarkable statement for a post-Dtr writer, who suggests that the unorthodox practice of worshiping the deity on hilltops was common in David's day.

Absalom's entering Jerusalem from the south at the same time that David is descending out of sight to the east. The two scenes with Ziba and Shimei that follow fill the space between the Mount of Olives and the Jordan River. After this, the narrator turns his attention, and ours, back to Absalom and his grand entrance into Jerusalem, and makes the interconnection between the two in the figure of Hushai. Thus begins the deadly contest between Ahithophel and Hushai.[63]

Before the central drama unfolds, in which the counsels of the two royal advisors are pitted against each other, we have two short vignettes. In the first, Hushai, David's friend, must win Absalom's confidence that he has indeed defected from David and will faithfully serve his son (2 Sam 16:16-19). In the second scene, Ahithophel gives advice to Absalom that he is to make a public display of having sex with the 10 concubines of David that had foolishly been sent by him to keep the palace. The purpose is not to strengthen Absalom's claim to the throne by taking his father's wives, as many commentators suggest, but to make the breach between David and his son irreparable and thereby strengthen his cause against his father's rule. Of course, the scene is intended to make a strong link back to the actions of David in the Bathsheba affair, even to the point of having Absalom's actions take place on the roof of the palace as a parallel to David's viewing Bathsheba from the same roof.[64] In rather ironic fashion, the narrator states that both David and Absalom regarded the advice of Ahithophel as comparable to the word of God. Such wise counselors have replaced the prophets and oracles within the realm in directing affairs of state.[65] This action also sets the scene for what follows in the contest between Ahithophel and Hushai.

The characterization of the advice offered by the two counselors is a brilliant piece of wisdom narrative and illustrates the difference between wise counsel and foolish flattery. The advice of Ahithophel is clear and decisive,

---

63. Again, one may note in the sagas the role of wisdom and the speeches of wise men as they play out in disputes between feuding parties.

64. It is not clear when the actions of Absalom regarding the concubines take place because the advice that Ahithophel offers in 2 Sam 17:1-4 is presented as a continuation of the previous advice and calls for immediate action while David is still in flight. But as we have seen, space and time are not of primary concern in the writer's construction of the narrative.

65. In Herodotus, the role of advice from wise counselors, as well as omens, plays an important role in his narrative. See R. Lattimore, "The Wise Adviser in Herodotus," *Classical Philology* 34 (1939): 24-35.

and it fits the situation precisely. David is in flight with a burdensome entourage of dependents and thus most vulnerable to attack. A select force of 12,000 would easily throw the whole of David's company into a panic, and panic is what wins battles. His description of David's condition as weary and discouraged fits exactly what has been given in the preceding narrative. Ahithophel intends to kill only David and so avoid needless escalation of the war and a quiet unification of the land under Absalom's rule. He uses only one simple simile to make his point of national unity and harmony. The fact is that with David dead the large mercenary force would be immediately unemployed and would either come to terms with the new ruler or would have to seek employment elsewhere.

Hushai counters this proposal by immediately disparaging Ahithophel's advice; *this time* it is not good. He then completely distracts Absalom's attention from the facts of the situation. He emphasizes the known expertise of David and his elite forces in military matters and how they are enraged and ready for a fight and that David would have taken every precaution not to camp with the people. We know that this description of David's present situation, whatever his past achievements might have been, is quite false. He pictures the first attack as favoring David and Absalom's forces suffering the first panic and rout, constantly harping on David's military prowess. Hushai proposes instead the enlistment of a massive army led personally by Absalom, who has no proven military competence and who would be most vulnerable in a battle. Such a large army of conscripts with so little experience against battle-hardened and expert soldiers is a counsel of disaster, and Ahithophel knows it. But Absalom is won over by the long, flowery speech, full of similes and flattery, with Absalom at the head of a great victorious army doing what conquering kings do to their enemies, so that he loses sight of the real objective as laid out by Ahithophel: peace and unity.

To understand the full significance of the presentation of this contest, it is necessary to compare it with the account of the northern tribes' defection from Rehoboam in 1 Kgs 12:1–20. A number of recent studies have suggested that the theological statement in 2 Sam 17:14b, "For Yahweh had ordained to frustrate the good counsel of Ahitophel in order that Yahweh might bring ruin upon Absalom," is part of a secondary revision of the account of Absalom's revolt, perhaps by the hand of Dtr. This view is contrary to the earlier opinion of von Rad, who saw it as integral to the whole narrative and fundamental to the author's outlook.[66] Little attention, however,

---

66. Von Rad, "Historical Writing in Ancient Israel," 199–202.

has been given to the fact that both this text itself and its larger context bear a close resemblance to 1 Kgs 12:15, "For it was a turn of affairs brought about by Yahweh that he might fulfill his word, which he spoke by Ahijah the Shilonite to Jeroboam the son of Nebat," in a similar narrative setting. In both stories in which the remark is embedded, we have situations of rebellion or threatened rebellion. In both cases, advice is sought from the previous king's senior advisors, whose views are crucial to the outcome. In both cases, the young king chooses the wrong advice, which is based on flattery rather than sound judgment, and finally in both the royal decision is attributed to divine intervention. In my judgment, there can be little doubt that a direct literary relationship exists between the two stories.

Once this general similarity is recognized, then the differences in the treatment of the counseling motif and ideological perspectives become significant. To begin with, the statement in 1 Kgs 12:15 suggests that divine intervention brought about the whole situation as a fulfillment of Ahijah's prophecy, which in turn is related to DtrH's larger historiographic scheme. In 2 Sam 17:14, however, the matter is entirely different. Divine intervention is not related to prophecy or to a scheme outside the story itself but clearly refers back to the scene in 15:31 in which David receives the news about Ahithophel's defection, which leads to his cry of desperation: "Please make foolish Ahithophel's advice, O Yahweh, my God." Immediately following this, David encounters Hushai at the place where God is worshiped and sends him on a mission to "frustrate" the counsel of Ahithophel. It is Hushai's brilliant achievement of persuading Absalom to take bad advice that is seen as the culmination of divine activity. This divine activity is seen precisely in subverting the "good" advice of Ahithophel, whose word is regarded as the "word of God" (16:23). But "good" here is not what Dtr would call "good in the eyes of Yahweh"; it is good because it is the kind of advice that would produce successful results. And it is the word of God not because it reflects the will of God as in prophecy but because its quality of pragmatic wisdom is godlike.[67] By contrast, the advice of the elder statesmen in 1 Kgs 12 is good both morally and pragmatically, and it is this advice that Rehoboam rejects even before he listens to the folly of the younger men.

Furthermore, the rather simple motif in 1 Kgs 12 of good advice by the older counselors being rejected in favor of the bad advice by the young foolish contemporaries of the king is made by the *David Saga* into a very subtle and much more elaborate narrative. Now it is a contest between two

---

67. See also 2 Sam 14:17, 20.

of the older king's counselors, one who offers good advice and the other who deliberately subverts that good (though morally bad) advice by persuading Absalom to act foolishly. The author has skillfully produced a narrative that is a mirror image of that of DtrH. In the *David Saga*, God defeats the "good" advice and the "word of God" in order to save the throne of David from this revolt by all the men of Israel.

If we now ask about the relationship of the two stories to each other, it seems to me clear that the story in the *David Saga* is later than and dependent on DtrH, for the following reasons. First, the much more complex and subtle development of the counseling motif in the *David Saga* could hardly be reduced to the simple form that we have in DtrH. Second, the recognition of divine intervention in the particular coincidence of circumstances and as answer to prayer is not a feature of DtrH, but it is a mark of the Yahwist in Gen 24, increasingly regarded as a late text. Third, in the rebellion of Sheba in 2 Sam 20, the sequel to the Absalom rebellion, there is the rallying cry "We have no portion in David and we have no inheritance in the son of Jesse; everyman to his tents, O Israel" (2 Sam 20:1). This is an almost verbatim quotation taken from 1 Kgs 12:16, where it appears in very similar circumstances in the revolt against the rule of Rehoboam. Finally, given the other numerous examples of literary dependence by the *David Saga* on the Dtr corpus, the probability of literary dependence in this case also is very high.

Once Hushai knows that he has won the contest of wits, he sends word by the two messengers, the sons of the priests, indicating what both Ahithophel and he had advised and warned David to take due precaution and cross the Jordan River before any preemptive attack could be made. The account of how the two messengers escape from pursuers by being hidden in a well while a woman sends Absalom's men in the wrong direction is an imitation of a similar episode in the story of the spies in Jericho in Josh 2. The messengers reach David and persuade him to take action, so during the night all the people are safely transported across the river. This finally gives them a line of defense against sudden attack such as that suggested by Ahithophel. They then proceed to Mahanaim, where they can set up camp, regroup, and allow some form of protection for all of the dependents that have come with them. In the meantime, Ahithophel sees that his advice was not followed and discerns what the consequences will be, so he returns to his home and commits suicide.

At the same time that David is setting up his base camp at Mahanaim, Absalom is now crossing the Jordan with the full army of Israel, and he sets

up his camp in Gilead (2 Sam 17:24-26). At its head, Absalom has appointed Amasa in place of Joab, who was David's commander of the conscripts. The author thus makes it clear that there is a rivalry between these
two, just as there was between Abner and Joab, and this anticipates the
working out of this rivalry at the end of the revolt. The narrator now engages in an aside that details the pedigree of Amasa and his relationship to
that of Joab. What is remarkable is that they are actually cousins, and both
are grandsons of the notorious Nahash, the Ammonite king.[68] Because
Amasa's father is not an Israelite[69] but an Ishmaelite, he is not even Judean
or Israelite! Zeruiah is identified as Joab's *mother*, a daughter of Nahash,
but what is curious about this is that his father's name is not given and
Joab and his brothers are always known as the "sons of Zeruiah." One
would certainly expect a designation such as this to refer to the father and
not the mother. By contrast, Amasa is otherwise referred to as "Amasa, son
of Jether" (his father) not "son of Abigal" (his mother).[70] Consequently, the
narrator has taken some liberties with the designation "sons of Zeruiah,"
because he may have found it in his sources of David's heroes. The pedi-
grees of these leaders would also suggest that the origin of the military
leaders under David both before he became king and during his reign, as
well as under Absalom and Solomon, were all as foreign mercenaries.

While David is in Mahanaim, he receives material support from three
leaders of the region (2 Sam 17:27-28). The first is Shobi son of Nahash,
who is probably to be understood as a vassal king in place of his brother
Hanun (2 Sam 10:1-5) and who has restored good relations with David;
the second is Machir son of Ammiel from Lodebar, who earlier sheltered
Mephibosheth (2 Sam 9:4-5); and the third is Barzillai the Gileadite, in
whose region Absalom is now encamped. This last one will appear again at

---

68. This seems to be confirmed by the reference to Nahash the Ammonite in the
following unit (v. 27). Nahash is viewed as an older contemporary of David, yet
Joab and Abishai, his grandsons, are David's contemporaries who have been with
him since the start of his military career. The narrator, however, is not concerned
about these chronological niceties. Similar genealogical notes are likewise scattered
throughout the sagas and play an important role in the narrative.

69. This is an obvious scribal correction, as seems clear from the parallel in
1 Chr 2:17.

70. Some scholars want to follow 1 Chr 2:13-17 and make Jesse the father of
Abigal and Zeruiah in place of Nahash, but this is clearly a "correction" on the part
of the Chronicler. It is difficult to explain why a scribe would substitute Nahash for
Jesse.

the end of the war to receive the king's gratitude for his support (2 Sam 19:31–40). These three leaders bring provisions for all the people in David's entourage, which is always a problem for a large military force on the move. The episode also has the literary function of making interconnections with other literary units both before and after, which is so characteristic of this writer.

David's Victory and the Death of Absalom

The account of the battle and its aftermath is given in 2 Sam 18. David reviews the troops and appoints the senior officers, with Joab, Abishai, and Ittai the Philistine sharing command of the forces with equal rank. David offers to go out with the troops, but this is a foolish gesture and he is persuaded not to do so. Once the king is struck down, then the battle would be lost and the largely mercenary force would have nothing more for which to fight, and they would be dispersed or defect to the enemy. David, of course, fears for the fate of Absalom for precisely the same reason, that is, that the professional commanders would seek to kill Absalom quickly to end the revolt, and this is why he wants to be in direct command to prevent harm coming to his son. However, because, in this narrator's view, David has not led his troops into battle since he became king but always left it to the commanders to do his fighting for him, he is in a very weak position to change that practice now. All he can do is place his generals under a public order to be lenient toward Absalom for his sake.

The description of the battle is very brief and completely confused, with the result that there is little point in trying to make some logistic or strategic sense of it. Battles are not fought in forests, and at any rate there was no "forest of Ephraim" in the Transjordan region. If it is meant to correspond to the region of Gilead, then the rugged slopes that rise up from the Jordan valley that are covered with brush cannot possibly serve as a battle field, though they may provide some cover to those fleeing from battle in the open. But pursuit into a region such as this is as dangerous for the pursuer as the pursued. This makes the body count of 20,000 under these circumstances a completely artificial figure with no connection to reality. The disaster for Absalom's forces is undoubtedly intended to contrast with the projected result of Ahithophel's scheme of a sudden attack in which David alone would be killed and there would be minimum loss of life.

What follows now is a description of the death of Absalom during the battle in the forest. There are a number of obscure aspects to the details of the account that make unclear exactly what the narrator intends to portray in this event. Contrary to popular assumption, there is no indication that Absalom was in flight when the accident happened, because the fighting took place in the woods. It is also assumed that it was Absalom's hair that was caught in the branches of the tree, based on the description of his massive head of hair in 2 Sam 14:26, but the text itself does not make the connection specifically. It is enough to understand from the description that through an unusual accident Absalom found himself defenseless, abandoned, and at the mercy of his foes. Against the command of David, which was common knowledge to all, Joab stabbed Absalom in the heart with three darts, and then Joab's armor-bearers gave him the coups de grace. This ended any further reason for fighting, and Joab blew the trumpet to end the conflict.[71]

The remarks about Absalom's burial are also curious because the spot where he is buried in a large pit is in the middle of a forest and it is marked by a large cairn of stones as a memorial to the decisive battle.[72] However, neither the location of the battle nor the memorial seems appropriate *in the middle of a forest.* This sort of memorial is hardly accessible to public view. By contrast, Absalom had set up for himself a pillar in the Valley of the Kings and designated it as Absalom's stele, which the narrator says survives "to this day." This reference to some object as witness to a past event is a technique often used by earlier biblical writers, including Dtr, to heighten the verisimilitude of the narrative. Its use, however, betrays the fact that the account was written long after an event in the distant past. Memorializing of this sort is entirely literary and is therefore a fiction like the rest of the account. Any number of standing stones in the region could serve the purpose in the minds of later readers of the story. The remark that Absalom erected this memorial because he had no son seems to contradict the statement in 2 Sam 14:27 in which it is said that he had three sons. The "error" in either the one or the other passage is often attributed to a "redactor," as though editors are more prone to mistakes and corruptions of the text than authors.

After the digression that deals with the burial of Absalom and the remarks about his earlier memorial, the narrative takes up again in 18:19

---

71. Joab's blowing the shofar to end hostilities is a common motif in the *David Saga.* See also 2 Sam 2:28, 20:22. It is never used in this way in Dtr.

72. It is also a typical feature of sagas to mark a decisive victory with a memorial on the spot where the opposing leader or villain was killed.

where it left off in v. 16. The motif of the messenger who brings news from the battle front is greatly elaborated here (2 Sam 18:19–19:1). Ahimaaz son of Zadok, whom we know from earlier in the story as a trusted messenger of the king (2 Sam 15:36, 17:17–21), appeals to Joab to bear the message of victory to the king, but Joab is concerned about what he will say about the death of Absalom, and so he sends a Cushite runner to break the news to David.[73] Once he is sent, then Ahimaaz repeats his request to run to inform the king, and because Joab assumes that the Cushite runner will easily arrive ahead of Ahimaaz, he permits him to go. Ahimaaz, however, chooses the better route and is able to overtake the Cushite and arrive first.

The contest between the messengers is viewed from the perspective of David waiting at the city gate with a watchman posted on the roof as lookout (18:24–27). The scene is reminiscent of a scene in the story of Eli in 1 Sam 4:12–18 in which Eli is also sitting by the gate to receive word of the battle. Eli is blind and so he needs the help of another to see for him what is going on. The narrator in the David story is imitating this episode but uses two messengers that come to David directly, whereas in the Eli story the messenger brings the bad news to the city and it is only a second person who comes to inform Eli. In the case of the defeat at the hands of the Philistines, the news is all bad, of both the death of the two sons and the capture of the ark, and this results in Eli's death. The result of the victory over Absalom is both good news of the military victory and bad news of the death of Absalom, David's favorite son. As we have seen above, it is the style of this author to take up a motif in an earlier narrative and develop it with greater artistic subtlety.

The two messengers present two different accounts of the events (2 Sam 18:28–32). The purpose of the first messenger to arrive, Ahimaaz, is to prepare David for the shock of the bad news. He brings the good news of the victory first, but David does not celebrate until he has heard about Absalom. Here, Ahimaaz tries to shelter David by pretending that he had not seen what actually happened, only that something was wrong. Thus, he allows the Cushite to finally deliver the bad news, that Absalom has been killed. The Cushite takes the attitude of his superior Joab, that the death of Absalom is a great benefit, although he does not disclose Joab's direct hand in the matter. Instead of a victory celebration, David retreats to a room in the

---

73. See the remarks by Redford on Cushite runners as military messengers (*Egypt, Canaan, and Israel,* 305–6). Note also the use of coinage in 18:11–12. Both are obvious anachronisms.

gate tower to engage in prolonged mourning for his son Absalom (2 Sam 19:1-9[18:33-19:8]).

What are we to make of this "tenderness" of David toward his son's death? A number of scholars have adopted the view that, because in their opinion the so-called Succession Narrative is an apology for David's rule, the point of the account must be to exonerate David from any responsibility in the death of his son Absalom and to lay the blame entirely on Joab. Thus, McCarter states:

> It is clear that the narrator is working very hard here to show his audience that David was not responsible for the death of Abishalom. As always in chaps. 13-20, David appears as a gentle man and loving father, referring to his murderous rebel son—whom he knows to be seeking his life (16:11)—with obvious affection as "young Abishalom." . . . His order of protection for Abishalom is reported so pointedly (18:5) and repeated so specifically (18:12) that we cannot doubt it is regarded by the narrator as of primary importance. The narrator is attempting to evoke sympathy for David, probably addressing himself to former supporters of Abishalom's cause in the aftermath of the revolt. David loved Abishalom, says the narrator. Abishalom's killing was not David's doing. . . . It was Joab, acting independently and in deliberate violation of his orders, who had the young man put to death. If Joab did so on the basis of a careful appraisal of the situation and fear of the long-range political consequences of sparing Abishalom's life, we are not told this. . . . He is important because the audience's acquaintance with his behavior will exonerate David. When the audience has been made aware of what actually took place on the day of the battle in the Forest of Ephraim, they will understand that David is not to be blamed for Abishalom's death and, therefore, that he has not forfeited his claim on the loyalty of those Israelites who followed Abishalom.[74]

I have quoted this position at length because it is still followed by many and because nothing could be further from the intentions of the author as reflected in the text. As I have argued throughout this analysis, this narrative of the revolt is not an apology that is addressed to an audience contemporary with the events; instead it is a fiction meant to portray a hopelessly dysfunctional monarchy that is torn apart by civil war and rebellion within the royal house itself.

Throughout the whole account of the revolt, the narrator makes it quite clear what his view is of David in this situation. First, David allows Absalom

---

74. McCarter, *II Samuel*, 410.

to return from exile without dealing seriously with the issue of the murder of his brother. The whole matter is treated as beyond the issue of the courts, and any system of justice and is reduced to a matter of David's personal relationship with his son. In the restitution of Absalom, David is easily manipulated by Joab. Once Absalom is reinstalled within the royal household, he assumes the role of crown prince without David's designating him as such or practicing any supervision or control of his most ambitious son. What happens as a result is blamed on David's obsessive love for Absalom, the heir apparent to the exclusion of all the rest of his sons and family in much the same way that David indulged his firstborn, Amnon. David's complete neglect of a system of justice and proper jurisprudence in the land, in violation of the principles of Deuteronomy, gives to Absalom the opportunity to foment a revolt against the crown. Absalom has support not only among the common citizenry of Israel and Judah—his revolt begins in Hebron, the heartland of Judah—but also among the military leaders, such as Amasa, and the foremost of David's senior counselors, Ahithophel. All of this completely contradicts the presentation of Dtr that David is a shepherd of his people, beloved by all Israel and Judah and all his servants, and that he reigns with justice and equity.

When David is forced to flee before Absalom, he does so reluctantly, and even though he speaks of leaving Jerusalem in haste, the whole procession moves out of the city and toward the Jordan at an incredibly slow pace, without any real sense of urgency or leadership. David acknowledges Absalom as already being king and even seems to offer him aid by encouraging Ittai to stay behind in Jerusalem and join him. He seems to show little concern for his family by deliberately leaving 10 of his many concubines behind in Jerusalem and putting them at great risk. He is rescued by Hushai, his friend, whom Absalom is a fool to trust. But it is also clear from Hushai's speech that what he says David will do, because David is an expert military leader and will not spend the night with his people but will lead his troops against any assault by Ahithophel. David, however, does not do this and must be warned of possible attack and to take the necessary precautions. David is easily persuaded against leading the troops in battle, and his total preoccupation with his concern for Absalom makes him a major liability. Thus, David's forces are victorious in spite of him, and all he can do is lament Absalom's death with no regard for all those who have risked their lives for him.

The narrator speaks most directly to David's behavior and his self-indulgent mourning for Absalom in the speech of Joab, who tells it as it is.

David's grieving for Absalom has turned victory into defeat and has shown
no gratitude or love toward those who have saved him and his large family
of sons, daughters, wives, and concubines. If David persists in this self-
absorbed grief, he will loose all of his support and it will be worse for him
that ever before. This threat seems to pull David out of his stupor, but he
does little more that make a public appearance, the most minimal gesture.
David's actions are so obviously inadequate and weak in this whole affair
that one cannot imagine that the narrator is intending to portray David in
a positive light.

David's restoration to his throne and palace in Jerusalem is dealt with in
a number of stages corresponding to his initial flight to Transjordan. The
initiative is taken by Israel after much deliberation throughout the tribes
(2 Sam 19:11-12[10-11]): better a live king who has after all led them
against their enemies in the past than a dead king who could not give them
victory. It is significant that Absalom is described as the one whom the Israelites *anointed* (v. 12[11]), just as they had anointed David in Hebron
(2 Sam 5:3), which ironically makes Absalom Yahweh's anointed no less
than David. The designation *anointed one* (*messiah*) is simply a political
equivalent of the term *king* and nothing more. Thus, both Absalom and David can be Yahweh's anointed at the same time over the same people recognized by different groups. When David learns of Israel's deliberations, he
immediately uses the information to negotiate with the elders of Judah to
support his return and be the first to escort him over Jordan because he is
himself a Judean. At the same time, David harbors deep resentment at
Joab's bullying him and seeks again to replace him, this time with none
other than Amasa, the defeated general of the Judean-Israelite forces. David
shows no loyalty to his own troops who saved his life and would replace
them with troops of his erstwhile enemy Judah under Amasa, who takes up
the offer and comes down to the Jordan to meet the king. This is the way
that professional and mercenary soldiers behave; one day they work for
one side, the next day for the other side.

The next literary unit to deal with David's restoration is his encounter
with members of the house of Saul, namely, Shimei, Ziba, and Mephibosheth (2 Sam 19:18-32[17-31]). This parallels the corresponding events
during David's retreat. These we have discussed together earlier, and we
need not repeat those remarks here.[75] Nevertheless, it is appropriate to
draw attention to one detail, David's rebuke to Abishai, who is prepared to

75. See above under Mephibosheth, pp. 280-287.

kill Shimei "because he has cursed Yahweh's anointed." David lumps Abishai together with Joab as the "sons of Zeruiah" and labels them his adversaries (2 Sam 19:23-24[22-23]; cf. 2 Sam 3:39). This motif of rebuking Abishai for suggesting that he kill David's opponents occurs elsewhere, as we have seen. In the first instance (1 Sam 26:8-11), Abishai threatens to kill Saul as David's enemy, but he is restrained lest he should "put forth his hand against Yahweh's anointed." In the second instance (2 Sam 16:9-12), Abishai threatens Shimei because he is cursing the king, but David restrains him. Now when Shimei comes to David to seek reconciliation, Abishai recalls the earlier instance of Shimei's cursing but also the first rebuke by David with his reference to "Yahweh's anointed." David's blunt dismissal of Abishai reveals him to be completely inconsistent, to invoke the law about cursing the king or to disregard it whenever it politically suits him. Furthermore, the two loyal commanders, Joab and Abishai, who have saved his life, have now been labeled as his adversaries.

The scene between David and Barzillai of Gilead (2 Sam 19:33-42[32-41]) balances the parallel scene in which Bazillai and other supporters of David bring him provisions when he first arrives in their region (2 Sam 17:27-28). Barzillai joins the escort to bring the king's party across the Jordan. David expresses his gratitude to Barzillai and invites him to join his party and live in Jerusalem, the capital; but Barzillai politely declines and sends Chimham, "your servant" (perhaps his son), in his place. The narrator makes it fairly clear that Barzillai had nothing to gain by accepting such an offer.

No sooner does David cross the Jordan than a dispute breaks out between the leaders of Judah and the leaders of Israel over the right of escort (2 Sam 19:43-45[42-44]). Judah asserts that it has the superior claim, using the argument of closer kinship that David had himself suggested. Israel makes its claim to priority because it has a greater share in the kingdom with 10 tribes and because of the fact that it first made the suggestion of escorting the king in his return. This creates a bitter dispute between the two regions over a matter of royal protocol, a dispute for which David himself was responsible that he does nothing to diffuse. The development of regional disunity, which leads into a second revolt, reveals David's complete ineptitude in maintaining the unity and harmony of the state.

At this point, we must pause a moment and think about why it takes David and his entourage so long (in terms of narrative length, 19:12[11]-20:3) to get from Mahanaim to Jerusalem. There is, of course, the literary parallel with the flight from Jerusalem to the Jordan, which is also drawn out and filled with episodes that have their counterparts in the narrative of David's return. Yet, in stark contrast to the first crossing of the Jordan, which took place in haste in the middle of the night, in the return it seems as though everyone comes down to the Jordan to help the king get across the river. There is obviously some point in making the events focus so much on just this particular piece of geography. This has, of course, nothing to do with trying to understand "whether the sequence of scenes corresponds to their historical occurrence."[76] Instead, it seems to me to be a parody of another great occasion of Jordan crossing, that of the Israelites crossing of the Jordan under Joshua. Here the focus is not on the ark as the means by which the king and his people are brought across the Jordan. Indeed, David sends a message to the two priests, Zadok and Abiathar, who are the custodians of the ark, to persuade the elders of Judah to meet him at the Jordan, but he says nothing about bringing the ark to the Jordan. What David has in mind is a kind of "Roman triumph" in this great escort of the king back to Jerusalem. As though to draw further attention to this parody, the writer notes that after David finally crossed the Jordan he went to Gilgal (the first stop of the Israelites after the Jordan crossing under Joshua), but David has only half the people of Israel with him. David's efforts at this grandiose procession only lead to dissension and another revolt.

The Sheba Revolt

The second revolt against David (2 Sam 20:1–22) is instigated by Sheba son of Bichri, a Benjaminite, who is described as a troublemaker (איש בליעל).[77] Once again, the narrator imitates the narrative of the revolt of the Northern tribes against Rehoboam with an almost verbatim cry of defiance (v. 1): "We have no share in David, and no inheritance in the son of Jesse, every man to his tent, O Israel!"[78] In the case of the later revolt, there were serious grievances that led to the separation of the states, but here it seems a quite trivial matter of protocol that should have been easily resolved. The representatives from Israel withdraw from the large group that accompanied the king to Jerusalem while the men from Judah remain loyal. There is, however, a very curious ambiguity about the tribe of Benjamin. Is it to be reckoned with Israel or with Judah? On the one hand, it

---

76. Hertzberg, *I and II Samuel,* 364.
77. Cf. 1 Sam 10:27.
78. Cf. 1 Kgs 12:16.

seems to be part of the contingent that did escort David across the Jordan with the representatives from Judah, and this seems to be reflected in the statement by the men of Israel that they have 10 shares in David, which would make Benjamin and Judah the other 2. Yet it is Sheba of Benjamin who starts the revolt by declaring that they have no share in David. This confusion also seems to be reflected in the later revolt against Rehoboam, in which Ahijah's prediction to Jeroboam (1 Kgs 11:27–39) is that he is to have control over 10 tribes, but to the house of David is given only 1 tribe, Judah, which seems to leave one tribe (Benjamin?) unaccounted for. In the account of the revolt itself, the distinction is primarily between Israel and Judah, but in what looks like a later supplement (1 Kgs 12:21–24), Judah and Benjamin are coupled together against the rest of Israel. It appears that the account of the revolt against David reflects this same confusion. It is even more puzzling that Sheba is described by Joab as a man from the highlands of Ephraim (2 Sam 20:21), as though there is some uncertainty about the border between Benjamin and Ephraim. All of this reflects a very late construction of the whole account.

After David has returned to Jerusalem, before he can respond to the threat of the revolt, he must attend to the 10 concubines who were violated by Absalom because of his own lack of foresight (2 Sam 20:3; cf. 16:20–23). These are removed from having any future standing in the royal harem or any sexual privileges but instead are ostracized and kept in seclusion for the rest of their lives, living as widows. The question is why does the narrator draw special attention to David's response to this "human tragedy" as some commentators describe it? It cannot be that David is just following custom law, because the whole situation is quite exceptional. Rather, it means that this very harsh treatment of these unfortunate women reflects the general callousness of David and the fact that they are viewed as expendable, given David's large harem of wives and concubines and the endless supply of more to take their place. They are simply one more group within the kingdom that suffers as a result of David's folly. There are no laws that restrict the behavior of the king and the royal family.

The action of the narrative now returns to the revolt of Sheba and the murder of Amasa by Joab (2 Sam 20:4–13). Amasa, who is the new general of the army of citizen conscripts, is called on by David to raise an army of regulars from throughout Judah in just 3 days and bring them to Jerusalem, a task that could hardly be accomplished in such a short time. When he fails to do so, David becomes impatient and orders Abishai to muster David's own standing army in Jerusalem along with the mercenaries and go after Sheba before he can take refuge in some fortified city and use it as a base against the king. Abishai proceeds with the Greek mercenaries (Cretans and peltasts) and the elite troops, together, apparently, with the deposed commander Joab,[79] and at Gibeon they meet Amasa. The narrative does not make clear whether he was accompanied by troops or alone. At any rate, Joab pretends to befriend him, and, much as he did in the earlier instance with Abner, he stabs Amasa with a concealed weapon. From this point on, Joab again assumes the command of the whole army. In order not to distract the soldiers who are now called on to follow their new commander, Joab, the body of the fallen general Amasa is dragged into a nearby field and covered. The troops now continue to pursue Sheba.

The final scene of the revolt (2 Sam 20:14–22) has Sheba holed up with a small band of his own clan of Bichrites in the northern city of Abel Beth-Maʿacah[80] before he has had time to muster the Israelite conscripts. The advantage of David's having a standing army of elite troops and mercenaries is that it can move so quickly into action, and Joab now has Sheba under siege in this city. The final drama plays out between the wise woman of Abel and Joab, in which a bargain is struck that for the head of Sheba the rest of the city will be spared. When the head has been thrown over the wall, the revolt is over and Joab wisely gives the trumpet's call to end hostilities and return home. Apart from the wonderful narrative interplay between the woman and Joab,[81] which is not our concern here, a feature that is worthy of note is the way in which the whole successful prosecution of this campaign resulting in a single death of the leader and no additional bloodshed (apart from Amasa) matches so closely the advice of Ahithophel in the earlier revolt, in which the advice was not followed by Absalom. David's first wish to use the conscript army under Amasa, instead of the elite force under Joab, is closer to the bad advice of Hushai that proved disastrous for Absalom. Once again, David does not lead the army but remains in Jerusalem.

In this episode of the revolt, which is presented at the end of David's career before the final days leading to the succession under Solomon, the narrator intends to show that the whole of David's reign was under the control of the mercenary army that he created when in exile from the court of Saul.

---

79. For the textual problems, see McCarter, *II Samuel*, 426–27.

80. This was the major city of the region that Zvi Maʿoz identifies with the archaeological site of Tel Dan. See Z. U. Maʿoz, *Dan Is Bāniyās, Tel Dan Is Abel-Beth-Maʿacha* (Archaostyle Scientific Research Series 2; Qazin: Archaostyle, 2006).

81. The woman of Abel is reminiscent of the earlier woman of Tekoa.

Once having created a force such as this, it came under the complete control of the two brothers of Zeruiah, Joab and Abishai, who were too much to handle and impossible to replace during his lifetime. The army was efficient but also quite brutal, and the account of the revolt strongly suggests an isolation of the royal court from the life of the people. Throughout David's career, the *David Saga* always portrays David as remaining at home while the troops under Joab do the fighting for him. The verisimilitude of the *David Saga*, in contrast to Dtr's idealized and heroic David, has beguiled scholars into accepting the account as historical reporting by an observer within the court and thus treating it as a historical source for the period instead of acknowledging it as a fiction of the late Persian period.

The Final Struggle for Succession to the Throne

Before we can consider the account of Solomon's succession to the throne, we must once again address the much-debated question of the relationship of the larger *David Saga* to DtrH, because this unit contains some very clear markers of Dtr style and language that are now embedded in the larger narrative. This is especially the case for 1 Kgs 2:1–4 and 10–12. As I argued in the last chapter, these verses are so clearly in the form and character of Dtr that they cannot be denied to this author.[82] The speech in 2:5–9, however, does not belong to Dtr but is closely tied to the whole of the *David Saga*. Yet 2:5–9 is so dependent on 2:1–4 that one must resort to various stratagems to save the priority of the supposed Succession Narrative. Similarly, 2:10–12 is the Dtr's regnal transition from David to Solomon, so that everything in the *David Saga* that comes after it depends on it.

The standard way of dealing with these problems for an earlier dating of SN, following Noth, is to attribute part of these formulae to SN instead of Dtr. The usual procedure, therefore, is to attribute 2:1–2 to SN and to see only vv. 3–4 as Dtr. But this will not do. The whole of 2:1–4 is quite incongruous with what has preceded and knows nothing of the very old David in the previous unit. The introductory statement, "As the time of David's death approached," would be redundant in the same source alongside the statement in 1:1, "Now King David was old and advanced in years." This can be seen in the parallel usage in Gen 24:1 and 47:29. In the case of Jacob in 47:29, the text states that "as the time of Israel's death approached" he called Joseph and made him take an oath to have him buried in the land

---

82. See above, pp. 267–268. See also the appendix, p. 361.

of Canaan. Of Abraham it is said that he was "old and advanced in years" (Gen 24:1) when he placed his servant under a similar oath to find a wife for Isaac from his kinsmen in Mesopotamia. Consequently, it is not likely that the two scenes introduced by 1 Kgs 1:1 and 2:1, both referring to the same person, David, belong to the same source or author. Furthermore, the expression in the statement of David, "I am about to part this earthly life" (2:1), closely related to the introductory remark about the approach of David's death, is also found in the speech of Joshua in Josh 23:14 (Dtr) as a parallel to the earlier statement, "I am old and advanced in years" (v. 2). Consequently, there is nothing in the language of 2:1-2 that argues against its attribution to Dtr and much that is in favor of it.[83]

Nevertheless, J. Rogers has argued that 2:1-2 should be regarded as pre-Dtr (= SN) and as an appropriate lead into vv. 5-9.[84] In fact, however, the *wĕgam* at the beginning of v. 5 makes the connection between the two parts very awkward.[85] If vv. 1-2 were part of a pre-Dtr original stock, then the exhortation to "be strong and be a man" should come after v. 5 and be together with v. 6. Rogers places great weight on the variation in terminology from the standard Dtr combination of חזק and אמץ, whereas here one finds חזק followed by היה לאיש, although this last combination is found in 1 Sam 4:9 (DtrH). Yet, if this exhortation of David is soon followed in DtrH by 1 Kgs 3, in which Solomon speaks of himself as an inexperienced youth, the slight variation in terminology to "be a man" is quite appropriate. Furthermore, it should be noted that *wĕgam* in 1 Kgs 2:5 introduces a new subject in the long speech of David quite different from what preceded it in vv. 2-4. This same technique is used three times by the author in 1:46-48 in the long speech of Jonathan son of Abiathar (vv. 43-48) in which he reports on a series of events, the last three introduced by the phrase "and moreover," *wĕgam*. It would appear that the later narrator used the same device to extend the earlier Dtr speech with his own addition in 2:5-9.

Kaiser attempts to overcome some of these objections by reconstructing a last testament of David out of 2:1-2, 5-9 which was a pro-dynastic addi-

---

83. See also the same pattern in Deut 31:2, where Moses announces his great age of 120 years and then exhorts the people in v. 6 and Joshua in v. 7 to "be strong and courageous." This is obviously a Dtr pattern.

84. J. S. Rogers, "Narrative Stock and Deuteronomistic Elaboration in 1 Kings 2," *CBQ* 50 (1988): 398-413.

85. It is not surprising that Rogers eliminates the *wĕgam* as redactional (ibid. 409 n. 32).

tion to CH prior to the Dtr additions in 2:3-4.[86] Kaiser must also reckon with *wĕgam* of v. 5 and the references to Solomon's wisdom in vv. 6 and 9 as later redactional glosses. But these references to Solomon's wisdom cannot have been added by Dtr because Solomon only acquired this wisdom through the events recorded in 1 Kgs 3, and it was not the cleverness of how to get rid of his enemies but the wisdom of how to govern well. The remarks of David and the subsequent actions by Solomon present the strongest contrast with Dtr's portrait of Solomon in chap. 3. As we have argued above, all of 2:1-4 belongs to Dtr, which fits very well with chap. 3, and vv. 5-9 are the later addition to this unit.

This brings us to consider the regnal transition formula in 1 Kgs 2:10-12. Opinions differ as to how to assign these verses, even though there is general agreement that at least part of them belongs to Dtr. In particular, the death and burial notice of v. 10 and the length of rule in v. 11 seem to correspond most directly to the transition formulas in DtrH.[87] It is the accession notice in v. 12 that deviates most noticeably from the usual form, but this is so for two reasons. First, 1 Kgs 2:10-12 is made to correspond directly with the Nathan oracle of 2 Sam 7:12 as its fulfillment:

2 Sam 7:12   When your days are ended and you sleep with your fathers, I will raise your offspring after you . . . and I will establish his kingdom.
1 Kgs 2:10-12 Then David slept with his fathers. . . . And Solomon sat upon the throne of David his father, and his kingdom was firmly established.

Second, if the regnal résumé did contain the usual notice naming the mother of the new king of Judah, as it does in the rest of Kings, in its present context the name of Solomon's mother would have been utterly redundant

---

86. O. Kaiser, "Das Verhältnis der Erzältung vom König David zum sogenannten Deuteronomistischen Geschichtswerk," 112-16.

87. Rogers ("Narrative Stock," 410-12) wants to retain v. 10 for his narrative stock (CH), based on the fact that death and burial notices of this sort are to be found in the Assyrian "Dynastic Chronicle" and therefore reflect widespread use in royal chronicles. If this "chronicle" were the model, then v. 11, containing the length of reign, would need to be included as well. However, this Assyrian text is an eclectic literary work like no other and belongs to the late 7th century, close to the time of the DtrH. The form within the Babylonian Chronicles mentions the death of the former ruler, the length of reign, and the accession of the new king, *but not his burial*. However, there is nothing to suggest that this convention was very widespread or very early, that is, not before the 7th century at the earliest. On these texts, see my *In Search of History*, 71-72, 79-92.

and could well have been eliminated. However, the fact that David's mother is not mentioned anywhere by Dtr is good reason to believe that Dtr did not even know of Bathsheba's existence. Third, there is also reason to believe that the regnal résumés for the Divided Monarchy are derived from Dtr's sources, that is, "the chronicles of the Kings of Israel/Judah," and that he did not have notices of this sort for Saul, David, and Solomon. So he merely improvised this notice, using elements from the others. The unit as a notice of succession is indivisible and must belong entirely to Dtr. If, therefore, both 2:1-4 and vv. 10-12 belong to DtrH, there is no other conclusion that can be drawn except that the *David Saga* is later than DtrH.

One solution for those who want to preserve the priority of SN is to consider all of 2:1-12 as secondary and see vv. 13ff. as a continuation of 1:53. But this will not do either because Adonijah's request for Abishag must presuppose David's death. Nor could Adonijah be put to death during David's lifetime, and the same applies to the expulsion of Abiathar, who was so loyal to David, as Solomon admits. David's remarks in 2:5-9 are very carefully constructed not to include these two figures. To overcome this problem, Würthwein resorts to the expedient of suggesting that the original death notice has been replaced by Dtr.[88] The substitution of a new death and burial notice by Dtr would have been a radical departure from his usual use of older sources, and to admit such inconsistent "redactional" activity is special pleading and makes anything possible.

Another of the principal issues in the debate about the relationship of Dtr to the narrative of the succession has to do with the reference to Abiathar and his fate in being expelled from the priesthood in 1 Kgs 2:26-27, with the concluding note that this event is the fulfillment of a prophecy in the time of Eli. Scholars have long viewed this as a Dtr addition, but they are divided as to how much of this unit is part of the later redaction. However, as I have already discussed at length above, all of the references to Abiathar belong to the late source, and the supposed fulfillment of the earlier prophecy has nothing to do with the original intention of the text in 1 Sam 2:27-36. It is the later narrator who has made use of a rather vague prophecy, which no longer had any relevance in the late Persian period, to give it a new connection within his own story of David. There is therefore nothing in 2 Kgs 2:26-27 that is Dtr, nor is Dtr present anywhere else in

---

88. E. Würthwein, *Die Bücher der Könige: 1 Könige 1-16* (ATD 11/1; Göttingen: Vandenhoeck & Ruprecht, 1985), 21. So also Kaiser, "Das Verhältnis der Erzältung vom König David," 118-19.

1 Kgs 1–2, apart from 1 Kgs 2:1–4, 10–12, which must be *earlier* than the rest of the narrative.

Let us now turn to a consideration of 1 Kgs 1–2 as a whole. Since the study of Rost, scholars have taken the subject of this unit, which is the succession to the throne of David, as the key to understanding the theme of the literary work as a whole and then use this theme to define its limits and its literary genre as a royal apology. As I have argued throughout this study up to this point, this has been a serious mistake, and this judgment applies to this unit as well. Although the question of succession dominates the narrative in 1 Kgs 1–2, this is only a subtheme within the larger work, albeit a very important one. The narrator is concerned with the whole career of David—his rise to power within the court of Saul and then his activity as a mercenary leader until he gains the throne, his rule over Judah and Israel and life in the court and royal family, the revolts against his rule, and finally the struggle for the succession to his throne among his sons. As with all of the other moments in David's career, but especially in the matter of the succession, the author sharpens his biting parody of Dtr's idealization of David and the theme of the divine promise of royal succession in 2 Sam 7.

The initial scene in 1 Kgs 1:1–4 is of an old and feeble monarch who has so little energy that even with a heavy covering of garments he cannot get warm. So it is suggested that perhaps a beautiful young woman can heat him up, and Abishag the Shunammite is brought to him to get him aroused, but to no avail. She remains a virgin. The point of this scene is not to suggest that because David no longer has his virility he is now unfit to rule and must give way to a successor. That theory is mere conjecture for which there is no evidence. The point, instead, is the fact that an absolute monarch, who has many wives and concubines in his royal harem, can, in his dotage, command the presence of one more beautiful virgin to administer to his needs. Even in matters related to his own personal care, David is entirely in the hands of his servants. Thus, his feeble state raises the question of just who is in charge of the realm with such a powerless and rather pathetic ruler, and who will now control the succession to the throne. The situation is ripe for a showdown within the palace among the principal rivals to the throne.

The obvious prime contender for the throne is Adonijah, son of Haggith, who is next in line after Absalom, and, as the narrator presents his position in 1 Kgs 1:5–8, Adonijah clearly regards himself as the legitimate heir and assumes the role of crown prince, and David says nothing to him that would suggest otherwise. He also has the strong support of Joab the commander of the army and Abiathar the priest. In spite of this, however, there

is a split among the power brokers within the court circles; Zadok the priest
as rival to Abiathar, and Benaiah, son of Jehoiada, commander of the mercenaries, as rival to Joab, while Nathan the prophet and Shimei, leader of
the Benjaminites, and the elite corps of the army do not support Adonijah
but belong to the party of Solomon. Furthermore, in obvious anticipation of
the imminent death of his father, Adonijah prepares a great celebration
feast at Enrogel, southeast of Jerusalem, and invites his supporters, his
brothers, the king's sons, and the royal officials of Judah, but he excludes
the rival party and Solomon his brother (vv. 9–10).[89] Thus, the narrator
sets the scene for a power struggle between two principal factions. All of
this happens under David's nose, and he knows nothing about it.

The situation is clearly grave for those who are not invited to Adonijah's
feast, because it signals a threat, which so often in circumstances such as
these would result in the elimination of the rival faction once the new king
had ascended the throne. That, at any rate, is how the situation is understood by the Solomon supporters, and Nathan takes the lead to address the
crisis. He puts forward a plan to Bathsheba, the mother of Solomon, in
which she now plays a leading role (vv. 11–14). First, Nathan deliberately
misrepresents the feast of Adonijah as reflecting a political coup in which
he has already assumed the kingship without David's knowledge and therefore represents it as an act of rebellion. But the narrator gives no indication
that this actually happened. The intent is to turn the king against the crown
prince for usurping the royal power prematurely. Second, Nathan invents a
promise made to Bathsheba by the king under a solemn oath that her son
would become king, which David clearly did not make. The plan is that,
while Bathsheba is reporting both these matters to the king, Nathan then
will also come in and confirm her statements.

The fact that the author of this story has attributed to Nathan the
prophet this kind of palace plot to manipulate the succession away from
the rightful heir and crown prince to the successor of his own choice, Solomon, is quite remarkable and deeply ironic. This is the same Nathan who
conveyed to David the divine oracle in which Yahweh promises to David a
"secure dynasty" and continuity on the throne after him (2 Sam 7:4–17),
but without naming the heir. Now, this same prophet invents a promise
that David is supposed to have made to Bathsheba, namely, that Solomon
will be his heir, a promise that he clearly did not make or make public at
any time. This is also the same prophet who condemned David for his

---

89. Feasts of this sort likewise play an important role in Icelandic sagas.

adultery with Bathsheba but who is now a member of Solomon's party and collaborating with Bathsheba to make her son king. In place of any oracles there are only lies from this man of God. It is this prophet who privately decides that Solomon, when he is still an infant, is *Jedidiah* ("beloved of Yahweh") and therefore his favorite. The rest of the succession account to the final establishment of Solomon on the throne is a continuous parody on the theme of the divine promise to David, a caricature that makes a mockery of Dtr's royal ideology.

When Bathsheba enters the king's chamber, the narrator reminds us of David's old age and senility and the fact that he is being attended to by the beautiful Abishag. When Bathsheba humbly bows before the king, he abruptly asks her, "What do you want?" Bathsheba plays her role well and pretends to remind the king of what he supposedly forgot, his solemn oath to make her son Solomon king after him. She then proceeds to inform the king that Adonijah has already made himself king in violation of this oath, and his great feast is represented as an acknowledgement of this fact. Furthermore, Solomon was excluded from this celebration, which can only mean that, as soon as David dies, which is obviously imminent, the lives of Bathsheba and Solomon will be in jeopardy, apparently because of this oath that gives Solomon the right to the throne. Nathan then enters to confirm the events as he and Bathsheba have misrepresented them and then forces David to decide which party he will support. The final statement accuses David by implying his negligence in not previously declaring who is to succeed him on the throne: "Has this state of affairs proceeded from my lord the king and you did not inform your servants who should succeed you on the throne?" David's response to this implied incompetence is to fall back on Bathsheba's claim of a prior oath with a kind of pious flourish, "As Yahweh lives, who has rescued me from all my troubles," he then repeats the oath that Bathsheba has earlier suggested to him, as though it was something that actually happened in the past. The manipulation of the old man is quite pathetic. The statement of Bathsheba in response is quite ludicrous in the circumstances: "May my lord King David live for ever!" All of this is a parody on the divine oath to David and David's prayer in response that we have in 2 Sam 7.

David then summons the leaders of this conspiracy, Zadok the priest, Nathan the prophet, and Benaiah the commander of the foreign mercenaries and palace guard, and he instructs them that they together are to carry out the coronation, with anointing of holy oil from the sanctuary. The details are laid out in such a way, even to the point that Solomon will ride on the king's own mule–the king himself will not be present, just as though he has already died–and they will make the formal acclamation "Long live King Solomon!" and he will sit on David's throne. This is tantamount to David's abdication. David further declares: "He [Solomon] shall be king in my place, and I have appointed him as leader (*nāgîd*) over Israel and Judah." Throughout Dtr, the term *nāgîd* is always used to refer to Yahweh's choice of the leader of his people (1 Sam 9:15-16, 10:1, 13:13-14) or the recognition by the people's representatives of Yahweh's choice (1 Kgs 5:2), but according to this late narrator it is David who assumes this divine prerogative to appoint the *nāgîd* of his choice. In this case, the representatives of the people of Israel and Judah have nothing to say in this decision. They are not even present. And in a completely cynical fashion, it is Benaiah son of Jehoiada, the commander of the foreign mercenaries, who adds the final confirmation: "So be it! May Yahweh, the God of my lord the king, confirm it." But we have had no such word from Yahweh, no oracle or divine confirmation, but only the word of a military commander. In reality, he becomes the king-maker.

There are some interesting parallels between this episode and that of the royal coup in 2 Kgs 11:4-16, in which a certain Jehoiada, who is both priest and the commander of the Carian mercenaries, organizes a royal coup to put the young prince on the throne. He too is anointed, this time in the temple itself; he receives the crown and the conspirators all shout, "Long live the king!" This is followed by the assassination of Queen Athaliah at the hands of the mercenary guard after they drag her out of the temple. In both cases, it is Greek mercenaries who are involved. The Carians of Asia Minor are known from the Saite period as forming the royal bodyguard to the pharaohs in Egypt, and the account thus belongs to this period, while the peltasts and Cretans belong to the late Persian period, so the relationship of the two narratives is clear. The account in 2 Kgs 11:4-16 is no earlier than Dtr and could be somewhat later, and 1 Kgs 1-2 must be considerably later and dependent on 2 Kgs 11:14-16. Now Benaiah is consistently called the son of Jehoiada, as though to make a connection with the Jehoiada of the other story and suggest that both stories have to do with conspiracies to gain the throne through the use of a foreign mercenary guard.[90] In the David story, however, the narrator is careful to distinguish the role of military commander from that of the priest.

---

90. The name Benaiah son of Jehoiada probably derives from the exploits of David's heroes in 2 Sam 23:20-23. The reference to Benaiah's role as commander of the "bodyguard" (v. 23b) is likely a later addition.

The anointing of Solomon is reported as planned (1 Kgs 1:38–40), with the addition that the people of the city enter into the spirit of the occasion and begin a great celebration. They are merely pawns in the game. They have had no say in the anointing itself and merely follow the lead of these prominent persons as reflecting the will of David. Meanwhile in Adonijah's feast nearby, the sound of the trumpet and the noise is interpreted by Joab as an ominous sign of trouble, and Jonathan son of Abiathar arrives to bring news of the events. He reports at length just what has happened, including the facts that it is David who has made Solomon king, so it cannot be contested, and that Solomon has the support not only of Zadok the priest and Nathan the prophet but also of Benaiah the head of the Greek mercenary guard. Adonijah may have Joab in his camp, but he has no troops. It is now too late to muster any because Solomon already sits on the throne. As for all of David's servants, it is significant that they repeat to David the same words used by Benaiah, taking their cue from the military commander, which amounts to an oath of allegiance to Solomon: "Your God make the name of Solomon more famous than yours, and make his throne greater than your throne" (v. 47). Then the narrator states that "David bowed upon his bed," which suggests that David is now on his deathbed. A similar expression is used of Jacob when he too is at the point of death (Gen 47:31b), and this is immediately followed in the original Joseph story by Gen 50:1–3 to indicate that Jacob has indeed died. The Yahwist, in Gen 48:1–2, 8–22, has his father briefly revive so that he can bestow a final blessing on the two sons of Joseph.[91] It would appear that the author of the *David Saga* is imitating the Yahwist in granting David some final words even after he is supposed to have died.

David, in his final words, refers back to the theme of the divine promise in 2 Sam 7:12, but with some significant differences. David states (1 Kgs 1:48), "Blessed be Yahweh, the God of Israel, who has today permitted one [of my offspring][92] to sit on my throne, and I am still alive to see it with my

---

91. See my *Prologue to History*, 318, 320–23. The Priestly Writer, after including a much longer addition in Gen 49, adds a parallel blessing to the twelve tribes and a charge to them regarding his burial in Machpelah, and then repeats the motif about dying in his bed.

92. The reading here follows the LXX, "one of my offspring." Many commentaries follow the MT, "one to sit," but this hardly seems fitting. As John Gray states, "Since someone had to succeed David in any case, there seems no particular point in his gratification at being succeeded; the point is that it gratified him to be succeeded by one of his sons, which he regarded as the crowning blessing" (*I and II*

own eyes." This is often considered as a "redactional" addition by Dtr to an older narrative, but this is quite unlikely. The allusion is based on 2 Sam 7:12, 13b: "When your life comes to an end and you rest with your ancestors, I will set up after you one of your own offspring, one from your own body, and I will confirm his kingdom . . . and will fix his royal throne in perpetuity." There are two important differences in perspective between these two statements. The first is that the former statement (1 Kgs 1:48) has in view only the immediate successor, who was one of a number of possible sons, and not a succession in perpetuity. Adonijah's succession would have fulfilled the same wish. By contrast, the divine promise in 2 Sam 7:12, 13b and the prayer of thanksgiving of David in 2 Sam 7:18-29 has to do with the future dynasty *in perpetuity* and not with the immediate succession of the next king.

The second and more important difference between the original promise and the fulfillment expressed by David, is that in the original promise the fulfillment comes only *after* David's death, not while he is still alive. The point that the author seems to underline is that the fulfillment of the divine promise to David was the result of a palace coup brought about by one son against another with the manipulation of David himself. It seems to make a mockery of the original promise theme. Ironically, the statement that David himself lived to witness the fulfillment of the promise through Solomon's coronation could also have been said about Absalom's sitting on David's throne while he was still alive. Both occasions are the result of a coup.

Once again, the scene shifts to Adonijah's party, and now there is a panic in which all of its members disperse. Adonijah feels particularly threatened and seeks asylum at the altar.[93] Adonijah accepts the fact that Solomon is now king and addresses him as "King Solomon." He is in the same position that Bathsheba complained to David that she and Solomon would be in if Adonijah had become king (1 Kgs 1:23). Adonijah requests from Solomon an oath that he will not kill him, but all he receives from him is some statement that if he proves to be "honorable," nothing will happen to him. It will not be difficult to find something dishonorable in the future of which to accuse him. But Solomon can hardly do away with his brother while David is still alive and so close to his own coronation. He will bide his time.

Kings: A Commentary [OTL; Philadelphia: Westminster, 1963], 92 note e). See also G. H. Jones, *1 and 2 Kings*, 104-5.

93. On asylum and its connection with the "altar" and sanctuary, see Exod 21:12-14.

What is remarkable about Solomon's coronation is that nothing is said about the role of any of the other sons of David in these events. We hear of them at the feast of Adonijah as though they all expected him to succeed David (v. 9). The same applies to the royal officials of Judah who were also in Adonijah's entourage but are nowhere to be found at Solomon's coronation. The Chronicler was well aware of this serious lack of protocol and in his own version of these events, has all of the leaders of the people and all of the sons pledging allegiance to Solomon (1 Chr 23:1-2, 28:1-2, 29:22-24). He makes absolutely certain that Solomon is the divine choice that is intended in the deity's promise to David (1 Chr 22:6-18) and that David has made this clear beforehand to all the leaders of the people. The contrast between the two accounts could not be sharper.

As I have indicated above, 1 Kgs 2:1-4 is Dtr's formulation of David's farewell speech to Solomon. By incorporating it into his own work, the later author has made the opening statement about David's approaching death (v. 1a) quite redundant. To this speech the later narrator adds a series of remarks (vv. 5-9) that are totally out of character with what has gone before.[94] First, David mentions his longstanding difficulties with Joab, recalling his murders of Abner and Amasa and blaming him for the shedding of innocent blood during his reign when he himself has been guilty of the same (vv. 5-6). The justice that David himself failed to exercise he now lays on Solomon. In a similar fashion, David recalls a grievance that he has with Shimei when he cursed David during his retreat from Absalom, and even when he later swore to spare him, he does not hold his son to the same oath. In both cases, David suggests to Solomon that he use his "wisdom" to find a way to dispatch both of them. The "wisdom" that Solomon will need to murder both of these men without a trial,[95] the former because he was a supporter of Adonijah and the latter on a flimsy pretext, even though he was a supporter of Solomon, makes a complete mockery of the young and innocent Solomon in 1 Kgs 3, in which Solomon in great humility asks the deity for wisdom and understanding in order to govern God's people and "to discern between good and evil" (v. 9). It is scarcely conceivable that the author of 1 Kgs 3 (Dtr) could have had before him the text of 1 Kgs 2.

---

94. Kaiser, following Würthwein, wants to attribute all of 2:1-9 to Deuteronomists. See above, n. 88.

95. Even Ahab and Jezebel at least make the show of having a public trial in the case of Naboth.

As indicated above, the transition formula in 1 Kgs 2:10-12 originally followed directly on vv. 1-4 as Dtr's transfer of power from David's reign to that of Solomon, and it is the author of the *David Saga* who builds on this in 1 Kgs 2:13-46. The content of this narrative unit focuses exclusively on the theme of how the kingdom of Solomon was secured by him (v. 12; cf. v. 46). The major obstacle to Solomon's security lies in the latent threat of his rival Adonijah and his supporters, and he must determine how these must be eliminated. Because Adonijah was given a promise that nothing would happen to him if he remained honorable (1:52), a pretext had to be found to accuse him of perfidy. This the unfortunate Adonijah provides with the naive assistance of Bathsheba (2:13-25). He comes to Bathsheba to make what he believes is a simple and reasonable request through her to Solomon. He first acknowledges to her that he has accepted the fact that he will not be king even though he had every reason to expect it, indeed "all Israel had set their expectations on him" (v. 15). However, as things turned out, it was not to be. Some scholars take the statement of Adonijah, "for it was his from Yahweh," to be an affirmation by the narrator of Solomon's divine legitimacy, but this is hardly likely. It is much more an acknowledgement of his fate. Adonijah could not have known the kind of intrigue that took place to deprive him of his rightful status. Ironically, he is speaking to one of those most responsible for this turn of events.

Now Adonijah puts forth his request; it is that he be given Abishag the Shunemmite as a wife. This request seems entirely reasonable because the narrator has been at pains to point out that she is still a virgin, and there has been no consummation of a union between David and Abishag, so she was no more than an attendant or nurse to him. She could not reasonably be considered one of David's concubines. There was no reason that she should be consigned to a status of permanent widowhood for such a duty. The narrator also makes it quite clear that even Bathsheba sees nothing offensive in the request and consents to relay it to the king. She characterizes it as merely "one small request" (v. 20). If Abishag was actually regarded as a member of his father's harem, then the request would have been scandalous and not treated so lightly by Bathsheba, but it is never suggested as such.

Solomon, however, seizes on this request as the pretext that he needs, that this is tantamount to asking for the kingdom itself. The exaggeration is ludicrous. In Solomon's response, he is quick to acknowledge that his elder brother, with his supporters, Abiathar and Joab, had the better claim to the throne. This is the threat that he must eliminate. Now he uses this simple pretext to have Adonijah murdered without trial or any self-defense.

As justification for this murder, Solomon appropriates the language of the divine promise to David in 2 Sam 7:12–13 to refer to himself: "And now, as Yahweh lives who has established me and placed me on the throne of David my father, and who has founded a dynasty for me, as he promised, Adonijah shall be put to death today" (v. 24). The execution is carried out by Solomon's henchman and commander of the mercenaries, Benaiah.

The other two supporters of Adonijah must now also be dealt with because of their guilt by association. They had nothing to do with Adonijah's request, only that they earlier supported Adonijah as the legitimate and expected heir. In Abiathar's case, he is exiled to his estate in Anathoth; the charge against him: "You deserve to die, but on this day I will not put you to death because you carried the ark of lord Yahweh before David my father and you shared in all the hardships that my father endured." He is deprived of his office for no just cause and could hardly have been a danger to Solomon, and he must now live with a constant threat over his head. This is the final reward for his lifelong loyalty to David. It is a case of blatant injustice. The case against Joab is perhaps a matter of justice deferred, although the narrator makes the point that, although he was a supporter of Adonijah, he had not previously supported Absalom and stood by David in his greatest hour of need. But David had instructed Solomon to find an appropriate occasion to carry out a vendetta against him, and Solomon does so. Joab seeks asylum at the altar in the sanctuary, which according to the law in Exod 21:13–14 and Deut 19:1–13 will not protect him against the avenger of blood (a kinsman of the murdered man). The intervention of Solomon, however, is entirely arbitrary except to remove the possibility of blood-guilt from the Davidic house for complicity in leaving the matter of Joab's murders unresolved for so long. But in the process of establishing his throne, Solomon has acquired his own share of blood-guilt. Benaiah carries out the execution of Joab and then replaces him as commander of the army just as Zadok replaced Abiathar as the leading priest.

The only one of Solomon's party who did not fare so well is Shimei. This was because David had a longstanding grudge against him because of his curses against David at the time of his flight from Absalom. In spite of the fact that Shimei subsequently became reconciled to David and received an oath from David protecting him during his lifetime, David laid on Solomon an obligation to find an opportunity to settle the old score against him. This, of course, empties the words of rebuke by David against Abishai of any sincerity (2 Sam 16:10–12). Solomon, on the other hand, has some moral obligation toward Shimei for Shimei's support, but with the other major opponents now dead or in exile, he could deal with Shimei, a leader of the house of Saul, with impunity. He places him under what amounts to house arrest with total restriction of movement within the confines of Jerusalem and therefore isolation from his Benjamin power base, and when he violates this restriction for a quite-reasonable cause, to reclaim lost property (two runaway slaves), Solomon uses this as a pretext to murder him.

The speech of Solomon that justifies his verdict of death to Shimei is loaded with pious hypocrisy. He reminds Shimei of "all the evil that you did to David my father" (v. 44), which consisted of the one episode of cursing but no significant damage, and ignores the fact that Shimei and his men were the first to invite the king back on his return to the land after the revolt. He then interprets his own action against Shimei as divine retribution for his behavior, as though to absolve himself of the bloody act. He invokes the theme of the divine promise to David, "King Solomon shall be blessed, and the throne of David shall be secure (*kwn*) before Yahweh in perpetuity," which refers back to the language of 2 Sam 7:16: "Your house and your kingdom shall be made firm forever before me, your throne shall be secure (*kwn*) in perpetuity," as well as to the prayer of David in which he requests divine blessing on his dynasty forever (2 Sam 7:29). This same cynical use of the divine promise by Solomon occurs also in 2:24, in which, in passing sentence on his brother Adonijah, he refers to the promise to David and its fulfillment in his succession as justification for putting his brother to death. The series of actions leading to the elimination of all possible threats to Solomon's throne is concluded by the statement "Thus was the kingdom made secure in the hand of Solomon" (v. 46b), which is a sinister restatement of the Dtr conclusion in 2:12b and the theme of the divine promise as a whole. I cannot understand how anyone can see in these texts a pro-Solomonic redaction.[96]

Summary

As we have seen in the above literary analysis, the *David Saga* makes use of the prior history of Dtr as a framework for his own story of David's reign, just as he did with the account of David's service in the court of Saul and his subsequent adventures as a leader of mercenaries. He begins with

---

96. Equally perplexing is the ascription of these texts to Dtr. See Rogers, "Narrative Stock," 398–405; and Würthwein, *1 Könige 1-16*, 6–8.

the very brief record of David's becoming king of Israel in Hebron and creates out of this one state two separate and rival kingdoms, Judah and Israel, with a protracted war between David and an invented fourth surviving son of Saul, Ishbosheth. He also introduces into the story of David Joab and Abishai, the sons of Zeruiah, as the commanders of his professional army and the real power behind the throne. They do all the fighting while David stays at home. Their rival and counterpart in Israel is Abner, who kills Joab's youngest brother in the opening battle between the two camps. Later, when Abner attempts to defect to David and bring the rest of the Israelites over to his side and to replace Joab as the joint commander, Joab murders him, demonstrating that David is completely powerless to control his military commanders. This theme continues throughout the whole of the *David Saga* until Joab is finally murdered by another commander of foreign mercenaries, Beniah, under orders from Solomon, and Beniah thus replaces Joab as supreme commander of the forces.

Without Abner, Ishbosheth is defenseless, protected by a single female servant who falls asleep on the job, and Ishbosheth is easily murdered. This leads to a revised version of David's coronation over all Israel, in which the elders of Israel make a covenant (that is, a political agreement) with David to be their king. The later revolt of Absalom, in which Israel anoints David's son in Hebron, reveals how tenuous this arrangement can be. The author of the *David Saga* has nothing to say about David's conquest of Jerusalem and the move of his court to this place, but he assumes this transition for the rest of his story of David. However, the *David Saga* does take up Dtr's account of the triumphal return of the ark to Jerusalem in 2 Sam 6 and turns it into a highly ambiguous event in which the deity strikes dead one of the those who had care of the ark. This leads David to park the ark for three months in quarantine in a Philistine's house just outside Jerusalem—as though there had never been any earlier wars against the Philistines—and with no consecrated persons to care for it, and yet a most capricious deity blesses the Philistine's household! When David sees that nothing has happened to the Philistines, he continues to bring the ark the rest of the way into Jerusalem. The *David Saga* revision even mars this joyous celebration by turning David's behavior into sexually provocative dancing, which is criticized by Michal, the daughter of Saul, leading to permanent estrangement between David and Michal.

As we argued above, Dtr considers David to have spent his whole life fighting the wars of Yahweh against the nations surrounding Israel so that the promise to David regarding his perpetual dynasty in 2 Sam 7 comes at the end of his life. The author of the *David Saga* completely revises this chronology by transferring chap. 8 to a position after chap. 7 and then inserting a large block of new episodes in chaps. 9–20 that is meant to cover most of his reign. The first of these episodes deals with the oath that David made with Jonathan to treat his offspring well after his death. It is discovered that Jonathan's son, Mephibosheth, survived the Philistine massacre of Saul's family, and David brings him to court to keep his oath. However, David shows no emotion or great affection for this lone survivor of Jonathan's family, in spite of the grief expressed by David in his lament in 2 Sam 1:19–27. David's subsequent treatment of Mephibosheth in the matter of his servant Ziba's slander manifests a rather callous injustice and speaks volumes about his total insensitivity. It is similar to his treatment of Michal, his first wife who loved him and risked her own life to save his. To speak of David's "tenderness" in the *David Saga*, as some do, is to overlook so many signals of the opposite sentiment.

The *David Saga* cleverly builds into Dtr's series of David's wars with the nations a new war with the Ammonites. Dtr had no account of such a war but only a rather vague reference to a war in the summary list of victories in 2 Sam 8:12. This gave the author freedom to shape this event as he wished. He first creates a *casus belli* in the insult of the Ammonite king to David's envoys (2 Sam 10:1–5), which then leads to the Ammonites' joining forces with the Arameans and Joab and Abishai's inconclusive victory over these joint forces. A second war follows against the Arameans, which was a displacement from Dtr's series of wars and which originally had nothing to do with the Ammonites. As we argued above, the Ammonite war is intended as a stark contrast to Saul's holy war against the Ammonites and its king, Nahash, the former king whom this story identifies as David's friend. This long, drawn-out war becomes the context for the Bathsheba affair.

Because this Ammonite war is covered in such extended detail, spanning three chapters, in stark contrast to the brief reports in Dtr, the author is suggesting that he is recounting what really goes on in supposed holy wars of this sort. The ark of God may be in the camp with the conscript soldiers, and some of them, such as the pious Hittite Uriah, may take the deuteronomic strictures very seriously, but King David is quite oblivious to all of that. He enjoys the comfort of his palace and thinks nothing of seducing a wife of a loyal soldier in the field, although he has many wives and concubines at his disposal. He cares nothing for Bathsheba; his only concern is with the inconvenient pregnancy that eventually leads him to have the husband, Uriah, murdered. As I have argued above, the author of the *David Saga* draws widely from the whole of DtrH in his characterization of David's actions, modeling him on the worst kings of Israel, Ahab and Jeroboam, as well as the rejected Saul, and in the end, through the prophet Nathan, he condemns the whole dynasty of David to ultimate destruction: "the sword shall not depart from your *house* forever" (2 Sam 12:10). This is in complete contradiction to the Nathan oracle in 2 Sam 7:13. Even though Solomon, as the second son of Bathsheba by David, is identified as "Jedidiah" ("Beloved of Yahweh") by Nathan and becomes his favorite, he is never recognized as the heir apparent by David; and it is ultimately only through Nathan's deceit that Solomon gains the throne.

After David's victory over the Ammonites, in which he himself actually does nothing but receive all of the spoils of war, the *David Saga* focuses almost entirely on life within the royal court (chaps. 13–19), about which Dtr says nothing at all. The picture that the author paints is a most distressing one. The sons of David, like their father, show themselves to be completely unworthy of ruling the people of Israel. First, there is the rape by Amnon, the crown prince, of his half-sister Tamar (2 Sam 13:1–22), about which David does nothing because Amnon is his favorite. Then there is the revenge murder of Amnon by Absalom, the brother of Tamar (13:23–39), again the result of David's negligence, and this leads in turn to Absalom's exile. When Absalom is finally restored from exile through the machinations of Joab and the wise woman of Tekoa (2 Sam 14), he wins David's affection and favor in place of Amnon as the crown prince, which gives him the chance to plot a rebellion to replace David as king (2 Sam 15–17). This leads to a disastrous civil war (chap. 18), which Absalom loses through his own stupidity and which David wins because he has so little to do with the outcome. Even so, David's complete political ineptitude in resolving disputes between Judah and Israel leads to another civil war (chaps. 19–20), which is won by his professional army and the sons of Zeruiah, whom he despises but cannot control. Why would any people wish to be ruled "forever" by such an unjust, chaotic, and dysfunctional monarchy? That clearly is the *theme* of this presentation of David's court. It is a question not just of succession but about the very nature of the institution itself.

The issue of the Davidic dynasty as a viable institution for the governance of the people comes to a head in the final episode of the succession in 1 Kgs 1–2. Once again, the *David Saga* builds into Dtr's simple transition of the monarchy in 2 Sam 2:1–4, 10–12 a complex series of events that portray David's complete ineptitude in the face of a palace intrigue and the struggle between the party of the crown prince Adonijah and the party of Solomon the son of Bathsheba, who had no reasonable right to the throne. David is easily won over to Solomon's side by lies invented by Nathan the prophet and uttered by Bathsheba, with the collaboration of Zadok the priest and Benaiah commander of the palace guard of foreign mercenaries. This leads to Solomon's anointing by Zadok the priest and Nathan the prophet to become king while David is still alive, which amounts to a military coup. David's final words to Solomon before his death, according to the *David Saga*, were to settle old scores against Joab and Shimei, which he could not do himself (1 Kgs 2:5–9). This is in stark contrast to Dtr's royal exhortation to Solomon to keep the Law of Moses.

The inauguration of Solomon's reign in 2:13–46 after David's death is marked by the murders of Adonijah, Joab, and Shimei, carried out by Benaiah, and the expulsion of Abiathar for no other reason than the fact that he was an earlier supporter of the crown prince Adonijah. All of this bloodshed and misery is justified by appeals to the divine promise to David as the way by which the Davidic dynasty was established. It can only be read as a deliberate critique of the whole royal ideology. The contrast in Solomon's behavior with what follows in 1 Kgs 3:1–15, in which Dtr has Solomon humbly asking the deity for wisdom in order to discern between right and wrong that he might govern his people wisely, could not be more pronounced. The end of the *David Saga*, therefore, marks the complete subversion of Dtr's David story and its royal ideology.

Conclusion

Our investigation of the story of David reveals that there are two competing presentations of David's rise to power and reign as king in place of Saul: the one, by Dtr as an integral part of his larger history of the people of Israel; the other, the *David Saga*, as an extensive revision that was limited in scope to the career of David and the succession by Solomon. Both have radically different ideologies regarding the nature of the state and the institution of the monarchy. In my concluding remarks, I want briefly to pull together these themes in both works. I regard these two literary works as the products of authors and not just "collectors" or "editors" of traditional material, although each of them employed quite-different genres, the one using historiography and the other using saga. We have already seen that in medieval literature the two genres could coexist, with saga making use of historiography as a framework for its storytelling, and this is what I believe to be the case here.

Understanding Dtr's David within
His Larger History of Israel

Let me begin by looking at the presentation of David within DtrH. We have already seen from the sociohistorical and archaeological evidence that there is little historical basis for believing in a united kingdom of David and Solomon. It is much more likely that Saul was an early ruler of a petty "kingdom" or chiefdom within the tribal district of Benjamin, and traditions of the region remembered him as a champion, fighting against outposts of Philistines in the northern highlands. In a similar fashion, David was leader of a band of warriors who conducted successful skirmishes in the southern highlands against the Philistines and was able to secure for himself a foothold in Hebron and possibly later in Jerusalem as a petty ruler or chieftain. In neither case can we speak of the founding of a state; nor is it likely that David or Saul had any original connection with each other. They may have been contemporaries, and in terms of chronology, they can only be dated rather vaguely to the 10th century B.C.E. Furthermore, during the period in which there was a separate and distinct state of Israel, there is no reason to believe that the term *Israel* stood for anything

other than the inhabitants of this particular region in the northern highlands of Palestine. It was only some time after the demise of the state of Israel that the designation "people of Israel" could be used in a wider sense
to include the people of Judah as well. When exactly this came about is still
a matter of debate, but in my view it is unlikely that it occurred much before the deuteronomic movement at the end of the monarchy.

Consequently, it was Dtr who took up various northern traditions, probably mediated through the Benjaminites, having to do with Moses and the
giving of the law in the wilderness, the settlement of the land, and the stories of the judges. From these, he fashioned an account of the origins of the
people of Israel and their history up to the reign of Saul. All of this was
viewed as having taken place under the guidance and intervention of Yahweh, the God of Israel. What was clearly necessary, in Dtr's view, was to integrate the origins of the Judean state into this sacred history of Israel if
there was to be a common historical tradition and a common identity
within the "people of Israel" under the one deity Yahweh, the God of Israel.
The way in which he did this was to fashion the story about David as one
who began his military career in the service of Saul, and it was David and
not Jonathan, Saul's son, as in the Saul tradition, who had so much success
against the Philistines. Because Saul's kingdom is in Benjamin and David is
from Judah, Dtr had to invent the story of the falling out between David
and Saul to account for David's return to the heartland of Judah in the
southern highlands, from which he then rises as king of the land.

The ideological claim that David was king over "all Israel" and not just
over Judah gives rise to the theme of the king as Yahweh's chosen leader
(*nāgîd*) of his people, Israel. Within the story of Saul in 1 Sam 9–14, it is
Saul who becomes the first divinely elected king and the one to bring deliverance from the Philistines to the people of Israel. However, Dtr then has
the deity reject Saul and his house in favor of another, David, because of a
trivial cultic irregularity, and this eventually allows David to become king
of all Israel in place of Saul. To strengthen this claim, Dtr has David marry
a daughter of Saul and also receive the friendship of Jonathan, the heir to
the throne. Both Jonathan and Saul explicitly acknowledge David to be the
future king over Israel (1 Sam 23:16-17, 24:21). Because Saul and all of his
sons die on Mount Gilboa, David alone is the obvious choice to succeed
Saul and he is immediately anointed king by all the tribes of Israel. David
is also recognized as Yahweh's *nāgîd*, his chosen leader to succeed Saul. In
this way, by making David the successor to Saul, Dtr has created the myth

of a "united kingdom" of Israel. It is this united kingdom that becomes transferred to Jerusalem as its capital.

Furthermore, the ark of the covenant, which in DtrH had been brought from the wilderness across the Jordan under Joshua and had eventually been placed in the sanctuary in Shiloh until its capture and exile among the Philistines, David brings back to Jerusalem in triumph. This object is for Dtr the symbol of a covenant between the people Israel and Yahweh, and through the divine promise to David and the commitment that his off-spring will build the "house" for the ark, as Yahweh's single and permanent abode, Jerusalem henceforth becomes the religious as well as political cap-ital of *Israel*. It is left to Solomon to take up the task of building the temple as permanent dwelling for the ark of Yahweh, which symbolizes the con-nection between Jerusalem and the prehistory of Israel up to that point. Even when the kingdom is eventually split after Solomon, Jerusalem, in theory, always remains this spiritual capital, according to Dtr.

Once it becomes clear that the David story is crucial to articulating Ju-dah's place within the people of Israel, the "house of David" is no longer viewed as a marginal petty kingdom, a small fraction of the size of the larger Israelite state, in which Judah was the junior partner of an alliance under the Omrides. For Dtr, Judah and Jerusalem stand at the very center and core of Israel's existence. All that Israel accomplished under the Om-rides as a military and bureaucratic power in the region Dtr imitates and at-tributes to David and Solomon, and to this he adds the achievements of the Arameans at the height of their power. Thus, David, as a king of all Israel, restores the ark and is given the promise of a perpetual dynasty that cannot be revoked, and he becomes the model king for all of the kings of both Is-rael and Judah, the standard of a just and righteous king by which their ac-tions are judged. Without Dtr's story of David, which so many scholars have failed to recognize as the center within the larger DtrH,[1] there is no clear connection between the earlier part of the history and the later part, and it becomes merely a didactic tale of obedience to Yahweh. Though the deuteronomic law of Moses plays a fundamental role in DtrH, what is equally important for Dtr is the question of national identity, because with-out this connection of the Davidic dynasty and Jerusalem with Israel, the

---

1. See D. J. McCarthy, "II Samuel 7 and the Structure of the Deuteronomistic His-tory," *JBL* 84 (1965): 131-38, as an exception.

northern tradition of the Mosaic law would have little relevance for Judah and the Jews.

As I have pointed out above, it is remarkable how completely Dtr sublimates the entity of Judah in favor of the "people of Israel" as his focus, even during the reigns of David and Solomon. According to our analysis, David becomes king of all the tribes of Israel at the very beginning of his reign in Hebron and reigns over "Israel" for 40 years (1 Kgs 2:11). Judah is completely absorbed into this polity and only becomes a distinct political entity when the kingdom becomes divided at the death of Solomon. Even so, Judah remains one tribe within the larger people of Israel and the history of Israel is for Dtr the history of both kingdoms, whose fundamental unity is expressed by the synchronized chronology. The questions arise, therefore, whether Dtr conceived of Israel as having a destiny beyond the demise of the two states and what role the house of David played in his view of that destiny. This takes us into the very thorny debate about the dating of DtrH, whether an early version belongs to the time of Josiah and a later revision was written in the Exile or whether all of it is exilic or later in date. I do not wish to get bogged down in this debate at the end of this study. My only point here is to emphasize that, whatever position one wishes to argue, Dtr's treatment of David is pivotal to the discussion of Israelite identity.

David's Rise to Power within the David Saga

David's rise to power as successor to Saul is presented by Dtr in a most positive light, as we have seen, and this is the view that still predominates in all the popular presentations of David. This prejudice in David's favor persists in spite of all the efforts throughout the *David Saga*'s attempts at a radical revision of this image of the founder of Judah's monarchy. From the very outset of David's career under Saul, the *David Saga* interprets David as treacherous, having been anointed as king by Samuel in secret while Saul was still on the throne. This casts a shadow over all of his actions within Saul's service and makes his relationship with Jonathan completely disingenuous. While Jonathan makes a covenant of loyalty with David "before Yahweh," he knows nothing about David's treasonous anointing by Samuel, and David uses Jonathan's affection to his own advantage. Saul is deeply suspicious of David's intentions as a threat to his own dynasty and frustrated by Jonathan's naivety. Thus, the falling out between Saul and David and David's subsequent flight is construed in an entirely different way by Dtr and the *David Saga*.

The account of David's flight from Saul to Judah in the *David Saga* is drawn out to include a final encounter between David and Samuel, which includes a parody of Saul's original meeting with Samuel, to Saul's complete discredit. There is also a prolonged scene of parting between David and Jonathan (a doublet of an earlier scene in Dtr), which anticipates David's later dealings with Jonathan's son Mephibosheth when David becomes king. It is a doublet to the two short scenes in Dtr between David and Jonathan, but in this presentation it is David who manipulates Jonathan's affection for him and who is placed in grave risk for David's benefit. David also makes the entirely unnecessary and thoughtless visit to the sanctuary at Nob, which compromises its priesthood and leads to the massacre of the entire community. The one priest who escapes, Abiathar, joins David, who then admits his mistake. Saul's massacre of the priests of Nob is often misunderstood as propaganda against the house of Saul in favor of the house of David as the destined leader of Israel, but this is not the intention of the author of the *David Saga*. Instead, it is the portrait of a ruler who is driven mad by his obsession with the realization of loss of the dynastic succession, which leads to the slaughter of the innocents. It is not the house of Saul that is being condemned—Jonathan, the heir apparent, is a most commendable figure—but the institution of the monarchy as such, which is under scrutiny. Kings and tyrants routinely behave in this way against perceived threats to their rule.

While Dtr presents David's little band of warriors as a boon to the small towns of Judah against marauding Philistines, the *David Saga* suggests that they are a scourge and would be happy to help Saul rid them of this group. This is illustrated in particular by the episode involving the large southern estate of Nabal, which is threatened by David and his men when Nabal refuses to pay for their unauthorized "protection." A massacre of the entire household is narrowly averted by Nabal's clever wife, Abigail, who quickly arranges for the gift of provisions that was "requested" and then flatters him with pious talk about his future destiny as king and his need to refrain from blood guilt and to fight the "wars of Yahweh," none of which corresponds to his present activity or to his future service under the Philistines or, indeed, to the whole period of his reign. The speech of Abigail, which is loaded with clichés of Dtr's royal ideology anticipating 2 Sam 7, is deeply ironic and intended as a parody on the earlier presentation of David's rise to power. The sudden death of Nabal allows David to take Abigail as one of his wives and whenever she is mentioned in the subsequent narrative she is always identified as Nabal's wife, as a constant reminder of this episode.

The doublet to Dtr's version of David's sparing Saul's life (1 Sam 24) is the *David Saga*'s account in 1 Sam 26, which is presented in an entirely different fashion. David and his men are no longer hiding in a cave to escape being found by Saul's search party, but they have now become an elite force of 600 professional mercenaries—the core of David's later personal army during his reign—and they take the initiative in their encounter with Saul's larger force of 3,000. There is nothing humble or conciliatory about David's manner, only the veiled threat of taking his forces outside Saul's reach and joining the enemy. And in place of Saul's acknowledgement of his injustice to David, his attempt at reconciliation and his recognition that David will indeed be the future king, the *David Saga* merely has Saul trying to persuade David to return to his service rather than have him go elsewhere and when David refuses, Saul grudgingly acknowledges his future success.

As a consequence of David's final encounter with Saul, David immediately sets out to join forces with the Philistines. In contrast to his attempt to seek political asylum with Achish of Gath in Dtr's account, in this doublet version of the *David Saga* he is warmly received by Achish, enlisted as a mercenary force, installed in a southern city of Ziklag, which becomes his personal domain, and is given a free hand to raid and massacre villages of the region. It is true that he avoids raiding Judean villages because he has future ambitions in ruling Judah, and so he must deceive his master, but the author hardly regards his behavior as commendable. Indeed, as we have seen, the *David Saga* makes clear that all of David's words and actions are entirely governed by his own interests and political ambitions. His word and even his oath are completely untrustworthy. In this portrayal, the author seems to raise a disturbing question: can the actions by David of deceit and shedding of innocent blood be justified because they are perpetrated against those outside Deuteronomy's understanding of the chosen people?

As though to drive home the point even more clearly, the final episode of David's life in exile before Saul's death has to do with the raid of the Amalekites on Ziklag, in which the city is destroyed and all the families are taken captive. The author is at pains to make clear two points about this disaster. The first is that the blame for the successful attack by the Amalekites is placed squarely on David's shoulders, because in his haste to support Achish in the upcoming campaign against Israel he did not take any precautions to protect the city against a possible raid, and this almost leads to full rebellion. The second is that whereas David was accustomed to massacring the aboriginal population, such as the Amalekites, in his raids of plunder, the Amalekites in contrast killed none of their captors. The dramatic rescue of David's and his men's own kin in the subsequent pursuit, followed by the slaughter of Amalekites, with no captives taken, leads to the acquisition of much booty, which is hardly treated as *ḥerem* but is regarded as David's personal property, which he distributes as payment to his troops and as political gifts to Judean leaders for future considerations. For the *David Saga*, there is always a glaring gap between the religious ideology of Dtr and political reality, and David's rise to power was no exception.

The David Saga *as a Radical Revision*
of Dtr's View of the State

In contrast to Dtr, who speaks of David's subjects as the people of Israel, the author of the *David Saga* maintains the distinction throughout between Judah and Israel as two separate polities.[2] He introduces the notion that David first became king of Judah in Hebron (2 Sam 2:4); and he then revises Dtr's dating formula in 2 Sam 5:4-5, in which David reigns over Judah alone for 7 and a half years and over Israel for 33 years, so that he becomes king of Israel in Hebron for only 6 months before he moves to Jerusalem. The clear implication is that he was king of two different polities at the same time. Furthermore, he invents a fourth son of Saul, who is king over Israel for 2 years and with whom David carries on a war. Even after Ishbosheth's death, David does not become king of Israel for another 5 years! This duality of states is reflected in the rest of the *David Saga*, no more clearly than at the end of the Absalom revolt and the return of David to Jerusalem, when conflict breaks out over which political entity has the prior claim over David, Judah or Israel. Furthermore, Benjamin, as a tribe that continues to have special allegiance to the house of Saul, inhabits a very ambiguous position within the larger political framework. In this way, the author establishes a direct continuity between the political conditions during David's reign and the eventual political division after Solomon's death.

Consequently, the ideology of an "all Israel" state is completely subverted. This is further emphasized in a number of ways. There are many foreigners in the realms of both Saul and David, and they are in positions of authority, such as Doeg the Edomite among the officers of Saul, the Hittite

---

2. See A. Alt, "The Formation of the Israelite State in Palestine," in *Essays on Old Testament History and Religion* (Oxford: Blackwell, 1966), 171-237, esp. pp. 205-37. Alt construes the distinction made by the *David Saga* as historical and builds his theory about state formation accordingly. He did not have the benefit of contemporary archaeological evidence as a counterweight to the biblical text.

soldiers among David's servants, and the black African runner in David's army. Indeed, most of David's elite forces appear to be made up of foreign mercenaries. Contrary to the principles of Deuteronomy, there seems to be no concern whatever about racial purity or taboos on intermarriage with non-Israelites. As stated above, David's raids against "aboriginal" villages or neighboring nations have nothing to do with religious principles but only involve booty and political power. Above all, it is the ark as the supreme symbol of the deity dwelling among the people of Yahweh in DtrH that is treated by the author of the *David Saga* so cavalierly. In the story of the ark's restoration to Jerusalem, it is regarded as a dangerous talisman. Handled in the wrong way, it can cause great trouble, as it does for Uzzah, one of the keepers of the ark, on its trip to Jerusalem, by killing him and interrupting its joyous return. Yet, when placed in the house of a Philistine for three months, it brings nothing but good luck, and David now wants it back for himself. This is hardly what Dtr intended by his invention of the ark of the covenant. The complete parody of the ark as a sacred object symbolic of the divine presence occurs again in the story of David's flight from Jerusalem in the Absalom revolt. As we have seen above, the appearance of the two priests and the band of Levites carrying the ark down into the Wadi Kidron on the east side of Jerusalem while David's entourage is crossing the stream appears to completely trivialize the parallel in Joshua's crossing of the Jordan. In David's case, the ark does not go on with the people but is sent back to Jerusalem, as though it might be bad luck.

Another telling reference to the ark is in the story of the Bathsheba affair. This story is set within the context of David's war with Ammon, which is related to David's feud with the king of Ammon over an act of personal dishonor toward David's messengers. We are told by Uriah the Hittite that the ark is in the camp of the Israelites, as though the war were being construed as a holy war. The foreigner Uriah is scrupulous in maintaining all the taboos associated with holy war, while David, who takes no part in this campaign, violates all these taboos with impunity. The whole conduct of the war is in utter disregard for the deuteronomic laws of holy war. War is merely intended for booty and the enrichment of the crown.

Furthermore, even the notion that Israel is a collection of twelve tribes is used as a mark not of the people's unity but of their division. Even David encourages the distinction between Judah and Israel, by emphasizing that it is the people of Judah who are his kin and his own flesh and blood, not the Israelites (2 Sam 19:12-14[11-13]). In the dispute that follows between Israel and Judah over who has priority in the royal protocol of escorting the king, the delegation from Israel speaks of having 10 shares in David (2 Sam 19:44[43]), which must be a vague reference to the 10 tribes and relative size to Judah's 1 share. This argument, however, carries no weight, and the revolt of a group of Israelites follows, with the rallying cry "We have no portion in David," which is the same as the cry that led to the permanent division of states in the later revolt under Rehoboam. *According to the David Saga there never was a unity of tribes, and even as late as the Persian period the author does not recognize the identity of the Jew as an Israelite.*

The Significance of Genre

In the introduction to this volume, I posed the problem of genre as it has to do with the *David Saga*, and I suggested that its closest literary analogy was the Icelandic saga; and throughout my discussion of the *David Saga*, I have drawn attention to the numerous similarities between this late version of the David story and the old Norse sagas. I further argued throughout my analysis of the Dtr stratum that the David story is an integral and indeed quite central part of DtrH as a whole, and therefore in form Dtr's David story is historiography. Because I have also argued that the *David Saga* was directly dependent on DtrH, my thesis entails the further claim that there was a quite-deliberate shift in genre from historiography to saga. This completely reverses the notions of Gunkel and von Rad, among others, who viewed the rise of historiography as moving from saga to history, with the Succession Narrative at the very apex of Israelite historiography.[3] However, the Icelandic sagas clearly demonstrate that the reverse of this development, from history to saga, was true in their case, and this was also true of the David story.

Consequently, we must ask what significance this kind of shift in genre might have on our understanding of the David story in general and the *David Saga* in particular. As indicated above, the base text of Dtr's David story is historiography, and the primary function of ancient historiography, particularly in the form of archaic history, which had to do with the origins of nations and states, is ideological.[4] It articulates national identity and the origins of customs and norms by which the society is to live. There can be

---

3. See my *In Search of History*, 209–20.

4. For a discussion of archaic or antiquarian history see my *Prologue to History: The Yahwist as Historian in Genesis* (Louisville: Westminster John Knox, 1992), 86–99; idem, "Is There Any Historiography in the Hebrew Bible? A Hebrew-Greek Comparison," *JNSL* 28/2 (2002): 1–25.

little doubt that DtrH as a whole and Dtr's David story in particular, as I have identified it, is meant to serve this function. It takes what are admittedly the northern traditions, from Moses to the kingship of Saul and the traditions of the Kingdom of Israel, which constitute the largest part of the history, and combines these with the rather sparse traditions of Judah to make the story of a common identity, the people of Israel. To do this, David, the founding figure of the Kingdom of Judah, becomes the linchpin. I have argued above that originally the traditions of Saul and David had no connection with each other and that it was Dtr who forged the ideological connections to create a common identity and destiny, with David as the ideal ruler and the temple of Jerusalem as its common religious center.

The *David Saga* takes up this historical base and creates out of it a saga of David's career, yielding a more lively and realistic portrayal of David's rise to power and reign. He does not attempt to fill his account with the artifacts and manners of a bygone age, which is quite beyond his grasp, but he places his characters in the setting and garb of his own age to make them familiar and alive to his audience. As I indicated in the introduction to this book, this is what the Icelandic sagas did with their founding traditions: they filled in the gaps left by the bare historical record in order to tell the "truth" about that age as they understood it. When the author sets about to tell the truth about kings and their courts as he knows them in his own time and supposes, not unreasonably, that these notions had always been true in every previous age, this creates a clash between the idealization of the historical tradition and the realism of the saga. The result is parody of several major themes of DtrH. The "real" David is no better than any of the other kings that followed and comparable in his actions to the worst; and he was directly responsible for the demise of the monarchy and the house of David itself. There never was a truly "united" monarchy, and it was always prone to factional conflict. Furthermore, Dtr's notion of ethnic purity is contradicted by the quite-mixed population and intermarriage of the whole region, just as the author knew it in his own day. The ark, which is so central to Dtr's program of integrating the ancient traditions of Israel into Judean ideology, is treated as an ancient fetish that is of no consequence, because it no longer has any role in his own day, if it ever had one in the past. For all of Dtr's talk about David's complete obedience to the laws and statutes of Yahweh as given through Moses (i.e., Deuteronomy) and David's exhortation to Solomon to do the same, their behavior, as well as the behavior of all of the rest of the sons of David, completely ignores or violates Deuteronomy's injunctions.

The fundamental error that has dominated the interpretation of the David story since the time of Wellhausen has been to read the whole as historiography, based on two or more supposed historical sources contemporary with the events themselves, and then form-critically to find Near Eastern genres, such as the royal apologies, as the models by which to interpret these hypothetical sources. Scholars were so convinced by the realism of the story that they thought it must be historical. At the time that this perspective arose and for a long time afterward, there was no external evidence from archaeology or history to contradict this viewpoint, and even when it did arise it was interpreted in a way that confirmed rather than questioned the prevailing view. It is now acknowledged, however, that a state such as the one reflected in the *David Saga* could not possibly have been in existence in Judah and Jerusalem in the 10th century and many indicators point to the late Persian period instead. Consequently, the *David Saga* cannot be treated any longer as historiography. The realistic quality of the *David Saga* is no guarantee of its historicity, just as Euripides's plays may be regarded as much more "realistic" than those of Aeschylus in their treatment of the heroic age, but they are no more historical. Moreover, to misconstrue the *David Saga* as historiography instead of saga is to misunderstand its purpose as "serious entertainment." Unlike DtrH, it is not intended to construct a narrow ethnic identity based on a divinely appointed institution, but instead its purpose is to replace DtrH with a more "realistic" view of life in a cosmopolitan world. As in the case of *Njals Saga*, the *David Saga* seeks to overcome nostalgia for an idealized past with a reality of what a monarchy of this sort would be like transplanted into the late Persian period. In this form of saga, it seeks to subvert and satirize the older historical and ideological tradition of Dtr. This is particularly the case with the royal ideology of the eternal house of David.

The Royal Ideology of the David Saga and DtrH Compared

The greatest revision in the *David Saga* is the author's consistent subversion of the royal ideology of Dtr. As we have seen above, Dtr establishes the basis for his royal ideology in the theme of the divinely chosen king and leader (*nāgîd*) of Yahweh's people Israel to give them victory over the Philistines, and so Samuel anoints Saul to be the future king (1 Sam 9:16, 10:1). However, because of Saul's one error in following Samuel's instructions, Samuel later informs Saul that his dynasty is rejected and that another leader (*nāgîd*) will replace him (1 Sam 13:13-14). This new leader turns out to be David, who replaces Saul as the great champion over the Philistines and whom Saul quickly recognizes as a threat to his dynasty (1 Sam 18). Eventually, after the death of Saul and all his possible heirs, all the tribes of Israel recognize David by his leadership in the wars of Yahweh as the divine choice and thus as his *nāgîd* over Israel, and they proceed to anoint him as king. However, during Saul's lifetime David always recognizes him as the only anointed one and never violates his status, which is the ideological basis for the continuity of kingship over all Israel.

This viewpoint was radically altered by the addition of the story of Saul's battle against the Amalekites (1 Sam 15), in which, as a consequence of Saul's disobedience to Samuel's explicit instructions to wipe out everything alive, Yahweh has specifically nullified Saul's status as the anointed one and given it to another, and in the subsequent episode Samuel proceeds to Bethlehem to surreptitiously anoint David. As a consequence, David receives the spirit of Yahweh to accomplish the mighty deeds in the subsequent narrative. This verdict of Saul's rejection is later confirmed by Samuel to Saul before the final battle against the Philistines, in which his death and the deaths of his sons will be the proof of his rejection (1 Sam 28:16-19). This post-Dtr revision, however, creates some problems for the account of David's period of service to Saul, because David's anointing is clearly an act of treason, which Samuel seems to openly acknowledge. It allows one to interpret all of David's actions as less than genuine loyalty to Saul and secretly treacherous. This may not have been the intention of the author of 1 Sam 15:1-16:13, but it appears to be the way in which the addition was interpreted by the author of the *David Saga*.

The theme of Yahweh's anointed is an important one within the *David Saga*. In the first scene introduced by this author, Jonathan, the crown prince, in a gesture of friendship, makes a sworn covenant of loyalty with David and invests him with all the regalia of his lofty position, that is, his personal armor, with which David then proceeds to lead the people in battle in Jonathan's place. Of course, Jonathan knows nothing of the secret anointing by Samuel. Again, when David meets with Jonathan at the beginning of his flight, he feigns complete innocence and sets Jonathan up to help him at great risk to Jonathan (1 Sam 20). It is Saul, rather than Jonathan, who seems to discern David's true intentions regarding the future of the kingdom. In Abigail's speech to David in the *David Saga* (1 Sam 25:28-31), she seems to know all about David's ambition to become king, as well as the secret anointing by Samuel, and uses Dtr language to flatter David in order to avoid a massacre of her household. The use of this kind of ideological jargon, applied to the leader of a band of ruffians bent on slaughter, is a complete subversion of these themes. Again, in the *David Saga*'s parallel to David sparing Saul's life (1 Sam 26), the phrase "Yahweh's anointed" comes up repeatedly, mimicking its use in 1 Sam 24:6, 10, but now it rings hollow, because David is also Yahweh's anointed in place of Saul. His concern for the inviolability of Yahweh's anointed seems to reflect self-interest more than respect for Saul. There is clearly no sincerity in his words.

In the *David Saga*'s version of David's ascent to the throne, David is first anointed as king over "the house of Judah" as a distinct polity. Nothing is said by way of an acknowledgement of the deity's choice. It is merely a political act. It does not matter that a son of Saul has also been made king of Israel at the same time. As we have seen above, the author of the *David Saga* has modified the earlier version of Israel's making David king by construing it as an event distinct from the anointing seven years earlier, and the anointing is the consequence of the elders of Israel's making a political agreement (*bĕrît*) with David. Furthermore, during the revolt of Absalom, we also have the situation in which Israel makes Absalom king and anoints him in Hebron, so that there are two "anointed ones." When Absalom is dead, the Israelites decide to simply revert to the old agreement (2 Sam 19:9-10). When Solomon is anointed king, it is done by members of Solomon's own party in the palace coup, with the result that again there are two kings, "anointed ones," at the same time. Furthermore, it is David and not Yahweh who decides who will be the leader (*nāgîd*) over Israel and Judah, usurping the divine prerogative.

We have also seen how completely the *David Saga* subverts and parodies the divine promise to David in 2 Sam 7, the cornerstone of Dtr's royal ideology. This can be seen especially in the account of Solomon's succession to the throne. First, the divine promise to David of a sure and perpetual dynasty as mediated through Nathan, the prophet, is in stark contrast to the promise invented by Nathan, which David is supposed to have given to Bathsheba that her son would succeed to the throne. The deception works and David orders Zadok the priest, Nathan the prophet, and Benaiah, the head of the palace guard, to proceed to anoint Solomon as king. In this way, Solomon is made king *before* David's death, contradicting the Nathan oracle, which speaks of securing David's dynasty *after* his death. And once David is dead, then Solomon himself sets about to secure his hold on power by a series of murders, and in two cases justifies his actions by making direct reference to the divine promise to David and misappropriating it for himself (1 Kgs 2:24, 45). After the murder of the last one of the house of Saul, the narrator concludes with a statement full of irony: "So the kingdom was established in the hand of Solomon" (v. 46b). It is uttered sardonically, as though it were the fulfillment of the Nathan prophecy in 2 Sam 7:15-16.

Also basic to Dtr's royal ideology is his idealization of David's reign as one of justice and righteousness, in which David's behavior is the model for all the future kings of Israel and Judah. As we have seen in our study of the *David Saga*, this view of David and his household is so completely subverted by repeated acts of violence: murders, rape, adultery, civil war, and bloodshed. It is not just in the case of the Bathsheba affair, in which David's actions are comparable to those of Ahab, the worst king of Israel according to Dtr, and in which the judgment is passed on him that the sword will never depart from his household/dynasty. The negative view of David begins with his violent rise to power and it includes the unremitting acts of injustice and bloodshed that persist in his family throughout his reign. A portrayal of this sort could never serve as a model of what the monarchy should be, "doing what is pleasing in the sight of Yahweh."

Final Remarks

What is it that the author of the *David Saga* is trying to say? He is not just trying to entertain his audience, any more than the anonymous authors of the Icelandic sagas were merely good storytellers. The artistry of the *David Saga* is serious and it is playing to a sophisticated audience of the late Persian period that is familiar both with the national tradition as reflected in DtrH and with the power politics of the Persian Empire. The whole cast of players in the *David Saga* is clothed in this period garb, and each particular act and scene is set in this time and place. With all the grand dreams about the revival of a Davidic empire from the Euphrates to the border of Egypt, the audience is confronted by a question: Is this what you want? This question is implied by the author's consistent and unrelenting attack on Dtr's central theme of the divine promise to David, which became the basis of messianism in the later period. For the author, the *messiah* or "anointed one" is nothing more than the product of a political action taken by those in authority, the elders of the people, or the result of a military coup, a status that can be just as quickly withdrawn or rescinded. And religious officials in the form of prophets and priests are just as likely to be involved in power politics as anyone else. The same applies to the use of religious texts, such as the divine promise to David, that are cited as justification for im-moral actions, such as murder and assassination.[5]

Included within the vision of a future messianic age are the deutero-nomic notions of a pure state that involves racial cleansing and the exclu-sion of foreigners and infidels. The author of the *David Saga* undermines these ideas by populating David's state with all kinds of foreigners. There is the Philistine Obededom who has an estate on the outskirts of Jerusalem, whose household is blessed by Yahweh, because of the presence of the ark. This is in stark contrast to Dtr's portrayal of the ark in Philistine territory, where it causes so much trouble. And then there is Uriah the Hittite, who is far more devout than David in his obedience to the law of Yahweh but who pays for it with his life. One can find many other foreigners throughout the whole saga, not least of whom are the numerous foreign mercenaries who are at the very center of power. For the author of the *David Saga*, it is totally unrealistic to think of an ethnically pure state such as this. Given also the fact that David freely intermarried with foreign wives without any divine ex-pression of disapproval, it would appear that the author was not in agree-ment with the policy of Ezra to annul mixed marriages.

Furthermore, the author does not seem to subscribe to the ideology of a greater Israel as a single identity inclusive of both Israel and Judah. He con-sciously goes against Dtr by recognizing Judah and Israel as distinct poli-ties throughout David's reign, and he even suggests the same for Benjamin and for other regions of the country. His view of the make-up of David's state (by which he means the ethnicity of his own state) is a very cosmo-politan one, in which people are judged for who they are, regardless of eth-nic or tribal affiliations. His outlook may well reflect a kind of "secular" wisdom perspective that is competing with the more "doctrinaire" views of his time. What is remarkable is that it found a firm response, which re-sulted in its uncontested place within the Dtr corpus of Samuel–Kings, and it took a quite-distinct work, namely, that of the Chronicler, to excise the *David Saga* from his own historical record and restore the pious image of David and Solomon and the unity of Israel.

---

5. This is not the place to enter into an extensive revision of the scholarly discus-sion about the biblical notions of the Messiah. One need only compare the under-lying literary assumptions reflected in a classical study such as as T. N. D. Mettinger, *King and Messiah* (CBOTS 8; Lund: Gleerup, 1976), with this study to realize how extensive a revision of this sort would need to be.

This gives us a different picture of competing ideologies and radically different understandings of social identities during the late Persian and early Hellenistic periods within the province of Jehud and the surrounding region and among those who were part of the same intellectual and religious tradition, broadly speaking. With the appropriate placement of the *David Saga* as a competing narrative by a highly gifted writer within this time frame and one who was willing to take such surprising liberties with the "historical" tradition that he had received, there are some interesting new possibilities for understanding the history of the biblical tradition in this and later periods.

Appendix:
The Division of Sources
(Dtr and the David Saga)

The outline of Dtr's story of David and Saul in *account A* can be seen in the following components.

1. *1 Sam 16:14-23.* David enters Saul's employment both as a musician who can relieve Saul's troubled spirit and also as an accomplished warrior.

2. *1 Sam 18:5-9*, (10-11), 12-16.* David is sent out on military missions and is very successful, to the extent that he wins greater praise from the people than Saul does, and this kindles a jealousy within Saul against David. This leads to the first instance in which David, while playing the lyre for Saul, is threatened by his spear. David is sent on more military missions and continues to be successful.

3. *1 Sam 18:17-30.* David is twice offered Saul's daughters in marriage. In the case of Merab, Saul reneges on his promise and gives his daughter to another. But in the case of Michal, who loves David dearly, David purchases her hand with the bride-price of 100 foreskins of the Philistines.

4. *1 Sam 19:1-17.* There are a series of threats against David that lead to the final break with Saul and his flight. First, Jonathan, Saul's son, learns of his father's intentions to kill David and so warns David. He also speaks to his father and wins for David a temporary reprieve. But no sooner is David restored to Saul's presence than he is threatened again by Saul's spear while playing the lyre and flees to his house. There his wife Michal urges him to leave and helps him to escape, while deceiving the messengers of Saul who have come to take him.

5. *1 Sam 21:11-16[10-15].* David's first impulse is to flee to Achish, king of Gath, for asylum, but his reputation as a warrior for Saul is too well known and he must leave Achish's court.

6. *1 Sam 22:1-5; 23:1-5, 15-18, 24b-28.* David now goes to Adullum in Judah and gathers his family and a band of 400 followers. He puts

his family under the protection of the king of Moab, while he and his men remain in Judah. During this period, they assist the town of Keilah against the marauding Philistines. David also receives a visit from Jonathan, who encourages him, acknowledges that David will be the future king, and makes a covenant of loyalty with him. David is pursued by Saul but manages to evade him.

7. *1 Sam 24:1-23[23:1-24:22].* Saul again pursues David in Engedi, and while he is in a cave relieving himself, Saul comes under David's control. But David refuses this chance to kill Saul and spares him. As a consequence, Saul admits that he was in the wrong, acknowledges that David will indeed be the king, and extracts from David an oath that he will not harm any of Saul's offspring. This ends contact between David *and Saul.*

8. *1 Sam 28:1a, 4; 31:1-13.* The final showdown takes place between Saul and the Philistines, in which Saul and his sons, including Jonathan, are killed.

9. *2 Sam 1:1*, 2-4, 11-12, 17-27.* David learns of the deaths of Saul and Jonathan and mourns their loss.

10. *2 Sam 2:1-2aα, 3; 5:1-2, 3b, (4).* David is anointed as king over all Israel in Hebron.

11. *2 Sam 5:6-12, 17-25; 8:1.* David captures Jerusalem, makes it the capital of the realm, and builds a palace. He then proceeds to defend his realm against the Philistines.

12. *2 Sam 8:2-14, 10:15-19.* David fights a series of foreign wars against the neighboring states.

13. *2 Sam 6:2-3a, 5, 15, 17-19.* David restores the ark to Israel and places it in Jerusalem.

14. *2 Sam 7:1-10a, (10b-11aα), 11aβ-29.* David receives the divine promise of a perpetual dynasty.

The following components belong to the additions made to Dtr by the *David Saga* in *account B*:

1. *1 Sam 17:1-18:4, 6a*.* The story of David and Goliath (17:1-58) and the subsequent covenant between Jonathan and David (18:1-4).

2. *1 Sam 19:18-21:10[9], 22:6-23.* David's flight to Samuel (19:18-24) and his return to Saul's court and meeting with Jonathan (20:1-21:1). David seeks help from the priests of Nob, which subsequently leads to their massacre (21:2-10, 22:6-23).

3. *1 Sam 23:6-14, 19-24a.*   The people of Keilah fail to provide safe asylum for David (23:6-14), and the Ziphites assist Saul in trying to track down David in Judah (23:19-24a).
4. *1 Sam 25:1-44.*   The story of David and Abigail.
5. *1 Sam 26:1-25.*   The second time David spares Saul's life.
6. *1 Sam 27:1-28:2, 29:1-11.*   David among the Philistines.
7. *1 Sam 30:1-31.*   David's pursuit of the Amalekites and rescue of the inhabitants of Ziklag.
8. *2 Sam 2:4-4:12.*   David becomes king of Judah and conducts a military campaign against Ishbosheth for control of Israel.
9. *2 Sam 1:1aβb, 5-10, 13-16; 2:2aβb; 5:3a, (4), 5, 13-16.*   These small additions integrate the *David Saga* into Dtr's account.
10. *2 Sam 6:1, 3b-4, 6-14, 16, 20-23.*   This represents the *David Saga*'s revision of the return of the ark in Dtr.
11. *2 Sam 8:16-18, 20:23-25.*   Lists of David's officials.
12. *2 Sam 9-20; 1 Kgs 1:1-52; 2:5-9, 13-46.*   Otherwise known as the Court History or Succession Narrative. This includes the restoration of Mephibosheth (2 Sam 9); the Ammonite war and the Bathsheba affair (10:1-14, 19b; 11-12); Amnon's rape of Tamar, his murder by Absalom, and Absalom's exile (chap. 13); Absalom's return and restoration (chap. 14); Absalom's revolt and death (chaps. 15-18); David's return to Jerusalem (chap. 19); the revolt of Sheba (chap. 20); the succession of Solomon (1 Kgs 1-2).

Bibliography

Ackroyd, P. "The Succession Narrative (So-Called)." *Int* 35 (1981): 383–96.

Adcock, F. E. *The Greek and Macedonian Art of War.* Berkeley: University of California Press, 1957.

Alt, A. *Die Staatenbildung der Israeliten in Palästina* (Leipzig: Alfred Edelmann, 1930). [Also published as "The Formation of the Israelite State in Palestine." Pp. 171–237 in *Essays on Old Testament History and Religion,* trans. R. A. Wilson. Oxford: Blackwell, 1966.]

_____. "Das Königtum in den Reichen Israel und Juda." *VT* 1 (1951): 2–22. [Also published as "The Monarchy in the Kingdoms of Israel and Judah." Pp. 241–59 in *Essays on Old Testament History and Religion,* trans. R. A. Wilson. Oxford: Blackwell, 1966.]

Aly, W. *Volkmärchen, Sage und Novelle bei Herodot und seinen Zeitgenossen: Eine Untersuchung über die volkstümlichen Elemente der altgriechischen Prosaerzählung.* Göttingen: Vandenhoeck & Ruprecht, 1921.

Andersson, T. M. *The Problem of Icedandic Saga Origins: A Historical Survey.* New Haven, CT: Yale University Press, 1964.

_____. *The Growth of the Medieval Icelandic Sagas (1180–1280).* Ithaca, NY: Cornell University Press, 2006.

Auld, A. G. "Prophets through the Looking Glass: A Response to Robert Carroll and Hugh Williamson." *JSOT* 27 (1983): 41–44.

Auld, A. G., and C. Y. S. Ho. "The Making of David and Goliath." *JSOT* 56 (1992): 19–39.

Bailey, R. C. *David in Love and War: The Pursuit of Power in 2 Samuel 10–12.* JSOTSup 75. Sheffield: JSOT Press, 1990.

Barthélemy, D. "Trois niveaux d'analyse." Pp. 47–54 in *The Story of David and Goliath: Textual and Literary Criticism* by Barthélemy et al. OBO 73. Göttingen: Vandenhoeck & Ruprecht / Fribourg: Éditions Universitaires, 1986.

Barthélemy, D., D. W. Gooding, J. Lust, and E. Tov. *The Story of David and Goliath: Textual and Literary Criticism.* OBO 73. Göttingen: Vandenhoeck & Ruprecht / Fribourg: Éditions Universitaires, 1986.

Beaulieu, P.-A. *The Reign of Nabonidus King of Babylon 556–539 B.C.* New Haven, CT: Yale University Press, 1989.

Biram, A., and J. Naveh. "An Aramaic Stele Fragment fron Tel Dan." *IEJ* 43 (1993): 81–98.

_____. "The Tel Dan Inscription: A New Fragment." *IEJ* 45 (1995): 1–18.

Birch, B. *The Rise of the Israelite Monarchy: The Growth and Development of 1 Samuel 7–15.* SBLDS 27. Missoula, MT: Scholars Press, 1976.

Blum, E. "Das Ende der Thronfolgegeschichte." Pp. 4–37 in *Die sogenannte Thronfolgegeschichte Davids,* ed. A. de Pury and T. Römer. OBO 176. Freiburg: Universitätsverlag, 2000.

Byrne, R. "The Refuge of Scribalism in Iron I Palestine." *BASOR* 345 (2007): 1–31.

Campbell, A. F. *Of Prophets and Kings: A Late Ninth-Century Document (1 Samuel 1–2 Kings 10)*. CBQMS 17. Washington, DC: Catholic Biblical Association, 1986.

Cancik, H. *Grundzüge der hetittischen und alttestamentlichen Geschichtsschreibung.* Wiesbaden: Harrassowitz, 1976.

Caspari, W. "The Literary Type and Historical Value of 2 Samuel 15–20." Pp. 59–88 in *Narrative and Novella in Samuel: Studies by Hugo Gressmann and Other Scholars 1906–1923*, ed. David M. Gunn. Sheffield: Almond, 1991.

Chadwick, R., P. M. M. Daviau, and M. Steiner. "Four Seasons of Excavations at Khirbat al-Mudayna on Wadi ath-Thamad, 1996–1999." *ADAJ* 44 (2000): 257–70.

Cody, A. "Le titre égyptien et le nom propre du scribe de David." *RB* 72 (1965): 381–93.

Cook, J. M. *The Persian Empire.* New York: Schocken, 1983.

Cross, F. M. *Canaanite Myth and Hebrew Epic: Essays in the History of the Religion of Israel.* Cambridge, MA: Harvard University Press, 1973.

Culley, R. C. *Studies in the Structure of Hebrew Narrative.* Philadelphia: Fortress / Missoula, MT: Scholars Press, 1976.

Dalley, S. "Foreign Chariotry and Cavalry in the Armies of Tiglath-Pileser III and Sargon II." *Iraq* 47 (1985): 31–48.

De Geus, C. H. J. *The Tribes of Israel: An Investigation into Some of the Presuppositions of Martin Noth's Amphictyony Hypothesis.* Assen: Van Gorcum, 1976.

Dever, W. G. "Archaeology and the 'Age of Solomon': A Case Study in Archaeology and Historiography." Pp. 217–51 in *The Age of Solomon, Scholarship at the Turn of the Millennium*, ed. L. K. Handy. Leiden: Brill, 1997.

_____ . *What Did the Biblical Writers Know and When Did They Know It?* Grand Rapids: Eerdmans, 2001.

Dietrich, W. *David, Saul und die Propheten: Das Verhaltnis von Religion und Politik nach den prophetischen Überlieferungen vom frühesten Königtum in Israel.* 2nd ed. BWANT 122. Stuttgart: Kohlhammer, 1992.

_____ . *Die frühe Königszeit in Israel: 10. Jahrhundert v. Chr.* Biblisch Enzyklopädie 3. Stuttgart: Kohlhammer, 1997.

_____ . "Das Ende der Thronfolgegeschichte." Pp. 38–69 in *Die sogenannte Thronfolgegeschichte Davids*, ed. A. de Pury and T. Römer. OBO 176. Freiburg: Universitätsverlag, 2000.

Dietrich, W., and T. Naumann. *Die Samuelbücher.* Erträge der Forschung 281. Darmstadt: Wissenschaftliche Buchgesellschaft, 1995.

_____ . "The David-Saul Narrative." Pp. 276–318 in *Reconsidering Israel and Judah: Recent Studies on the Deuteronomistic History*, ed. G. N. Knoppers and J. G. McConville. Sources for Biblical and Theological Study 8. Winona Lake, IN: Eisenbrauns, 2000.

Dion, P. E. "Aramean Tribes and Nations of First Millennium Western Asia." Pp. 1281–94 in vol. 2 of *Civilizations of the Ancient Near East*, ed. J. Sasson. 4 vols. New York: Scribners, 1995.

Dodd, E. R. "Homer." In *Fifty Years of Classical Scholarship*, ed. M. Platnauer. New York: Barnes & Noble, 1954.

Driver, S. R. *Notes on the Hebrew Text of the Books of Samuel.* Oxford: Clarendon, 1913.

Edelman, D. V. *King Saul in the Historiography of Judah.* JSOTSup 121. Sheffield: Sheffield Academic Press, 1991.

Eissfeldt, O. *The Old Testament: An Introduction.* New York: Harper & Row, 1965.

Fales, F. M. "Kilamuwa and the Foreign Kings." *WO* 10 (1979): 6–22.

Faust, A. "Abandonment, Urbanization, Resettlement and the Formation of the Israelite State." *NEA* 66 (2003): 147–61.

Finkelstein, I. "The Emergence of Israel: A Phase in the Cyclic History of Canaan in the Third and Second Millennia BCE." Pp. 150–78 in *From Nomadism to Monarchy,* ed. I. Finkelstein and N. Na'aman. Jerusalem: Israel Exploration Society, 1994.

_____ . "The Archaeology of the United Monarchy: An Alternative View." *Levant* 28 (1996): 177–87.

_____ . "Bible Archaeology or Archaeology of Palestine in the Iron Age? A Rejoinder." *Levant* 30 (1998): 167–74.

_____ . "State Formation in Israel and Judah: A Contrast in Context, a Contrast in Trajectory." *NEA* 62 (1999): 35–52.

_____ . "Omride Architecture." *ZDPV* 116 (2000): 114–38.

_____ . "Addendum: Ben-Tor's Dating of Hazor X–VII." *TA* 27 (2000): 240–44.

_____ . "The Rise of Jerusalem and Judah: The Missing Link." *Levant* 33 (2001): 105–15.

_____ . "Gezer Revisited and Revised." *TA* 29 (2002): 262–96.

_____ . "The Philistines in the Bible: A Late-Monarchic Perspective." *JSOT* 27 (2002): 131–67.

_____ . "[De]formation of the Israelite State: A Rejoinder on Methodology." *NEA* 68 (2005): 202–8.

_____ . "The Last Labayu: King Saul and the Expansion of the First North Israelite Territorial Entity." Pp. 171–87 in *Essays on Ancient Israel in Its Near Eastern Context: A Tribute to Nadav Na'aman,* ed. Y. Amit et al. Winona Lake, IN: Eisenbrauns, 2006.

_____ . "Shechem in the Late Bronze and the Iron I." Pp. 349–56 in *Timelines: Studies in Honour of Manfred Bietak,* ed. E. Czerney et al. Orientalia Lovaniensia Analecta 149. Leuven: Peeters, 2006.

Finkelstein, I., and N. Na'aman. "Shechem of the Amarna Period and the Rise of the Northern Kingdom of Israel." *IEJ* 55 (2005): 172–93.

Finkelstein, I., and E. Piasetzky. "Recent Radiocarbon Results and King Solomon." *Antiquity* 77 (2003): 771–79.

Finkelstein, I., and N. A. Silberman. *The Bible Unearthed.* New York: Simon & Schuster, 2001.

_____ . "The Bible Unearthed: A Rejoinder." *BASOR* 327 (2002): 67–68.

_____ . *David and Solomon: In Search of the Bible's Sacred Kings and the Roots of the Western Tradition.* New York: Free Press, 2006.

_____ . "Temple and Dynasty: Hezekiah, the Remaking of Judah and the Rise of the Pan-Israelite Ideology." *JSOT* 30 (2006): 259–85.

Finkelstein, I., L. Singer-Avitz, Z. Herzog, and David Ussishkin, "Has David's Palace in Jerusalem Been Found." *TA* 34 (2007): 142-64.

Finley, M. I. *The World of Odysseus.* New York: New York Review of Books, 2002.

Garlan, Y. *War in the Ancient World: A Social History.* New York: Norton, 1975.

Garsiel, M. "The Story of David and Bathsheba: A Different Approach." *CBQ* 55 (1993): 244-62.

Goldwasser, O. "An Egyptian Scribe from Lachish and the Hieratic Tradition of the Hebrew Kingdoms." *TA* 18 (1991): 248-53.

Gooding, D. W. "An Approach to the Literary and Textual Problems in the David-Goliath Story." Pp. 55-86 in *The Story of David and Goliath: Textual and Literary Criticism* by Barthélemy et al. OBO 73. Göttingen: Vandenhoeck & Ruprecht / Fribourg: Éditions Universitaires, 1986.

Gordon, R. P. "In Search of David: The David Tradition in Recent Study." Pp. 285-97 in *Faith, Tradition, and History: Old Testament Historiography in Its Near Eastern Context,* ed. A. P. Millard, J. K. Hoffmeier, and D. W. Baker. Winona Lake, IN: Eisenbrauns, 1994.

Gray, J. *I & II Kings: A Commentary.* OTL. Philadelphia: Westminster, 1963.

Grayson, A. K. *Assyrian and Babylonian Chronicles.* Locust Valley, NY: J. J. Augustin, 1975. Repr. Winona Lake, IN: Eisenbrauns, 2000.

_____ . *Assyrian Royal Inscriptions.* Vol. 2. Wiesbaden: Harrassowitz, 1976.

_____ . "Assyria and Babylonia." *Orientalia* 49 (1980): 140-93.

Gressmann, H. "The Oldest History Writing in Israel." Pp. 9-58 in *Narrative and Novella in Samuel: Studies by Hugo Gressmann and Other Scholars 1906-1923,* ed. David M. Gunn. Sheffield: Almond, 1991.

Griffith, G. T. *The Mercenaries of the Hellenistic World.* Cambridge: Cambridge University Press, 1935.

Grønbaek, J. H. *Die Geschichte vom Aufstieg Davids (1 Sam. 15-2 Sam. 5): Tradition und Komposition.* Acta theologica Danica 10. Copenhagen: Prostant & Munksgaard, 1971.

Gunkel, H. "Die isrealitische Literatur." Pp. 53-112 in *Die orientalischen Literaturen,* ed. P. Hinneberg. 2nd ed. Berlin: Teubner, 1925.

_____ . "Geschichtsschreibung im A.T.," in *RGG* 2:1348-54.

_____ . "Geschichtsschreibung im A.T.," in *RGG*[2] 2:1112-15.

Gunn, D. M. "Narrative Patterns and Oral Tradition in Judges and Samuel." *VT* 24 (1974): 286-317.

_____ . "David and the Gift of the Kingdom." *Semeia* 3 (1975): 14-45.

_____ . "Traditional Composition in the 'Succession Narrative.'" *VT* 26 (1976): 214-29.

_____ . "On Oral Tradition: A Response to John Van Seters." *Semeia* 5 (1976): 155-61.

_____ . *The Story of King David: Genre and Interpretation.* JSOTSup 6. Sheffield: JSOT Press, 1978.

_____ . *The Fate of King Saul: An Interpretation of a Biblical Story.* JSOTSup 14. Sheffield: JSOT Press, 1980.

Hallberg, P. *The Icelandic Saga.* Lincoln: University of Nebraska Press, 1962.

Halpern, B. *David's Secret Demons: Messiah, Murderer, Traitor, King.* Grand Rapids: Eerdmans, 2001.

Hawkins, J. D. "Karkamish and Karatepe: Neo-Hittite City States in North Syria." Pp. 1295–1307 in vol. 2 of *Civilizations of the Ancient Near East,* ed. J. M. Sasson. 4 vols. New York: Scribners, 1995.

Herrmann, S. "Die Königsnovelle in Ägypten und in Israel." *WZK-MUL* 3/1 (1953–54): 51–62.

Hertzberg, H. W. *I and II Samuel: A Commentary.* OTL. Philadelphia: Westminster, 1964.

Hoffner, H. "Propaganda and Political Justification in Hittite Historiography." Pp. 49–62 in *Unity and Diversity: Essays in the History, Literature, and Religion of the Ancient Near East,* ed. H. Goedicke and J. J. M. Roberts. Baltimore: Johns Hopkins University Press, 1975.

_____ . "Histories and Historians of the Ancient Near East: The Hittites." *Orientalia* 49 (1980): 283–332.

Holladay, J. S. "Red Slip, Burnish, and the Solomonic Gateway at Gezer." *BASOR* 277/278 (1990): 23–70.

Hollaway, S. W. "Use of Assyriology in Chronological Apologetics in *David's Secret Demons.*" *SJOT* 17 (2003): 245–67.

Ishida, T. "Solomon's Succession in the Light of the Inscription of Kilamuwa, King of Yʾdy-Samʾal." Pp. 167–74 in *History and Historical Writing in Ancient Israel: Studies in Biblical Historiography.* Leiden: Brill, 1999.

_____ . "The Succession Narrative and Esarhaddon's Apology." Pp. 175–85 in *History and Historical Writing in Ancient Israel: Studies in Biblical Historiography.* Leiden: Brill, 1999.

Jamieson-Drake, D. W. *Scribes and Schools in Monarchic Judah: A Socio-Archeological Approach.* JSOTSup 109. Sheffield: Almond, 1991.

Jones, G. H. *The Nathan Narratives.* JSOTSup 80. Sheffield: JSOT Press, 1990.

Kaiser, O. "Das Verhältnis der Erzählung vom König David zum sogenannten deuteronomistischen Geschichtswerk: Am Beispiel von Kön 1–2 untersucht. Ein Gespräch mit John Van Seters." Pp. 94–122 in *Die sogenannte Thronfolgegeschichte Davids,* ed. A. de Pury and T. Römer. OBO 176. Freiburg: Universitätsverlag, 2000.

Kellogg, R. "Introduction." Pp. xv–lvii in *The Sagas of Icelanders: A Selection.* London: Penguin, 2001.

Kenyon, K. *Royal Cities of the Old Testament.* New York: Schocken, 1971.

Keys, G. *The Wages of Sin: A Reappraisal of the Succession Narrative.* JSOTSup 221. Sheffield: JSOT Press, 1996.

Klein, R. W. *1 Samuel.* WBC 10. Waco, TX: Word, 1983.

Koch, K. *The Growth of the Biblical Tradition:The Form-Critical Method,* trans. S. M. Cupitt. London: Black,1969.

Lattimore, R. "The Wise Adviser in Herodotus." *Classical Philology* 34 (1939): 24–35.

Lemaire, A. "The United Monarchy: Saul, David and Solomon." Pp. 85–109 in *Ancient Israel,* ed. H. Shanks. Engelwood Cliffs, NJ: Prentice-Hall, 1988.

Lemche, N.-P. "From Patronage Society to Patronage Society." Pp. 106–20 in *The Origins of the Israelite States*, ed. V. Fritz and P. R. Davies. JSOTSup 228. Sheffield: Sheffield Academic Press, 1996.

_____. *The Israelites in History and Tradition*. Louisville: Westminster John Knox, 1998.

Levenson, J. D. "1 Samuel 25 as Literature and History." *CBQ* 40 (1978): 11–28.

Lönnroth, L. *Njáls Saga: A Critical Introduction*. Berkeley: University of California Press, 1976.

Luckenbill, D. D. *Ancient Records of Assyria and Babylonia*. 2 vols. Chicago: University of Chicago Press, 1926–27.

Lust, J. "The Story of David and Goliath in Hebrew and Greek." Pp. 5–18 in *The Story of David and Goliath: Textual and Literary Criticism* by Barthélemy et al. OBO 73. Göttingen: Vandenhoeck & Ruprecht / Fribourg: Éditions Universitaires, 1986.

Magnusson, M., and H. Palsson, *Njal's Saga*. Harmondsworth, UK: Penguin, 1960.

Maʿoz, Z. U. *Dan Is Bāniyās, Tel Dan Is Abel-Beth-Maʿacha*. Archaostyle Scientific Research Series 2. Qazin: Archaostyle, 2006.

Mauchline, J. *1 and 2 Samuel*. NCB. London: Oliphants, 1971.

Mazar, A. *Archaeology of the Land of the Bible: 10,000–586 B.C.E.* New York: Doubleday, 1990.

Mazar, E. "Did I Find King David's Palace?" *BAR* 32/1 (2006): 16–27, 70.

McCarter, P. K. *I Samuel*. AB 8. Garden City, NY: Doubleday, 1980.

_____. " 'Plots, True or False': The Succession Narrative as Court Apologetic." *Int* 35 (1981): 355–67.

_____. *II Samuel*. AB 9. Garden City, NY: Doubleday, 1984.

McCarthy, D. J. "II Samuel 7 and the Structure of the Deuteronomistic History." *JBL* 84 (1965): 131–38.

_____. "An Installation Genre?" *JBL* 90 (1971): 31–41.

McKenzie, S. L. *The Trouble with Kings*. VTSup 42. Leiden: Brill, 1991.

_____. "The So-Called Succession Narrative in the Deuteronomistic History." Pp. 123–35 in *Die sogenannte Thronfolgegeschichte Davids*, ed. A. de Pury and T. Römer. OBO 176. Freiburg: Universitätsverlag, 2000.

_____. *King David: A Biography*. New York: Oxford University Press, 2000.

_____. "Why Didn't God Let David Build the Temple? The History of a Biblical Tradition." Pp. 204–24 in *Worship and the Hebrew Bible: Essays in Honour of John T. Willis*, ed. M. P. Graham, R. R. Marrs, and S. L. McKenzie. JSOTSup 284. Sheffield: Sheffield Academic Press, 1999.

Mettinger, T. N. D. *Solomonic State Officials*. Lund: Gleerup, 1971.

_____. *King and Messiah: The Civil and Sacred Legitimation of the Israelite King*. CBOTS 8. Lund: Gleerup, 1976.

_____. *The Dethronement of Sabaoth*. CBOTS 18. Lund: Gleerup, 1982.

Mildenberger, F. *Die vordeuteronomistische Saul-Davidüberlieferung*. Ph.D. diss., Tübingen Universität, 1962.

Miller, J. M. "The Moabite Stone as a Memorial Stela." *PEQ* 104 (1974): 9–18.

Miller, P. D., and J. J. M. Roberts, *The Hand of the Lord: A Reassessment of the "Ark Narrative" of 1 Samuel*. Baltimore: Johns Hopkins University Press, 1977.

Na'aman, N. "The 'Conquest of Canaan' in the Book of Joshua and in History." Pp. 218-81 in *From Nomadism to Monarchy: Archaeological and Historical Aspects of Early Israel*, ed. I. Finkelstein and N. Na'aman. Jerusalem: Israel Exploration Society, 1994.

_____. "Hazael of ʿAmqi and Hadadezer of Beth-rehob." *UF* 27 (1995): 381-94.

_____. "The Contribution of the Amarna Letters to the Debate on Jerusalem's Political Position in the Tenth Century B.C.E." *BASOR* 304 (1996): 17-27.

_____. "Sources and Composition in the History of David." Pp. 170-86 in *The Origins of the Ancient Israelite States*, ed. V. Fritz and P. R. Davies. JSOTSup 228. Sheffield: Sheffield Academic Press, 1996.

_____. "Historical and Literary Notes on the Excavations of Tel Jezreel." *TA* 24 (1997): 122-28.

_____. "Ittai the Gittite." *BN* 94 (1998): 22-25.

_____. "Habiru-like Bands in the Assyrian Empire and Bands in Biblical Historiography." *JAOS* 120 (2000): 621-24.

_____. "Three Notes on the Aramaic Inscription from Tel Dan." *IEJ* 50 (2000): 92-104.

_____. "In Search of Reality behind the Account of David's Wars with Israel's Neighbours." *IEJ* 52 (2002): 200-224.

_____. "The Sources Available for the Authors of the Book of Kings." Pp. 105-20 in *Recenti tendenze nella ricostruzione della storia antica d'Israele*, ed. M. Liverani. Rome: Accademia nazionale dei Lincei, 2005.

_____. "When and How Did Jerusalem Become a Great City? The Rise of Jerusalem as Judah's Premier City in the Eighth-Seventh Centuries B.C.E." *BASOR* 347 (2007): 21-56.

Niemann, H. M. *Herrschaft, Königtum und Staat: Skizzen zur soziokulturellen Entwicklung im monarchischen Israel*. Tübingen: Mohr Siebeck, 1993.

Noll, K. L. *The Faces of David*. JSOTSup 242. Sheffield: Sheffield Academic Press, 1997.

_____. "Is There a Text in This Tradition? Readers' Response and the Taming of Samuel's God." *JSOT* 83 (1999): 31-51.

Noth, M. *The Deuteronomistic History*. JSOTSup 15. Sheffield: JSOT Press, 1981.

_____. *The History of Israel*. 2nd ed. New York: Harper & Row, 1960.

_____. "David and Israel in II Samuel VII." Pp. 250-59 in *The Laws of the Pentateuch and Other Essays*. Edinburgh: Oliver & Boyd, 1966.

Nubel, H.-U. *Davids Aufstieg in der frühe israelitischer Geschichtsschreibung*, Ph.D. diss., Rheinische Friedrich-Wilhelms-Universität, 1959.

Olmstead, A. T. *The History of the Persian Empire*. Chicago: University of Chicago Press, 1948.

Parke, H. W. *Greek Mercenary Soldiers: From the Earliest Times to the Battle of Ipsus*. Oxford: Clarendon, 1933.

Perlit, L. *Bundestheologie im Alten Testament*. WMANT 36. Neukirchen-Vluyn: Neukirchener Verlag, 1969.

Pfeiffer, R. H. *Introduction to the Old Testament*. New York: Harper & Row, 1941.

Pisano, S. *Additions or Omissions in the Books of Samuel*. OBO 57. Freiburg: Universitätsverlag, 1984.

Pury, A. de, and T. Römer, eds. *Die sogenannte Thronfolgegeschichte Davids.* OBO 176. Freiburg: Universitätsverlag, 2000.

Rad, G. von. "The Beginnings of Historical Writing in Ancient Israel." Pp. 166-204 in *The Problem of the Hexateuch and Other Essays*, trans. E. W. Trueman Dicken. New York: McGraw-Hill, 1966. [This is an English translation of "Der Anfang der Geschichtsschreibung im alten Israel." *Archiv für Kulturgeschichte* 32 (1944): 1-42.]

_____ . "The Tent and the Ark (1931)." Pp. 103-24 in *The Problem of the Hexateuch and Other Essays*. Edinburgh: Oliver & Boyd, 1966.

_____ . *Old Testament Theology.* Vol. 1. New York: Harper & Row, 1962.

Redford, D. B. *Egypt, Canaan, and Israel in Ancient Times.* Princeton: Princeton University Press, 1992.

Rofé, A. "The Battle of David and Goliath: Folktale, Theology, Eschatology." Pp. 117-51 in *Judaic Perspectives on Ancient Israel*, ed. J. Neusner et al. Philadelphia: Fortress, 1987.

Rogers, J. S. "Narrative Stock and Deuteronomistic Elaboration in 1 Kings 2." *CBQ* 50 (1988): 398-413.

Römer, T. C. *The So-Called Deuteronomistic History: A Sociological, Historical and Literary Introduction.* London: T. & T. Clark, 2005.

Rost, L. *Die Überlieferung von der Thronnachfolge Davids.* BWANT 3/6. Stuttgart: Kohlhammer, 1926. [Trans. M. D. Rutter and D. M. Gunn as *The Succession to the Throne of David.* Sheffield: Almond, 1982.]

Rudnig, T. A. *Davids Thron: Redaktionskritische Studien zur der Thronnachfolge Davids.* BZAW 358. Berlin: de Gruyter, 2006.

Sharon, I., A. Gilboa, A. J. T. Jull, and E. Boarette. "Report on the First Stage of the Iron Age Dating Project in Israel: Supporting a Low Chronology." *Radiocarbon* 49 (2007): 1-46.

Simean-Yofre, H. "רחם *rḥm*," in *TDOT* 9:340-355

Smith, H. P. *The Books of Samuel.* ICC. New York: Scribners, 1899.

Steiner, M. L. *Excavations by Kathleen M. Kenyon in Jerusalem 1961-1967: The Settlement in the Bronze and Iron Ages.* Copenhagen International Series 9. London: Sheffield Academic Press, 2001.

Stoebe, H. J. *Das erste Buch Samuelis.* KAT 8/1. Gütersloh: Gütersloher Verlagshaus, 1973.

_____ . *Das zweite Buch Samuelis.* KAT 8/2. Gütersloh: Gütersloher Verlagshaus, 1994.

_____ . "רחם *rḥm* pi. to comfort," in *TLOT* 2:734-39.

Tadmor, H. "Autobiographical Apology in the Royal Assyrian Literature." Pp. 36-57 in *History, Historiography and Interpretation: Studies in Biblical and Cuneiform Literatures*, ed. H. Tadmor and M. Weinfeld. Jerusalem: Magnes, 1983.

Thomas, R. *Oral Tradition and Written Record in Classical Athens.* Cambridge: Cambridge University Press, 1989.

_____ . *Literacy and Orality in Ancient Greece.* Cambridge: Cambridge University Press, 1992.

Thompson, T. L. *Early History of the Israelite People: From the Written and Archaeological Sources.* Leiden: Brill, 1992.

Thucydides. *The Peloponnesian War*, trans. R. Warner. Harmondsworth: Penguin, 1972.

Toorn, K. van der. *Scribal Culture and the Making of the Hebrew Bible*. Cambridge, MA: Harvard University Press, 2007.

Tov, E. "The Composition of 1 Samuel 16-18 in the Light of the Septuagint Version." Pp. 97-130 in *Empirical Models for Biblical Criticism*, ed. J. H. Tigay. Philadelphia: University of Pennsylvania Press, 1985.

_____. "The Nature of the Differences between MT and the LXX," Pp. 19-46 in *The Story of David and Goliath: Textual and Literary Criticism* by Barthélemy et al. OBO 73. Göttingen: Vandenhoeck & Ruprecht / Fribourg: Éditions Universitaires, 1986.

_____. *Textual Criticism of the Hebrew Bible*. Minneapolis: Fortress, 1992.

Ussishkin, D. "Excavations at Tel Lachish 1973-1977: Preliminary Report." *TA* 5 (1978): 1-97.

_____. "Excavations at Tel Lachish 1978-1983: Second Preliminary Report." *TA* 10 (1983): 97-175.

_____. "Notes on Megiddo, Gezer, Ashdod, and Tel Batash in the Tenth and Ninth Centuries B.C." BASOR 277/78 (1990): 71-91.

_____. "The Credibility of the Tel Jezreel Excavations: A Rejoinder to Amnon Ben Tor." *TA* 27 (2000): 248-56.

_____. "Solomon's Jerusalem: The Text and the Facts on the Ground." Pp. 103-15 in *Jerusalem in the Bible and Archaeology: The First Temple Period*, ed. A. G. Vaughn and A. E. Killebrew. Atlanta: Society of Biblical Literature, 2003.

Van Seters, J. "The Terms 'Amorite' and 'Hittite' in the Old Testament." *VT* 22 (1972): 64-81.

_____. *Abraham in History and Tradition*. New Haven, CT: Yale University Press, 1975.

_____. "Oral Patterns or Literary Conventions in Biblical Narrative." *Semeia* 5 (1976): 139-54.

_____. "Problems in the Literary Analysis of the Court History of David." *JSOT* 1 (1976): 22-29.

_____. "Histories and Historians of the Near East: Ancient Israel." *Orientalia* 50 (1981): 137-85.

_____. *In Search of History: Historiography in the Ancient World and the Origins of Biblical History*. New Haven, CT: Yale University Press, 1983. Repr. Winona Lake, IN: Eisenbrauns, 1997.

_____. "Love and Death in the Court History of David." Pp. 121-24 in *Love and Death in the Ancient Near East: Essays in Honor of Marvin H. Pope*, ed. J. H. Marks and R. M. Good. Guildford, CT: Four Quarters, 1987.

_____. "Joshua's Campaign of Canaan and Near Eastern Historiography." *SJOT* 4/2 (1990): 1-12.

_____. *Prologue to History: The Yahwist as Historian in Genesis*. Louisville: Westminster John Knox, 1992.

_____. *The Life of Moses: The Yahwist as Historian in Exodus-Numbers*. Louisville: Westminster John Knox, 1994.

_____. "Creative Imitation in the Hebrew Bible." *SR* 29 (2000): 395-409.

_____ . "The Court History and DtrH: Conflicting Perspectives on the House of David." Pp. 70-93 in *Die sogenannte Thronfolgegeschichte Davids*, ed. A. de Pury and T. Römer. OBO 176. Freiburg: Universitätsverlag, 2000.

_____ . "The Silence of Dinah (Genesis 34)." Pp. 237-47 in *Jacob: A Plural Commentary of Gen. 25-36. Mélanges offerts à Albert de Pury*, ed. J.-D. Macchi and T. Römer. Geneva: Labor et Fides, 2001.

_____ . "Is There any Historiography in the Hebrew Bible? A Hebrew-Greek Comparison." *JNSL* 28/2 (2002): 1-25.

_____ . "The Formula *lešakken šemo šam* and the Centralization of Worship in Deuteronomy and DH." *JNSL* 30 (2004): 1-18.

_____ . *The Edited Bible: The Curious History of the "Editor" in Biblical Criticism.* Winona Lake, IN: Eisenbrauns, 2006.

_____ . "The 'Shared Text' of Samuel-Kings and Chronicles Re-examined." Pp. 503-15 in *Reflections and Refractions: Studies in Biblical Historiography in Honour of A. Graeme Auld*, ed. R. Rezetko et al. VTSup 113. Leiden: Brill, 2007.

_____ . "David: Messianic King or Mercenary Ruler?" Pp. 27-39 in *Community Identity in Judean Historiography: Biblical and Comparative Perspectives*, ed. G. N. Knoppers and K. A. Ristau. Winona Lake, IN: Eisenbrauns, 2009.

_____ . "David the Mercenary." In *Israel in Transition: From Late Bronze II to Iron IIA (c. 1250-850 BCE)*, vol. 2: *The Texts*, ed. L. L. Grabbe. European Seminar in Historiography 8. London: T. & T. Clark, forthcoming.

_____ . "Israel and Egypt in the 'Age of Solomon.'" In *Walls of the Prince: Egypt and Canaan in Antiquity. Papers in Honor of John S. Holladay Jr.*, ed. E. B. Banning. Toronto: Benben, forthcoming.

Vaux, R. de. "Titres et fonctionaires égyptiens à la cour de David et de Salomon." *RB* 48 (1939): 394-405.

_____ . *Histoire ancienne d'Israël*, vol. 2: *La période des Juges*. Paris: Gabalda, 1973.

Veijola, T. *Die Ewige Dynastie: David und die Entstehung seiner Dynastie nach der deuteronomistichen Darstellung.* Suomalaisen Tiedeakatemian Toimituksia Annales Academiae Scientiarum Fennicae Series B 193. Helsinki: Suomalainen Tiedeakatemia, 1975.

Walker, C. B. F. "Babylonian Chronicle 25: A Chronicle of the Kassite and Isin II Dynasties." Pp. 397-417 in *Zikin Šumim: Assyriological Studies Presented to F. R. Kraus on the Occasion of His Seventieth Birthday*, ed. G. van Driel et al. Leiden: Brill, 1982.

Waterfield, R. *Xenophon's Retreat: Greece, Persia and the End of the Golden Age.* Cambridge: Harvard University Press, 2006.

Wedgewood, C. V. *The Thirty Years War.* New York: New York Review of Books, 2005.

Weiser, A. "Die Templebaukrise unter David." *ZAW* 77 (1965): 153-68.

_____ . "Die Legitimation des Königs David: Zur Eigenart und Entstehung der sogen. Geschichte von Davids Aufstieg." *VT* 16 (1966): 325-54.

Wellhausen, J. *Prolegomena to the History of Ancient Israel.* Gloucester, MA: Peter Smith, 1973.

_____ . *Die Composition des Hexateuch und der Historischen Bücher des Alten Testaments.* 4th ed. Berlin: de Gruyter, 1963.

White, M. C. *The Elijah Legends and Jehu's Coup.* Brown Judaic Studies 311. Atlanta: Scholars Press, 1997.

Whitelam, K. W. *The Invention of Ancient Israel: The Silencing of Palestinian History.* London: Routledge, 1996.

Whybray, R. N. *The Succession Narrative: A Study of II Sam. 9-20 and I Kings 1 and 2.* Studies in Biblical Theology 2nd Series 9. London: SCM, 1968.

Wightman, G. J. "The Myth of Solomon." *BASOR* 277/278 (1990): 5-22.

Willi-Plein, I. "Michal und die Anfänge des Königtums in Israel " Pp. 401-19 in *Congress Volume Cambridge 1995,* ed. J. A. Emerton. VTSup 66. Leiden: Brill, 1997.

_____. "1 Sam 18-19 und die Davidshausgeschichte." Pp. 138-77 in *David und Saul im Widerstreit: Diachronie und Synchronie im Wettstreit,* ed. W. Dietrich. OBO 206. Freiburg: Academic Press / Göttingen: Vandenhoeck & Ruprecht, 2004.

Williamson, H. G. M. "Jezreel in the Biblical Texts." *TA* 18 (1991): 72-92.

Wolf, H. M. *The Apology of Hattušiliš Compared with Other Self-Justifications,* Ph.D. diss., Brandeis University, 1967.

Würthwein, E. *Die Bücher der Könige: 1 Könige 1-16.* ATD 11/1. Göttingen: Vandenhoeck & Ruprecht, 1985.

Yalichev, S. *Mercenaries of the Ancient World.* London: Constable, 1997.

Zobel, H.-J. "aron," in *TDOT* 1:363-74.

Index of Authors

Index of Scripture